CHRISTIAN FAITH AS RELIGION

A Study in the Theologies of Calvin and Schleiermacher

Paul E. Capetz

University Press of America,® Inc.
Lanham • New York • Oxford

Copyright © 1998
University Press of America,® Inc.
4720 Boston Way
Lanham, Maryland 20706

12 Hid's Copse Rd.
Cumnor Hill, Oxford OX2 9JJ

Library of Congress Cataloging-in-Publication Data

Capetz, Paul E.
Christian faith as religion : a study in the theologies of Calvin and
Schleiermacher / Paul E. Capetz.
p.   cm.
A revision of the author's thesis, University of Chicago, 1996.
Includes bibliographical references and index.
1. Christianity—Essence, genius, nature—History of doctrines. 2.
Religion—Philosophy—History. 3. Calvin, Jean, 1509-1564. 4.
Schleiermacher, Friedrich, 1768-1834. 5. Liberalism (Religion)—
Protestant churches—History of doctrines. I. Title.
BT60.C37 1998   230'.044'0922—dc21   98-38313 CIP

ISBN 0-7618-1243-1 (cloth: alk. ppr.)
ISBN 0-7618-1244-X (pbk: alk. ppr.)

In memory of
Louise M. Whetstone
1900-1988

Contents

Abbreviations

Acknowledgments

Introduction

Chapter 1
**The Interpretation of Religion as a Problem
in Protestant Theology**   1

> *From the Reformation to the Enlightenment*
> *The Neo-Orthodox Critique of Liberal Theology*
> *Revising the Neo-Orthodox Historiography*
> *The Historical Thesis and the Method*

Chapter 2
Calvin's Interpretation of Religion   29

> *Defining "Piety" in an Age of Reform*
> *The Religious Ideal of Human Existence*
> *Pagan Testimonies to the Religious Character of Human Existence*
> *Summary*

Chapter 3
Calvin on the Christian Faith   71

> *The Reformation and the Question of True Religion*
> *Faith and the Restoration of Piety*
> *The History of True and False Religion*
> *Summary*

Chapter 4
Schleiermacher's Interpretation of Religion   109

Beyond Orthodoxy and Rationalism
The Young Schleiermacher: From Pietism to Romanticism
The Mature Schleiermacher: From the "Speeches" to the
    "Glaubenslehre"
Summary

Chapter 5
Schleiermacher on the Christian Faith   153

The Positivity of Religion
Identifying the Place of Christianity among the Religions
Christian Faith according to the Principles of the Protestant
    Church
Summary

Chapter 6
Christian Faith and Religion: From Calvin to Schleiermacher 197

The Comparison of Classical and Liberal Protestant Theology
What is Christian Faith?
What is Religion?
Conclusion

Afterword   237

Bibliography   263

Index   301

Abbreviations

ANF   *The Ante-Nicene Fathers.* Ed. Alexander Roberts and James Donaldson. 10 vols. Edinburgh: T. & T. Clark, 1867-72. Reprint ed., Grand Rapids: Wm. B. Eerdmans, 1980-1983.

BO   Friedrich Schleiermacher, *Brief Outline on the Study of Theology.* English translation of the 2d ed. of KD (1830). Trans. Terrence N. Tice. Richmond: John Knox Press, 1966.

CF   Friedrich Schleiermacher, *The Christian Faith.* English translation of the 2d German ed. (1830-31). Ed. H. R. Mackintosh and J. S. Stewart. Edinburgh: T. and T. Clark, 1928. Reprint ed., Philadelphia: Fortress Press, 1976.

CO   *Ioannis Calvini opera quae supersunt omnia.* Ed. Wilhelm Baum, Edward Cunitz, and Edward Reuss. 59 vols. *Corpus Reformatorum,* vols. 29-87. Braunschweig: C.A. Schwetschke and Son (M. Bruhn), 1863-1900.

Crouter   Friedrich Schleiermacher, *On Religion: Speeches to its Cultured Despisers.* English translation of the first ed. of *Reden* (1799). Trans. Richard Crouter. 2d ed. Cambridge Texts in the History of Philosophy. Cambridge: Cambridge University Press, 1996.

Gl.   *Glaubenslehre.* Friedrich Schleiermacher, *Der christliche Glaube nach den Grundsätzen der evangelischen Kirche im Zusammenhange dargestellt.* 7th ed., based on the 2d (1830-31). Ed.

Martin Redeker. 2 vols. Berlin: Walter de Gruyter, 1960. Cited by section (§) and subsection.

Gl.¹   The first edition of *Gl.* (1821-22). Ed. Hermann Peiter. 2 vols. Berlin and New York: Walter de Gruyter, 1984.

Inst.   John Calvin, *Institutio christianae religionis.* Cited in the 1559 ed. by book, chapter, and section according to the text in OS, vols. 3-5.

KD   Friedrich Schleiermacher, *Kurze Darstellung des theologischen Studiums zum Behuf einleitender Vorlesungen.* 3d, critical ed., based on the 2d (1830) with notes indicating variations from the first ed. of KD (1811). Ed. Heinrich Scholz (1910). Reprint ed., Darmstadt: Wissenschaftliche Buchgesellschaft, 1961.

KGA   Friedrich Schleiermacher, *Kritische Gesamtausgabe.* Ed. Hans-Joachim Birkner, Gerhard Ebeling, Hermann Fischer, Heinz Kimmerle, and Kurt-Victor Selge. Berlin and New York: Walter de Gruyter, 1980-. Cited by part, volume, and page.

Latin Works   *Latin Works of Huldreich Zwingli.* Ed. Samuel Macauley Jackson et al. 3 vols. Vol. 1, New York: G.P. Putnam's Sons, 1912. Vols. 2-3, Philadelphia: Heidelberg Press, 1922-1929. Vol. 1 carried the title *The Latin Works and the Correspondence of Huldreich Zwingli.* Vols. 2 and 3 have been reprinted with the titles *On Providence and Other Essays* and *Commentary on True and False Religion* (Durham, North Carolina: Labyrinth Press, 1983, 1981).

LCL   *The Loeb Classical Library.*

LW   *Luther's Works.* American ed. Ed. Jaroslav Pelikan and Helmut T. Lehmann. 55 vols. St. Louis: Concordia Publishing House, Philadelphia: Fortress Press, 1955-1986.

McNeill   John Calvin, *Institutes of the Christian Religion.* English translation of the 1559 ed. Ed. John T.

McNeill and trans. Ford Lewis Battles. 2 vols. Library of Christian Classics, vols. 20-21. Philadelphia: Westminster Press, 1960.

MPG *Patrologiae Cursus Completus.* Series Graeca. Ed. J. P. Migne. 161 vols. Paris, 1857-66.

MPL *Patrologiae Cursus Completus.* Series Latina. Ed. J. P. Migne. 221 vols. Paris, 1844-1900.

NPNF *Nicene and Post-Nicene Fathers.* Ed. Philip Schaff. 14 vols. New York: Christian Literature Co., 1886-1890. Reprint ed., Grand Rapids: Wm. B. Eerdmans, 1980-1983.

Oman Friedrich Schleiermacher, *On Religion: Speeches to its Cultured Despisers.* English translation of 3d ed. of *Reden* (1821). Trans. John Oman (1893). New York: Harper and Row, 1958. Reprint ed. with a foreword by Jack Forstman, Louisville: Westminster/ John Knox Press, 1994.

OS *Ioannis Calvini opera selecta.* Ed. Peter Barth, Wilhelm Niesel, and Dora Scheuner. 5 vols. Munich: Chr. Kaiser, 1926-52.

OtGl. Friedrich Schleiermacher, *On the Glaubenslehre: Two Letters to Dr. Lücke.* English translation of *Sendschr.* Trans. James Duke and Francis Fiorenza. American Academy of Religion Texts and Translations Series 3. Chico: Scholars Press, 1981.

Reden Friedrich Schleiermacher, *Reden über die Religion.* Critical ed. by G. Ch. Bernhard Pünjer. Braunschweig: C. A. Schwetschke and Son (M. Bruhn), 1879. Based on the first ed. (1799), Pünjer indicates the changes in the 2d (1806) and 3d (1821) editions; aside from minor revisions, the 4th ed. (1831) was a reprint. Cited by edition and page.

Sendschr. *Schleiermachers Sendschreiben über seine Glaubenslehre an Lücke* (1829). Ed. Hermann Mulert. Studien zur Geschichte des neueren Protestantismus, Quellenheft 2. Giessen: Alfred

Töpelmann (J. Ricker), 1908.

SW   *Friedrich Schleiermachers sämmtliche Werke.* Ed.
        Ludwig Jonas, Alexander Schweizer, Friedrich Lücke
        et al. 31 vols. Berlin: Georg Reimer, 1835-1864.
        Cited by division, volume, and page.

WA   *D. Martin Luthers Werke: Kritische Gesamtausgabe.*
        Weimarer Ausgabe. Weimar, 1883-.

Werke *Huldreich Zwinglis sämtliche Werke.* Ed. Emil Egli et
        al. *Corpus Reformatorum*, vols. 88ff. Berlin, 1905-;
        reprinted and series resumed, Zurich: Theologischer
        Verlag, 1984-.

Acknowledgments

This book is a revised version of my 1996 dissertation submitted to the faculty of the Divinity School of the University of Chicago. I wish to acknowledge with gratitude the professors without whose assistance this work would never have seen the light of day. B. A. Gerrish closely supervised the dissertation at each phase of its development and inspired me with his vision of historical theology as an academic discipline of eminent ecclesial significance. His commitment to the historical interpretation of Protestantism as a single unit of study that embraces the two epochs of classical and liberal theology made it possible for me to conceive the topic of this comparative inquiry. Langdon Gilkey, my first reader, taught me—by precept as well as by example—to be an appreciative student of diverse systems of theology by identifying their underlying religious concerns. Susan E. Schreiner, my second reader, introduced me to the late medieval context of classical Protestant theology. Each of these teachers has taught me to appreciate the riches of the Protestant heritage, old and new.

Mention should also be made of two other professors at Chicago who assisted me with this project. David Tracy read the initial formulation of the proposed thesis and his incisive questions helped me to clarify the theological and philosophical issues involved in the topic. Hans Dieter Betz gave me the benefit of his critical reading of portions of the dissertation and encouraged me to revise it for publication. Furthermore, I am deeply indebted to Douglas F. Ottati, my former colleague at Union Theological Seminary in Virginia, for innumerable insights that grew out of our many conversations together both in the classroom and outside of it.

I wish to thank the following publishers for allowing me to cite their English versions of primary sources when I have been unable to come up with a better translation of my own. Material reproduced from Calvin, *Institutes of the Christian Religion*, translated by Ford Lewis Battles and edited by John T. McNeill (Library of Christian Classics series) and Schleiermacher, *On Religion: Speeches to its Cultured*

Despisers, translated by John Oman with a foreword by Jack Forstman, has been used by permission of Westminster/John Knox Press. Material reproduced from Schleiermacher, *On Religion: Speeches to its Cultured Despisers*, translated and edited by Richard Crouter (Cambridge Texts in the History of Philosophy) has been used by permission of Cambridge University Press.

A number of persons have greatly assisted me in the technical preparation of the manuscript. I wish to thank Dale Dobias for his bibliographical labors, Carol Ann Stewart for her editorial assistance, Kimberly Vrudny for formating the text, Jeanyne Slettom for proofreading, and Christi Wirth-Davis for preparing the index. Mary Ann Nelson and Sandy Gustafson also helped out at crucial points along the way. I am especially appreciative of the faculty, staff, and students at United Theological Seminary of the Twin Cities for their commitment to critical theological scholarship on behalf of the church. Without their constant encouragement, I should never have been able to complete this project.

There are too many debts of a non-academic sort to family and friends for me to name them all. Here I mention only my grandmother, Louise M. Whetstone, with whom I enjoyed many of my earliest conversations about religious questions and who taught me to appreciate religions other than my own. She died in the year that I began to work on the dissertation, and it is to her memory that this book is lovingly dedicated.

Introduction

The history of Protestant theology since the eighteenth century is the chronicle of various attempts to interpret the classical Christian heritage in relation to modern thought. Paul Tillich writes:

> More than two centuries of theological work have been determined by the apologetic problem. "The Christian message and the modern mind" has been the dominating theme since the end of classical orthodoxy. The perennial question has been: Can the Christian message be adapted to the modern mind without losing its essential and unique character?[1]

Whereas theology in the nineteenth century gave expression to the confidence that the Christian message could be translated into the categories of modern thought without loss of its theological substance, Protestant theology in the twentieth century has been characterized by intense criticism of the inherited ways of building a bridge between the Enlightenment and the church's classical tradition.

The crucial issues may be illustrated by contrasting the divergent ways the concept "religion" has typically been employed in nineteenth- and twentieth-century Protestant theology. Beginning with Schleiermacher, liberal theologians were concerned with defining the nature of religion as a necessary dimension of human experience in relation to which the specific character of Christian faith was to be clarified. But for theologians after Barth, the appropriateness of "religion" as a category of theological interpretation could no longer be taken for granted.[2]

The "dialectical" or "neo-orthodox" theologians, whose thought was forged in the trenches of World War I and severely tested by the rise of fascism in Europe, viewed with suspicion the legacy of liberal theologians from the nineteenth century who identified Christian faith as a form of human religion. To their mind, religion was the most sublime expression of the arrogance and self-assertion of bourgeois civilization that led to the tragedy of August 1914. Hence, the times called for a radical break with inherited modes of thinking so that the Christian message might be able to speak a prophetic word of judgment and healing to a culture in ruins.[3]

The classic statement of this position is Barth's discussion in the *Church Dogmatics* (1.2) entitled "The Revelation of God as the Abolition of Religion."[4] In Barth's perspective, Christian faith is the antithesis of human religion. Barth argued that the gospel calls for faith in God's unique self-revelation in Jesus Christ, whereas religion is the reliance of the human being upon its own powers to master the ultimate conditions of existence. Hence, a genuinely Christian theology must repudiate religion in the name of faith. For Barth, the liberal attempt to interpret Christian faith in relation to the general phenomenon of human religion was an expression of its desire to ground faith in something outside itself. Since the gospel has its foundation in revelation, subsuming Christian faith under a general category of religion threatens both its integrity and its truth.

Continuing the theological criticism of religion initiated by Barth, Bonhoeffer called for a "non-religious interpretation" of the gospel as he sat in a Nazi prison. Unlike Barth, who viewed religion as an expression of the sinful character of human existence apart from faith, Bonhoeffer spoke of religion as a stage in the development of human history which was now being superseded by the thorough secularization of the modern West. In this radically new situation of a "world come of age," Bonhoeffer called upon the church to face the challenge of "a completely religionless time" by asking itself how to speak of "God" in a secular idiom. Although the strength of liberal theology is that it did not try to put the clock back, its mistake lay in seeking to carve out "a space for religion in the world," thereby allowing the world to dictate Christ's place in it.[5]

In spite of their differing emphases, both Barth and Bonhoeffer shared the conviction that theology in their time must make a decisive break with the liberal method of interpreting Christian faith as a form of religion.[6] It was a hallmark of their theological programs, moreover, that the repudiation of religion was regarded as an essential element of the Reformation heritage which was now being rediscovered after its loss during the era of liberal theology when the concept "religion" had been employed to secure a place for Christianity in the modern world. To be sure, not all Protestant thinkers of this generation joined with Barth and Bonhoeffer in dispensing with the concept "religion." Nonetheless, those theologians (e.g., Tillich) who maintained continuity with the liberal past by continuing to speak of Christian faith as a form of religion stood against the stream.[7]

When the history of Protestant theology in the first half of the twentieth century is written from the perspective of a later age, the neo-orthodox antithesis between Christian faith and religion may be more significant for what it reveals about the generation of theologians who came to prominence between the two world wars than as a lasting constructive contribution to Protestant theology. Be that as it may, this movement deserves to be understood on its own terms as a creative response to the pressing challenges facing the Protestant churches in Europe after the breakdown of the bourgeois culture of the nineteenth century and the theological efforts at mediation between Christian faith and the modern mind representative of that culture's questions and concerns.

Neo-orthodoxy has long since been eclipsed by a multitude of other theological schools and movements which have addressed themselves to the challenges arising in the second half of the twentieth century. For our purposes, two interrelated developments are especially noteworthy. Since the end of World War II, Protestant theology has embraced the new opportunities for ecumenism with other Christian traditions exemplified by the Second Vatican Council (1962-65) and increasingly opened itself to respectful dialogue with representatives of various non-Christian religious traditions. These encounters have occasioned for many Protestant thinkers a reconsideration of their own Reformation heritage in relation to other expressions of Christian faith, as well as raised larger questions about the meaning and truth of Christian faith in relation to other expressions of human religion.[8]

In the North American context, the new theological and religious pluralism has found institutional expression. It is not uncommon to find Roman Catholic and Protestant scholars working together on the same theological faculty and addressing a shared ecumenical agenda. Moreover, the founding of departments of religious studies in colleges and universities, where the primary task is to understand the various religions on their own terms apart from theological commitments, illustrates the new attitude of openness to non-Christian religious traditions.[9] As a result of the new situation, Protestant theology today is less concerned with defending its continuity with the Reformation and more interested in speaking from the broader context of the ecumenical church. Furthermore, Protestant theology has been profoundly affected by the methodological discussion concerning the proper scope of religious studies as a field of academic inquiry and the relation, if any, between a theological and a non-theological approach to the study of religion.

In the light of this new situation, it is not surprising that the neo-orthodox opposition between Christian faith and religion is no longer in vogue among Protestant thinkers.[10] Indeed, the formulation of the central issues within Protestant theology has undergone a significant transformation since the neo-orthodox era that reflects its participation in the ecumenical movement and its attention to the developing field of religious studies. Nonetheless, the neo-orthodox criticism of liberal theology continues to exert an important influence upon current debates among Protestant theologians, especially in matters pertaining to theological method.

Lindbeck's call for a "postliberal" theology is indicative in this respect. In contrast to the neo-orthodox theologians who argued on inner-theological grounds that the liberal interpretation of Christian faith as religion represents a distortion of the Protestant heritage, Lindbeck argues on explicitly non-theological grounds that the understanding of religion typically employed by liberal theologians is philosophically deficient. In place of the liberal "experiential-expressive" model of religion, Lindbeck proposes a "cultural-linguistic" view of religion as being more adequate in light of the non-theological approaches to the study of religion.

Lindbeck summarizes the "experiential-expressive" understanding of religion in the following terms:

> (1) Different religions are diverse expressions or objectifications of a common core experience. It is this experience which identifies them as religious. (2) The experience, while conscious, may be unknown on the level of self-conscious reflection. (3) It is present in all human beings. (4) In most religions, the experience is the source and norm of objectifications: it is by reference to the experience that their adequacy or lack of adequacy is to be judged.[11]

The issue, as Lindbeck puts it, is "whether it is conceptually and empirically better to picture religions in expressivist fashion as products of those deep experiences of the divine (or the self, or the world) which most of us are accustomed to thinking of as peculiarly religious, or whether one should opt for the converse thesis that religions are producers of experience." In the "cultural-linguistic" approach, "religions are seen as comprehensive interpretive schemes . . . which structure human experience and understanding of self and world." According to the new paradigm, a religion is "a communal phenomenon that shapes the subjectivities of individuals rather than being primarily a manifestation of those subjectivities."[12]

In Lindbeck's view, theologians in the liberal tradition incorrectly assume "that the scholarly study of religious phenomena on the whole supports the crucial affirmation of the basic unity of religious experience."[13] The claim he advances is that "a cultural-linguistic approach is preferable . . . provided the aim is to give a nontheological account of the relations of religion and experience."[14] Still, Lindbeck writes as a theologian who is especially concerned about the implications of differing theories of religion for the status of theological doctrines.[15] Whereas the liberal theologian "interprets doctrines as noninformative and nondiscursive symbols of inner feelings, attitudes, or existential orientations," the postliberal theologian understands doctrines as "communally authoritative rules of discourse, attitude, and action."[16] Hence, Christian doctrines do not express a pre-linguistic religious experience to which all persons in principle have access; rather, they shape the religious experience of Christians. Lindbeck recommends the theology of Barth as exemplary of a postliberal understanding of the relation between language and experience suggested by a "cultural-linguistic" model of religion.[17]

At first glance, this seems like an odd strategy for commending a theology such as that of Barth who was committed, above all, to freeing Christian faith from dependence on a concept of religion developed apart from revelation.[18] But it does give indication of the degree to which Protestant criticism of the nineteenth-century effort to correlate Christian faith with modern thought has undergone an important reformulation in response to the non-theological study of religion. Whereas the neo-orthodox theologians had argued that the liberal attempt to interpret Christian faith as religion signified a substantive departure from the Protestant heritage, the postliberal theologians contend that liberal theology succumbed to an erroneous concept of religious experience that reflects the philosophical assumptions of the modern "turn to the subject."[19] Accordingly, the postmodern "linguistic turn" in contemporary philosophy, by arguing that there is no universal standpoint unaffected by language and culture from which to describe "common human experience" and its generic features, thus poses a significant non-theological challenge to the liberal tradition's apologetic enterprise.[20]

There may, indeed, be good philosophical reasons for criticizing Schleiermacher's legacy in relation to recent non-theological understandings of religion. Since liberal theology understands itself to be intrinsically correlational and thus beholden to the two norms of theological appropriateness and philosophical adequacy, theologians in this tradition cannot afford to ignore these philosophical criticisms.[21] It is important, however, to distinguish a theological objection to liberal theology from a philosophical criticism of it. While the liberal attempt to delineate an essential religious dimension of common human experience may face a crucial challenge from contemporary philosophical criticisms of modern thought, this is not the same as rejecting the attempt as theologically inappropriate to a Protestant interpretation of Christian faith.

The conflation of these two issues in contemporary Protestant debates about theological method is illustrated by Thiemann's argument against "foundationalism" in theology coupled with his call for a revival of the classic Protestant doctrine of "revelation" represented by Luther and Barth. "The most pervasive form of foundationalism in modern theology is that which seeks to ground theological language in a universal religious experience."[22] By contrast, the doctrine of revelation bears witness to "the central Christian conviction that faith's knowledge of God is a gift of God's grace."[23] He explains:

> Many theologians who refuse to employ the concept of revelation still undertake to defend belief in God's prevenience by an argument which asserts the universality of a "religious dimension" of human experience. These arguments for *homo religiosus* serve as the functional equivalents of doctrines of revelation because . . . they are theoretical justifications for Christian belief in the priority of God's gracious reality. Theologians who employ these arguments seek to demonstrate that human beings are inherently in relation to God.[24]

Thiemann is concerned to argue both that attempts by modern theologians to delineate a religious dimension of common human experience are philosophically incoherent (thus failing to meet the criterion of adequacy) and that they are theologically deficient since they neglect the doctrine of revelation (thus failing to meet the criterion of appropriateness). He explains:

> Few theologians then are willing to argue that theology can dispense with such defenses of God's prior reality, and yet most theologians apparently want to discard the doctrine of revelation. But without further clarification it is not clear how the former can be affirmed while the latter is denied.[25]

That the philosophical and theological questions are closely intertwined for Thiemann is evident from his discussion of Schleiermacher's argument for an immediate experience of God constitutive of human existence as such.[26]

Since Protestant theologians in the twentieth century have expressed so much ambivalence about their liberal inheritance from the nineteenth century, it may be helpful to step back from the methodological debates of contemporary theology in order to ask a historical question about the relation of modern Protestant thought to its classical heritage in the controverted question of Christian faith as religion. As Protestant theology seeks to orient itself in the new situation of theological and religious pluralism with which it is confronted at the close of this century, historical theology has an important contribution to make by clarifying both the relations of modern theology to its sources in the Reformation and the relations within modern theology of neo-orthodoxy to its liberal predecessor.

The purpose of this historical inquiry is to examine the topic of Christian faith as religion in the theologies of John Calvin (1509-1564) and Friedrich Schleiermacher (1768-1834) in order to test the neo-orthodox claim that liberal theology represents a departure from the Reformation heritage. Through the comparison of Calvin and Schleiermacher, whose achievements may be taken as representative of the two epochs of Protestant theology, this book endeavors to demonstrate that Protestant theology in both its classical and liberal forms has availed itself of a critical concept of religion as a tool for the theological interpretation of Christian faith. The history of Protestant theology from its classical to its liberal form can be properly understood only when the lines of continuity between the two epochs of Protestant theology are correctly drawn. Moreover, the correct historical understanding of this relation is important beyond the circle of Protestant theologians, since the origins of the modern non-theological study of religion are inextricably bound up with developments in modern Protestantism as it defined itself in relation to the Enlightenment.[27]

This inquiry poses two distinct yet related questions to the theologies of Calvin and Schleiermacher: first, what is the meaning and significance of the phenomenon of human religion in general? and, second, what is the meaning and significance of the Christian faith as a particular religion among others? Through close examination of their interpretations of Christian doctrine, the argument is advanced that the sharp antithesis between Christian faith and religion, so characteristic of neo-orthodox theologians, is not conducive to an understanding of the way these concepts have been employed in either classical or liberal Protestant theology. Furthermore, it does not allow for an adequate historical account of how the question of Christian faith as religion was reformulated in the modern world as the tradition of the Reformation encountered the Enlightenment. In the execution of this argument, I take seriously the theological objections raised by the neo-orthodox and utilize their criticisms of liberal theology to frame the contours of this historical examination.

While the mode of this investigation is exegetical and historical, its ultimate design is theological and constructive. In this sense, it exemplifies a hermeneutical understanding of "historical theology" as a historical discipline of eminent theological significance. As a historical discipline, it holds itself accountable to the critical-historical method of inquiry. But as a sub-discipline within the larger theological enterprise, it assumes responsibility for contributing to the explicitly theological task of the Christian church by means of its historical labors. Historical theology examines the past informed by the questions of contemporary theology. For its part, constructive theology allows its own formulation of questions to be criticized by historical study. In this hermeneutical model, historical theology apart from constructive theology is irrelevant just as constructive theology apart from historical theology is empty.

The reader needs to keep in mind two important limitations of this historical study. First, it does not seek to defend the liberal tradition's understanding of religion on philosophical grounds. It leaves open the possibility that the legacy of Schleiermacher is vulnerable to philosophical criticism in its formulation of an argument for a religious dimension of human experience as such. In keeping with the logic of their own correlational conception of the theological enterprise, contemporary theologians working in the liberal tradition are obligated to take the strictly philosophical challenges to their theological formulations with utter seriousness. If this theological tradition is to be further developed in relation to the non-theological study of religion, new constructive formulations are required that clarify how an appeal to common human experience can be defended that incorporates the important insights of the postmodern "linguistic turn" in philosophy.

Second, in this study questions of theological method are subordinated to substantive issues of theological interpretation. The reason for this subordination of formal issues to material issues lies in my conviction that the strictly methodological or formal questions of theology do not permit of adjudication apart from explicit attention to the material or substantive questions of theological interpretation. Disagreements *about* theology reflect, in this view, differing answers to the questions *of* theology. Hence, debates about method can sometimes beg the crucial issue if these formal questions are treated in isolation from the larger theological frameworks of which they are a part.[28]

This book examines the development of the question of Christian faith as religion in one strand of Protestant theology: the Reformed tradition of Calvin. The comparison of Schleiermacher with Calvin is designed to demonstrate that liberal theology's attempt to delineate a necessary religious dimension of common human experience in relation to which Christian faith is to be understood is a modern formulation of a theological concern that had already been articulated during the

Reformation.[29] This treatment of Christian faith and religion as a material issue of theological interpretation is thus intended to shift the contemporary debate in Protestant theology away from excessive preoccupation with questions of method and back to substantive concerns, such as those raised by the neo-orthodox theologians. It is also designed to assist in the disentangling of philosophical and theological criticisms, especially since contemporary critics of Schleiermacher's legacy have invoked explicitly non-theological arguments in support of their theological objections. Although this study does not attempt a normative proposal for understanding Christian faith as religion, it does lay a historical foundation for further constructive reflection.

The focus of this study, then, is on theology's criterion of appropriateness in order to assess the liberal tradition's claim to be an authentic heir to the Reformation heritage in the modern world. Through the comparison of Schleiermacher with Calvin, the substantive continuity of liberal theology with the Reformation is delineated in spite of a shift in the formulation of the question of Christian faith as religion. If the theological method of liberal theology should turn out to be a fitting formal expression of its material interpretation of Christian faith, criticisms of the liberal attempt to delineate a religious dimension of human experience must take sufficient notice of this relation of theological content and method so as not to obscure the crucial issues faced by Protestant theology in a new situation of ecumenism and religious pluralism.[30] The important methodological questions of constructive theology, including that of its relation to the discipline of religious studies, may profitably be taken up anew once Protestant theologians have a deeper understanding of the contemporary situation in which they find themselves and its relation to their theological heritage that only the long perspective of historical study can provide.

NOTES

1. *Systematic Theology*, 3 vols. (Chicago: The University of Chicago Press, 1951-1963), 1:7.
2. Gerhard Ebeling observes that "the relation between the gospel and religion has become one, if not, indeed, the central, problem of the history of theology in our century." "Evangelium und Religion," in *Theologie in den Gegensätzen des Lebens*, vol. 4 of *Wort und Glaube* (Tübingen: J. C. B. Mohr [Paul Siebeck], 1995), p. 28. I am indebted to Hans Dieter Betz for drawing my attention to this most recent volume of Ebeling's essays. Secondary literature originally published in a foreign language has been cited according to standard English translations where these are available. In those cases where no

translation exists, the translations given are mine. Translations of primary texts are my own except where reference to an English translation is explicitly made.

3. The terms "liberal" and "neo-orthodox" are broad designations which cannot be used with precision since they embrace theologians who sometimes differed greatly among themselves in their development of a shared set of themes and concerns. Furthermore, not all theologians who are so characterized applied these terms to themselves. In general, however, "liberal" may be taken to describe "the spirit and attitude of those who sought to incorporate in Christian theology the values of freedom of thought, tolerance, and the humanitarian motives in modern Western culture." Daniel Day Williams, "Liberalism," in *A Handbook of Christian Theology: Definition Essays on Concepts and Movements of Thought in Contemporary Protestantism*, ed. Arthur A. Cohen and Marvin Halverson (Nashville: Abingdon Press, 1958), p. 207. By contrast, "neo-orthodox" describes "a response to the developing crisis of the Western world. . . . When, therefore, the self-confidence of that culture began to wane, and its foundations to collapse after the First World War, an understandable response occurred from the more sensitive Christian leaders. This response (e.g. in Karl Barth and Emil Brunner) was a passionate attempt to locate the sources of the Christian message and the ground of its hope beyond a culture in crisis." Langdon Gilkey, "Neo-Orthodoxy," in *A Handbook of Christian Theology*, p. 256.

4. Karl Barth, *The Doctrine of the Word of God*, vol. 1.2 of *Church Dogmatics*, trans. G. T. Thomson and Harold Knight (Edinburgh: T. & T. Clark; New York: Charles Scribner's Sons, 1956), §17, pp. 280-361.

5. Dietrich Bonhoeffer, *Letters and Papers from Prison*, rev. ed., ed. Eberhard Bethge and trans. Reginald H. Fuller (New York: Macmillan, 1967), pp. 138-43 (letter of 30 April, 1944) and pp. 167-72 (letter of 8 June, 1944).

6. The differing views of Barth and Bonhoeffer are appropriated as mutually complementary resources in the construction of a contemporary "theological critique of religion" by Hans-Joachim Kraus, *Theologische Religionskritik*, Neukirchener Beiträge zur systematischen Theologie 2 (Neukirchen-Vluyn: Neukirchener Verlag, 1982).

7. "[T]he impact of Barth on Germany was so great that when I returned to Germany in 1948, I was immediately criticized by my friends for still using the word 'religion.' It had been, so to speak, eradicated from the theological discussion in Germany." Paul Tillich, *A History of Christian Thought: From its Judaic and Hellenistic Origins to Existentialism*, ed. Carl E. Braaten (New York: Simon and Schuster, 1967-68), p. 404. It is very difficult to sort out the substantive issues in the controversies between Barth, Bonhoeffer, and Tillich on account of their lack of agreement on a common definition of "religion." An attempt in this direction, however, has been made by Benkt-Erik Benktson, *Christus und die Religion: Der Religionsbegriff bei Barth, Bonhoeffer und Tillich*, Arbeiten zur Theologie 9, zweite Reihe (Stuttgart: Calwer Verlag, 1967).

8. Gilkey points out the historic importance of the decolonization of the non-Western world after World War II for understanding the cultural and social context of the new religious pluralism in theology. "Plurality: Christianity's New Situation," in *Through the Tempest: Theological Voyages in a Pluralistic*

Culture, selected and edited by Jeff B. Pool (Minneapolis: Fortress Press, 1991), pp. 21-24.

9. The close relation between the secularization of the modern West to which Bonhoeffer called attention and the development of "religious studies" as distinct from "theology" must not be overlooked, since the modern study of religion proceeds from the axiom that "religion should be approached as being something eminently *human.*" Walter H. Capps, *Religious Studies: The Making of a Discipline* (Minneapolis: Fortress Press, 1995), p. 8

10. Beginning in the 1960's, many Protestant theologians gave expression to their decisive break with neo-orthodox modes of thought. William Hamilton, for example, wrote: "If by definition religion equals sin, and you then say revelation ought to be against religion, you may bring some delight to careless readers, but you have not forwarded theological clarity very much." "The Death of God Theologies Today," in *Radical Theology and the Death of God,* ed. Thomas J. J. Altizer and William Hamilton (Indianapolis: The Bobbs-Merrill Company, 1966), p. 39.

11. George A. Lindbeck, *The Nature of Doctrine: Religion and Theology in a Postliberal Age* (Philadelphia: The Westminster Press, 1984), p. 31. Lindbeck draws his characterization of the "experiential-expressive" theory of religion from Roman Catholic theologian Bernard Lonergan, *Method in Theology* (New York: Herder and Herder, 1972), pp. 101-24 (Lindbeck, p. 42, n. 1). The ecumenical character of contemporary theological debate is illustrated by the fact that Lindbeck ascribes this liberal model of religion to both Catholic and Protestant theologians.

12. Ibid., pp. 30, 32-33.

13. Ibid., p. 32.

14. Ibid., p. 30.

15. Lindbeck's reflections upon the relation between theories of religion and doctrine emerged out of his own extensive involvement in ecumenical dialogue. Ibid., p. 7.

16. Ibid., p. 18.

17. Ibid., p. 135.

18. See also Garrett Green, "Challenging the Religious Studies Canon: Karl Barth's Theory of Religion," in *The Journal of Religion* 75 (October 1995): 473-86. Would Barth claim he has a "theory of religion" that can be evaluated apart from his dogmatics?

19. William C. Placher explains his own initial attraction to Lindbeck's postliberal paradigm by saying "that it offered the best account of how to do theology, given the philosophical views I found most persuasive." *Unapologetic Theology: A Christian Voice in a Pluralistic Conversation* (Louisville: Westminster/John Knox Press, 1989), p. 7. The postliberal appeal to explicit modes of philosophical argument makes connection with the more implicit philosophical polemic against the liberal notion of religious experience found in the neo-orthodox theologians themselves. Lindbeck says that Barth avoided "the experiential-expressive turn to the subject" characteristic of modern philosophy, but does not mention his affinity for Feuerbach's anti-theological theory of religion. *The Nature of Doctrine,* p. 24. Barth's appropriation of

Feuerbach within the framework of his own theology is well summarized by
Reinhart Gruhn, "Religionskritik als Aufgabe der Theologie: Zur Kontroverse
'Religion statt Offenbarung?'" in *Evangelische Theologie* 39 (1979): 234-55.

20. The postliberal theologians acknowledge the necessity and even
legitimacy of "*ad hoc* apologetics" as distinct from a "systematic" or
"foundational" use of apologetics which is held to be characteristic of the liberal
tradition. Ronald F. Thiemann writes of "nonfoundational" theology's non-
systematic use of apologetics: "In the process of seeking justification it will
surely on occasion need to engage in conversation with positions external to the
Christian faith. Though the Christian faith has its own integrity, it does not exist
in a vacuum. The doctrine of God, Christology, anthropology, et. al., are all
influenced by concepts and categories derived from non-Christian sources. But
such borrowings are employed for distinctive Christian uses and sustained by
distinctive Christian practices and thus are no longer *systematically* ruled by the
original context. They are annexed for Christian purposes and ruled by the new
Christian context." *Revelation and Theology: The Gospel as Narrated Promise*
(Notre Dame: University of Notre Dame Press, 1985), pp. 74-75. Thiemann
explains: "This is the way Karl Barth conceives of Christian use of non-
Christian concepts." Ibid., p. 173, n. 7. This formulation of theology's relation
to philosophy, as well as the explicit appeal to a concept of religion defended on
non-theological grounds, suggests the possibility of a rapprochement between
the traditions of Schleiermacher and Barth inasmuch as it is acknowledged that
both positions correlate an interpretation of Christian faith derived from the
witness of scripture and tradition with insights into human existence indebted to
sources outside the circle of faith. The crucial question for the postliberals is the
character of this correlation, i.e., whether philosophy or theology has the upper
hand. In his typology of various kinds of theology, Hans W. Frei describes both
Schleiermacher and Barth as theologians who seek to relate Christian theology
positively to modern culture without sacrificing the integrity of the church's
confession of faith as expressed in its first-order doctrinal statements: "The third
and fourth types—represented by Schleiermacher and Barth—usually thought
to be at opposite poles, are very close under this typology and its topical center."
Types of Christian Theology, ed. George Hunsinger and William C. Placher
(New Haven and London: Yale University Press, 1992), p. 6.

21. For this formulation of correlational theology as obligated both to
criteria of appropriateness and adequacy, see David Tracy, *Blessed Rage for
Order: The New Pluralism in Theology* (New York: The Seabury Press, 1978),
p. 57, n. 4; also Schubert M. Ogden, "What Is Theology?" in *On Theology* (San
Francisco: Harper and Row, 1986), p. 4, who speaks of criteria of
appropriateness and credibility.

22. *Revelation and Theology*, p. 73. Thiemann agrees with Lindbeck's view
of the relation between liberal theology's interpretation of Christian doctrine
and its theory of religion: "This expressive or symbolic view of Christian
language and the urge toward foundationalism thus usually go hand in hand."
Ibid.

23. Ibid., p. 3.

24. Ibid.

25. Ibid., p. 4.

26. "Schleiermacher does not take the Christian claim to revelation to be 'beyond controversy'; its plausibility must be shown by an appeal to a formal, universal, precognitive form of experience which serves as the logical foundation for the particular Christian claim. . . . Like the reformers, Schleiermacher believes that our relation to God is given by God's grace, but he feels compelled to defend that conviction by arguing *first* that the God-relation is a universal element of human nature and *second* that the grace-given character of the relation is established by the marks of immediacy. The argument from absolute dependence is Schleiermacher's attempt to put the Christian belief in the prevenience of God's grace on a firmer universal footing." Ibid., p. 29.

27. For a discussion of Schleiermacher's role in the emergence of the modern study of religion, see Capps, *Religious Studies*, pp. 13-18.

28. To put it in other words, the formal questions of method should be understood as relatively abstract in relation to the concrete material issues with which a theological system is engaged. Gilkey writes: "[A] method in theology is not a neutral tool for theological discovery such that its loss alone spells theological frustration, and its reappearance, whatever the context, augurs success. Rather, a method is itself a part of that wider whole which is expressed in an entire philosophical or theological system. . . . Thus methods 'fit' the systems which they explain, and make little sense outside them." *Naming the Whirlwind: The Renewal of God-Language* (Indianapolis and New York: The Bobbs-Merrill Company, 1969), p. 190. In a discussion of Barth and Schleiermacher, James M. Gustafson makes a similar point when analyzing the relation of formal questions of theological method ("the philosophy of theology") to material issues of theological interpretation ("the substance of theology"). "In all of these works and in others, the philosopher of theology was also the investigator of the substance of theology. It is apparent to the reader of such works that the two tasks deeply inform each other, that something in intention like an experiment is taking place in which there are alterations in methods and procedures as a result of attempting to deal with substantive theological problems. Just as the most instructive work in literary criticism includes the discussion of texts in the light of the methods that are being espoused, so also instructive work in theology shapes method not only in relation to general philosophical questions but also in relation to the texts or the ideas to which the method is to be applied." *Ethics from a Theocentric Perspective*, vol. 1, *Theology and Ethics* (Chicago: The University of Chicago Press, 1981), p. 65. Tracy also acknowledges that his own "revisionist" model for theology is not "purely methodological or formal." *Blessed Rage*, p. 81; p. 109, n. 1.

29. B. A. Gerrish writes: "It is not forsaking either the sixteenth or the twentieth century if one turns to the nineteenth, since the question of nineteenth-century Protestant thought was precisely that of tradition and the modern world: What is to be done with the Reformation heritage in a world of which Calvin never dreamed?" *Tradition and the Modern World: Reformed Theology in the Nineteenth Century* (Chicago and London: The University of Chicago Press,

1978), p. x.

30. In my review of the collection of essays edited by James O. Duke and Robert F. Streetman entitled *Barth and Schleiermacher: Beyond the Impasse?* (Philadelphia: Fortress Press, 1988), I suggest that the proper way to approach the methodological issues between Barth and Schleiermacher is through a material comparison of the two theologians' differing interpretations of the meaning and significance of the Reformation heritage. *The Journal of Religion* 70 (July 1990): 467-69.

Chapter 1

The Interpretation of Religion as a Problem in Protestant Theology

From the Reformation to the Enlightenment

The Protestant Reformation began as a critique of disputed religious practices within Western Christianity. When, as legend has it, Luther posted his "Ninety-Five Theses" on the door of the Wittenberg church in 1517, he hoped to open a debate that would issue in the reform of religious life. But by the time of his death in 1546, Latin Christendom was divided against itself and the religious unity that had provided Western Europe with cultural cohesion for well over a thousand years was lost. Although the religious concerns of the Protestant Reformers were thoroughly medieval, the historical effects of their activities contributed to the eventual dissolution of medieval society. Over the next two centuries, a distinctively modern, secular civilization arose to take its place. With the Enlightenment's demand for a civilization freed from the domination of ecclesiastical interests—symbolized politically by the French Revolution of 1789—the modern world came into its own.

From the Reformation to the Enlightenment, Western civilization underwent its most profound transformation since Augustine had forged the medieval religious synthesis out of the cultural chaos occasioned by the demise of the Roman Empire. The development of Protestantism as a distinct variation of this Augustinian religious heritage coincides with the transformation of the West from its medieval to its modern form. For that reason, the history of Protestant theology itself can be divided into two epochs: the classical period, in which the Protestant alternative to Catholic theology was initially formulated, and the modern period, in which this Protestant theological heritage was reformulated in response to the challenges that the Enlightenment posed to the medieval view of the world.

As a consequence of the transition from the medieval to the modern situation, the two epochs of Protestant theology were characterized by differing religious questions and concerns. The Reformation arose in response to the anxiety felt by religious persons in the late medieval period when they considered their standing before God on Judgment Day. As an answer to this fear of eternal damnation, Luther's doctrine of "justification by faith alone" was intended to assure the guilty conscience of God's merciful forgiveness. By contrast, the shift to a modern worldview generated a new religious anxiety. Instead of asking how we may escape God's wrath, the modern person is more inclined to wonder whether God exists at all. In response to this new religious question raised by the Enlightenment, modern theologians have tended to reinterpret Luther's "faith" so as to provide an assurance that human life does have some ultimate meaning and purpose even in a cosmos that does not seem to require God as an explanatory principle. The historical task of describing the development of Protestant theology from its original sixteenth-century formulation to its modern reformulations must take seriously this shift in the religious questions to which it sought to respond.[1]

Whereas the Reformation was the crisis *within* medieval religion, the Enlightenment was the crisis *of* medieval religion.[2] In the sixteenth century both Catholic and Protestant took it for granted that Christianity is the true religion of humankind. At stake in the dispute was, rather, the question: Which interpretation of Christian faith is true? Each side accused the other of teaching "false religion" as a consequence of having departed from the ancient truth that had been divinely revealed. By contrast, the Enlightenment suggested another possibility: perhaps both Catholicism and Protestantism are simply differing expressions of medieval superstition. In this case, the antidote to superstition is to be found in the enlightened reason.[3] Hence, in addition to pointing out that the religious question underwent a significant change from the Reformation to the Enlightenment, it must also be noted that the criteria for criticism of religious traditions underwent tremendous development as well.

This means that the Reformation and the Enlightenment were religious crises in the West that, in each instance, occasioned serious reflection upon the meaning of the concept "religion" itself and the criteria for determining its truth.[4] In the classical period, Protestants defended their doctrine of justification by faith alone as the original form of the Christian message. On the basis of this reformulation of the Catholic doctrinal tradition, they proceeded to reform the church's practices so as to bring them into conformity with "true religion" as revealed in scripture. By contrast, their modern descendants sought to understand the nature of religious experience itself in a world where scientific inquiry had rendered discourse about God problematic. Moreover, they asked anew what it means to confess the apostolic faith in the face of historical-critical inquiry that threatened to undermine the authority of the Bible and the church's doctrinal traditions.

Calvin and Schleiermacher have been chosen for a comparative study in order to illustrate this historical shift in the theological question because each theologian makes a methodical use of the concept "religion" in his systematic presentation of Protestant doctrine. An investigation of both theologians with respect to their interpretations of religion and Christian faith as religion can illuminate this movement from classical to modern Protestant theology in response to the two crises of religion in the Western world. Such comparative analysis contributes to clarification of the general historical question regarding the shifts within Western religion from the medieval to the modern period.

Apart from purely historical interest, however, the comparison is important for reasons of a theological nature. While the historian may determine from a vantage point outside of a given tradition that its encounter with modernity has effected certain transformations within it, it is another thing altogether to understand how persons within that tradition make sense of such changes. Whereas the historical question is descriptive (How has a tradition changed?), the theological question is normative (How are changes in the tradition to be evaluated?). Among Protestant theologians in the modern world, there is widespread agreement that the Enlightenment has been the occasion for tremendous change within the tradition of the Reformation. But there is no consensus regarding how the transition from classical to modern Protestantism is to be evaluated.

By analyzing neo-orthodoxy's assessment that the line of continuity with the classical heritage of Protestantism had been severed in the modern era, the relation between the descriptive question of history and the normative question of theology can be investigated. Since Schleiermacher was the towering figure whose name, more than any other, was associated with the new course that Protestant theology had set for itself in response to the Enlightenment, it is not surprising that critical scrutiny has focused on his work and its historical effects upon the nineteenth century as a whole.[5] For this reason, the historical task of undertaking a comparison of Schleiermacher with Calvin is of more than historical interest since it involves the question of the normative self-understanding of Protestant theology in the twentieth century in relation to the two epochs of its own heritage.

The Neo-Orthodox Critique of Liberal Theology

According to Karl Barth (1886-1968) and Emil Brunner (1889-1966), modern theology signifies a momentous "defection" from the Reformation heritage. Schleiermacher and his progeny, they argued, took Protestant theology down the wrong path by turning its attention away from the divinely revealed Word of God in Christ and toward human religious experience. Accordingly, the great chasm separating modern theology from the theology of the Reformation can be succinctly formulated as the choice between divine revelation or human religion.

On account of their understanding of the antithetical relation between classical and modern Protestant theology, Barth and Brunner felt compelled to repudiate the tradition of liberal theology in which they had been educated. In so doing, they believed they were recovering the great themes of the Reformation: *sola gratia, sola fide,* and *sola scriptura.* In their judgment, liberal theology had lost (or, at least, badly obscured) precisely these themes. The problem lay in the attempt on the part of modern theologians to come to terms with the Enlightenment. Schleiermacher bore the brunt of their criticism, not because he was the worst offender, but because he was the most brilliant.

Brunner launched his polemic against Schleiermacher in 1924 with a book entitled *Mysticism and the Word.* The subtitle clearly indicates the case against Schleiermacher that its author was concerned to prosecute: "The Contrast between the Modern Interpretation of Religion and Christian Faith, illustrated by the Theology of Schleiermacher." Brunner's argument with Schleiermacher is based upon his premise that there are two fundamentally opposed ways of being religious: "mysticism" and "faith." Mysticism is the yearning for an experience of union between the finite and the infinite. It is a hallmark of mysticism that the experience of the soul's union with God defies the light of conceptual clarification and seeks refuge in the elusiveness of the symbol. In opposition to mysticism, faith depends upon the Word for its very existence and encourages the examination into the truth that Christian theology has always represented. Schleiermacher's ill-fated significance for modern Protestantism is that he substituted the mystical understanding of religious experience for the faith that trusts and obeys God's Word. By confusing religious experience (mysticism) with Christian faith, and then proceeding to build a theology based upon this confusion, Schleiermacher has brought a Trojan horse into the heart of the Protestant camp. In Brunner's assessment, his theological generation was confronted with a decision between mortal enemies: either Christ or modern religion.[6]

Brunner was convinced that the question regarding the nature of religion constitutes the real heart of Schleiermacher's theology. As a result, the general concept of religion determined the content of Schleiermacher's dogmatics to the detriment of its *Christian* character. In contrast to Schleiermacher's "religion," Brunner opposes the "biblical-Reformation" view of faith. Whereas religion is mere subjective feeling, faith arises out of the objective proclamation of God's truth. Consequently, Brunner describes Schleiermacher's theology as "expressionistic," giving words to an experience that does not refer to anything beyond itself.

Brunner wiped his hands of Schleiermacher once and for all after delivering his negative verdict. He scarcely considered Schleiermacher a Christian at all, let alone a Protestant theologian! Indeed, he expressed amazement that the liberal theologians of the nineteenth century who prided themselves on their historical consciousness could have considered Schleiermacher the renewer of Reformation theology. The only solution to this riddle that Brunner can propose is that the apologetic interest in defending religion against modern atheism had so possessed their souls that they forgot to consider *which* religion it was they were anxious to defend.[7]

Barth's criticism is different both in its shape and its tone. In Barth's judgment, Schleiermacher was the greatest Protestant theologian since the Reformation. Indeed, throughout the course of his life Barth returned again and again to reconsider Schleiermacher's work, ever wanting to give his old adversary the benefit of the doubt and even leaving open the possibility that the future of theology may still belong to him after all.[8] Yet in spite of this generosity of spirit, Barth never reversed his judgment upon Schleiermacher and the responsibility he bears for the problematic character of modern Protestant theology.

Barth believed that Schleiermacher led theology down a dangerous path leading in the end to a subjectivistic anthropocentrism that stands in striking contrast to the theological objectivity of the Reformers. According to this view, Schleiermacher's program for theology, with its concern to interpret Christian faith as a distinct type of religious experience, is antithetical to a theology based upon God's revelation in Jesus Christ. In Barth's theology, the concept "religion" has predominantly negative overtones. Barth defines religion as "the realm of man's attempts to justify and to sanctify himself before a capricious and arbitrary picture of God."[9] Human religion, therefore, represents the perennial attempt at justification by works. Opposed to the works of religion is the grace of revelation upon which faith stands. Armed with this antithetical understanding of religion (justification by works) and revelation (justification by faith), Barth levels his critique at Schleiermacher and the liberal tradition for replacing revelation with religion, which is tantamount to placing one's confidence in works-righteousness.

Barth does concede, however, that there is a sense in which Christianity can be called a religion. Religion is the way human beings receive revelation. Revelation is an event that "has at least the form of human competence, experience and activity. And it is at this point that we come up against the problem of man's religion."[10] Indeed, Barth affirms that "[t]he Church is the locus of true religion, so far as through grace it lives by grace."[11] Even with respect to this formulation, however, Barth remains cautious lest the recognition of an inescapably human dimension become the occasion for theology to abandon its true basis and proper theme. The real issue, he tells us, is whether what we know of human religion

> must serve as a norm and principle by which to explain the revelation of God; or, *vice versa*, does it mean that we have to interpret the Christian religion and all other religions by what we are told by God's revelation?[12]

Barth finds the chief hallmark of modern Protestantism to lie in a subversion of this crucial relationship between religion and revelation:

> [R]eligion has not to be understood in the light of revelation, but revelation in the light of religion. To this common denominator the aims and programmes of all the more important tendencies of modern theology can be reduced.[13]

On account of this fateful subordination of revelation to religion, liberal Protestant theology is "religionism."

Barth characterizes modern theology as "apologetic" because, in his eyes, its form and content are constituted by the attempt to answer Christianity's "cultured despisers." The problem with apologetics, however, is that what may at first appear as a laudable effort to commend the church's faith to the world turns out to be, upon closer inspection, a lack of faith in the efficacy of God's Word to create faith when and where the Spirit wills.[14] At the root of the new development in modern theology, Barth judges that "originally and properly the sin was one of unbelief."[15] The sacrifice of revelation for religion is, then, the original sin of liberal theology:

> That it really lost revelation is shown by the very fact that it could exchange it, and with it its own birthright, for the concept "religion."[16]

Believing that "religionism" is an abandonment of authentic biblical faith as proclaimed by the Reformers, Barth spent his tremendous energies and talents attempting to clear the ground for a theology that hearkens solely to God's Word revealed in Jesus Christ as the scriptures attest it. In this concern, he saw himself as a loyal son of the Reformation.

There are, however, tendencies in the works of the Reformers themselves, as Barth acknowledges, that have played into the hands of liberal theologians. One such example is Calvin's use of the term *religio*.

> After the humanistic fashion, Calvin spoke of the *religio christiana* even in the title page of his *chef d'oeuvre*. But when he did so he was not conscious of making *christiana* the predicate of something human in a neutral and universal sense.[17]

Barth clearly recognizes the influence of Renaissance humanism on the style of Calvin's language. Yet he believes this is simply Calvin's way of speaking and that humanism exercises no substantive influence upon the concept "religion" in his theology. Religion, for Calvin, is "a normative concept which he has derived from Holy Scripture, and in which the universal is sublimated in the particular, religion in revelation, and not *vice versa*."[18]

Although Barth judges Calvin to have been influenced by the Renaissance only as regards the form of his thought, he is quite certain that modern theology has been influenced by the humanistic outlook in both its form and its substance.

> The period of the 16th-18th centuries was in its own way a great period, when European man resumed the powerful offensive which had been made by Graeco-Roman antiquity, beginning to discover himself as a man, his nature, his possibilities and capacities, humanity. The discovery of "religion" belonged, of course, to the same movement. It was in the nature of things that theology should have its part in that discovery.[19]

In a fundamental sense, "the problem of human religion" is simply "the problem of man in general." Nonetheless, by substituting religion for revelation, theology thus "fell prey to the absolutism with which the man of that period made himself the centre and measure and goal of all

things."[20] Unlike Calvin, who was "able quietly to incorporate this
problem into his discussion and exposition," the anthropocentric
theology of the modern period isolated "piety from the Word of God ...
making of it a distinct and prior chapter."[21]

Barth's criticism of "religionism" is tied to his understanding of
"natural theology." Natural theology is the attempt to know God
through means other than God's revelation to human beings. When
Barth speaks of "revelation" he means, quite strictly, God's revelation
in Jesus Christ. This christological restriction is crucial because it
enables him to reject any suggestion of a universal revelation of God to
human beings apart from Christ, even if one should argue, as Brunner
himself tried to do, that God's revelation in the creation cannot properly
be perceived apart from Jesus Christ.[22] Barth believed the only way to
secure the authentically Christian character of theology (i.e., that
theology is obedient reflection upon God's word to us and not speech
about the human being in a loud voice!) is to insist upon this
epistemological restriction. Thus his controversies with other
theologians, including his erstwhile comrade Brunner, revolved around
the issue of the sources for theology's knowledge about God.

By means of this epistemological concentration upon Jesus Christ
as the sole locus of God's revelation, Barth diagnosed natural theology
to be the malady afflicting Roman Catholic and liberal Protestant
theology alike. In his judgment, it is the perennial threat to Christian
theology against which the Reformers sought to secure the church's
faith.[23] This polemic against natural theology lies at the heart of Barth's
construal of the Reformation heritage, and of the Reformed tradition of
Calvin in particular. He believed the defense of revelation to be
particularly strong in the Reformed tradition's insistence that genuine
knowledge of God is only to be found in the biblical witness to Christ.[24]
His opposition to human religion, then, reflects the consequent resolve
of the Reformed theologian to withstand natural theology in the name
of God's exclusive revelation in Jesus Christ.

"There is an obvious difference," Barth contends, "between
regarding religion as the problem of theology and regarding it as only
one problem in theology." By the same token, he continues, "there is an
obvious difference between regarding faith as a form of human piety
and regarding it as a form of the judgment and grace of God." This
"obvious difference" is the decision that has to be made between
religion and revelation. For Barth, "one of the most difficult historical
puzzles" is to explain how "in the manifestations of modern
Protestantism in the 19th and 20th centuries, as it developed from its
16th and 17th century root, the great characteristic decisions have all
gone on the side of the first alternatives."[25] Nonetheless, what may be

a puzzle for the historian demands of the theologian a decision:

> Until better instructed, I can see no way from Schleiermacher, or from
> his contemporary epigones, to the chroniclers, prophets, and wise
> ones of Israel, to those who narrate the story of the life, death, and
> resurrection of Jesus Christ, to the word of the apostles—no way to
> the God of Abraham, Isaac, and Jacob and the Father of Jesus Christ,
> no way to the great tradition of the Christian church. For the present
> I can see nothing here but a choice. And for me there can be no
> question as to how that choice is to be made.[26]

Barth and Brunner both conclude that there is the sharpest possible
discontinuity in the ways religion has been interpreted in classical and
liberal Protestant theology. Whether the contrast is drawn, as with
Barth, between revelation and religion or, with Brunner, between faith
and religious experience, the verdict is the same: liberal Protestantism
represents a radical departure from the theological substance of the
Reformation in its employment of religion as a concept for the
interpretation of Christian faith. In each construal of the problem, the
liberal understanding of Christian faith as religion is not merely
different from that of classical Protestantism, but opposed to it.

This historical analysis of Protestant theology's development from
its classical to its modern form played an important role in the self-
understanding of the neo-orthodox theologians who saw themselves
called to re-establish their continuity with the Reformers by rejecting
the line of Schleiermacher. The descriptive judgment of an antithetical
relation between the two epochs of Protestant theology thus supplied a
warrant for the normative judgment to reject religion as a category for
the theological interpretation of Christian faith. Nonetheless, Barth and
Brunner both admit that their descriptions of radical discontinuity leave
them with an unsolved historical riddle on their hands. Barth says it is
"one of the most difficult historical puzzles" to explain how the
Reformation of the sixteenth century could have produced its own
antithesis in the liberal theology of the nineteenth century. Brunner
expresses astonishment that the historically-minded liberal theologians
could have been so blind to the discrepancy between their own
interpretation of Christian faith and that of the original Reformers.

The historical student of Protestantism must make a decision: either
to find the adequate historical explanation that would solve the riddle of
radical discontinuity between classical and liberal Protestantism
uncovered by the neo-orthodox or to pose the historical question in a
different manner. In the latter case, a revision of the categories
employed by the neo-orthodox theologians is required.

Revising the Neo-Orthodox Historiography

After the neo-orthodox consensus within Protestant theology began
to unravel in the second half of our century, theologians took up anew
the questions raised by the liberals in the nineteenth century.[27] This
altered situation in theology also occasioned a reconsideration of the
neo-orthodox view of the historical relation between the two epochs of
Protestant theology. In this context, the question of Schleiermacher's
standing in the tradition of the Reformation was examined afresh.[28]

No one in recent years has done more to challenge the neo-
orthodox historiography than B. A. Gerrish. At the heart of Gerrish's
revised interpretation of the two epochs of Protestant theology is a re-
examination of the notion of "tradition." Gerrish wants to understand a
tradition (in this case, the tradition of the Reformation) as a living,
dynamic movement through time.[29] To say that traditions are dynamic
is to admit that traditions change over the course of time. Precisely
because they are dynamic, the question of continuity within a tradition
is not so simple a matter as repeating in the twentieth century the
slogans of the sixteenth. Those who merely repeat what has been said
before may actually be saying something quite different from what was
originally meant.[30] Just because the rhetoric of Barth and Brunner may
at times sound more like Luther or Calvin than does that of their
nineteenth-century predecessors does not mean that they actually are
closer in substance to the Reformers. Traditions change along with the
changing circumstances of the people who transmit them. For that
reason, it is always a difficult matter to hazard a guess as to how the
Reformers themselves might have answered the distinctively modern
challenges faced by Schleiermacher.

Gerrish goes further, however, than simply saying that, in fact,
traditions do change. He finds something characteristically Protestant in
the notion of "continuity as a kind of change."[31] Not only did Luther
recast the inherited doctrinal tradition of Catholicism in the name of
fidelity to that tradition itself, but even Calvin's attitude toward the
tradition of Luther is best described as one of critical deference: Calvin
felt free to learn from Luther as well as to criticize him.[32] And in his
reply to Cardinal Sadoleto on behalf of the Genevans, Calvin retorted
that unquestioned allegiance to the tradition of one's ancestors is a poor
defense of religion.[33] In this view, fidelity to a tradition (*traditio*) lies
less in unswerving loyalty to whatever has been handed down from the
past (as *traditum*) than in a critical appropriation and creative
transformation of the past (as *tradendum*) for the sake of the present and
the future.

In view of this "Protestant" notion of tradition as a sort of faithful change, Gerrish reminds us that the great liberal theologians of the nineteenth century understood themselves as doing in their own day what Luther and Calvin did in theirs: revising the received tradition so as to hand it down in the best form for a new age.

> If the liberal Protestants claimed the right to a critical use of tradition, they were in principle claiming nothing more than did Luther and Calvin; Protestantism was revisionary from the first.[34]

It is precisely this deferential yet critical posture toward the Reformation heritage that Gerrish finds exemplified in Schleiermacher's understanding of the task of theology as a further development of the Protestant tradition.[35] As Schleiermacher affirmed, "The Reformation still goes on!"[36] To understand Schleiermacher's relation to the classical Protestant heritage, it is necessary to examine how he sought to develop it in fidelity to what he discerned to be its enduring significance for Christianity.

But there is another, more precise sense in which Gerrish wants to re-examine the question of Schleiermacher's standing as a Protestant theologian: Schleiermacher was a pastor of the Reformed church who took his own origins in the Reformed tradition seriously.[37] To be sure, he was not interested in being Reformed in any narrowly confessional sense, since the Prussian state church in which he served was a "union" of the Lutherans and the Reformed. Consequently, he aimed at being a Protestant (*evangelisch*) theologian in a broad, appreciative spirit of ecumenism. Nonetheless, when it came to precise differences of doctrine between them, Schleiermacher professed his allegiance to "the Reformed school."[38] Hence, the question of Schleiermacher's relation to the Reformation should not necessarily be formulated as that of Schleiermacher's relation to Luther, as Gerrish points out has often been the case.[39] It ought, rather, to be formulated as that of Schleiermacher's relation to Calvin.[40]

Gerrish's interest in comparing Schleiermacher with Calvin has been focused primarily on questions regarding the theme, method, and shape of Protestant dogmatics. Since Calvin's *Institutes of the Christian Religion* and Schleiermacher's *The Christian Faith* are the best exemplars of the genre of dogmatics in the two epochs of Protestant theology, comparison of these works illustrates in a singularly clear fashion what was involved in the "paradigm shift" from classical to liberal theology.[41] The constructive question Gerrish seeks to illuminate through his historical analysis is what it means for modern theologians to undertake the task of Protestant dogmatics once all the dogmas of the past (including those of the sixteenth century!) have been thoroughly historicized.[42]

Though both Calvin and Schleiermacher understand the properly dogmatic task of Protestant theology to consist in giving an ordered or systematic presentation of the Christian faith which aims to show the logical interconnections among the church's various doctrines, the chief difference between the classical and the liberal paradigms has to do with the way this common understanding of the dogmatic task is implemented. Calvin's *Institutes* is not a biblical commentary; still, Calvin's dogmatic procedure is to give a systematic arrangement to the doctrinal principles he has discovered through his exegesis of the Bible. By Schleiermacher's time, however, biblical exegesis had become more sharply differentiated from dogmatic theology as a distinct discipline in its own right. In his encyclopedic survey of theological studies, Schleiermacher classified biblical exegesis as the first part of historical theology whereas he assigned dogmatics to the final part of historical theology. This means that exegesis of the Bible is concerned to understand the earliest stage of the development of Christian doctrine while dogmatics is concerned with the state of the church's doctrine in the present historical moment (hence, Schleiermacher's description of it as a part of the larger enterprise of historical theology).[43] Unlike Calvin's, therefore, Schleiermacher's dogmatics is not an attempt to systematize the results of biblical exegesis. It is, rather, an effort to illustrate how the inherited doctrines "hang together" as expressions of the living faith experienced by Protestant Christians.[44] As sources for his description of this experience of faith, Schleiermacher turned to the classical Lutheran and Reformed confessions since these documents contain the purest expressions of the Protestant spirit by virtue of their historical proximity to the originating events of the Reformation.

In spite of these differences in the classical and the liberal paradigms, Gerrish finds a striking similarity in the methodological ideal for Protestant dogmatics that the two Reformed theologians strive to emulate. That ideal may be described (to play on the title of Kant's famous book) as the pursuit of "theology within the limits of piety alone."[45] While Calvin's central theme is the knowledge of God, it is always a knowledge of God in relation to oneself. The knowledge with which faith is concerned is not the "empty speculation" of the philosophers but, rather, that which is framed by piety (*pietas*). "Indeed," Calvin explains in the opening pages of his *Institutes*, "we shall not say that, properly speaking, God is known where there is no religion or piety."[46] Schleiermacher's most apparent link to his Reformed ancestor lies precisely in his own use of the term "piety" (*Frömmigkeit*) to indicate the theme of dogmatics. Eschewing speculation (*Weltweisheit*) as much as Calvin, Schleiermacher makes it a methodological principle that all statements within a system of Christian doctrine must be interpreted in strict relation to the Christian religious affections.[47] While Calvin turns directly to the Bible as the immediate source for his theology framed by piety, Schleiermacher employs the Protestant confessions. Nonetheless, the crucial commonality here is to be discerned in their understanding of dogmatics as a *descriptive* enterprise that refrains from speculative knowledge of God by insuring that the interpretation of doctrine never loses touch with the concrete experience of faith in Christ as this is actually known among Protestant Christians.[48]

Since both Calvin and Schleiermacher aspire after a descriptive account of Protestant faith that excludes "speculation" by keeping to the rule of "piety alone," the first task that faces each theologian is to delineate the nature of piety or religion. Gerrish writes:

> In Calvin, as in Schleiermacher, the theme of *pietas*, broadened into an account of *homo religiosus*, has become the first item on a carefully structured dogmatic agenda, and it continues to regulate the agenda by its exclusion of speculation from beginning to end. [49]

In striking contrast to the neo-orthodox assessment, Gerrish concludes that it is precisely the experiential character of Schleiermacher's theology that "contains the clue to reappraising him as a church theologian in the legitimate succession of Luther and Calvin."[50] Gerrish thus proposes a revised framework for comparing the classical and liberal paradigms of Protestant theology within which the differing ways Calvin and Schleiermacher seek to implement a common ideal for the dogmatic task can be explored.

By asking what it means to do "theology within the limits of piety alone" in the classical and liberal paradigms, it becomes evident that there is an important similarity in the formal structure according to which Calvin and Schleiermacher shape their dogmatic systems. Both divide their dogmatics into two parts, corresponding to the distinction between the doctrine of creation and the doctrine of redemption. This distinction allows them to organize their dogmatic treatises around two *foci*: a relation to God as creator and a relation to God as redeemer. Within this framework, each theologian interprets the universal phenomenon of human religiousness as a response, however inadequate, to the relation to God as creator constitutive of human existence as such. The distinctive character of Christian faith is that the relation to God is shaped and formed by the redemptive relation to Jesus Christ. In faith God is known as the redeemer, who brings the human being into appropriate relation to its creator. Thus "faith" is the actualization of "piety" which is the religious ideal for human existence.

Calvin speaks of a "twofold knowledge of God" (*duplex cognitio Dei*), referring to the difference between knowing God as the creator and providential sustainer of all things and knowing God as the redeemer in the face of Christ. Both aspects are essential to the complete dogmatic explication of *Christian* faith. Schleiermacher, too, divides his dogmatic treatise into two parts: a description of the religious consciousness as it is determined by the antithesis of sin and grace (redemption) and a description of the religious consciousness as it is presupposed by, as well as contained in, the antithesis of sin and grace (creation and preservation). In both accounts, an adequate explication of specifically Christian faith requires for its completeness a consideration of the universally human relation to God implied in the doctrine of creation. To be sure, the Christian's redemptive experience of faith cannot be deduced from the universally human experience of dependence upon God's creative and sustaining power; yet it is equally certain that the distinctive character of Christian faith cannot be understood apart from this general human experience of dependence upon God for our very existence in relation to whom some religious response is inescapable.

This recognition of the common shape of their dogmatic systems has implications for a contemporary reassessment of the ways in which the neo-orthodox theologians posed the question of Schleiermacher's relation to Calvin. If both Reformed theologians posit a religious response to God as constitutive of human existence simply as such and proceed to elucidate this religious aspect of our common human experience as a necessary, though not a sufficient, step toward clarifying the distinctively Christian religious response of faith, then the great alternatives before which Brunner and Barth placed their generation may have been based on a misleading comparative framework.

In response to Brunner, Gerrish argues that the attempt to pit "biblical-Reformation" faith against Schleiermacher's "religion" is wrongheaded:

> The propriety of [Brunner's] move may well be questioned. It would surely make more sense to compare what Calvin says of faith with what Schleiermacher says of faith, and what Schleiermacher says of religion or piety with Calvin's term *pietas*—or perhaps with the *sensus divinitatis* suggested to him by the natural theology of an "eminent pagan" (Cicero).[51]

Furthermore, Gerrish disputes whether a Barthian description of Calvin as a "christocentric" theologian is really an accurate standard against which to measure the Reformed character of Schleiermacher's theology:

> It was certainly a monstrous interpretation when Karl Barth spoke of christology as a "great disturbance" in Schleiermacher's dogmatics. And yet it can hardly be established that Schleiermacher was really a christocentric theologian in the strictest sense. . . . It all depends on the meaning assigned to the term "christocentric." But this much, at least, may be said with assurance: According to Schleiermacher, the religiousness of Christians, like everyone else's, is as such constituted by their humanity, not by their relation to Christ, who is rather the source of its Christianness and its peculiar strength. And since Calvin, like Schleiermacher, found that he needed to talk about *homo religiosus* before he could expound faith in Christ, might it be useful to ask if Schleiermacher's theology is perhaps *not* christocentric— and therefore *gut calvinistisch*?[52]

From the perspective provided by this revised posing of the problem, the alleged discovery of an unbridgeable chasm that separates classical and liberal theology on account of the antithetical nature of the concepts religion and faith, on the one hand, or religion and revelation, on the other hand, can only seem mistaken. It suggests that the historical puzzle of the relation between the two epochs of Protestant theology that so baffled Barth and Brunner may be the result of reading back into history their own formulation of the crucial issues they confronted after the First World War.

It is not insignificant, I think, that Barth and Brunner themselves came from the Reformed tradition. The great neo-orthodox theologians who stood in the Lutheran tradition, such as Tillich and Bultmann, did not make Schleiermacher the direct target of their criticisms of the liberal tradition.[53] Perhaps the controversy concerning Schleiermacher should be seen, at least in part, as a question within Reformed theology in the twentieth century about the legacy of Calvin's tradition in the modern world.[54] The verdict of the neo-orthodox theologians stood in striking contrast to that of Schleiermacher's pupil, Alexander Schweizer, who believed that Schleiermacher had revived a distinctively Reformed consciousness in his execution of the dogmatic task of Protestant theology.

> Only Schleiermacher, working in the spirit of the Reformed school, took up Reformed dogmatics anew and furthered it in such a way that it can belong to a united church without losing its identity.[55]

Barth was aware of Schweizer's claim and it troubled him.

"Embarrassing for Brunner and me," he wrote, "if it were so! That it is not so—I would very much like to be fully convinced of that! But this is not, for the time being, raised so far above all doubt that one could immediately build one's house on it."[56]

The cumulative weight of these observations amply justifies a reconsideration of Schleiermacher as a theologian in the tradition of Calvin, especially in the pivotal issue of religion and Christian faith where the neo-orthodox claimed to have uncovered the greatest discontinuity between classical and liberal Protestant theology. By adopting Gerrish's dynamic understanding of tradition, the comparison of Reformed theologians from the classical and liberal epochs of Protestantism need not be constricted from the start by an exceedingly narrow notion of what it means to stand in the line of continuity with a received religious tradition. The notion of "continuity as a kind of change" frees the theologian from the equally unsatisfying extremes either of defending Schleiermacher, on the supposed ground that there is complete agreement between him and Calvin, or of rejecting Schleiermacher, because complete identity between him and Calvin cannot be found.

In order to understand the relation between Calvin and Schleiermacher as theologians in a common tradition of theological reflection, therefore, it is necessary to trace *development*, the ways in which important ideas, motifs, themes, concerns, and questions are carried over into new circumstances, reformulated in response to new challenges, and reworked into a new form for the purposes of a different situation.[57] Ideally, such a perspective ought to rule out anachronistic readings of the past that suppress the genuine differences between the various spokespersons in a tradition while making possible an appreciation for new developments of old material. Viewed in this light, traditions are seen as less static and more flexible—in a word, more complex.

This appreciation of the complexity of an inherited religious tradition, however, does not make the evaluative task of constructive theology any easier. It still remains to decide who has developed the tradition in the most appropriate manner and to defend that decision to others. But the task of historical theology does not extend that far. The historian is obligated only to remove the blinders from our eyes when we look back upon the past so that the complexity of the inherited theological tradition is not obscured by facile generalizations. Yet precisely the acknowledgment of historical complexity opens up new possibilities for constructive theology which faces the challenge of putting the received tradition in a form relevant to contemporary circumstances.[58] In this manner, the descriptive enterprise of historical study may be of service in the normative task of constructive theology by providing alternative ways of construing the lines of continuity and change within an inherited tradition.

The Historical Thesis and the Method

The task of this historical study is to compare the systematic function of the concept "religion" in the dogmatic theologies of the two Reformed theologians who best represent the classical and liberal epochs of Protestant theology. The exegetical analysis is designed to clarify how this concept is defined and used by Calvin and Schleiermacher for the purpose of giving a theological explication of the meaning and truth of Christian faith from a Protestant perspective.

In the examination of each theologian the concept "religion" is clarified in relation to the concepts "faith" and "revelation" as these function within the context of their systematic frameworks. In response to the criticisms of Brunner and Barth, it is argued that the neo-orthodox antithesis between "religion," on the one hand, and "revelation" and "faith," on the other, does not allow for an accurate exegesis of the theologies of either Calvin or Schleiermacher. Hence, the burden of this inquiry is to demonstrate that, on strictly historical grounds, the neo-orthodox case against Schleiermacher is flawed in its use of a misleading comparative framework. But the consequence of this faulty historiography is that the presentation of Calvin's theology, to which the neo-orthodox make their appeal, is distorted in the process as well.

By contrast, Calvin and Schleiermacher are shown to be in fundamental agreement on two counts. First, both theologians affirm that the general phenomenon of religion is rooted in the essential nature of human experience. Accordingly, not only religion but also human existence itself is misunderstood apart from recognition of the religious character of common human experience. Second, Christian faith is the fulfillment of human religion through its actualization of the religious ideal given with human existence itself (piety). Hence, faith is not the antithesis of religion, but its perfection.

Furthermore, both Reformed theologians understand "revelation" in a double sense: as God's "original revelation" constitutive of human experience simply as such and as God's "decisive revelation" in Jesus Christ constitutive of Christian faith.[59] This twofold meaning of revelation explains why "religion" and "faith" are not antithetical concepts in the theologies of Calvin and Schleiermacher. The human being is essentially religious because human existence itself is constituted by a relation to God.[60] While this original revelation of God to the human being does not suffice to account for the distinctive character of Christian faith, the latter cannot be properly understood without reference to the former.

The operative assumption of this study is that Calvin and Schleiermacher are best compared as thinkers within a common tradition of theological reflection when their theologies are examined with respect to the questions: what is religion? and, what is Christian faith? By inquiring of them how they answer these distinct yet related questions, Calvin and Schleiermacher are shown to be theologians who address a similar set of concerns within the context of two very distinct religious crises in the history of Western Christianity. This means, at the very least, that there is an important formal similarity in their interpretations of Christian faith as religion. Nonetheless, it will be argued that there are important material similarities in their definitions of religion and Christian faith as well. But the delineation of these formal and material similarities is not intended to obscure the fact that there are also significant differences between the classical and liberal exemplars of Reformed theology. The claim to be advanced is that these differences can be accurately clarified from a strictly historical perspective only after the neo-orthodox historiography has been set aside in favor of a new comparative framework.

In the nature of the case, comparative analysis is difficult work. Two words of caution need to be stressed at the outset. First, the theologies of Calvin and Schleiermacher are more or less internally coherent presentations of Christian doctrine. This means that the concepts "religion" and "faith" cannot be abstracted from their logical contexts in these theologies and simply compared with one another apart from consideration of their relation to the whole of which they are parts. In other words, the task is to undertake a comparison of two systematic proposals for understanding what it means to be a Protestant Christian, each of which has integrity in itself. For that reason, the procedure will be to examine each theologian individually, first, with respect to the question of the nature and significance of human religiosity and, second, with respect to the question of the nature and significance of the Christian faith. The two chapters devoted to each theologian are intended as interpretations of how the concepts "religion" and "faith" are used in their respective theologies apart from direct comparison. It is only in the final chapter that the comparative endeavor itself is undertaken.

Secondly, an attempt is made to compare comprehensive interpretations of Christian faith from two very different historical periods in which people were asking different religious questions and employing different criteria by which to evaluate the competing religious answers given to these questions. It would be difficult enough to compare two systematic theologies from the same era (e.g., Tillich and Barth). But a double challenge arises in this study. Thus the comparative endeavor of the final chapter will attempt to respect the differences in the religious questions and the evaluative criteria of the two epochs of Protestant theology.

These considerations alone might suggest that the obstacles to comparison are too great to yield any significant results. Indeed, one of the lessons to be learned is just how difficult good historical comparison really is. One can err either by focusing on similarities in such a way that important differences are obscured or by accentuating the differences in such a way that crucial similarities are ignored.[61] It is to be hoped that this particular effort at historical comparison of systematic theologies will neither obscure the differences nor ignore the similarities.

From this perspective, Schleiermacher's theology is best understood as a creative development of Calvin's legacy in response to a new set of challenges to which Calvin himself did not need to respond. If this argument is valid, it follows that the neo-orthodox attempt to pit the Reformation against liberal theology rests on a distorted reading of the historical record. To be sure, this revised account of the historical development from classical to modern theology does not answer the normative or hermeneutical question: What is the best way to continue the tradition of the Reformation after the Enlightenment? But it does imply that any constructive proposal for contemporary theology has to be judged according to its own intrinsic merits and may not rest its case on a caricature of the Protestant tradition, old or new.

NOTES

1. Note how three Lutheran theologians characterize the change in the religious question. Ernst Troeltsch gave this description: "For Luther, the being of God, the curse of sin, the existence of hell, were beyond question. What was problematical was only the application of grace and deliverance to one's own self, *fiducia specialis*. For the modern world, confronted with the new cosmology of the natural sciences, and the modern anti-anthropomorphic metaphysics, it was precisely the being of God which was the problematical point, while, on the other hand, it was beyond question that to be once certain of the being of God would be to have found the meaning and goal of life, salvation and grace. In these circumstances, the general principle of the 'new way' discovered by Luther was infinitely more important than his special dogmatic goal. . . . Everywhere the idea of faith has triumphed over the content of faith." *Protestantism and Progress: The Significance of Protestantism for the*

Rise of the Modern World, Fortress Texts in Modern Theology (Philadelphia: Fortress Press, 1986), pp. 97-98. Bonhoeffer wrote: "Man has learnt to deal with himself in all questions of importance without recourse to the 'working hypothesis' called God." "[W]e cannot be honest unless we recognize that we have to live in the world *etsi deus non daretur*. And this is just what we do recognize—before God! . . . The God who lets us live in the world without the working hypothesis of God is the God before whom we stand continually. Before God and with God we live without God." *Letters and Papers from Prison*, pp. 168, 188. And Tillich said: "The act of accepting meaninglessness is in itself a meaningful act. It is an act of faith." "The Lutheran courage returns but not supported by the faith in a judging and forgiving God. . . . The courage to be is rooted in the God who appears when God has disappeared in the anxiety of doubt." *The Courage to Be* (New Haven and London: Yale University Press, 1952), pp. 176, 189-90.

2. For a discussion of the ways in which the modern experience affected the shape of Western religion, see Hugh McLeod, *Religion and the People of Western Europe, 1789-1970* (Oxford: Oxford University Press, 1981).

3. The new mood is well illustrated by the critical inquiries of David Hume (1711-1776). See *Hume on Religion*, edited with an introduction by Richard Wollheim (Cleveland and New York: Meridian Books, 1963).

4. Ebeling points out that Augustine was the first Latin thinker to coin the phrase "true religion" (*vera religio*). "Augustine created the hitherto unknown combination of words *vera religio*, thereby bringing together the concept of religion with the question of truth, something that was completely foreign to antiquity. The consequence was that there can be only *one* true religion, while of necessity there is a multitude of *religiones falsae* opposed to it." "Evangelium und Religion," in *Wort und Glaube*, 4:32; see Augustine, *De vera religione* (*MPL* 34:122-71).

5. Ogden speaks of Schleiermacher's revision of the inherited Protestant theological tradition as a "paradigm shift" with which modern theology is still coming to grips. "Response to Josef Blank: Biblical Theology in the New Paradigm," in *Paradigm Change in Theology: A Symposium for the Future*, ed. Hans Küng and David Tracy (New York: Crossroad, 1989), p. 288. The idea of a "paradigm shift" is taken from Thomas S. Kuhn, *The Structure of Scientific Revolutions*, 2d ed. (Chicago: The University of Chicago Press, 1970). Kuhn defined a "paradigm" as "an entire constellation of beliefs, values, techniques, and so on shared by the members of a given community" (p. 175). A "paradigm shift" is the gradual replacement of one paradigmatic model for the interpretation of reality by another. See the essay by Hans Küng, "Paradigm Change in Theology: A Proposal for Discussion," in *Paradigm Change in Theology*, p. 7.

6. Emil Brunner, *Die Mystik und das Wort: Der Gegensatz zwischen moderner Religionsauffassung und christlichem Glauben dargestellt an der Theologie Schleiermachers* (Tübingen: J.C.B. Mohr [Paul Siebeck], 1924), p. 10.

7. Ibid., pp. 11-12.

8. "Concluding Unscientific Postscript on Schleiermacher" (1968), in *The*

Theology of Schleiermacher: Lectures at Göttingen, Winter Semester 1923-24, ed. Dietrich Ritschl, trans. Geoffrey W. Bromiley (Grand Rapids: Eerdmans, 1982), pp. 261-79.

9. *Church Dogmatics,* 1.2, p. 280.

10. Ibid., pp. 280-81.

11. Ibid., p. 280.

12. Ibid., p. 284.

13. Ibid., p. 291.

14. See Barth's discussion of Schleiermacher in his *Protestant Thought: From Rousseau to Ritschl,* translated by Brian Cozens from eleven chapters of *Die protestantische Theologie im 19. Jahrhundert* (Harper and Row, 1959; repr., New York: Simon and Schuster, 1959), pp. 306-54.

15. *Church Dogmatics,* 1.2, p. 293.

16. Ibid., p. 294.

17. Ibid., p. 284.

18. Ibid. "Therefore the concept of *religio* as a general and neutral form has no fundamental significance in Calvin's conception and exposition of Christianity." Ibid., p. 285.

19. Ibid., p. 293.

20. Ibid.

21. Ibid., pp. 293-94.

22. *Natural Theology, Comprising "Nature and Grace" by Professor Dr. Emil Brunner and the reply "No!" by Dr. Karl Barth,* trans. Peter Fraenkel, with an introduction by John Baillie (London: Geoffrey Bles: The Centenary Press, 1946). A very lucid account of the Barth-Brunner debate is given by Heinz Zahrnt, *The Question of God: Protestant Theology in the Twentieth Century,* trans. R. A. Wilson (New York: Harcourt, Brace, & World, 1969), pp. 55-68; see also pp. 85-122 for a fuller account of Barth's development.

23. Barth views natural theology, not works righteousness, as the basic problem of Catholic theology. "I believe that because of it it is impossible ever to become a Roman Catholic, all other reasons for not doing so being to my mind short-sighted and trivial." *The Doctrine of the Word of God,* vol. 1.1 of *Church Dogmatics,* 2d ed., trans. G. W. Bromiley (Edinburgh: T. and T. Clark, 1975), p. xiii.

24. In an early essay, Barth identified the "scriptural principle" as the epistemological hallmark of Reformed doctrine. "The Doctrinal Task of the Reformed Churches" (1923), in *The Word of God and the Word of Man,* trans. Douglas Horton (Harper Paperback, 1957; repr. ed., Gloucester, Mass.: Peter Smith, 1978), pp. 240-41. He later took the Gifford Lectures as an opportunity to explain why a Reformed theologian must oppose natural theology. *The Knowledge of God and the Service of God, according to the Teaching of the Reformation, recalling the Scottish Confession of 1560,* trans. J. L. M. Haire and Ian Henderson (London: Hodder and Stoughton, 1938). For an assessment of Barth's relation to the Reformed tradition, see Alasdair I. C. Heron, "Karl Barths Neugestaltung der reformierten Theologie," in *Evangelische Theologie* 46 (1986): 393-402.

25. *Church Dogmatics,* 1.2, p. 284.

26. "Concluding Unscientific Postscript," pp. 271-72.

27. The best analysis of the demise of neo-orthodoxy remains, in my judgment, that of Gilkey, *Naming the Whirlwind*, pp. 73-106.

28. Especially noteworthy in this connection is the superb study by Richard R. Niebuhr, *Schleiermacher on Christ and Religion: A New Introduction* (New York: Charles Scribner's Sons, 1964). Niebuhr locates Schleiermacher's understanding of religion within the lineage of Augustine, Calvin, and Jonathan Edwards: "[E]ven the most polemical interpreter of Schleiermacher's theological thinking cannot overlook the fact that his statement of the religious situation is not essentially different from that with which the Augustinian-Reformed tradition has long since made the Western world familiar" (p. 193). The new willingness to reconsider Schleiermacher found expression at a major symposium held at Vanderbilt Divinity School (1968), the contributions to which were published in *Schleiermacher as Contemporary*, ed. Robert W. Funk, vol. 7 of *Journal for Theology and the Church* (New York: Herder and Herder, 1970).

29. As Jaroslav Pelikan so well puts it: "Tradition is the living faith of the dead, traditionalism is the dead faith of the living." *The Vindication of Tradition* (New Haven: Yale University Press, 1984), p. 65.

30. Ebeling writes: "The only way in which we can say today, in a strict sense, what was said in the past is to say it today in a new and different way. ... If, by way of pure repetition, we were to say today the same thing that was said 2,000 years ago, we would only be imagining that we were saying the same thing, while actually we would be saying something quite different. If proclamation were not at each moment a new interpretation of what was proclaimed in the past, it would not be proclamation of what was proclaimed in the past." *The Problem of Historicity in the Church and its Proclamation*, trans. Grover Foley (Philadelphia: Fortress Press, 1967), p. 26.

31. *Tradition and the Modern World*, p. 3.

32. "The Pathfinder: Calvin's Image of Martin Luther," in *The Old Protestantism and the New: Essays on the Reformation Heritage* (Edinburgh: T. & T. Clark Limited, 1982), pp. 27-48.

33. *Tradition and the Modern World*, p. 5. See John Calvin and Jacopo Sadoleto, *A Reformation Debate: Sadoleto's Letter to the Genevans and Calvin's Reply*, edited with an introduction by John C. Olin (Harper and Row, 1966; repr. ed., Grand Rapids: Baker Book House, 1976), p. 90.

34. *Tradition and the Modern World*, p. 7.

35. "Continuity and Change: Friedrich Schleiermacher on the Task of Theology," in *Tradition and the Modern World*, pp. 13-48. Gerrish prefaces his essay on Schleiermacher's understanding of the theological task with this epigraph from Calvin: "Our constant endeavor, day and night, is not just to transmit the tradition faithfully, but also to put it in the form we think will prove best." *Defensio contra Pighium* (*CO* 6:250), cited in "Continuity and Change," p. 13.

36. Cited by Martin Redeker, *Schleiermacher: Life and Thought*, trans. John Wallhausser (Philadelphia: Fortress Press, 1973), p. 198. Schleiermacher indicated his "progressive" interpretation of Protestantism when he wrote: "It is

an essential characteristic of the Protestant view of the Christian Church that we think of it as a whole in movement which is capable of progress and development." *Die christliche Sitte nach den Grundsäzen der evangelischen Kirche im Zusammenhang dargestellt* (1884), *SW* 1,12:72.

37. "Continuity and Change," p. 15.

38. *Sendschr.*, p. 30. Schleiermacher describes himself as "a theologian who descends entirely from the Reformed school and does not believe that this may be set aside even in the contemporary state of ecclesiastical union." Ibid. (*OtGl.*, p. 55).

39. For examples of research into the relation of Schleiermacher to Luther, see Georg Wobbermin, "Gibt es eine Linie Luther-Schleiermacher?" in *Zeitschrift für Theologie und Kirche* 12 (1931): 250-60; Gerhard Ebeling, "Luther und Schleiermacher," in *Internationaler Schleiermacher-Kongreß Berlin 1984*, ed. Kurt-Victor Selge (Berlin: Walter de Gruyter, 1985), 1:21-38; and Paul Seifert, "Schleiermacher und Luther," in *Luther: Zeitschrift der Luther-Gesellschaft* 40 (1969): 51-68. Gerrish has also made a contribution to this question in his article "Doctor Martin Luther: Subjectivity and Doctrine in the Lutheran Reformation," in *Continuing the Reformation: Essays on Modern Religious Thought* (Chicago and London: The University of Chicago Press, 1993), pp. 38-56, esp. pp. 52-56.

40. Though granting the naturalness of a comparison between Luther and Schleiermacher ("The one stood related to classical Protestant theology much as the other stood related to liberal Protestant theology, and they have every claim to be ranked as German Protestantism's most eminent theologians"), Gerrish asks whether the assumption that the Reformation is to be identified with Luther isn't "one of those misleading academic presuppositions that shut off a potentially fruitful avenue of inquiry?" "[S]imply to identify the Reformation with Luther is to assign to Luther a status he did not have in Schleiermacher's own eyes and, at the same time, to miss the distinctive role he did assign to Calvin." "From Calvin to Schleiermacher: The Theme and Shape of Christian Dogmatics," in *Continuing the Reformation*, pp. 181-82.

41. Williston Walker praises the *Institutes* as "the ablest doctrinal treatise that the Reformation produced," whose power "was speedily recognized by friend and foe alike. No theological exposition since the *Summa* of Aquinas has had so profound an influence or gained so lasting a fame." *The Reformation* (New York: Charles Scribner's Sons, 1900), p. 243. The editors of the English translation of Schleiermacher's *The Christian Faith* say that it is, "with the exception of Calvin's *Institutes*, the most important work covering the whole field of doctrine to which Protestant theology can point." This statement was made before Barth began work on his monumental *Church Dogmatics*. "Editors' Preface," *The Christian Faith*, p. v. Gerrish has examined this question in his essay, "From Dogmatik to Glaubenslehre: A Paradigm Change in Modern Theology?" in *Continuing the Reformation*, pp. 239-48.

42. See Gerrish's article "The Possibility of a Historical Theology: An Appraisal of Troeltsch's Dogmatics," in *The Old Protestantism and the New*, pp. 208-29. Along this line is the important study by Walter E. Wyman, Jr., *The Concept of Glaubenslehre: Ernst Troeltsch and the Theological Heritage of*

Schleiermacher, American Academy of Religion Academy Series 44 (Chico: Scholars Press, 1983).

43. *KD*, §85, 88, and 97.

44. Schleiermacher defines dogmatics as the study of the *Zusammenhang* ("coherence") of Christian doctrine in a particular period. Gl., §19.

45. "Theology within the Limits of Piety Alone: Schleiermacher and Calvin's Notion of God," in *The Old Protestantism and the New*, pp. 196-207. The allusion is to Immanuel Kant, *Religion Within the Limits of Reason Alone* (1793), translated with an introduction and notes by Theodore M. Greene and Hoyt H. Hudson (New York: Harper and Row, 1960).

46. *Inst.*, 1.2.1 (McNeill, 1:39).

47. Of the two major reasons Schleiermacher gave for his appreciation of the *Institutes*, the first is that, as a work of theology, it always seeks to make contact with the religious affections; the second is that it exemplifies the systematic coherence in presenting doctrine he himself so admired. *An Herrn Hofprediger Dr. Ammon über seine Prüfung der Harmsischen Sätze* (1818), *SW*, 1,5:345; see also his *Geschichte der christlichen Kirche* (1840), *SW*, 1,11:602, where he speaks of the *Institutes* in the following terms: "A strict connection between the academic-critical and the actual religious elements is maintained by a keen method and great systematic scope." In Schleiermacher's view, dogmatic statements have a twofold value: the ecclesial and the academic (*wissenschaftlich*). Gl., §17.

48. In a passage where Calvin explains that the truth of scripture's message can only be confirmed in our hearts through the internal testimony of the Holy Spirit, he makes a statement that comes very close to Schleiermacher's own description of his theological method in general. Calvin writes: "Such, then, is a conviction that requires no reasons; such, a knowledge with which the best reason agrees—in which the mind truly reposes more securely and constantly than in any reasons; such, finally, a feeling that can be born only of heavenly revelation. I speak of nothing other than what each believer experiences within himself—though my words fall far beneath a just explanation of the matter." *Inst.*, 1.7.5 (McNeill, 1:80-81). Compare this with Schleiermacher's statement: "I looked neither right nor left to any philosopher but simply investigated the feeling common to all pious Christians and sought to describe it." *Sendschr.*, p. 25.

49. "From Calvin to Schleiermacher," p. 190. Both theologians use "the concept of piety to monitor or police the dogmatic system." "Theology within the Limits of Piety Alone," p. 197.

50. *A Prince of the Church: Schleiermacher and the Beginnings of Modern Theology* (Philadelphia: Fortress Press, 1984), p. 23.

51. "Continuity and Change," p. 24.

52. "From Calvin to Schleiermacher," pp. 180-81. Niebuhr clarifies the difference in the meaning of "christocentrism" when applied to Schleiermacher's theology in these terms: "We have here a species of Christocentrism, though it is not the Christo-centrism of Karl Barth's *Church Dogmatics*." "A word of caution is required here, however. The reader will not find Schleiermacher justifying all that he says about God and man by his

doctrine of Christ. Christology is not the archimedean point by means of which *The Christian Faith* moves all the other doctrines of theology before the reader's view. It is not the absolute center about which everything else revolves. So far as the doctrinal, objective content of his thinking is concerned, Schleiermacher's theology like that of Calvin and others before him has more than one center and does not pretend to exhibit the artificial simplicity of the circle. . . . For the sake of distinguishing Schleiermacher's manner of theological reflection, therefore, from the attitude and method that style themselves as Christo-centric in the above-mentioned material and objective senses, we may call it Christo-morphic." *Schleiermacher on Christ and Religion*, pp. 161, 211-12. In a note, Niebuhr goes on to explain: "Schleiermacher makes no attempt, for example, to derive a knowledge of God from the disclosure of God exclusively circumscribed by the figure of Jesus. His doctrine of God has more than one source, and while this fact may be adjudged a weakness by Barthian critics, it nevertheless places Schleiermacher in a substantial theological tradition. In this tradition, Christ is the reformer of man's knowledge of God and of himself. Christ is not the sole objective center of that knowledge, for neither God nor man can be 'extracted,' as it were, from Jesus Christ. But in the presence of Jesus Christ, God and man emerge anew in human understanding and existence. On this score, Schleiermacher is closer to, and more faithful to, Calvin than is Barth." Ibid., p. 212, n. 2.

53. Oddly, Tillich claims Schleiermacher for the Lutheran tradition over against Barth's Reformed tradition: "Barth rightly appeals to the Reformed tradition. . . . In contrast to this I consciously place myself in the German Lutheran tradition. . . . In this line stand Schleiermacher and Hegel." "Answer to Karl Barth," in *The Beginnings of Dialectic Theology*, ed. James M. Robinson (Richmond: John Knox Press, 1968), p. 158. Elsewhere, however, Tillich does acknowledge Schleiermacher as "a follower of Calvin." *History of Christian Thought*, p. 407. Barth detected in Bultmann's theology the same errors he found in Schleiermacher. Writing to Bultmann, he explained: "[W]ith you I simply feel myself finally replaced under the same bondage in Egypt that . . . we are supposed to have left with the rejection of Schleiermacher and the new allegiance to the theology of the reformers." *Karl Barth-Rudolf Bultmann, Letters 1922-1966*, ed. Bernd Jaspert, trans. Geoffrey W. Bromiley (Grand Rapids: Eerdmans, 1981), p. 58 (letter of 27 May, 1931). Bultmann acknowledged his positive appreciation of Schleiermacher: "I myself put Schleiermacher in the sequence from Jeremiah to Kierkegaard. Yes, I do." But this high estimate of Schleiermacher was not uncritical: "Naturally I will not invalidate in the case of Schleiermacher the duty of criticism which I recommend in the case of Paul." Ibid., p. 6 (letter of 32 December, 1922). Interestingly, Bultmann praised Barth's *Römerbrief* by placing it squarely in the lineage of Schleiermacher. "Karl Barth's *Epistle to the Romans* may be characterized by one sentence, the phraseology of which he would disagree with, but which would still be valid in terms of the usage that has been prevalent in the present time: The book attempts to prove *the independence and the absolute nature of religion*. It thus takes its place, even though it is in the form of a commentary, in the same line with such works as Schleiermacher's *On*

Religion and Otto's *The Idea of the Holy*, with modern attempts to demonstrate
a religious a priori, and finally with the Letter to the Romans itself, which, with
its radical contrast of works and faith, basically has no other intention than this.
However different all these attempts may be in detail, they seek to give verbal
expression to the consciousness of the uniqueness and absoluteness of religion."
"Karl Barth's *Epistle to the Romans* in its Second Edition," in *The Beginnings
of Dialectic Theology*, p. 100. Bruce L. McCormack replies: "Bultmann was
right: Barth would not have accepted the terms employed in this description.
Barth was not in the least interested in demonstrating a religious a priori; quite
the contrary. We might accurately put Barth's concern by saying that he was
interested in proclaiming the independence of revelation. . . . Still, Bultmann's
reading was not simply mistaken. Barth's attempt to establish the independence
of revelation *did* belong to a tradition of thought whose source lay in Friedrich
Schleiermacher's effort to make religion independent of metaphysics and
ethics." "Revelation and History in Transfoundationalist Perspective: Karl
Barth's Theological Epistemology in Conversation with a Schleiermacherian
Tradition," in *The Journal of Religion* 78 (January 1998): 19.

54. At least one scholar not otherwise inclined to include Schleiermacher
within the canon of the Reformed tradition has been forced to concede the
weight of Gerrish's argument. John H. Leith, *An Introduction to the Reformed
Tradition: A Way of Being the Christian Community*, rev. ed. (Atlanta: John
Knox Press, 1981), p. 139, Appendix D.

55. Alexander Schweizer, *Glaubenslehre der evangelisch-reformirten
Kirche dargestellt und aus den Quellen belegt* (Zurich: Orell, Füssli, and
Comp., 1844-47), 1:91.

56. "Brunners Schleiermacherbuch," *Zwischen den Zeiten* 2 (1924): 60.

57. Heiko Oberman advocates a shift from a "causal" to a "contextual"
reading of history, by which he means that the historian's task is "to place ideas
in their context and point to their characteristics and their changing structures."
The goal of this contextual reading is to provide "a perspective for measuring
the changes in the configuration of questions and answers." *Forerunners of the
Reformation: The Shape of Late Medieval Thought Illustrated by Key
Documents* (Philadelphia: Fortress Press, 1966, 1981), p. 39.

58. For a recent analysis of the requirements of any responsible act of
interpretation when the complexity and ambiguity of a historical tradition are
fully acknowledged, see David Tracy, *Plurality and Ambiguity: Hermeneutics,
Religion, Hope* (San Francisco: Harper and Row, 1987).

59. I have borrowed these terms from Ogden who writes: "'Revelation' in
one sense of the word properly designates the original event that is constitutive
not only of Christian existence but also of human existence in general or simply
as such." "If this is correct, however, there also is no great difficulty in
accounting for the appropriateness of theology's characteristic acknowledgment
throughout most of its long history of something like a 'natural revelation'—or,
as I prefer to say, following Friedrich Schleiermacher, 'original revelation.' ...
Yet if there are the best of reasons for acknowledging that revelation in one
sense of the word is the original presentation of God to every human
understanding, clearly this is not the only, or even the primary sense of

'revelation.' . . . [W]hat the New Testament itself says about revelation includes the further idea that it has occured decisively in the special event of Jesus Christ, and that it takes place again and again in the present in the witness and faith of which this event is the principle as well as the origin. Consequently, from the New Testament down to our own time, the primary sense of 'revelation' in Christian theology has not been 'original revelation' but what I call 'special revelation,' and, more exactly, 'decisive revelation,' which is to say, the re-presentation of God that has taken place and continues to take place through the particular strand of human history of which Jesus is the center." "On Revelation," in *On Theology*, pp. 25, 28-29. One could also make this distinction by speaking of "natural" and "historical" revelation.

60.   Although critical of modern theology's attempt to delineate a religious dimension of common human experience, Thiemann does recognize that this approach gives expression to a doctrine of revelation: "To be human is to be religious, and to be religious is to be in relation to God. Such an argument functions in the broadest sense as an account or doctrine of revelation." *Revelation and Theology*, p. 4.

61.   A good comparison allows for the discernment of the relevant analogies between the terms being compared, i.e., the "similarities-in-difference" and the "continuities-in-discontinuity." David Tracy, *The Analogical Imagination: Christian Theology and the Culture of Pluralism* (New York: Crossroad, 1981), p. 420f.

Chapter 2

Calvin's Interpretation of Religion

Defining "Piety" in an Age of Reform

Calvin did not doubt that human beings are, by nature, religious creatures. For that reason, he assumes that reflective persons will want to concern themselves with a discussion of "true religion" since the question gets at the heart of what it means to be a human being. In his own day, the controversy about the nature of true and false religion arose as a conflict within Western Christianity itself regarding the reform of the church and the proper principles on which reform ought to be based. Catholic and Protestant contended for the right to claim continuity with the legacy of Augustine and, of course, the Bible. And though it was taken for granted by both sides that the Christian faith in some form is the true religion of humanity, the debate between them regarding *which* form is the true religion forced each party to clarify and to defend the grounds for its position.

Calvin never wrote a separate treatise on religion in the manner of Schleiermacher's *Speeches*. He did, however, compose a thoughtful and well-ordered exposition of Christian doctrine as taught among the Protestants. In the final edition of his *Institutes* (1559), he devotes the first five chapters of Book I to a preliminary definition of religion that establishes the terms of the discussion to follow. In these "introductory chapters," as they are called by Peter Barth[1], Calvin articulates a coherent set of ideas about the nature of being authentically religious and develops their implications for the analysis of religion as it is actually practiced. Since the concepts contained in these introductory chapters inform Calvin's discussion throughout the *Institutes*, clarity regarding their meaning and use can serve to illuminate the structure of his theology as a defense of the Protestant interpretation of Christian faith as the true religion.[2]

The task of this chapter is to expound Calvin's understanding of the religious ideal for human existence (piety) and to see how he argues that the normative criteria for true religion are objectively given in the order of nature itself. In the next chapter, attention is directed to Calvin's exposition of Christian faith as the instrument whereby true religion may be restored in a world that has turned away from the clear evidence of nature to embrace religious fabrications of its own making.

The argument of this chapter is twofold: first, piety, according to Calvin, ought to have been the fitting human response to the abundant testimonies of God's goodness found in the natural order; second, even when piety is wanting, the evident human need to worship something bears witness to an innate sense of obligation toward God that cannot be eradicated, as the writings of the pagan philosophers from antiquity amply testify. Thus there is a natural knowledge of God's goodness and a corresponding sense of obligation toward God that account for the origins of religion among human beings; though this knowledge should have been sufficient to instill piety, it serves in the present context of religious confusion to remind persons of their responsibility for false religion and to arouse them to the pursuit of true religion.

The Religious Ideal of Human Existence

When Calvin was converted to the Protestant cause, he put his vast humanist learning in the service of the Reformation. Previously, he had harbored the ambition of making a name for himself in the world of letters. His first publication was not a theological treatise but a commentary on a work by the Stoic philosopher Seneca, for which Calvin himself had to pay the printing costs.[3] But after his "sudden conversion," as he would later call it, the young scholar channeled his energies into theological pursuits.

> By the secret reins of his providence, God set another direction for my course in life. At first, since I was too stubbornly addicted to the superstitions of the Papacy to be easily rescued from so deep a quagmire, by a sudden conversion to teachability (*subita conversione ad docilitatem*) God subdued a heart which, for my age, was overmuch hardened. Having thus received some taste of true piety, I was inflamed with such desire to make headway in it that, while I did not give up other studies altogether, I pursued them with less interest. And not a year had gone by before all who were desirous of purer doctrine came to me for instruction, even though I was just a novice and a beginner myself.[4]

The so-called "conversion" was as much a change of direction in Calvin's understanding of his vocation as it was a change of mind regarding the disputed religious questions of the day. Now he understood himself called to assist in the reform of the church by turning his attention to theological studies; moreover, he had come to agree with the Protestants that Luther was right: the sources of abuse in the church were doctrinal and, therefore, the humanist call for a reform of morals and a revival of classical learning voiced, for example, by Erasmus and Jacques Lefèvre missed its target. If one hoped to see the authentic Christian religion restored to its pristine purity, as the Catholic humanists certainly did, then the doctrinal issue would have to be faced squarely: Augustine's doctrine of grace, which all parties agreed represented the genuine teaching of scripture, had been perverted by an insidious Pelagianism that sought to conceal its true colors by balancing grace and merit. The corrupt practices of the papacy were a symptom of a deeper corruption of the church's doctrine.

It would be a mistake to assume, however, that Calvin was any the less indebted to classical learning or to humanist styles of thought after he began to wield his pen on behalf of the Protestant cause.[5] Indeed, Calvin's distinctive contribution to the Reformation cannot be assessed accurately apart from consideration of the way he brought the concerns of humanist scholarship to bear on the development of Protestant theology.[6] Like the humanists generally, Calvin rejected the scholastic method of doing theology that had been so much a part of the intellectual world of medieval Catholicism. The humanists held scholastic theology in disdain, in large measure, because they believed its academic style of argument obscured the simple purity of Christ's teachings. But their concern for eloquence of style never led the humanists to reject the content of scholastic doctrine itself. By contrast, Calvin's conversion meant that the reformulation of the church's inherited doctrinal traditions would have to be at the center of his own concern with reform.[7]

The *Institutes* represents the fruit of this engagement with the substance of doctrine on the part of the converted humanist scholar. Calvin's original purpose in composing the *Institutes* was not merely apologetic. To be sure, he was concerned to defend the Protestants who were threatened with persecution (Calvin himself had been forced to flee France as a result of the so-called "affair of the Placards" in 1534). But he wrote his manual of Protestant doctrine chiefly with a didactic purpose in mind: to instruct persons in the doctrine of true religion. In a letter to King Francis I of France with which Calvin prefaced the first edition of his *Institutes* (1536), he said that his intention in writing the book was "to hand on certain rudiments through which those who are touched by some interest in religion might be trained to true piety."[8] The full title indicates that its purpose is to provide a "summary of piety" (*pietatis summa*) and whatever is necessary to know about "the doctrine of salvation" (*doctrina salutis*).[9]

Coupled with the Protestant concern for true doctrine is the humanist quest for the proper form in which to express it. Calvin's humanist heritage is reflected in his attempt over the years to find the most appropriate pedagogical arrangement for instruction in Protestant theology. The first edition of the *Institutes* was modeled after Luther's *Small Catechism* (1529). It contains six chapters devoted to discussions of the Decalogue (*de lege*), the Apostles' Creed (*de fide*), the Lord's Prayer (*de oratione*), Baptism and the Lord's Supper (*de sacramentis*), the five "false sacraments," and the meaning of Christian liberty in the church and society. The work underwent many revisions until reaching its definitive form in 1559, at which point Calvin judged that he had finally found the method of presentation best suited to his purposes: "Although I did not regret the labor spent, I was never satisfied until the work had been arranged in the order now set forth."[10]

The final edition of the *Institutes* is not merely an expanded version of the original catechetical treatise upon which Calvin had embarked in 1536 and which had been revised by him over the years. It merits the honor of being called the first full-scale "systematic theology" of the Protestant Reformation.[11] Not only had the catechetical model been left behind, but the work was now composed of four books, each of which contains approximately twenty chapters. There was, moreover, a new reason given for its purpose: to train theological students preparing for the ministry. Calvin's intent was to give those called to preach the gospel a key with which to open the door to scripture's meaning so that its doctrine might be preached correctly:

> I believe I have so embraced the sum of religion (*religionis summa*) in all its parts, and have arranged it in such an order, that if anyone rightly grasps it, it will not be difficult for him to determine what he ought especially to seek in Scripture, and to what end he ought to relate its contents.[12]

Among the benefits of providing an ordered presentation of doctrine, Calvin explains, is that he will now be freed from the need to engage in lengthy digressions in his biblical commentaries, provided, of course, that students come to their exegetical studies equipped with a knowledge of the *Institutes*. What was originally a book of catechetical instruction thus became in its final edition the exemplar of a new genre of Protestant theological literature intended to complement the catechism and the biblical commentary.[13]

In the 1559 edition Calvin introduced a new principle of arrangement by which the whole work is structured. Although divided into four books, the *Institutes* now sets forth scripture's doctrine according to a "twofold knowledge of God" (*duplex cognitio Dei*) as creator and redeemer that provides the mature work with its organizational plan.

> It is one thing to feel that God as our maker supports us by his power, governs us by his providence, nourishes us by his goodness, and attends us with all sorts of blessings—and another thing to embrace the grace of reconciliation offered to us in Christ.[14]

Calvin's point is that scripture teaches a twofold knowledge of God that should be reflected in the logical arrangement of doctrine. Viewed from the perspective of this new principle of a "twofold knowledge of God," Book I deals with the knowledge of God the creator, whereas the other three books treat the knowledge of God the redeemer.[15]

Combined with this structural principle of a "twofold knowledge of God" that Calvin introduces in 1559 is another principle that had been important ever since 1536: The knowledge of God, which is the proper theme of Christian theology, is necessarily accompanied by a corresponding knowledge of ourselves. Indeed, every edition of the *Institutes* opens with the statement, "Nearly all the wisdom we possess, that is to say, true and sound wisdom, consists of two parts: knowledge of God and of ourselves (*cognitio Dei et nostri*)."[16] What this entails, as Dowey observes, is of great methodological importance for the way Calvin goes about the properly dogmatic task of theology.

> The introductory words of the *Institutes* . . . are to be understood as one of Calvin's basic epistemological propositions—one he never violated. They are not, however, a systematic postulate, but an a posteriori principle true to the Biblical picture of God and man. For Calvin, God is never an abstraction to be related to an abstractly conceived humanity, but the God of man, whose face is turned "toward us" and whose name and person and will are known. And correspondingly, man is always described in terms of his relation to this known God: as created by God, separated from God, or redeemed by him. Thus, every theological statement has an anthropological correlate, and every anthropological statement, a theological correlate.[17]

Accordingly, Calvin's mature theology is best understood as governed by two principles: the structural principle of a "twofold knowledge of God" as creator and redeemer and the epistemological principle that all knowledge of God must be correlated with an appropriate knowledge of ourselves.[18]

The insistence that the knowledge of God go hand in hand with a knowledge of ourselves reflects the anti-scholastic polemic of humanism that wants to insure the eminently practical character of theological knowledge. In this view, theology is not to be an abstract discipline that tickles the mind with theoretical subtleties; its goal, rather, is to transform the heart and to edify human life.[19] Calvin's principle that the knowledge of God (as creator and redeemer) has to be accompanied by a corresponding knowledge of ourselves (as created and fallen-redeemed) prevents theology from engaging in idle speculation. Calvin defines "speculation" as a quest for knowledge of God arising from intellectual curiosity and not from the existential concern for our appropriate response to God ("knowledge which . . . merely flits in the brain").[20]

The antithesis of speculation is a knowledge framed by "religion" or "piety," which is directly concerned with the consequences for human self-understanding and practice ("a knowledge of God . . . which will be sound and fruitful if we duly perceive it, and if it takes root in the heart").[21] Calvin's notion of piety is the rule by which he insures the eminently practical character of theology's knowledge of God and safeguards it from speculative intrusions. "Indeed, we shall not say that, properly speaking, God is known where there is no religion or piety."[22]

Given Calvin's polemic against speculation and his commitment to circumscribe theology's knowledge of God quite strictly by "religion or piety," the fact that the first five chapters of Book I are devoted to clarifying the meaning of piety and religion is significant. Not only did Calvin find in 1559 the proper order of arrangement for which he had so long been searching; but also he prefaced his presentation of scripture's twofold knowledge of God with a prologue on the human being as a religious creature.[23]

The argument is advanced, moreover, that the human being is naturally religious and, indeed, that the very order of nature should have been sufficient to lead us to the practice of true religion since the creation contains abundant testimony of the creator's goodness toward his creatures. The presence of this discussion in the opening chapters, however, has occasioned much debate in the secondary literature about the question whether Calvin has a "natural theology," especially since Brunner appealed to Calvin in support of his own proposal for a "Christian natural theology," to which Barth responded with his unequivocal *"Nein!"*[24] Since this question has so permeated the scholarly research, it cannot be avoided even if the issue is "religion," not "natural theology."[25] Still, a proper grasp of the formal structure of the 1559 *Institutes* sets the stage for understanding the place of this prologue on the natural religiosity of the human being within Calvin's mature dogmatic system.[26]

It is not until the sixth chapter of Book I that the knowledge of God the creator as taught by the scriptures is introduced. Prior to chapter six, Calvin expounds the knowledge of God the creator as taught by the natural order. In the important passage where Calvin first alerts readers that he plans to present doctrine according to a "twofold knowledge of God," he explains:

> First, as much in the fashioning of the universe as in the general teaching of Scripture, the Lord shows himself to be simply the Creator. Then in the face of Christ he shows himself the Redeemer. Of the resulting twofold knowledge of God we shall now discuss the first aspect; the second will be dealt with in its proper place. [27]

God reveals himself to be the creator *both* in the natural order *and* in the teaching of scripture. Moreover, near the end of this section, Calvin inserts another important observation concerning his method in the first five chapters. Although he could easily adduce scriptural supports for his argument regarding nature's testimony to its maker, his present purpose is to put them aside until chapter six so that he may restrict himself to other modes of argument:

> These I now intentionally pass over, for they will find a more appropriate place where I shall discuss from the Scriptures the creation of the universe. Now I have only wanted to touch upon the fact that this way of seeking God is common both to strangers and to those of his household, if they trace the outlines that above and below sketch a living likeness of him.[28]

Clearly, Calvin has made a decision to let his argument rest on other warrants for the time being before turning to an exposition of the knowledge of God as taught by the Bible. Here in the introductory chapters he wants to draw our attention to the knowledge of God that nature itself teaches since God shows himself to be the creator "as much in the fashioning of the universe (*tam in mundi opificio*) as in the general teaching of scripture (*quam in generali Scripturae doctrina*)."[29] This way of seeking God is shared by believers and unbelievers alike (*exteris et domesticis communem hanc esse viam quaerendi Dei*).[30]

Among the puzzles of the "natural theology" debate is the way scripture was pitted against nature as a source for the knowledge of God. Yet Calvin had concluded from his exegetical studies that the Bible itself teaches a natural knowledge of God which accounts for the intrinsically religious character of human existence.[31] Two points are easily confused in this discussion. First, there is Calvin's conviction that nature is, in principle, sufficient to instruct us in the duties of piety toward God. Second, there is the candid recognition that Calvin's views on what nature actually teaches about God and piety are, in large measure, derived from the Bible.[32] Nonetheless, Calvin believes that scripture teaches a "revelation" of God in nature and he does not see his attempt to take this seriously as being at odds with a Protestant commitment to the Bible.[33] Indeed, the purpose of the introductory chapters is to convince us that false religion in its various manifestations is at odds with the essential or "created" character of human existence. Nature teaches plainly enough the lessons of true religion; the problem is that the sinful human being has turned away from nature's tutelage. This is the clear meaning of the scripture, as Calvin reads it.[34]

Since the present concern is simply to understand what Calvin sees as the religious ideal of human existence, it is necessary to bracket the actuality of sin and the consequent need for redemption in order to set forth the contours of his understanding of the human being in its original created state. And this is exactly what Calvin himself does in these opening chapters:

> Here I do not yet touch upon the sort of knowledge by which persons, in themselves lost and accursed, apprehend God the Redeemer in Christ the Mediator; but I speak only of the primal and simple knowledge (*prima et simplex Dei notitia*) to which the very order of nature would have led us if Adam had remained upright (*si integer stetisset Adam*).[35]

Like pre-modern theologians generally, Calvin assumes that the fall of the first human pair as narrated in Genesis was a historical event that dramatically altered the religious situation of all subsequent generations. Precisely for that reason, however, the story has more than mere historical import since it points to a fundamental distinction between two modes of human existence: what humanity ought to be like according to the blueprint of its creator and what humanity has actually become on account of the perversity of its own vain imagination.[36]

It is important to bear this distinction in mind when reading the introductory chapters because Calvin moves back and forth from a discussion of the religious ideal to an evaluation of human religious practice in the light of that ideal. Still, the crucial point is that the character of human religion after the fall can only be understood when measured by the religious ideal exemplified by Adam before he turned away from the clear lessons of nature. When the human being truly comes to know the discrepancy between its ideal created state and its actual fallen condition, false religion is exposed for what it is: human existence in contradiction with itself.

Calvin points to a "seed of religion" (*semen religionis*) implanted in each human breast: "As experience bears witness, God has sown a seed of religion in all persons."[37] The metaphor of a seed suggests a potentiality in human nature for being religious that may grow and blossom, but need not; it can fail to take root or its development may be thwarted. Calvin laments that, for the most part, the seed of religion has not germinated, with the result that "no correct piety remains in the world."

> Scarcely one person in a hundred is encountered who nourishes it after it has been conceived in his heart and no one, moreover, in whom it matures, let alone comes to fruition in its time.[38]

Nonetheless, the innate capacity to be religious is given to human beings, regardless of what they do with it.[39]

Calvin also says that all persons have a natural awareness of God or, as he calls it, a "sense of divinity" (*divinitatis sensus*): "We hold it to be beyond controversy that there is within the human mind, indeed by natural instinct (*naturali instinctu*), a sense of divinity."[40] This is not a propositional knowledge but a "feeling of nature" (*a naturae sensu*).[41] "For the Lord manifests himself by his powers, the force of which we feel within ourselves and the benefits of which we enjoy."[42] Ideally, the seed of religion should blossom into piety since this is fitting to our sense of divinity. Calvin says this sense of God's powers is "a proper teacher of piety, from which religion is born."[43]

In the opening line of the *Institutes*, Calvin sets forth his conviction that knowledge of God and knowledge of self are the two principal parts of wisdom. Moreover, the two are so inextricably bound that Calvin confesses an inability to discern "which one precedes and gives birth to the other."[44] On the one hand, knowledge of self leads to knowledge of God.[45] On the other hand, knowledge of God is required in order to know oneself truly.[46] But however they may actually be related to one another, Calvin insists that, pedagogically speaking, the order of right teaching (*ordo recte docendi*) demands that he begin with the knowledge of God and then proceed to discuss knowledge of self.[47] Nonetheless, the two belong inseparably together.[48]

Calvin does not believe that it is possible for the finite human mind to grasp the essence of God *a se*. For that reason, God is known only through his works. This is how the infinite God accommodates himself to the finite capacity of his creatures.[49] The knowledge that we can have from God's self-disclosure in his works is a knowledge of God's character. Unlike those who play with frigid speculations and ask, "What is God?," the pious mind asks, "What is God like and what is our appropriate response?"

> Now I understand the knowledge of God to be that by which we not only conceive that there is some God, but indeed that by which we grasp what is important for us to know of him, what is proper to his glory and, finally, what is helpful.[50]

The knowledge of God with which piety is concerned is the engaged knowledge of one whose awareness of dependence upon God involves the question of proper worship of God.[51]

Everything within the created order is a "mirror" reflecting the grandeur of the creator. Nonetheless, the human being is unique since it alone is able to reflect God's glory in an act of self-conscious gratitude.[52] The capacity for understanding was given that persons may know their maker since this is the chief end of human life. In one of his commentaries Calvin writes, "Certainly nothing is more absurd than that [human beings] do not know their author, having been endowed with understanding primarily for this purpose."[53]

Calvin understands the human being as a microcosm, a "little world" reflecting the grandeur of the larger world.

> [The human being] is a rare specimen of the power, goodness, and wisdom of God, containing in itself enough miracles to occupy our minds, if only it does not bother us to pay attention.[54]

Within this microcosm, there is abundant evidence that points to God. To understand oneself aright means to find God within. Indeed, the apostle Paul has testified that God "is not far from any of us" since we feel God as the power that quickens us.[55]

To be sure, there is enough light of the divine wisdom within so that there is no need to seek any further for God.[56] Nonetheless, the divine light shines forth abundantly in the macrocosm as well. The skillful ordering of the universe, too, is a sort of mirror in which to contemplate God who is otherwise invisible.[57] Since our proper end is to know God, the creator has given sufficient testimony to himself in the visible works of nature.

> Lest the access to happiness be closed to anyone, not only has [God] placed that which we've called a seed of religion in the minds of human beings, but he has so disclosed himself in the entire working

of the world and daily makes himself known that they cannot open their eyes without being compelled to see him.[58]

Just as God has left a witness to himself in the human heart, so too has he engraved his signature in each of his works. Wherever we look, there are certain and unmistakable marks of the divine glory to behold. While God's essence is beyond the grasp of the most learned philosopher, even unlearned folk have no excuse for ignorance since the order of nature is "a testimony of divinity too evident to escape the notice of even the dullest race."[59]

Whether human beings look within or gaze upon the external works of nature, God instructs us that we are his creatures. Though it is not possible to understand what God is *a se*, the creation testifies to God's benevolence.

[I]f the cause be sought by which he was once led to create these things and is now moved to preserve them, we shall find that his goodness alone is the cause.[60]

This knowledge of God's goodness takes root in the heart where it gives rise to piety: "Our mind cannot apprehend God without rendering to him some worship."[61] Nonetheless, this worship is not sufficient unless it is recognized that God deserves reverence as the source of all good things. Since God's goodness is the sole source of everything, gratitude is our appropriate response: "I call piety reverence combined with love for God which the knowledge of his benefits elicits."[62]

Calvin employs two metaphors, in particular, to express piety's perception of God as the giver of all good gifts. According to the first metaphor, God is the overflowing "source" or "fountain" whence comes every good thing.

Still, it will not be sufficient simply to hold that there is one who ought to be honored and adored by all, unless we are persuaded that he is the fountain of all good things (*fons omnium bonorum*), lest we seek something elsewhere than in him.[63]

In Calvin's other favorite metaphor, God is the solicitous "father" who seeks his children's well-being.[64] Only when the creator and sustainer of all things is acknowledged as a loving parent will creatures realize that their true good lies in God alone. Apart from this assurance of God's bounty there can be no genuine service of God.

For until human beings perceive that they owe all things to God, that they are nurtured by his paternal care, that he is the author of all their

goods, that apart from him nothing is to be sought, they will not
submit themselves to him with willing service; indeed, unless they
establish their genuine happiness in him, they will never devote
themselves to him truly and completely from the heart.[65]

In knowing that God is the source of everything good, the pious mind
not only "understands that he governs all things" but also "gives itself
over to complete trust in him."[66] God wants his children to obey him
out of love for his goodness, not from fear of punishment. And, indeed,
the obedient children fear offending such a loving parent more than hell
itself.[67]

   When the seed of religion comes to fruition in a pious heart, service
of God is true and authentic:

   Without doubt, pure and genuine religion consists in faith united with
   an earnest fear of God, a fear which contains within itself willing
   reverence and carries with it legitimate worship . . . [68]

Such religion is the response that human beings ought to render on the
basis of a grateful acknowledgment of the goodness of God of which
they are the beneficiaries. This knowledge, which is the foundation of
true religion, is that "to which the genuine order of nature would have
led us if Adam had remained upright."[69] "For," as Calvin reminds us
later in the *Institutes*, "if testimonies of Scripture were lacking—and
they are very many and very clear—nature itself also exhorts us to give
thanks to the Lord."[70]

   Those who do not cultivate the seed of religion so that it blossoms
into filial piety toward God "degenerate from the law of their
creation."[71] Since persons are by nature religious, all are obligated to
the creator who sowed in them the seed of religion. There can be, then,
no evasion of responsibility in the matter of proper religion since none
can claim any exemption from the duties of piety.

   Indeed, lest anyone seek refuge in a pretext of ignorance, God himself
   has placed in all people a certain understanding of his divinity;
   constantly renewing the memory of it, he repeatedly instills new
   drops so that, since all people understand that there is a God and that
   he is their maker, they are condemned by their own testimony because
   they have not worshipped him and devoted their lives to his will.[72]

There is a contradiction involved in any attempt to deny our religious
obligation since knowledge of self inescapably involves knowledge of
God.[73] Indeed, some knowledge of God, however dim, is found even
among those peoples in whom the seed fails to come to full blossom.

And to prove his point, Calvin draws upon the philosophical discussions of religion from antiquity with which he was well acquainted.

Pagan Testimonies to the Religious Character of Human Existence

Calvin sees in the universality of religious phenomena "a tacit confession that the sense of divinity has been inscribed on the hearts of all."

> As that famous pagan says, there is no nation so barbaric, no race so savage, in whom this conviction is not fixed, that there is a God. And those who in other parts of their lives seem least to differ from the beasts, nevertheless, retain some seed of religion. [74]

"That famous pagan," as Calvin calls him, is none other than Cicero (106-43 B.C.E.), whose treatise *On the Nature of the Gods* is devoted to the question of proper religion. This text records a conversation between three philosophers who represent different schools of thought: the Epicurean, the Stoic, and the Academic schools. Throughout the dialogue the reader sees how these Hellenistic philosophers sought to distinguish proper religion from superstition by examining whether religious beliefs rest upon the solid foundation of certain knowledge or merely represent the received opinions of tradition. In his prologue Calvin appeals to Cicero's text in support of his own view that the presence of religion in all cultures bears witness to a universal knowledge of God.

That Calvin draws on the ancients ought to come as no surprise given his immersion in classical learning.

> Indeed, I confess that certain grains of piety have always been scattered throughout the world and that, without a doubt, God has somehow sowed by his own hand the brilliant thoughts found in the philosophers and profane writers.[75]

But his specific use of Cicero is of particular significance in two respects: first, it is a clear case of literary dependence on a classical author who investigated the meaning of religion. This is itself an indication that Calvin wrestled with defining "religion" apart from the related question of defining "Christian religion." Second, Calvin developed his own interpretation of religion in self-conscious debate with these ancient philosophies of religion. Understanding the ways, then, in which he both draws upon the insights of the pagan philosophers and departs from them gives a more sharply delineated picture of Calvin's thoughts on religion.[76]

Calvin shares two fundamental convictions that he finds in the ancient philosophers: first, true religion must be based on genuine knowledge of the deity's character and, second, we are first instructed in this knowledge by nature itself. But Calvin also has significant disagreements with the philosophers and, aside from appealing to them in support of his own arguments, he introduces their conflicting viewpoints to demonstrate the insufficiency of philosophy as a guide to the natural knowledge of God. Thus Calvin appeals to the pagans for corroboration of his conviction that all persons have a sense of religious obligation toward God at the same time that he uses their example to point his readers to the Bible for clarification of this aspect of our experience.[77]

Calvin's notion that nature has planted a "seed of religion" or a "sense of divinity" in the human heart is itself drawn from Cicero.[78] The Epicurean argues that there is an innate knowledge of the gods in the human mind:

> For what race or what group of people is there which does not have some preconception (*anticipationem*) of the gods apart from instruction (*sine doctrina*)?[79]

Belief in the existence of the gods is not based on the authority of mere tradition; it is, rather, taught by nature itself. Epicurus spoke of this as a *prolepsis*, whereby he meant "a certain form of knowledge which is inborn in the mind, and without which there can be no other knowledge, no rational thought or argument." According to the Epicurean, this innate knowledge of deity is the proper place to begin any debate about the meaning of religion.

> So you see that the foundation of our inquiry (*fundamentum huius quaestionis*) has been well laid. This is not a belief (*opinio*) which has been prescribed to us by some authority, or custom, or law. It rests on the firm consensus of all (*omnium firma consensio*) that we must admit the existence of the gods because we have in our minds inborn knowledge (*innatas cognitiones*) of them. Moreover, a belief which all share by nature must necessarily be true. It must be admitted, therefore, that the gods exist.[80]

The fact that "not only philosophers but even the unlearned" (*non philosophos solum sed etiam indoctos*) affirm the existence of the gods is proof of this innate knowledge.[81]

The similarity with Calvin is striking. Calvin, too, locates the origin of religion in a knowledge of God naturally implanted in the human soul. He says that it would be easier to alter the natural disposition (*naturae affectus*) of the human being than to wipe out the seed of religion.[82] The "light of nature" (*naturae lux*) would have to be extinguished before we could deny God.[83] The conviction of God's reality does not have to be acquired because the sense of divinity is already "engraved" (*insculptum*) on our hearts.

> We conclude that this doctrine is not one which must first be learned
> in school but is one of which each is his own teacher from the womb
> and which nature itself allows no one to forget . . . [84]

Calvin agrees with the ancients in this respect: the knowledge upon which proper religion ought to be based is first taught by the school of nature. Just exactly what nature teaches, however, is a point of dispute, as it was for the philosophers themselves.

Although Calvin has no hesitation in pointing to nature as the original source of our knowledge of God, he fears lest praise of nature lead to a forgetfulness of God to whom nature itself directs us. There are those, he tells us, "who do not hestitate to pervert the entire seed of divinity that has been sown in human nature in order to bury the name of God." Such people credit nature with having brought forth all things so that they do not have to give thanks to God: "They push God aside, with the cloak of nature brought forward, which is to them the artificer of all things."[85] The religious consequence of this self-sufficiency of nature would be that the human being is not bound by gratitude to the "fountain of all good things" for the gift of life and its many blessings.

Calvin finds this danger in the Epicurean doctrine. According to Epicurus, all things take their rise from the accidental collision of material particles. Even the gods themselves were brought forth by this natural process. Calvin finds support for his polemic in the argument of the Stoic who counters the atomistic philosophy with its implication of randomness at the heart of reality and its subordination of deity to blind nature. Indeed, the real drama in Cicero's dialogue consists in the exchange between the Epicurean and the Stoic philosophers.[86]

The Stoic infers from the harmony and beauty of nature's operations the existence of a wise artificer who governs the natural order. He asks: "How can [the Epicureans] assert that the universe has somehow been made by the blind and accidental collisions of particles of matter?" The Stoic goes on to mock the atomistic doctrine:

> If the clash of atoms can make a world, why can it not build a porch,
> or a temple, or a house or a city? These are much easier and less
> laborious tasks.[87]

For the Stoic, moreover, the human mind is an even greater attestation of a divine designer than the external works of nature. Just as reason betokens the soul's divinity, the rational "soul" animating nature is divine.[88] The clear evidence of design thus excludes the rule of chance and fortune and points, instead, to divine providence.

If, however, there is no divine intelligence, there is nothing superior to the human being, concludes the Stoic:

> If the gods do not exist, then what is there in the nature of things greater than the human being? For only the human being has reason and nothing can be greater than that.[89]

Calvin, of course, agrees and asks how we can point to "signs of divinity" in the human being (*divinitatis insignia in homine*) apart from recognizing their divine author.

> Now what reason will there be to think that the human being is divine and not to acknowledge the creator? Shall we, indeed, discern between right and wrong by means of that judgment implanted in us, yet there be no judge in heaven? Will there remain to us even in sleep some remnant of intelligence, but no God keeping watch in ruling the world? Shall we be considered the inventors of so many arts and useful things that God is defrauded of his praise?[90]

For the Stoic it is absurd (and presumptuous!) to deny the existence of an intelligence greater than the human being:

> It is a piece of foolish arrogance for the human being to think that there is nothing better than itself in the whole world. Hence, there must be something greater; therefore, God most certainly exists.[91]

And Calvin recalls that the apostle Paul had appealed to the pagan poet who exclaimed, "We are indeed his offspring."

> Because he has decorated us with such excellence, he has testified to us that he is our father. Just as from a common feeling (*ex communi sensu*) and, as it were, at the dictation of experience (*dictante experientia*), the profane poets called him the father of human beings.[92]

Clearly, Calvin finds in the Stoic doctrine confirmation of his own view that the design evident in the natural order points us to the providence of God so that no one may use "nature" as a pretext for ingratitude to nature's God.[93]

Although Calvin shares the Stoic polemic against Epicureanism, he wants to insure, nonetheless, that the proper distinction is drawn between the order of nature and its divine orderer so as not to fall into the pantheism of the Stoic doctrine.[94] Remarkably, though, this does not prevent him from making a concession that comes very near to the position from which he wants to distance himself:

> I confess, of course, that it can be said piously, provided that it proceeds from a pious mind, that nature is God (*naturam esse Deum*).[95]

Calvin hastens to add, however, that "it is a harsh and improper saying" since it is injurious "to involve God confusedly with the inferior course of his works." Nature, rather, is "the order appointed by God." Nonetheless, it can be said "piously" (*pie*) that "nature is God."[96]

The "pious" qualification is important since it gets to the heart of Calvin's concern. Debates about God should not be speculative exercises arising from mere intellectual curiosity. They are eminently practical matters having to do with the appropriate religious response to the knowledge of our maker with which we have been endowed by nature. A pious person can say that "nature is God" since God's providential rule is so intimately bound up with every detail of the natural order that there is no nature apart from God. When this is acknowledged, the false religious conclusion is avoided:

> Let us then remember, whenever we contemplate our own nature, that there is one God who so governs all natures that he would have us look unto him, direct our faith to him, and worship and call upon him. For nothing is more ridiculous than to enjoy the very remarkable gifts that attest the divine nature within us, yet to overlook the Author who gives them to us.[97]

Recognition of God's providence leads us to affirm that the natural order is nothing but the expression of God's will.

The distinction between speculation and a knowledge of God framed by "piety" has implications for what Calvin means by "atheism." Atheism can take two forms: the first is the intellectual denial that God exists; the second is the practical negation of a theoretical belief in God's reality. Regarding the first form, Calvin thinks that the denial of God involves the atheist in a self-contradiction since it is impossible to deny the sense of divinity within:

> Although there have been some in the past, and today not a few come forward who deny that God exists, nevertheless, in spite of

themselves, from time to time they have a feeling of what they wish
not to know.[98]

Atheism thus miscontrues human experience itself since it is unable to
account for the religious texture of our lives.

The second form of atheism consists in living in a manner that
exhibits no regard for the moral fabric of the universe. The fool who
said in his heart, "There is no God," was not a making theoretical point;
he was expressing an indifference to matters of right and wrong since
he does not expect to account for his deeds before the divine judge:

> David depicts them as absolutely denying that God exists, not because
> they take away his being but, since they strip him of his judgment and
> his providence, they shut him idly in heaven.[99]

This practical atheism, though it does not actually deny that God exists,
renders belief in God of no consequence for the way we conduct our
lives.

Once again, Calvin has in mind the Epicurean denial of
providence.[100] Epicurus believed that superstition arises from fear of
the gods. His antidote to superstition, not surprisingly, was to assure
people that the gods need not be feared since they are unconcerned with
human affairs.

> If we aspire for nothing more than to worship the gods in a pious
> fashion that is free of superstition, then what has been said is
> sufficient: the excellent nature of the gods should be worshipped in
> piety since their nature is eternal and blessed (for whatever is eminent
> deserves a proper veneration); and all fear of divine power or anger
> should be expelled (since it is clear that anger and favor alike are
> eliminated from a nature that is blessed and immortal; these having
> been removed, there is no fear hanging over us).[101]

The problem, as the Epicurean sees it, is that false notions lead us to live
in dread of the gods: "Who wouldn't fear an inquisitive busybody of a
god who forsees and thinks of and notices all things, and makes
everything his concern?"[102]

The Academic objects that such a notion would undermine
morality: "For how can there be sanctity if the gods do not attend to
human affairs?"[103] Calvin agrees.

> For nothing is less agreeable to God than to hand over the government
> of the world to Fortune after having abandoned it, to be blind to the
> evils of human beings, with the result that they indulge in license

without punishment. Each one who indulges himself without care, because the fear of heavenly judgment has been extinguished, denies that God exists.[104]

Calvin rejects the argument that fear is a sufficient explanation of religion's origin.[105] This view fails to distinguish a "proper fear" of God based on reverence from a "servile" fear of punishment.[106] Superstition is always a distortion of our proper fear of God and presupposes for its intelligibility the "firm conviction about God" implanted in each heart, "from which there emerges, as from a seed, the propensity toward religion."[107]

The Stoic explains that the etymology of "superstition" is derived from the activity of those who spend all their time in prayers and sacrifices so that their children might outlive them (*superstites*). The word "religion," on the other hand, refers to the activity of those who carefully review and examine all things pertaining to worship (*relegere*). Hence arose that distinction between "religious" and "superstitious," the former being a term of approbation and the latter a term of reproach.[108] Since the attempt to distinguish piety from superstition was of concern to the ancestors long ago just as it is now to philosophers, the received traditions merit our respect.

We ought to revere and worship these gods under the names which custom has bestowed upon them. But the best worship of them is the purest, holiest, and most pious, so that we always revere them with thought and speech that is pure, sincere, and uncorrupt.[109]

Though traditions can be corrupted through ignorance and superstition, the Stoic recommends an attitude of critical deference to the received religious customs, thereby affirming the possibility of a reasonable worship.

Calvin agrees that the word "religion" comes from the Latin *relegere* but he gives a different explanation of its etymology. For his part, Calvin thinks the word is opposed to unrestrained license in worship: piety (true religion) keeps itself (*relegit*) within proper limits. By contrast, superstition arises out of a misplaced zeal for religion; instead of being content with what is proper, it heaps up a useless pile of worthless things.[110] Superstition is the product of those who indulge in flights of speculation: "They do not apprehend [God] as he offers himself but imagine him as they have fabricated him out of their own rashness."[111] "In this respect, it doesn't much matter," Calvin tells us, "whether you conceive one God or many."[112]

Although Cicero does not categorically reject what custom

prescribes, his treastise on religion includes a skepticism about what mere mortals can truly know about the deity.[113] This skepticism comes to expression in the story of Simonides, narrated by the Academic:

> If you ask me what deity is and what it is like, I shall appeal to the authority of Simonides. When the tyrant Hiero put this question to him, he asked for a day in which to consider it. When Hiero asked him again the next day, he asked for two more days. And when he continued to double the number of days in this way, Hiero became curious and asked him why he did so. "Because the longer I consider the matter," he said, "the more obscure it seems to me."[114]

The Academic concludes that, since Simonides was in every way a wise man, wisdom consists in skepticism regarding a topic which far exceeds our capacities.

It was the diversity of perspectives on religion that led to this philosophical skepticism. Although "some praise the reply of Simonides," Calvin explains that he must draw a different conclusion:

> They gather a cloud out of human ignorance to hide their lack of piety,
> but this does not in the least excuse their flight from God.[115]

Of course, Simonides was wise to suspend judgment on a matter of which he himself was so patently ignorant. But Calvin sees in his example the proof that even the wisest of philosophers is not able to supply us with the proper knowledge of God upon which true religion must be founded.

In the introductory chapters of the *Institutes* Calvin draws upon the discussions of the ancient philosophers for his own theological purposes.[116] He is concerned to make two major points. First, there can be no evasion of responsiblity in the matter of true religion since nature has implanted in everyone a knowledge of God that should be sufficient to lead us to piety. In Calvin's view, the fact that the philosophers also recognized this principle serves as confirmation of his argument. But, second, the disagreements evident among the philosophers themselves show just how confused this original knowledge of God from nature has become. Like the ancients, Calvin believes that correct knowledge of God is the proper foundation of true religion. Indeed, it is this belief that gives his theology its epistemological emphasis.[117] Yet apart from a proper piety, there is no uncorrupted knowledge of God, which is how Calvin accounts for the deficiencies in philosophy.

Had it not been for Adam's fall, the order of nature would have been a sufficient school for piety. But after turning away from the manifold signs of the creator's goodness, human beings can no longer "read" and interpret nature correctly. "It appears," Calvin concludes, "that if people were taught only by nature, they would hold nothing certain or solid or clear, but would be so bound to confused principles as to worship an unknown god."[118]

> Thus is it in vain that so many burning lamps shine for us in the workmanship of the universe to illustrate the glory of its author. Although they illuminate us from all sides, they are nevertheless completely unable to lead us into the right path in and of themselves. Surely they incite some sparks. But they are suffocated before their fuller splendor is spread forth.[119]

As he turns from a consideration of the religious ideal to an analysis of the actual religious situation, there is a shift in Calvin's use of the term "nature." In the first sense, "nature" refers to the created goodness of the world; according to the second sense, however, "nature" refers to the negative effects of humanity's sin.[120] With respect to the original goodness of creation, sin is completely "unnatural." With respect to our actual condition, however, we might well say that sin has become "second nature" to us.

This distinction between the two senses of "nature" does a lot to clarify some of the ambiguities in the "natural theology" debate. First, it has to be affirmed that Calvin teaches a knowledge of God through the created order to which all human religion is a response, however inadequate. Whether we call this knowledge "natural" or "revealed," the meaning is clear: God has so disclosed himself in the works of creation that piety should be forthcoming. But, second, the lack of a grateful response to the creator's goodness prevents nature's witness to God from being clearly perceived. Although the knowledge of God shines forth through the created works of nature, our common human guilt has rendered us blind to what is actually there to be seen.[121]

The result of this inability to construe nature's religious message properly does not mean that a religious response to nature on the part of the creature is lacking. Indeed, our unquenchable need to worship something and our ineradicable sense of right and wrong testify that the light of nature has not been completely extinguished.

> There are two principal parts of the light which still resides in corrupt nature: first, some seed of religion is innate in all persons; then, the distinction between good and evil has been engraved on their consciences.[122]

What it does mean is that human beings are living in contradiction to the clear light of nature: "But what are the fruits that ultimately spring from it, except that religion degenerates into a thousand monsters of superstition, and conscience perverts every decision, so as to confound vice with virtue?"[123] While nature itself continues to be an unabated revelation of God's majesty, human "nature" has become too perverse to perceive it clearly.[124] For this reason, Calvin concludes:

> It is necessary that another and better help come forward that may properly direct us to the Creator of the world himself. Therefore, it was not in vain that he added the light of his Word by which to become known unto salvation.[125]

Summary

In the opening pages of the *Institutes*, Calvin gives us his analysis of *homo religiosus* and elaborates the principles that will serve him in the analysis of religion as it is actually practiced among human beings. Not only does he believe that nature is our first teacher in matters of religion, but he hammers out his interpretation of religion in conversation with the ancient philosophers who also shared this conviction. Yet it follows from his analysis that only a pious mind can perceive the signs of nature for what they truly are: testimonies of God's goodness toward his creatures. When the epistemological character of Calvin's theology is under consideration, therefore, it must be remembered that there is no genuine knowledge of God apart from piety.

Once human beings have turned away from nature's testimonies to God's goodness, scripture functions like a pair of glasses that enables us to see clearly again.

> Just as with elderly or bleary-eyed people and any whose eyes are weak if you present them with a very beautiful volume: although they recognize it to be something written, they can nevertheless barely make out two words. But with the aid of spectacles they will begin to read clearly. Thus Scripture, gathering up the otherwise confused knowledge of God in our minds (*confusam alioqui Dei notitiam in mentibus nostris*), having dispersed our darkness, clearly shows us the true God.[126]

Scripture serves as a lens that refocuses our confused knowledge of the creator. Hence, scripture does not supplement an otherwise pure and unsullied knowledge of God from nature.[127] It "re-presents" the knowledge of God as creator, thereby showing us to ourselves as we truly are: ungrateful recipients of God's liberality.[128]

Yet scripture not only shows us God as the world's creator but also—and most importantly—proclaims God as the world's redeemer. To know God as one's redeemer is that knowledge "which alone quickens dead souls."[129] It is this salvific knowledge of God that scripture contains which is "the proper doctrine of faith" (*propria fidei doctrina*).

> [S]ince we have fallen from life into death, the whole knowledge of God the Creator that we have discussed would be useless unless faith also followed, setting forth for us God our Father in Christ.[130]

Much of the problem with the "natural theology" debate is that the pivotal epistemological significance of Calvin's doctrine of faith, developed in Book III, is ignored. But when that is left out of the discussion, we get the misleading impression that Calvin has exhausted his doctrine of the knowledge of God in Book I, with the result that it becomes difficult to see how he relates "nature" to "scripture" as sources for the knowledge of God. Apart from the doctrine of "faith," however, the relations between these other two sources can never be properly grasped.[131]

Calvin introduces his *summa pietatis* by depicting the religious ideal of human existence (*pietas*). But the real controversy in the sixteenth century was the doctrine of salvation (*doctrina salutis*). It was Luther's doctrine of justification by faith alone that distinguished the Protestants from other advocates of reform who did not wish to repudiate the papal teaching. So the next question is: What is the relation between the Protestant doctrine of faith and *pietas* in Calvin's theology? As we shall see in the next chapter, Calvin believes that piety can be restored after Adam's fall only when the gospel is correctly preached and received with faith. And that's why this humanist convert to the Protestant cause wrote his *Institutes* in the first place: so that "those who are touched by some interest in religion might be trained to true piety."[132]

NOTES

1. Peter Barth, "Die fünf Einleitungskapitel von Calvins Institutio," in *Kirchenblatt für die reformierte Schweiz*, 40. Jahrg., nos. 11-13 (March 12, 19, and 26, 1925): 41-42, 45-47, 49-50. The term *Einleitung* suggests that the proper comparison is with Schleiermacher's "Introduction" to *The Christian Faith*, but this is clearly not Barth's intent.

2. Karl Holl approached Luther with a similar set of questions in his essay, *What Did Luther Understand by Religion?*, ed. James Luther Adams and Walter

F. Bense, trans. Fred W. Meuser and Walter R. Wietzke (Philadelphia: Fortress Press, 1977). Anticipating the charge of anachronism, Holl writes: "We do Luther no violence when we try to relate him to these questions" (p. 16).

3. *Calvin's Commentary on Seneca's De Clementia* (1532), with introduction, translation, and notes by Ford Lewis Battles and André Malan Hugo, The Renaissance Society of America—Renaissance Text Series 3 (Leiden: E. J. Brill, 1969). Calvin's commentary was not, however, the success he had hoped it would be. As one writer put it, "Calvin's career as a professional man of letters may be said to have begun and ended with this work." Alister E. McGrath, *A Life of John Calvin: A Study in the Shaping of Western Culture* (Oxford and Cambridge, Mass.: Blackwell, 1990), p. 60.

4. "Preface" to *Comm.* Psalms from 1557 (*CO* 31:21). The exact date of the conversion is disputed by scholars, though it is not to be dated later than the fall of 1533 when Nicolas Cop delivered his rectoral address in support of Lutheran ideas, an address which Calvin was believed to have written. On the meaning of Calvin's "conversion" and the complicated issues surrounding its interpretation, see Alexandre Ganoczy, *The Young Calvin*, trans. David Foxgrover and Wade Provo (Philadelphia: Westminster Press, 1987), pp. 241-66.

5. As one scholar points out, "[Calvin] remained no less humanistic in method and in his particular type of intellectual outlook." "It would be a mistake to imagine that Calvin's reading was limited to theologians; he had not ceased to steep his mind in the thought of antiquity even after his conversion." François Wendel, *Calvin: Origins and Development of His Religious Thought*, trans. Philip Mairet (New York: Harper and Row, 1963; repr., Durham: Labyrinth Press, 1987), pp. 44, 115.

6. On Calvin's relations to humanism, see Quirinus Breen, *John Calvin: A Study in French Humanism*, 2d ed. (Chicago: Archon Books, 1968), and "Humanism and the Reformation," in *The Impact of the Church Upon its Culture: Reappraisals of the History of Christianity*, vol. 2, *Essays in Divinity*, ed. Jerald C. Brauer (Chicago: University of Chicago, 1968), pp. 145-71.

7. "Those who chose to abolish scholastic doctrine as well as criticize scholastic method became Protestants." Steven Ozment, *The Age of Reform 1250-1550: An Intellectual and Religious History of Late Medieval Europe* (New Haven and London: Yale University Press, 1980), p. 307. Nonetheless, Richard Muller cautions against letting the Protestant polemic against scholasticism obscure Calvin's real indebtedness to the scholastic legacy. "It often appears from the *Institutes*, commentaries, treatises, and sermons that Calvin held a fundamentally negative view of scholastic theology, at times to the point of caricature, at the same time that his theology contained a measure of positive allusion to and indirect reliance on scholastic formulations. . . . In short, Calvin's overtly negative reaction to 'scholastici' conveys only a small part of his relationship to medieval scholastic theology, its method, its themes, and its distinctions. Alongside the rejection, there is also appropriation, sometimes explicit, often unacknowledged." "Scholasticism in Calvin: A Question of Relation and Disjunction," in *Calvinus Sincerioris Religionis Vindex: Calvin as Protector of the Purer Religion*, ed. Wilhelm H. Neuser and

Brian G. Armstrong, vol. 36 of Sixteenth Century Essays and Studies (Kirksville, Missouri: Sixteenth Century Journal Publishers, 1997), pp. 263-65.

8. "Prefatory Address to the King of France" (*OS* 3:9; McNeill, 1:9). The letter also accompanied every subsequent edition thereafter. See Harmannus Obendiek, "Die Institutio Calvins als 'Confessio' und 'Apologie,'" in *Theologische Aufsätze: Karl Barth zum 50. Geburtstag*, ed. Ernst Wolf (Munich, 1936), pp. 417-31.

9. The Latin text is found in *OS* 1:19-283 and *CO* 1, cols. 1-252. An English translation is available in *Institutes of the Christian Religion: 1536 Edition*, translated and annotated by Ford Lewis Battles (Grand Rapids: Eerdmans, 1975; rev. ed., 1986).

10. "John Calvin to the Reader," *OS* 3:5 (McNeill, 1:3). The other major revisions were in 1539, 1543, and 1550.

11. The question of the "systematic" character of Calvin's theology is a disputed one. William Bouwsma denies that Calvin at any stage of his career can be called a systematic theologian on account of his humanist leanings: "I cannot accept the received version of Calvin as a systematic thinker. . . . A systematic Calvin would be an anachronism; there are no 'systematic' thinkers of any significance in the sixteenth century." *John Calvin: A Sixteenth Century Portrait* (New York and Oxford: Oxford University Press, 1988), p. 5. Gerrish replies: "With Erasmus, [Calvin] shared in the sixteenth century's shift from a scholastic to a humanistic model for theology. . . . Nevertheless, in the final edition of his *Institutes* he left the topical method of Erasmus behind, and it is this that made Calvin not simply a systematic theologian but the preeminent systematician of the Protestant Reformation." *Grace and Gratitude: The Eucharistic Theology of John Calvin* (Minneapolis: Fortress Press, 1993), p. 16. Unlike Erasmus and Melanchthon, by 1559 "Calvin has come to think of order not as mere sequence but as logical or organic connection" (Ibid., p. 18). Bouwsma is rejecting a rationalistic notion of systematic theology according to which theological propositions are logically deduced from a central idea or doctrine (e.g., predestination). According to this definition, however, neither the theology of Calvin nor that of Schleiermacher would qualify as examples. The history of the various attempts to find the "central doctrine" of Calvin's theology is instructive in this respect, as Hermann Bauke points out in his study, *Die Probleme der Theologie Calvins* (Leipzig: J. C. Hinrichs, 1922), esp. p. 4. It should be recalled that Schleiermacher preferred the older term "dogmatics" to the more recent "systematic theology" since it acknowledges its connection with the received tradition as well as its practical purpose of providing leadership for the church. *KD*, §97.

12. "To the Reader," *OS* 3:6 (McNeill, 1:4). In the preface he wrote for the French edition (1560), Calvin acknowledges that exegesis can be difficult: "Although Holy Scripture contains a perfect doctrine, to which one can add nothing . . . yet a person who has not much practice in it has good reason for some guidance and direction, to know what he ought to look for in it, in order not to wander hither and thither, but to hold to a sure path, that he may always be pressing toward the end to which the Holy Spirit calls him." *OS* 3:7 (McNeill, 1:6).

13. "The differences in form between the last edition of 1559 and its predecessors are striking. . . . [I]t can almost be spoken of as a new work." W. de Greef, *The Writings of John Calvin: An Introductory Guide*, trans. Lyle D. Bierma (Grand Rapids: Baker Books and Apollos, 1993), pp. 201-202. Gerrish agrees: "Were it not for the final revision of the *Institutes* . . . there would be no compelling reason to name Calvin the preeminent systematician among the Reformers." "From Calvin to Schleiermacher," p. 190.

14. *Inst.*, 1.2.1; see also 1.6.1, 2; 1.10.1; 1.13.9, 11, 23, 24; 1.14.20, 21; and 2.6.1.

15. The crucial passage indicating the transition to the knowledge of God the redeemer is found in *Inst.*, 2.6.1.

16. *Inst.*, 1.1.1. Charles Partee points out that Budé, France's premier humanist in the sixteenth century, defined philosophy as knowledge of things divine and human. *Calvin and Classical Philosophy*, Studies in the History of Christian Thought 14 (Leiden: E. J. Brill, 1977), p. 10. In humanist fashion, Calvin described theology as an explication of "the Christian philosophy" (*la Philosophie Chrestienne*), employing an ancient designation that had been given new life by Erasmus. *OS* 3:7 (McNeill, 1:6). See also Josef Bohatec, *Budé und Calvin: Studien zur Gedankenwelt des französischen Frühhumanismus* (Graz: Verlag Hermann Böhlaus Nachf., 1950), pp. 32-33, 241-53. Bohatec writes: "Even the first foundational sentence of the *Institutes* . . . comes from the Christian French Humanism" (p. 241).

17. Edward A. Dowey, Jr., *The Knowledge of God in Calvin's Theology* (New York: Columbia University Press, 1952), pp. 19-20. Dowey speaks of "the principle of correlation" in Calvin's theology, "by which we learn the intimate connection that exists between the knowledge of God and ourselves" (p. 18). He acknowledges his indebtedness to Tillich, who first applied this term to Calvin's *Institutes* (p. 18, n. 62). Indeed, Tillich found methodological significance in Calvin's insistence upon the interconnection between knowledge of God and self: "In the initial sentences of his theological system Calvin expresses the essence of the method of correlation." *Systematic Theology*, 1:63. See also Dowey's more recent discussion, "The Structure of Calvin's Theological Thought as Influenced by the Two-Fold Knowledge of God," in Wilhelm H. Neuser, ed., *Calvinus Ecclesiae Genevensis Custos*, International Congress on Calvin Research 1982 (Frankfurt: Verlag Peter Lang, 1984), pp. 135-48. Mary Potter Engel insists that the celebrated "theocentric" character of Calvin's theology (expressed, in part, by his emphasis upon the knowledge of God as the theme of his *Institutes*) should not close our eyes to the necessary anthropological correlate of his theology: "Calvin never intended theology and anthropology to be mutually exclusive. Just as for Augustine God and the soul belong together, so for Calvin the knowledge of God and the knowledge of humankind belong together. . . . Calvin's theology is an ellipse with two foci, *theos* and *anthropos*." *John Calvin's Perspectival Anthropology*, American Academy of Religion Series 52 (Atlanta: Scholars Press, 1988), pp. 189, 191.

18. Not all commentators agree, however, that Calvin structures his theology according to the *duplex cognitio Dei*. T. H. L. Parker, for instance, believes that the fundamental organizing principle for the *Institutes*, even in

1559, is provided by the Trinitarian structure of the Apostles' Creed, reflected in Calvin's decision to divide the work into four books. "[I]t is a mistake to interpret this theological form of the *Institutio* as governed by the doctrine of the knowledge of God the Creator and the doctrine of God the Redeemer in Christ. In this way violence is done to Calvin's intention and his theology is misinterpreted. Rather, the twofold knowledge which governs the *Institutio* is that which has been the first sentence since 1536: '. . . the knowledge of God and the knowledge of ourselves.'" *John Calvin* (Tring: Lion Publishing, 1987; originally published 1975), p. 155. See also his study, *The Doctrine of the Knowledge of God: A Study in Calvin's Theology* (Edinburgh and London: Oliver and Boyd, 1952). The American edition, entitled *Calvin's Doctrine of the Knowledge of God* (Grand Rapids: Eerdmans, 1959), contains an appendix on Dowey's thesis (pp. 117-25). For discussions of the question, see Wendel, *Calvin*, pp. 112-22, especially p. 121; Dowey, "The Structure of Calvin's Theological Thought," pp. 142-44; Gerrish, "Theology within the Limits of Piety Alone," pp. 199-201; and the classic study by Julius Köstlin, "Calvins *Institutio* nach Form und Inhalt, in ihrer geschichtlichen Entwicklung," in *Theologische Studien und Kritiken* (1868): 7-62, 410-86, esp. 57-58.

19. Erasmus described "the Christian philosophy" (*Christiana Philosophia*) as "more truly seated in emotions than syllogisms (*in affectibus situm verius quam in syllogismis*), a life rather than an argument (*vita est magis quam disputatio*), inspiration rather than erudition (*afflatus potius quam eruditio*), a transformation rather than a system of reason (*transformatio magis quam ratio*)." *Paraclesis, id est adhortatio ad Christianae philosophiae studium*, in *Opera Omnia* (Leiden, 1704; repr. ed., London: The Gregg Press, 1962), 5:141. See also Bouwsma, *Calvin*, pp. 156-57, 159-60.

20. *Inst.*, 1.5.9 (McNeill, 1:61).

21. *Inst.*, 1.5.9 (McNeill, 1:61-62).

22. *Inst.*, 1.2.1 (McNeill, 1:39).

23. "The *Institutes* are a *tour de force* in many ways, but they are most remarkable in their break from the medieval way of doing theology. The opening of the *Institutes* resembles more a work of modern philosophy than a work of medieval theology. Calvin opens not with a discussion of the attributes of God, or proofs for his existence . . . but with a discussion of the interrelationship between the knowledge of God and the knowledge of man." Gerald J. Postema, "Calvin's Alleged Rejection of Natural Theology," in *Scottish Journal of Theology* 24 (November, 1971): 423. McNeill cites the statement of Descartes: "I hold that all those to whom God has given the use of this reason are bound to employ it in the effort to know him and to know themselves." *Oeuvres de Descartes*, ed. C. Adam and P. Tannery (Paris: L. Cerf, 1897-), 1:44 (McNeill, 1:37, n. 3). This, of course, is a reformulation of Augustine's famous statement: "I desire to know God and the soul. Nothing more? Nothing at all." *Soliloquies*, 1.2.7 (*MPL* 32.872 [*NPNF* 7:539]). In addition to pointing out that Calvin does not start with proofs for God's existence, it should also be noted that he does not begin with a discussion of the authority of scripture, either.

24. Brunner's exegesis of Calvin is found in *Natural Theology*, pp. 35-50,

with Barth's alternative exegesis found on pp. 94-109. For a survey of the debate's influence upon Calvin scholarship, see David C. Steinmetz, "The Theology of Calvin and Calvinism," in *Reformation Europe: A Guide to Research*, ed. Steven Ozment (St. Louis: Center for Reformation Research, 1982), pp. 219-22.

25. I want to make it clear, however, that my purpose is not to take sides in this debate since I think that the framework within which this entire discussion took place is skewed from the outset. "Natural theology" or "revelation" is not, in my judgment, the best question with which to approach Calvin. By contrast, I think that the twofold question of "religion" and "Christian faith as religion" is a much better question, but this is precisely what the neo-orthodox rejected when they sought to leap over the nineteenth century in order to return to the Reformation.

26. Serene Jones has recently proposed what she calls a "rhetorical" reading of the first three chapters of the *Institutes* that stands in striking contrast to the interpretation I am here suggesting. See her *Calvin and the Rhetoric of Piety*, Columbia Series in Reformed Theology (Louisville: Westminster/John Knox Press, 1995). She writes: "While it is true that Calvin treats a topic that contemporary theologians would describe as 'theological methodology,' he does not approach the subject in a manner typical of contemporary theologians" (p. 111-12). "Calvin intended these chapters on 'natural knowledge' to serve rhetorical functions that are not necessarily wedded to concerns for logical precision, conceptual clarity, or systematic rigor" (p. 159). Regarding chapter two where Calvin defines "piety," she denies that Calvin's purpose "is to give a straightforward definition of *pietas* and to present the reader with arguments in support of this definition." She writes: "While it is true that one of the text's functions lies in an expository analysis of *pietas*, my rhetorical reading has attempted to uncover other functions that the chapter serves as well, and when these additional functions are taken into consideration, a very different picture of Calvin's theology as a whole begins to emerge" (p. 147). Her objection to interpretations that seek to discern "a well-reasoned, carefully executed, logically constructed analysis of the character of 'religious knowledge'" is that they "mainly attend to the propositional components of the rhetoric" while they "overlook the great wealth of textual activity that . . . resists the limits of propositional analysis. . . . [I]f my analysis does nothing else, it should convince the reader that there is no central argument that neatly ties the chapter together" but "many different arguments taking place all at once" (p. 146). Her focus "is not on the argument as much as it is on the attitude of praise Calvin is trying to inculcate in his readers." Thereby she wants us "to appreciate more clearly Calvin's skill at shaping the Christian character of his readers" (p. 8). I would simply ask scholars to consider whether my interpretation sheds light on the logical structure of Calvin's theology as a whole in a way that does no violence to the multivalent character of Calvin's rhetoric. Sou-Young Lee has this to say: "Even though Calvin places much importance on pietas, it is difficult for us to find any trace that he attempted to describe pietas systematically. We catch only a glimpse of his understanding and thoughts on pietas scattered throughout his writings. Nevertheless, even though his references to pietas are not systematic

but sporadic, not synthetic but fragmentary, we can ascertain that the content is a mass of highly clear and consistent thinking." "Calvin's Understanding of *Pietas*," in *Calvinus Sincerioris Religionis Vindex*, p. 226.

27. *Inst.*, 1.2.1 (McNeill, 1:40).

28. *Inst.*, 1.5.6 (McNeill, 1:59).

29. *Inst.*, 1.2.1.

30. *Inst.*, 1.5.6.

31. In defense of his position against Barth's critique, Brunner says: "If it were possible to show that my theses are neither Thomist nor Neo-Protestant but adhere to the teaching of the Reformation, not much would remain of the objections which Barth has so far raised against them." Just a few lines later, however, he adds: "Calvin goes even further in the direction which Barth calls 'Thomism' or 'Neo-Protestantism' than I should dare to do." It is puzzling that this concession never led Brunner to re-examine his definition of "the teaching of the Reformation," since he identifies himself with "those who, in using the word 'Reformation,' think especially of Calvin." *Natural Theology*, pp. 35-36. This ambivalence toward what Calvin actually says reveals the inadequacy of the conceptual categories with which the neo-orthodox theologians approached the historical record: while Brunner appeals to Calvin for support in his debate with Barth, he must distance himself from those aspects of Calvin's theology that might lend credence to Schleiermacher! For his part, Barth believed it was necessary to go beyond the formulations of the Reformers in view of the infiltration of Nazi ideology into the heart of the Protestant church in Germany: "Of course the 'German Christians' have been very glad about the new discovery of what 'adheres to the teaching of the Reformation.' . . . If we really wish to maintain the Reformers' position over against that of Roman Catholicism and Neo-Protestantism, we are not in a position today to repeat the statements of Luther and Calvin without at the same time making them more pointed than they themselves did." Ibid., pp. 99, 101.

32. Barth downplays the significance of Calvin's discussion of religion in the *Institutes* by insisting that the concept of religion has been derived from Scripture. *Church Dogmatics*, 1.2, p. 284. There is an important half-truth in this observation. Calvin's understanding of religion is certainly influenced by his reading of the Bible and stands in the service of his broader concern to defend the Protestant doctrine of faith. But this is not the whole picture since it does not take seriously the way Calvin hammers out his concept of religion in conversation with the pagan philosophers and it obscures the fact that Calvin shares the conviction of the pagans that nature itself is our first teacher in matters of religion. "[Calvin] assumed that the awareness of nature's testimony belongs to Christian and non-Christian alike, and that he was thereby appealing to a common experience. Now this evidence was, in the formulation given to it by Calvin, derived from the philosophical discourses of pagan philosophers." Victor L. Nuovo, *Calvin's Theology: A Study of its Sources in Classical Antiquity* (Ph.D. diss., Columbia University, 1964), pp. 63-64.

33. In his Gifford Lectures, James Barr calls into question the exegetical foundation of Barth's theology by demonstrating the extent to which "natural theology" is implied throughout major portions of the Bible. As Barr correctly

58 Christian Faith as Religion

sees, this argument has serious implications for Barth's entire theology: "If it is true that natural theology in some way underlies the Bible, if it is used and therefore supported by some significant parts of the Bible, the effect upon Barth's total theological position must be devastating. And this not so much because it means that his position about natural theology is wrong. That may or may not be the case, but is not the point I wish to pursue. What it means is that his doctrine of scripture is wrong. His assessment of the Bible as the Word of God and as the arbiter of theological truth cannot tolerate the perception that natural theology is sanctioned by its presence there. . . . [I]t could not tolerate the gigantic theological error of natural theology within key portions of the scripture—for no portions were more key than the Law of Moses, the Psalms, and the writings and speeches of Paul—not at a time when it was being asserted that the rejection of natural theology was *the pivotal matter* of discrimination between one theology and another." Barr continues: "And this would have made a big difference. For one thing, it would have severely qualified Barth's claim that his theology was in positive continuity with the Reformation. He did . . . note the use of natural theology by both Luther and Calvin, but he could do this without strain because he appeared in other regards to be completely loyal to that movement, and could interpret his own shift of position concerning natural theology as an element of even greater loyalty to it. But to have made this shift of position, and accompanied it with an admission that the shift not only was a move away from the Reformers' own practice, but meant that Holy Scripture itself was mistaken about this key issue, this would have been too much for most of those who heard Barth's lectures with sympathy and appreciation. For of course Luther and Calvin, in so far as they did use natural theology, did so under the impression, which they shared with most traditional Christians, that scripture itself gave sanction to this." *Biblical Faith and Natural Theology: The Gifford Lectures for 1991 Delivered in the University of Edinburgh* (Oxford: Clarendon Press, 1993), pp. 103-5.

34. Brunner said of Barth: "[I]t seems to me a queer kind of loyalty to Scripture to demand that such a revelation should not be acknowledged, in order that the significance of biblical revelation should not be minimised." *Natural Theology*, p. 25; Odgen rephrased Brunner's point: "It is a strange kind of loyalty to scripture to deny for its sake what it itself plainly affirms." "On Revelation," p. 28.

35. *Inst.*, 1.2.1 (McNeill, 1:39-40). Calvin calls this knowledge "primal and simple" to distinguish it from the more complex knowledge of God the redeemer which has to take into account the experiences of human estrangement from and reconciliation with the creator.

36. Peter Brunner explains that the authentic religious response to the natural knowledge of God which was a possibility for Adam before the fall (*in principio*) remains a possibility in principle (*prinzipiell*) for us after the fall: "Adam's fall does not excuse me for not knowing God here and now on the basis of his original testimonies (*Urbezeugungen*). The possibility of knowing God on the basis of his original testimonies, which was valid in the beginning, remains valid in principle even here and now. The fact that I do not actually know God must never be construed as fate, thereby mitigating it; rather, it must

be exposed as guilt." "Allgemeine und besondere Offenbarung in Calvins Institutio," in *Evangelische Theologie*, 1. Jahrg. (1934): 197.

37. *Inst.*, 1.4.1; *Comm.* John 4:36 (*CO* 47:96).

38. *Inst.*, 1.4.1.

39. "It is one of the major components of Calvin's natural theology that he speaks of the human being as having been created with a capacity for religion (*Anlage zur Religion*)." Günter Gloede, *Theologia Naturalis bei Calvin*, Tübinger Studien zur systematischen Theologie 5 (Stuttgart: Verlag von W. Kohlhammer, 1935), p. 282.

40. *Inst.*, 1.3.1. Dowey calls the *sensus divinitatis* an "internal" or "subjective revelation" in which "the glory and majesty of God, by which he inspires fear and worship, are given directly to the mind." *The Knowledge of God*, pp. 53, 57. But Samuel J. Preus thinks "it would clarify matters simply to speak of such knowledge in Calvin's own language—as natural." "Zwingli, Calvin, and the Origin of Religion," *Church History* 46 (June 1977): 200.

41. *Inst.*, 1.4.2. "At the beginning of the *Institutio* there may be perceived a remarkable omission. The subject of the book is the knowledge of God; but Calvin does not lay the foundation for his building by first proving the existence of God who is to be known. . . . How different from St. Thomas Aquinas. . . . Calvin, however, presupposes the existence of God, on the very ground, the validity of which St. Thomas denies, that men have an innate knowledge of the existence of God. . . . [I]t is a more or less conscious feeling or idea that apart from the world of men there is Another; a feeling or idea that naturally is believed intellectually, and is disbelieved only in defiance of nature, and that naturally finds expression in worship." Parker, *Doctrine of the Knowledge of God*, pp. 7-8.

42. *Inst.*, 1.5.9.

43. *Inst.*, 1.2.1. Though "piety" (*pietas*) and "religion" (*religio*) are sometimes used synonymously, it is characteristic for Calvin to employ "religion" descriptively as a designation for the entire field of religious activity, whereas "piety" is always a normative term. When Calvin uses "religion" as a synonym for piety, it is usually modified by an adjective, e.g., "true religion." Compare this to Zwingli's differing usage of terms: "I take 'religion' in the sense that encompasses the entire piety of Christians: faith, life, laws, observances, and sacraments. Then, moreover, I distinguish religion from superstition by adding 'true' and 'false'." *De vera et falsa religione Commentarius* (1525), in *Werke*, 3:639. The difference in definition reflects contrasting approaches to the interpretation of religion. Preus speaks of Zwingli as exemplifying an approach to the interpretation of religion he calls "'historical' or empirical," in contrast to Calvin's approach which he describes as "'natural' or essentialist." The "historical" approach of Zwingli attends to "concrete, particular manifestations of religion elicited by specific divine activity" whereas the "natural" approach of Calvin finds "the roots of religion in a universal, innate human quality or attribute" (p. 189). Preus continues: "Zwingli would not talk about religion without reference to divine activity . . . Calvin differed: for him, religion was presupposed as a 'natural' human activity. No less than for Zwingli, of course, the word of God was supposed to establish

authentic religiousness; nevertheless, Calvin saw man expressing his fundamental humanity in his religiousness, whereas for Zwingli religion to a greater degree seemed to presuppose sin" (pp. 189-90). Perhaps Barth's affinities are more Zwinglian than Calvinist here. See also the study by Bernhard Pünjer, *History of the Christian Philosophy of Religion from the Reformation to Kant*, trans. W. Hastie (Edinburgh: T. and T. Clark, 1887), pp. 145-58.

44. *Inst.*, 1.1.1.

45. Calvin invokes the Delphic maxim "Know Thyself" to make his point that self-knowledge includes knowledge of God. "It was not without reason that the ancient proverb so strongly recommended knowledge of self to the human being." Inst., 2.1.1. See Eliza Gregory Wilkens, *The Delphic Maxims in Literature* (Chicago: The University of Chicago Press, 1929), p. 100. Erasmus called the maxim "the crown" of wisdom, "a saying which antiquity believed sent from heaven, and one in which the great authors took delight, holding it to epitomize the fullness of wisdom." *Enchiridion Militis Christiani*, in *Ausgewählte Werke*, ed. Hajo Holborn with Annemarie Holborn (Munich: C. H. Beck'sche Verlagsbuchhandlung, 1933), p. 40, cited according to the translation of Ford Lewis Battles, *Advocates of Reform: From Wyclif to Erasmus*, ed. Matthew Spinka, Library of Christian Classics 14 (London and Philadelphia: S.C.M. and Westminster Press, 1953), p. 310. For one ancient example, see Plato, *Protagoras*, 343a and b (*LCL*, p. 196f.).

46. The French edition of 1560 puts it this way: "In knowing God, one knows oneself as well" (C'est qu'en cognoissant Dieu, chacun de nous aussi se cognoisse"). *Institution de la Religion chrestienne*, 1.1.1, critical edition with introduction, notes, and variants by Jean-Daniel Benoit (Paris: Librairie Philosophique J. Vrin, 1957), 1:50.

47. *Inst.*, 1.1.3. Calvin doesn't tell us why this is "the correct order of teaching." Jones, however, takes his decision here as confirmation of a Barthian reading: "Barth's interpretation of Calvin is much closer to the interpretation my rhetorical reading renders. Calvin does suggest, finally, that divine knowledge must precede self-knowledge and that self-knowledge is incapable of generating any theologically positive content." *Calvin and the Rhetoric of Piety*, p. 113; see also pp. 106-7. She writes: "[B]ecause the function of his discussion of self-knowledge is more rhetorically than theologically substantive, it does not provide a substantive foundation upon which Calvin's dogmatic claims will be based. In short, Calvin uses apologetics in the service of dogmatics without allowing it to generate the norm for the content of dogmatics" (p. 114). But according to his own statement, Calvin could just as easily begin with knowledge of self.

48. Zwingli, too, had placed the correlation of knowledge of God with knowledge of self at the heart of his interpretation of religion. "Religion comprises two terms," he wrote: "the one toward whom religion reaches out and the one who by means of religion reaches out toward the other. . . . It is God toward whom religion reaches out and the human being who by means of religion reaches out toward him." Zwingli concludes that "religion cannot be discussed properly without first of all recognizing God and knowing the human

being." *De vera et falsa religione*, in *Werke*, 3:640.

49. God accommodates himself to our measure of understanding. In this case, the created works are his accommodation to us as creatures, as the Bible (with its twofold knowledge of God) is God's accommodation to us as sinners. *Inst.*, 1.5.1, 1.6.1, 1.17.13. See Dowey, *Knowledge of God*, pp. 3-17. Ford Lewis Battles writes: "[F]or Calvin, accommodation has to do not only with the Scriptures and their interpretation, but with the whole of created reality to which, for the Christian, Scripture holds the clue. The entire created universe and all its parts are naught but a grand accommodation on God's part of himself to the crowning glory (and subsequent shame) of that creation, namely man." "God Was Accommodating Himself to Human Capacity," in *Interpretation: A Journal of Bible and Theology* 31 (January 1977): 21.

50. *Inst.*, 1.2.1.

51. Tillich writes: "Calvin states more clearly than any of the other Reformers that God is known in an existential attitude." *History of Christian Thought*, p. 263. See also P. Lobstein, "La Connaissance religieuse d'après Calvin," *Revue de théologie et de philosophie religieuses* 42 (1909): 53-110. I am indebted to Lynne Krehbiel for assistance with the translation of this article.

52. *Inst.*, 1.5.3. Gerrish, "The Mirror of God's Goodness: A Key Metaphor in Calvin's View of Man," in *The Old Protestantism and the New*, pp. 150-59. Gerrish argues that the primary meaning of the *imago Dei* in Calvin's theology is this activity in which the human being reflects God's glory by thankfully acknowledging God as the giver of all good gifts. "While the entire created order reflects God's glory as in a mirror and in this sense 'images' God, man is distinguished from the mute creation by his ability to reflect God's glory in a conscious response of thankfulness. It is this, above all, that sets him apart from the brute beasts: they likewise owe their existence to God, but they do not know it" (p. 154). Brunner says that the *imago Dei* is "the seat of religion, of the knowledge of God and of God's worthiness to be worshipped." *Natural Theology*, p. 42.

53. *Comm.* Acts 17:27 (*CO* 48:415). In the *Genevan Catechism* (1545), knowledge of God is said to be the "chief end of human life" (*OS* 2:75).

54. *Inst.*, 1.5.3. Calvin notes that "long ago certain of the philosophers called the human a *mikrokosmos*, and not without good reason." Ibid. Cf. Aristotle, *Physics*, 8.2, in *Basic Works of Aristotle*, trans. Richard McKeon, (New York: Random House, 1941), p. 359; Cicero, *Tusculan Disputations*, 1.24-27 (*LCL*, pp. 64-79). See also Roy W. Battenhouse, "The Doctrine of Man in Calvin and Renaissance Platonism," in *Journal of the History of Ideas* 9 (1948): 447-71, and Charles Trinkaus, "Renaissance Problems in Calvin's Theology," in *Studies in the Renaissance* 1 (1954): 59-80.

55. *Inst.*, 1.5.3 (comment on Acts 17:26-27). "Now we see that all who do not know God do not know themselves, because they have God not only in the excellent gifts of their mind, but in their very existence. Since it does not belong to any but God to exist, all other things dwell in him." *Comm.* Acts 17:28 (*CO* 48:417). This reflects the Thomist view that God's essence is to exist, whereas the essence of creatures does not include their existence. *Summa Theologiae*, 1.3.4, in *Aquinas on Nature and Grace*, ed. A. M. Fairweather, Library of

Christian Classics: Ichthus edition (Philadelphia: Westminster Press, 1954), pp. 62-63.

56. Brunner writes: "God can be known from nature other than man, but also from man himself. Indeed, he is to be known especially from the latter. But above all from *experientia*, i.e. from the experience of his preserving and providential grace." *Natural Theology*, p. 38.

57. Peter Barth writes: "Corresponding to the general *sensus divinitatis* in humanity (which, of course, does not reach its goal!), God has revealed himself in a way which is fundamentally accessible to everyone: through the artful design of the world." "Die fünf Einleitungskapitel," p. 46.

58. *Inst.*, 1.5.1.

59. *Inst.*, 1.5.1.

60. *Inst.*, 1.5.6. Cf. Plato, *Timaeus*, 29D-30A, (*LCL, Plato*, 9:55) where the goodness of God is said to be his reason for creating the universe. Calvin considered Plato "the most religious" of all the ancient philosophers (*inter omnes religiosissimus*). *Inst.*, 1.5.11.

61. *Inst.* 1.2.1. Cf. Seneca's statement: "Whoever knows God, worships God." Ep. 95.47 (*LCL, Epistulae Morales*, 3:88f.). Also, Bohatec, p. 244.

62. *Inst.*, 1.2.1. Reminiscent of Melanchthon's phrase "To know Christ is to know his benefits." *Loci Communes Theologici*, in *Melanchthons Werke in Auswahl*, ed. Hans Engelland (Gütersloh: C. Bertelsmann Verlag, 1952), 2:1, p. 7. Indeed, Calvin's meaning is precisely this: "To know God is to know his benefits." In connection with Melanchthon's statement Bohatec cites a similar definition from the Hermetic literature, which was popular among humanists in Calvin's day: "Piety is the knowledge of God; the one who knows God, being filled with all good things, thinks divine thoughts" (p. 246). On the influence of Hermeticism at the time of the Reformation, see the brief summary by Mircea Eliade, *A History of Religious Ideas*, vol. 3: *From Muhammed to the Age of Reforms*, trans. Alf-Hiltebeitel and Diane Apostolos-Cappadona (Chicago: The University of Chicago Press, 1985), pp. 251-55. Eliade points out that Lefèvre, the Catholic reformer to whom Calvin turned for advice shortly before entering the Protestant camp, was a student of Hermeticism (p. 254). On Lefèvre's relation to Hermeticism, see Frances A. Yates, *Giordano Bruno and the Hermetic Tradition* (Chicago: The University of Chicago Press, 1964), pp. 170-72.

63. *Inst.*, 1.2.1. One could even say that *fons omnium bonorum* is Calvin's fundamental definition of deity. See Gerrish, *Grace and Gratitude*, p. 26, and especially pp. 31-38 for a discussion of the Platonic provenance of this idea in Calvin's theology.

64. "Father" is the regulative personal metaphor for God in the *Institutes*, even though Calvin recognized that the Bible itself did not exclude other metaphors for God, including "mother," e.g., *Comm.* Isa 42:12 (*CO* 37:69-70). See the probing essay by Jane Dempsey Douglass, "Calvin's Use of Metaphorical Language for God: God as Enemy and God as Mother," in *Archive for Reformation History* 77 (1986): 126-40. See also Gerrish, *Grace and Gratitude*, pp. 38-41.

65. *Inst.*, 1.2.1.

66. *Inst.*, 1.2.1.
67. *Inst.*, 1.2.2.
68. *Inst.*, 1.2.2.
69. *Inst.*, 1.2.1.
70. *Inst.*, 3.9.3 (McNeill, 1:715).
71. *Inst.*, 1.3.3.
72. *Inst.*, 1.3.1. Barr writes: "Calvin uses natural theology to prove the *impossibility of atheism*, a point which is not marginal but of central importance. Human beings had an innate religious instinct, which on Barthian terms might not amount to much, but for Calvin himself was a powerful basis of argument. Religion was for him, as it was not for Barth, a significant positive symbol. It was not by chance that his best-known work was called the *Institutes* 'of the Christian Religion.'" *Biblical Faith and Natural Theology*, p. 110.
73. "Calvin shows an unusually lively interest in the demonstration that the human being from birth, from nature—that is to say, simply on account of its being human—carries within something that compels it to conceive the idea of God (even if this idea is completely distorted). The human being dehumanizes and deceives itself and is guilty if it wants to eradicate this *divinitatis sensus* from its natural constitution and to deny it. The consciousness of God is given with the self-consciousness of the human being and is inseparable from it." Hans Engelland, *Gott und Mensch bei Calvin* (Munich: Chr. Kaiser Verlag, 1934), p. 16.
74. *Inst.*, 1.3.1.
75. *Comm.* John 4:36 (*CO* 47:96).
76. The question of Calvin's continuity and discontinuity with Cicero has been carefully explored by Egil Grislis, "Calvin's Use of Cicero in the Institutes I:1-5—A Case Study in Theological Method," in *Archive for Reformation History* 62 (1971): 5-37. Grislis contends that "in his use of classical sources Calvin's own theological perspective emerges more clearly. He exhibits an impressive agreement with classical thought, as represented by Cicero, and at the same time undertakes a basic reinterpretation of it from the standpoint of biblical revelation" (p. 5). Bohatec shares the same judgment: "It will not escape the attention of a careful reader that Calvin makes a connection with the guiding principles of antiquity and fills them with a Christian content" (p. 244).
77. "The relation of Calvin's theology to Antiquity is complex. It may be defined as one of repudiation and dependence. Calvin repudiated the doctrines of the ancient philosophers, yet claimed to find in Scripture the fulfillment of their essential task; namely, to guide man to a knowledge of God. . . . The very arguments that he used against ancient philosophers have antecedents in philosophical polemics of Antiquity. The virtues he claimed for Scripture's doctrine are the same that ancient philosophers reserved for sound philosophy." Nuovo, *Calvin's Theology*, pp. 1-2.
78. "Calvin discussed the source of religion in completely anthropological terms. Even though his *Institutes* was structured by the thesis that knowledge of God and man are reciprocal matters which cannot be treated in isolation . . . Calvin could locate and identify the basis of religion by referring to human nature alone—to the innate *sensus divinitatis*. The authority for this belief was

not Scripture but classical antiquity . . ." Preus, p. 197.

79. Cicero, *De natura deorum (LCL)*, 1.16.43.

80. *De natura deorum*, 1.17.44.

81. *De natura deorum*, 1.17.44.

82. *Inst.*, 1.3.1.

83. *Inst.*, 1.4.2.

84. *Inst.*, 1.3.3.

85. *Inst.*, 1.5.4.

86. For summaries of their philosophies, see P. H. DeLacy, "Epicureanism and the Epicurean School" and "Epicurus," in *The Encyclopedia of Philosophy*, ed. Paul Edwards (New York: The Macmillan Company and the Free Press, 1967), 3:2-3, 3-5; Philip P. Hallie, "Stoicism," in *The Encyclopedia of Philosophy*, 8:19-22. On the religious dimensions of their philosophies, see the older but still insightful work by Eduard Zeller, *Stoics, Epicureans, and Sceptics*, trans. Oswald J. Reichel, new and rev. ed. (New York: Russell and Russell, Inc., 1962), pp. 341-80 and 462-71.

87. *De natura deorum*, 2.37.94.

88. In antiquity, the Delphic maxim "Know Thyself" meant one of two things: first, it was a summons to know one's mortal limits so as to avoid inordinate pride and, second, it was an exhortation to recognize the divinity of the rational soul. Cicero uses it in this latter sense when he writes: "Therefore, the soul, I say, is divine." *Tusculan Disputations* 1.26.65 (*LCL*, p. 74f.). See Hans Dieter Betz, "The Delphic Maxim ΓΝΩΘΙ ΣΑYTON in Hermetic Interpretation," in *Hellenismus und Urchristentum*, vol. 1 of *Gesammelte Aufsätze* (Tübingen: J. C. B. Mohr [Paul Siebeck], 1990), p. 97.

89. *De natura deorum*, 2.6.16.

90. *Inst.*, 1.5.5.

91. *De natura deorum*, 2.6.16.

92. *Inst.*, 1.5.3, commenting on Acts 17:28 where a line from the poem *Phaenomena* by Aratus of Soli (3rd century B.C.E.) is cited. Elsewhere Calvin notes that the pagan poets gratefully attributed the invention of philosophy, the laws, and other useful things to the gods. *Inst.*, 2.2.15.

93. The Stoic affirms: "Nothing is more excellent than God; thus the world must be ruled by him; God is not obedient or subject to any nature, since he himself rules all nature." *De natura deorum*, 2.30.77.

94. On Calvin's attempt to steer a middle course between the Epicurean denial of providence and Stoic pantheism, see Susan E. Schreiner, *The Theatre of His Glory: Nature and the Natural Order in the Thought of John Calvin*, Studies in Historical Theology 3 (Durham: Labyrinth Press, 1991), pp. 16-21. The tension is to affirm God's active involvement with every detail of nature's operation without identifying God exclusively with the natural process.

95. *Inst.*, 1.5.5.

96. Calvin's comment stands in a tradition that goes back to Seneca: "Therefore you do nothing, O most ungrateful of mortals, you who say that you are indebted not to God but to nature, because there is no nature without God and no God without nature, but both are the same thing, differing in function." *On Benefits*, 4.7.2 (*Epistulae Morales, LCL*, 3:218f). Lactantius praised Seneca

for the insight that nature, if it is not mute, must be called "God": "Therefore Seneca, the sharpest of all the Stoics, says it better, who saw that 'nature is nothing other than God' . . . since God himself is nature." *The Divine Institutes*, 2.9 (*MPL* 6:299 [*ANF* 7.53]). Zwingli argued that the identification of God with nature could be used to combat polytheism: "Finally [they deride unjustly] Gaius Pliny who said that that which we call God was the power of nature. For being a most learned man he revolted at a multiplicity of gods and accordingly at the nomenclature involved. Hence he denied that there were gods, but he did not really deny, indeed he asserted, the existence of the Deity. For what he called nature we call the Deity. . . . He seems, therefore, to understand by nature that power which moves and unites or separates all things. And what is that but God?" *On the Providence of God*, in *Werke*, 6:3, pp. 97-99; according to the translation found in *Latin Works*, 2:145-6. Brunner recognizes Stoic influence in Calvin's use of the term "nature." *Natural Theology*, p. 36. Herman Bavinck writes: "There is no part of the world in which some spark of the divine glory does not glimmer. Though it be a metaphorical mode of expression, since God should not be confounded with nature, it may be affirmed in a truly religious sense that nature is God." "Calvin and Common Grace," in *Calvin and the Reformation*, Four Studies by Emile Doumergue, August Lang, Herman Bavinck, and Benjamin B. Warfield, ed. William Park Armstrong (Princeton Theological Review Association, 1909; repr., Grand Rapids: Baker Book House, 1980), p. 118.

97. *Inst.*, 1.5.6.

98. *Inst.*, 1.3.2.

99. *Inst.*, 1.4.2 (Ps 14:1; 53:1). David calls these fools "atheists," Calvin explains, "not because they conclude that there is no God by means of reasoned argument or formal syllogisms, as they say" but, rather, because "they have overthrown all order, so that there remains no distinction between right and wrong, no concern for integrity, and no affection for humanity." *Comm.* Ps 14:1 (*CO* 31:136). Whereas Calvin's "fool" is morally indifferent, Anselm's "fool" is simply stupid since he fails to understand that God's existence is self-evident to human reason. "An Address (*Proslogion*)," in *A Scholastic Miscellany: Anselm to Ockham*, ed. Eugene R. Fairweather, The Library of Christian Classics: Ichthus edition (Philadelphia: Westminster Press, 1956), pp. 74-75.

100. The Epicurean denial of providence was commonly identified with atheism in the Middle Ages. Thomas Aquinas wrote: "Some people completely deny providence, such as Democritus and the Epicureans, who assert that the world was made by accident." *Summa Theologiae* 1.22.2. Calvin often speaks of the Epicureans as "atheists," in spite of the fact that they never denied the existence of the gods. For a discussion about the meaning of "atheism" in Calvin's time, see Lucien Febvre, *The Problem of Unbelief in the Sixteenth Century: The Religion of Rabelais*, trans. Beatrice Gottlieb (Cambridge, Massachusetts: Harvard University Press, 1982). Febvre argues that theoretical atheism in the modern sense was not a real option in the 16th century which Febvre characterizes as "a century that wanted to believe" (this is the title he gives to his conclusion on pp. 455-64). Jones makes the interesting suggestion that "Calvin textually fashions a historically unprecedented 'atheistic' identity

... an identity that had as yet no explicit historical referent but would soon be occupied by one of modernity's most interesting characters, that very alive and popular foe known to later generations of Enlightenment theologians as the intellectual atheist. Would it not be one of history's ironies if here, in the *Institutes*, one could trace the conceptual roots of not only Puritan, Presbyterian, and Dutch Reformed identities, but the emergent identity of contemporary culture's great religious skeptic as well?" *Calvin and the Rhetoric of Piety*, pp. 174-75.

101.   *De natura deorum*, 1.17.45.

102.   *De natura deorum*, 1.20.54-55. This is, no doubt, precisely what the Epicurean would find objectionable in Calvin's view of deity.

103.   *De natura deorum*, 1.44.123.

104.   *Inst.*, 1.4.2.

105.   He mentions, in particular, Statius who had written that "fear first made the gods." *Inst.*, 1.5.4; Statius, *Thebaid*, 3.660 (*LCL, Statius* 1:500f.).

106.   On the distinction between "proper" and "servile" fear, see *Inst.*, 3.2.22-23, 26-27. The pious fear God, not punishment. *Inst.*, 3.2.26-27; also *Inst.*, 1.2.2.

107.   *Inst.*, 1.3.2. "Calvin could have called the fear of God an 'axiom' for the human being." Gloede, p. 284.

108.   *De natura deorum*, 2.28.72.

109.   *De natura deorum*, 2.28.71.

110.   *Inst.*, 1.12.1.

111.   *Inst.*, 1.4.1.

112.   *Inst.*, 1.4.3.

113.   "Cicero's realism took the human plight very seriously. Cicero described broken human existence and acknowledged a genuine and deep-seated confusion among men in regard to their knowledge of the gods." Grislis, p. 20.

114.   *De natura deorum*, 1.22.60.

115.   *Inst.*, 1.5.12.

116.   Grislis writes of Calvin's use of Cicero: "Calvin has established a vigorous dialogue between classical learning and biblical revelation—and that at such a strategic place as the opening sections of his main work. Here Calvin has found such a dialogue to be apologetically useful and theologically fruitful" (p. 36).

117.   In the 1539 edition of the *Institutes*, the first chapter is entitled *De cognitione Dei*, which is then elaborated in 1543 to read *De cognitione Dei, quae primum est religionis fundamentum: et unde vera eius regula sit petenda* ("On the knowledge of God which is the chief foundation of religion; and from which we ought to seek the true rule of religion"). *CO* 1:279.

118.   *Inst.*, 1.5.12 (an allusion to Acts 17:23).

119.   *Inst.*, 1.5.14.

120.   "As a result of this dual usage, the 'nature' of man is both his original, created goodness, from which any lapse is unnatural; and it is also the sinfulness or 'natural' disposition of man as against his created goodness." Dowey, *Knowledge of God*, p. 66.

121.   Dowey writes: "God did not stop revealing himself in nature at the Fall. The actual guilt of man in Calvin's theology is the result of actual rejection of

an actual revelation that remains clear." *Knowledge of God*, p. 73. Parker writes: "The revelation in creation and providence, however, does not cease to be revelation because man does not profit by it." *Doctrine of the Knowledge of God*, p. 38. Calvin clarifies his use of terms regarding nature and its corruption: "Let us remember to attribute our ruin to a distortion of nature (*depravatio naturae*) in order that we may not bring an accusation against God himself, the author of nature," and, "therefore, we say that the human being has been spoiled by a natural corruption (*naturalis vitiositas*) but one which did not arise from nature." *Inst.*, 2.1.10-11.

122. *Comm.* John 1:5 (*CO* 47:6). Peter Barth writes of the human situation *post lapsum*: "Even in this situation there can be no question that for Calvin the human being retains a dim feeling (*ein dunkles Gefühl*) for divinity." *Das Problem der natürlichen Theologie*, Theologische Existenz Heute 18 (Munich: Chr. Kaiser Verlag, 1935), p. 25f.

123. *Comm.* John 1:5 (*CO* 47:6). Even Karl Barth acknowledges that Calvin attributes to all persons a "seed of religion," yet he denies that this concept has any significance in his theology on account of sin: "Certainly Calvin ascribes to fallen man an inalienable *semen* of this religion. But over against it he sets the knowledge that this *semen* cannot ripen, let alone bear fruit in anyone. Therefore the concept of *religio* as a general and neutral form has no fundamental significance in Calvin's conception and exposition of Christianity. For him *religio* is an entity X, which receives content and form only as it is equated with Christianity . . . as it is taken up into revelation and fashioned by it." *Church Dogmatics*, 1.2, pp. 284-85. I would pose two questions to Barth: First, if this concept is of no consequence for Calvin's theology, why did he spend so much effort trying to elaborate it, especially in the final version of his *Institutes* when he was certain he had at last found the proper arrangement for Protestant dogmatics? And, second, how can Barth speak of the concept of religion in Calvin's theology as "neutral" given its obvious normative import as the proper human response to God's self-disclosure?

124. David C. Steinmetz analyzes Calvin's exegesis of Rom 1:18-32 and compares it with that of the medieval exegetical tradition. "Calvin and the Natural Knowledge of God," in *Calvin in Context* (New York and Oxford: Oxford University Press, 1995), pp. 23-39. Steinmetz shows how Calvin agrees with other commentators (e.g., Melanchthon, Bucer, and Bullinger) "that there is a general knowledge of God from creation . . . accessible to human reason apart from grace" even though "the natural knowledge of God is not saving" (p. 28). The novelty of Calvin's exegesis, however, consists in "focusing on the knowing subject and the noetic effects of sin. . . . Calvin breaks with the exegetical tradition since Augustine by distinguishing sharply between what is offered to natural reason and what is received. . . . The diffculty is not with what is shown to fallen human reason through the natural order; the difficulty is with human misperception because of sin" (p. 29). On account of this focus, Calvin creates a difficulty for himself: "In the judgment of Calvin's contemporaries, Paul does not stress an acute noetic impairment because of sin or distinguish sharply between what is revealed in nature and what is perceived by fallen human reason. . . . By stressing the damage human reason has incurred through

sin, Calvin makes the argument for moral responsibility of the pagans all the
more difficult to sustain" (p. 31). Steinmetz concludes: "In short, Calvin draws
a distinction between what is offered and received that becomes a guiding
principle of his thought. . . . Only when reason is illumined by faith, can it once
again see the world for what it is, a mirror of divine glory. On this fundamental
point Calvin is, I think, sometimes ambiguous, but never ambivalent" (p. 32).

125. *Inst.*, 1.6.1 (McNeill, 1:69-70).

126. *Inst.*, 1.6.1. See also *Inst.*, 1.14.1 and "Argumentum," *Comm.* Gen (*CO*
23:9-10), where this central metaphor of "spectacles" also occurs. Nuovo
writes: "Natural theology signified to [Calvin] that discipline whose task is to
demonstrate the divine moral government of the world from the experience of
natural and human events. 'Natural' is not the opposite of 'supernatural' or
'divine,' but of contrived, invented, established by custom: all vices to which,
according to Calvin, the ancients had succumbed. A natural theology of
Scripture, then, is no contradiction when understood in these terms. Thus,
Calvin conceived Scripture in one of its roles as the true guide and interpreter
of the common experience of nature and of human events, as the spectacles that
correct man's vision, that repudiate what is fictictious and that restore what is
natural and true and morally profitable." *Calvin's Theology*, p. 2.

127. Barth's real objection to Brunner consists in the suggestion that, after
Adam's fall, we might look to nature "for another source of revelation beside
Scripture, for one that would supplement Scripture." *Natural Theology*, p. 105f.
He explains: "It is true that, according to Calvin, the knowledge of God in
Christ includes a real knowledge of God in creation. Includes! This means that
it does not, as Brunner seems to think, bring forth a second, relatively
independent kind of knowledge . . ." (p. 108f.).

128. Again, I have borrowed terminology from Odgen who speaks of the
gospel as the "re-presentation" of the gift and demand of God's love. *The Point
of Christology* (San Francisco: Harper and Row, 1982). Against this idea that
scripture in any way "re-presents" an original knowledge of God, Jones argues:
"At first glance, it appears that Calvin is describing something like an innate,
prelinguistic religious experience that is universally present in all persons by
virtue of the divinely implanted 'seed of religion.' It is possible that having
asserted the presence of this seed, Calvin could then go on to discuss how the
language of scripture and doctrine simply expresses or names this innate but
prelinguistic knowledge. Instead, Calvin harshly announces that this innate
knowledge is useless because sin has made it impossible for even the faithful to
know God intuitively. Thus, Calvin argues, human beings are dependent on the
word or language of God as given in scripture to set the terms through which
knowledge of God is communicated. Although Calvin does not state this as
directly as one might hope, the implication of his discussion is that scripture and
its interpretation in doctrine together form the linguistic preconditions
necessary for an experience of the divine." *Calvin and the Rhetoric of Piety*, p.
204. This reading makes it impossible, in my judgment, to understand what
Calvin actually says, both about the Bible and about the "seed of religion." One
of the Bible's functions is, indeed, to confront us anew with the knowledge of
God as creator and of ourselves as God's creatures from which we have all

turned away. Otherwise, Calvin's metaphor of scripture as a "pair of spectacles" would be inappropriate. Thus, it is more accurate to say that scripture makes possible an *undistorted* experience of the divine after Adam's fall. But to interpret Calvin as claiming that there is no experience of the divine at all apart from scripture would undermine his own account of the phenomenon of false religion as a perversion of the divinely implanted "seed of religion."

129. *Inst.*, 1.6.1.

130. *Inst.*, 2.6.1 (McNeill, 1:341).

131. Trying to exegete Calvin through the lens of the "natural theology" debate of 1934, with the partial truths found on both sides, is (as Barth said of Brunner's exegesis) "enough to make one weep" (p. 109). John Baillie says it best in his introduction to the English translation when he asks, "Which of them is right? Or, if neither is entirely right, which of them comes nearer the truth, and where exactly does each go astray? And may there even be something amiss with the ground they occupy in common?" *Natural Theology*, p. 12. Dowey writes of the Barth-Brunner controversy: "Neither side used Calvin's own basic distinction, the *duplex cognitio Domini*, properly." *Knowledge of God*, p. 247. And E. David Willis writes of the ambiguity of the word "revelation" to refer to both creation and scripture: "If one means God's self-disclosure in non-Scriptural ways which can be appropriated by sinful men as an alternative source of saving knowledge, the answer must still be *no* in Barth's sense. If one means God's self-disclosure through the marks of justice and ordering power in creation, no matter how utterly incapable sinful men are, lacking Scripture, of appropriating this self-disclosure, then the answer must be *yes* as with Brunner." *Calvin's Catholic Christology: The Function of the So-called Extra Calvinisticum in Calvin's Theology*, Studies in Medieval and Reformation Thought 2 (Leiden: E. J. Brill, 1966), p. 120.

132. *OS* 3:9 (McNeill, 1:9).

Chapter 3

Calvin on the Christian Faith

The Reformation and the Question of True Religion

Calvin's understanding of religion can be fully appreciated only when viewed in the context of his theological work on behalf of the Reformation. However much Calvin, in humanist fashion, hammered out a definition of piety in conversation with the ancients, his theology is primarily indebted to Luther. For Calvin's "conversion" meant that, as a Protestant theologian, he would part company with his fellow humanists in the Roman camp regarding the diagnosis of the church's afflictions. Unlike reformers in the Erasmian mold, Calvin would have to call for a reform of doctrine as did Luther. Therefore, if the form of Calvin's thought is to be viewed as an expression of his humanist leanings, the substance of his thought has to be understood primarily in the light of the Protestant criticism of Catholic theology.

The definition of piety that Calvin forged in the "introductory chapters" of the 1559 *Institutes* is applied throughout the remainder of the work to illustrate how Protestant doctrine exemplifies the principles of true religion.[1] Calvin's primary source for his views on true religion is the Bible, interpreted through the lens of Luther's doctrine of justification by faith alone. Careful study of the scriptures, in Calvin's view, allows for the formulation of precepts that distinguish true from false religion. With these guidelines in hand, Calvin interprets the controversies of his own century as signifying the most recent chapter in the long history of true versus false religion. Thus the question of a correct statement of Christian doctrine is inextricably bound up with the definition of true religion.[2]

The task of this chapter is to investigate Calvin's understanding of Christian faith as true religion. More specifically, I shall attempt to sketch Calvin's concern to interpret Protestantism as the restoration of true religion within Christendom. While it is not my present purpose to give a detailed account of the various controversies that marked the religious crisis of the sixteenth century, it is pertinent to situate Calvin's criticism of the Roman church in the larger context of his understanding of the history of religion. In the course of the exposition, it will become apparent how Calvin addresses the issue of religious diversity, both within Christendom and beyond it.

The argument of this chapter is twofold: first, Calvin interprets faith as the instrument whereby true religion is restored after humanity's fall into false religion; second, true religion has a history of struggle with false religion which finds its contemporary manifestation in the Reformation. After the fall, the gospel reveals God's goodness anew, this time in the form of an assurance of forgiveness to sinners whose ingratitude had blinded them from recognizing the clear self-disclosure of God in the created order. Faith, in the Protestant sense, is the certainty of God's mercy as redeemer that re-establishes the proper foundation for piety. The Protestant interpretation of the gospel, therefore, separates the true from the false in religion according to its doctrine of faith.

Faith and the Restoration of Piety

The Protestants believed that "Pelagianism" was the problem afflicting the church of their day and that the fundamental source of ecclesiastical abuses, therefore, was doctrinal: the gospel of grace had been perverted into a law of works! To be sure, it was not the unabashed Pelagianism against which Augustine had fought but a subtle and, for that reason, more insidious sort since it concealed its true colors by speaking of grace *and* merit.[3] Consequently, the Protestants had no hesitation in identifying "works righteousness" as the hallmark of the false doctrine taught by the papacy and expressed in abusive practices such as the selling of indulgences.[4]

On account of their diagnosis of the situation, the Protestants countered what they took to be a "moralistic" appraisal of the basic problem needing to be addressed in their day. In contrast to the Catholic humanists, the Protestants advocated a reform of doctrine that would correct the faulty teaching of the church. In other words, the Protestants believed that underlying the obvious moral crisis of the church was a religious crisis.[5] Only a proper understanding of the gospel could illuminate the actual nature of this religious crisis and deliver the effective remedy with which to heal it.

Luther's personal religious crisis that eventually led to the break with the papacy arose from his own anxiety regarding personal salvation, an anxiety which was shared, however, by many of his contemporaries. He found the antidote to this anxiety in his exegetical discovery that the apostle Paul teaches the doctrine of "justification by faith alone," whereby the guilty sinner is assured of God's unconditional forgiveness for the sake of Jesus Christ and his righteousness. Hence, the "righteousness of God" revealed in the gospel (Rom 1:17) is not the absolute standard according to which God judges sinners and finds them wanting; rather, it is the righteousness that God gives to sinners as a gift in Christ, so that they need not fear his wrath on Judgment Day.[6] According to Luther's reading of the New Testament, the Christian who trusts in God's promise of mercy need not be suspended over the abyss of doubt regarding personal salvation. Indeed, certainty of salvation is what the Protestants believed the gospel had to offer the anxious medieval pilgrim who wavered between hope of heaven and fear of hell. Yet it was precisely this certainty, Luther believed, that was undermined with doubt by the official teaching of the church.[7]

Whereas Luther claimed that Roman Catholic theology was guilty of a relapse into Pelagianism, the Catholics replied, in turn, that Luther had invented a doctrine hitherto unknown to the ancients. Indeed, the charge of "novelty," with its ancient connotation of heresy, was the Catholic thorn in the Protestant flesh, since the nature of the Lutheran Reformation was not merely moral and pedagogical but, fundamentally, doctrinal. Luther was, after all, engaged in a thorough reshaping of the inherited theological tradition of Augustine.[8] But given the medieval assumption (shared by Catholic and Protestant alike) that innovation in teaching is to be avoided at all costs, the Protestants had to defend their position by appealing to the antiquity of their interpretation of the gospel. And this they did not only by claiming to stand in the authentic line of Augustine but also by testing the merely human opinions of tradition against the very words of God himself.

Since the church's teaching had become corrupt in his eyes, Luther advocated a return to "scripture alone" as the ancient norm by which the inherited doctrinal traditions might be criticized.[9] Unlike the radical reformers to the left of Luther and Zwingli, the Protestants did not reject the church's tradition altogether in the name of a simple return to scripture. But they did adopt a critical posture toward the received tradition of Catholic theology so that they sifted the true from the false in this tradition according to their biblical norm of justification by faith alone. Hence, they pitted scripture against tradition in order to rescue the biblical (and, in their view, Augustinian!) doctrine of grace from what they took to be the Pelagianizing tendencies of late medieval theology.[10]

For their part, Catholics saw in the Protestant criticism of the Roman doctrine an assault upon the divine inspiration of the church's authoritative tradition. According to the Catholic concept of "tradition," the possibility of pitting scripture against tradition did not exist since both are inspired by the same Holy Spirit (John 14:26). In this way the church assured the faithful that its doctrinal and moral teachings are simply the progressive unfolding of the gospel "once for all delivered to the saints" (Jude 3).[11] And, besides, the Catholics countered that the Protestant use of scripture to criticize the tradition was an instance of circular reasoning since it is impossible to acknowledge the authority of scripture apart from an implicit recognition of the authority of the church which canonized the scripture in the first place.[12]

From the Protestant perspective, what was at stake in the criticism of tradition by appeal to the more ancient norm of scripture was the religious issue of certainty regarding salvation. If scripture depends for its authority upon the merely human tradition of the church, then sinners have no direct assurance from God that they are forgiven for the sake of Jesus Christ. Calvin thus argues that the Protestant position on scripture is inextricably linked to the question of assurance for the troubled conscience.

> A very dangerous error generally prevails that scripture has only so much weight as is given to it by the consent of the church. As if the eternal and inviolable truth of God depended upon the decision of human beings! . . . But, if this is so, what will happen to miserable consciences seeking firm assurance of eternal life if all promises of it consist in and depend solely upon the judgment of human beings? [13]

Hence, the Reformers' defense of scripture's authority apart from the church's tradition was tied to their affirmation of the sole sufficiency of faith in God's promise of forgiveness taught by the scriptures.

Whereas nature would have been sufficient to instruct us in the duties of piety, Adam's decision to turn away from the manifold testimonies of God's fatherly favor has altered how we perceive the world around us:

> The natural order was, undoubtedly, that the fabric of the world should be the school in which we might learn piety, and from it pass over to eternal life and perfect happiness. But after our defection, in whatever direction we cast our eyes, above and below, God's curse appears. This curse . . . must fill souls with despair.[14]

The scripture is like a pair of glasses that make it possible for us to see the natural order once again as the "theatre" in which God displays his glory.[15] Just as God had originally disclosed his character through the created works, God now accommodates himself to sinners through the words of scripture.[16] After the fall, therefore, adhering to what God has chosen to reveal of his will in scripture is the only way that "speculation" in theology can be avoided.

Scripture teaches a twofold knowledge of God: it shows us that God is not only our creator but also—and now most importantly—that he is our redeemer.

> It was necessary, in passing from death to life, that they should know God, not only as a Creator, but as a Redeemer also; and both kinds of knowledge they certainly did obtain from the Word. In point of order, however, the knowledge first given was that which made them acquainted with the God by whom the world was made and is governed. To this first knowledge was afterwards added the more intimate knowledge which alone quickens dead souls, and by which God is known, not only as the Creator of the world, and the sole author and disposer of all events, but also as a Redeemer, in the person of the Mediator.[17]

In "re-presenting" the creator of the world, scripture gives us a sure rule by which to distinguish the true God from all the false gods fabricated out of the imaginative power of human speculation. Scripture's main point, however, is the good news wherein the creator assures his guilt-ridden children that he wills to be the redeemer "in order that he may again begin to be a father to us."[18]

Calvin shifts his basic metaphor from "seeing" to "hearing" as he moves from discussing God's accommodation of himself to finite minds through the created order to his accommodation of himself to sinful consciences through the scriptures:

> [H]owever fitting it may be for human beings to direct their eyes in earnest to the contemplation of God's works, since they have been placed in this most splendid theatre to be spectators of them, it is especially fitting that they lend their ears to the Word, in order to profit all the more.[19]

In the words of scripture God *speaks* to his wayward children whose vision has been so clouded by sin that they no longer *see* the signs of divine benevolence clearly set before them. In this altered situation, the proper response is to hearken obediently to his voice and to keep to the rule he has prescribed in the scriptures.

While we should obey everything that God says to us in the

scriptures, faith rests upon the gospel: the promise of God's mercy for the sake of Jesus Christ.

> We make the freely given promise of God the foundation of faith because upon it faith properly rests. Faith is certain that God is true in all things whether he command or forbid, whether he promise or threaten; and it also obediently receives his commandments, observes his prohibitions, heeds his threats. Nevertheless, faith properly begins with a promise, rests in it, and ends in it. For in God faith seeks life: a life that is not found in commandments or declarations of penalties, but in the promise of mercy, and only in a freely given promise. . . . Therefore, when we say that faith must rest upon a freely given promise, we do not deny that believers embrace and grasp the Word of God in every respect: but we point out the promise of mercy as the proper goal of faith.[20]

Faith leans upon the gospel since this is God's freely given promise to sinners that he is, indeed, a forgiving father. And the Protestant sermon is where this promise is heard and received in faith, when the Holy Spirit unites us with Christ so that we embrace his benefits.[21]

Calvin expressed the Protestant position well, therefore, when he defined "faith" as the wholehearted confidence in the divine goodness made known in the gospel:

> Now we shall possess a right definition of faith if we call it a firm and certain knowledge of God's benevolence toward us, founded upon the truth of the freely given promise in Christ, both revealed to our minds and sealed upon our hearts through the Holy Spirit.[22]

Faith and the gospel belong inseparably together and, for that reason, the apostle Paul speaks of the gospel as "the word of faith" (Rom 10:8). "Thence arises," Calvin explains, "that frequent correlation (*correlatio*) between faith and the gospel in the apostle," since "there exists no other sufficiently firm testimony of God's benevolence to us (*nullum aliud satis firmum divinae erga nos benevolentiae testimonium*), the knowledge of which faith seeks."[23]

According to Calvin, the religious crisis of the sixteenth century has two main aspects. First, there is the pursuit of "works righteousness," that is, the attempt to appease God's wrath resulting from our distorted knowledge of God's character. Second, there is the corresponding delusion about ourselves, namely, that we have the power within us to summon the righteousness with which to satisfy God's demand. These two aspects reflect the inseparability of knowledge of God and self in Calvin's theology: on account of sin, we lack both a certain knowledge of God's mercy and a sober estimate of our own abilities.

The necessity of faith in God's promise of mercy points to the basic epistemological problem after the fall: the sinner can only perceive God as a merciless judge, never as a benevolent and forgiving father. This is what Calvin means by "God's curse" which drives us to despair. Our perception of the world is filtered through the lens of the bad conscience we carry within us; hence, wherever we look we see evidence of God's anger toward us.[24] This perception is not altogether wrong. Conscience is a "sense of divine judgment" that "does not allow us to suppress within ourselves what we know, but pursues us until it leads to conviction."[25] Thus our guilt on account of sin leads us to fear God's just punishment. And this fear drives us to labor endlessly in an attempt to satisfy the divine justice, an attempt which, in the end, is futile since we can never be certain that we have done all we can.[26]

The attempt to justify ourselves not only betrays a lack of knowledge regarding God's grace; it shows how wanting in self-knowledge we are as well. While our conscience continues to appeal to right and wrong after the fall, it nonetheless misleads us with a false sense of our own goodness. Whereas people judge moral worth by external behavior, they forget that God takes into account the inward affections. Nothing escapes the gaze of God "who cares not for outward appearance as much as for purity of heart." In God's eyes, a desire to kill counts just as much as the act of murder itself; lust is a form of fornication and avarice is tantamount to theft.[27] Consequently, when we exhort ourselves to pursue virtue and declare war on the vices, this is nothing but self-deception. Adequate self-knowledge involves acknowledging the difference between our ideal, created condition and our actual, fallen condition.[28]

Only faith in the gospel makes it possible for sinners to see God once again as a gracious father.[29] Apart from faith's assurance of the divine goodness, the sinner can never give God the proper service which is the essence of true religion. We have faith, writes Calvin, "when the will of God is made known to us and we embrace it so that we are able to worship him as a father." "Hence the knowledge of God is required as necessary to faith," he argues, "for where there is no certain knowledge of God, there is no religion, piety is utterly extinct and faith is abolished."[30] "Obedience," he explains, "depends on faith, just as faith depends on the word" (*Obedientia . . . pendet ex fide, sicuti fides ex verbo*).[31]

> Therefore, in order that religion may have firm roots in our hearts, let this be the foundation of our faith: that God will always be

conciliatory toward us. For unless we are truly persuaded of his
mercy, no piety will ever flourish in us, however much we might feign
it . . . Thus, reverence for God and worship of him depend upon a
sense of his goodness and grace, for we shall not be able to worship
God from the heart . . . and there will be no genuine religion in us until
that persuasion is thoroughly and deeply rooted in our hearts: that he is
always ready to forgive as often as we take refuge in him.[32]

Calvin thus speaks of faith in God's grace as "the true logic of piety"
(*dialectica pietatis*): only when we are persuaded that God "is by nature
inclined to mercy" can we worship him aright, whereas "those who
distrust God must necessarily be always murmuring and rebelling
against him." Faith is "the root of true piety" because it "teaches us to
hope for and to desire all good things from God and it disposes us to
obey him."[33]

Calvin sometimes uses the terms "faith" and "piety"
synonymously, though at other times he speaks of faith as instrumental
to piety.[34] Still, there is no doubt as to his meaning: through faith in the
promise of God's mercy, we come anew to adequate knowledge of God
and of ourselves. We see God once again as "father" or "fountain of all
good things" and we know ourselves once again as the grateful
recipients of God's bounty, though now humbled by the recognition that
we are completely dependent upon God not only for the gift of life but
also for the gift of restoring us to authentic life. "Most assuredly,"
Calvin says, "we are redeemed by the Lord for this end: that we may
consecrate ourselves and all our members to him."[35] Put simply, the
purpose for which we were created is to reflect God's glory in praise.[36]

The gospel, according to Calvin, teaches a "double grace" (*duplex
gratia*): first, God forgives the sinner (justification) and, second, God
redirects the redeemed sinner toward a new life of *pietas*
(sanctification).

Christ was given to us by God's kindness, to be grasped and
possessed by us in faith, by participating in whom we may receive
above all a double grace: namely, that being reconciled to God by his
innocence, we might have in heaven instead of a judge a gracious
father; then, that being sanctified by his spirit we might practice
innocence and purity of life.[37]

Good works, then, do nothing to earn merit before God. "That person
will be justified by faith," writes Calvin, "who, cut off from the
righteousness of works, takes hold of the righteousness of Christ
through faith and, clothed in it, appears in the sight of God not as a
sinner but as righteous."[38] Additionally, faith in the grace of God leads

to genuine works of love on behalf of the neighbor, since faith is inherently active and, therefore, issues necessarily in love. Faith, in other words, "works through love" (Gal 5:6).[39] While the gospel frees us *from* the necessity of works as far as our relation to God is concerned, it also frees us *for* genuine works of love as far as the neighbor is concerned.[40] But instead of pursuing works out of an anxious concern with our own salvation, we gladly yield to the law's demands out of a grateful response to God's mercy shown us in Christ.

The law of God can be summarized by saying that "nothing is required to live a good life except piety and justice."[41] Calvin can just as well say that the law requires faith and love: faith designates our religious relation to God whereas love refers to our moral relation with the neighbor.[42] The two tables of the decalogue should be exegeted in light of this distinction between religion and morality:

> For God has divided his law into two parts, in which is contained the whole of righteousness, as to assign the first part to the duties of religion which particularly concern the worship of his majesty, and the second to the duties of love that refer to human beings.[43]

Calvin says that the worship of God is "the first foundation of righteousness." Morality without religion, therefore, is vain: "Not only is religion the chief part but the very soul" of righteousness.[44] Consequently, the first table "instructs us in piety and the proper duties of religion" before proceeding to spell out "how on account of the fear of his name we ought to conduct ourselves in human society."[45] This is what Christ, the law's "best interpreter," meant when he summarized the law as love of God and love of neighbor: "First, indeed, our soul should be completely filled with the love of God. From this the love of neighbor will flow spontaneously." Love is derived from piety which consists in "a good conscience and sincere faith" (1 Tim 1:5).[46] "Even if the life of a human being were perfect in all the virtues," Calvin explains, "unless it is referred to the worship of God, it can certainly be praised by the world, but in heaven it will be pure abomination, since the chief part of righteousness is to render to God his right and honor..."[47]

The Protestants believed that a moral reform of the church apart from a reform of doctrine would miss its mark since, from their viewpoint, the fundamental problem of the sixteenth century was religious: the church had encouraged sinners to confide in their own strength instead of relying upon the freely given promise of God to forgive us for Christ's sake. But if they departed from other reform-minded critics in their analysis of the underlying problem needing to be addressed, the Protestants were not, for that reason, indifferent to the moral consequences of the religious crisis. And this concern for the moral life becomes very evident in the prominent place that Calvin assigns to sanctification in his own theology.

> Now if it is true (which it most certainly is) that the whole of the gospel is contained under these two headings, repentance and forgiveness of sins, do we not see that the Lord freely justifies his own in order that he may at the same time restore them to true righteousness by the sanctification of his Spirit?[48]

Sanctification, like justification, is completely the work of God's spirit in the lives of the faithful who have learned to rely on grace.[49] But the Protestant reliance upon the gospel's assurance of salvation gives rise to a new zeal to conform to God's law that includes the inward affections as well as external deeds.[50] Thus the moral crisis in the church can be understood, the Protestants contended, only when placed in its larger religious context and the relation between justification and sanctification is correctly grasped. Works of love are not in any sense "meritorious" before God; they are simply expressions of the living faith by which we are united with Christ.

Calvin shows himself to be a good student of Luther when he affirms not only that the doctrine of "justification by faith alone" is the "main hinge on which religion turns" (*praecipuus sustinendae religionis cardo*) but also that "the entire doctrine of piety (*tota pietatis doctrina*) . . . rests on this foundation."[51] Luther's doctrine is thus the indispensable presupposition of Calvin's defense of true religion amid the controversies of the day. Though the Lutheran interpretation of the gospel arose in response to the anxious question regarding the soul's salvation, its answer to this question was intended to do away with the gnawing doubt about God's forgiveness that gave rise to this anxiety in the first place. In Calvin's theology, therefore, the central religious concern is not how to find a gracious God; it is, rather, how we ought to serve the gracious God revealed to us in the gospel.[52]

It is by participating in Christ's righteousness, which occurs when the gospel is heard and received in faith through the activity of the Holy Spirit, that we are enabled to stand justified before God's judgment. This gift of unmerited forgiveness allows sinners to see God once again as a gracious "father" who not only sustains his children with every good gift but also receives them back into his household after they have turned aside from the "fountain of all good things." The renewed perception of God as good—or, in the face of sin and guilt, as merciful—binds the once wayward human heart in loyal service to its creator and redeemer. The seed of religion finally comes to fruition and God's glory is reflected in a life of piety.[53]

The History of True and False Religion

Once the doctrine of faith is firmly grasped, careful exegesis of the scriptures can uncover the principles that illuminate the history of religion.[54] Scripture is the map that leads us through the ambiguous realm of mere opinion in religion to an "unambiguous faith" (*indubia fides*).

> In order that true religion may shine upon us, we ought to hold that it must take its beginning from heavenly doctrine and that no one can obtain even the least taste of right and sound doctrine unless he has been a student of scripture.[55]

True religion, founded upon the freely given promise of mercy, is always engaged in combat with false religion, which has its source in human speculation. But with scripture as our guide, we have the criteria with which to analyze the religious dynamics in any specific situation so that we can identify the true from the false in religion.

Calvin analyzes the nature of false religion and comes up with a sketch of its characteristic features. False religion is marked chiefly by three traits: idolatry, superstition, and hypocrisy. Calvin's portrait of false religion is the antithesis of his depiction of *pietas*.

Since human beings have thwarted "the seed of the knowledge of God that has been sown in their minds by the wonderful workmanship of nature," it cannot "come to a good and fair fruit."[56] As a result of a lack of trust in God, the heart becomes "a perpetual factory of idols" since the religious nature of the human being requires ultimate confidence in *something*.[57] But worship directed elsewhere than to the goodness of God is misguided.

> If idolatry is to be treated in general, this alone will be more than sufficient as a perpetual reason to condemn it: the entire worship of piety is owed to God alone and, for that reason, is profaned as soon as any part of it is conferred on creatures, whether angels, people, or stars.[58]

An idolatrous religion represents the height of confusion and disorder: "A religion in which God is not preeminent has no truth or soundness."[59]

Since the root of false religion is the suppression or distortion of the knowledge of God that is naturally implanted, superstition carries the connotation of human fabrications in the religious domain.[60] For Calvin, superstition suggests a refusal to keep within the proper bounds and a desire to exceed the established limits. Whereas true religion is the appropriate response to what God reveals of his will, "superstition fabricates for itself any god it pleases, and then invents various kinds of worship for it."[61] Since the knowledge of God is the beginning of true religion, "it follows, that where doctrine is either corrupted or disdained, there is no piety, at least not that which is approved by God."

> People will indeed boast of the name with their lips; but before God there is no religion, except that which is measured according to the rule of the Word.[62]

Superstition is virtually synonymous with falsehood in religion: "As our natures are prone to falsehood and vanity, the very first superstition will easily carry us away, unless we are held in check by this bond . . ."[63]

Just as true religion is founded upon the knowledge of God as God gives himself to be known by creatures, false religion is based upon human fabrication. Human *opinio* in religion is thus opposed to God's word. Calvin describes pagan religion as a "labyrinth" because it represents "a confused opinion concerning the nature of God."[64] When enduring human opinions assume the status of a venerable tradition, the respect we bring to our ancestors becomes another pretense for the perpetuation of falsehood in religion. Human opinion is "the mother of error" and, therefore, "the custom of the city or the consensus of antiquity is much too weak and fragile a bond of piety to follow in worshipping God."[65] Consequently, Calvin opposes any argument for religion based merely on the tradition of one's ancestors, since on that basis Jews, Turks, and Papists can all make their appeal.[66]

The unmistakable sign of superstition is the unchecked diversity in the religious beliefs and practices of humankind, a sure mark that true religion has been lost.[67] This diversity is testimony of the fact that, having forsaken the word of God, human beings fabricate gods and religions out of their own minds.

> In one respect we are certainly different, because each of us privately forges for ourselves some particular error. Nevertheless we are in another respect alike because each of us without exception abandons the one true God for preposterous trifles.[68]

On the one hand, there is a remarkable diversity (we would say "plurality") of religious traditions. On the other hand, the diversity is superficial since it takes its rise from idolatrous superstition.

Just as true knowledge of God necessitates true self-knowledge, false religion based on a distorted knowledge of God involves self-deception. Calvin's favorite word for this aspect of the religious crisis is "hypocrisy." Those persons engaged in idolatrous superstitions may evince some zeal for religion but they are, nonetheless, thoroughly deceived. Human beings "do not so carefully and anxiously seek various superstitions unless they are unwilling to come before God and to devote themselves to him without some deceit and hypocrisy." The roots of such hypocrisy are deep in the hearts of persons who "always deceive themselves and even wish to deceive God." Hypocrites refuse to acknowledge to themselves the truth of their situation: "It is certainly not because they have any doubt about what is right," Calvin explains, "but because they willfully deceive themselves."[69]

One of the chief ways by which hypocrites, with their zeal for religion, deceive themselves is through an excessive emphasis upon outward ceremonies. By this means they can neglect the foulness in their hearts, thus never penetrating to the root of their religious problem. In true piety, however, God is worshipped with the heart and the mind, which is to say "inwardly." At best, ceremonies are useful as an exercise of piety on account of human infirmity.[70] In their proper place, ceremonies ought to give outward expression to our inward invocation of God. "Religion has truly its proper seat in the heart," writes Calvin. "But from this root, confession afterwards arises as its fruit, so to speak."[71] Yet hypocrites uproot the ceremonies of religion from their grounding in a pious heart. They "tear apart things that are . . . inseparable: it is an impious divorce, when anyone only thrusts ceremonies upon God while being devoid of piety."[72] Hence, empty ceremonies are a sure mark of hypocrisy.

These three terms taken together—idolatry, superstition, and hypocrisy—fill out the description of false religion. Idolatry transfers to a creature, whether actual or make-believe, the worship that properly belongs only to God. Superstition points to the fabricated character of any religion that is based on mere human opinion and not upon God's self-revelation. Hypocrisy describes the self-deception of those who content themselves with empty ceremonies in place of genuine worship.

When Calvin exegeted the scriptures for the criteria with which to evaluate religion, he found two propositions that became axiomatic for him: first, after Adam's fall the restoration of true religion has always been based upon faith in the gospel, which is the assurance of God's promise of forgiveness; second, true religion is not confined within the boundaries of the visible church. If the Protestant affirms with the Catholic that *extra ecclesiam nulla salus* ("outside of the church there is no salvation"), this affirmation must be qualified by adding that there is no true church where the gospel is not correctly preached.[73]

Scripture narrates the history of Israel and the history of the apostolic era. Calvin reads this narrative as one continuous history of the true church engaged in combat with false religion. He understands the "faith" of the Old Testament patriarchs and prophets as *Christian* faith: the Jews believed in Christ and participated in the same covenant as do those who stand on this side, historically speaking, of the incarnation. For this reason, Calvin believes there is only one covenant that is the common subject-matter of both Old and New Testaments. The difference between them is not a difference in substance but a difference, rather, in their mode of administration.[74]

> The covenant of all the fathers does not in any way differ from ours with respect to substance and reality so that it is, in short, one and the same covenant. Yet the administration of them varies.[75]

The dispensation of the Old Testament, by which Calvin means the Jewish religion prior to the appearance of Jesus, was, in essence, the proclamation of the gospel of justification by faith alone.[76] The chief difference between the two dispensations is simply the clarity with which the gospel is proclaimed in the period of the New Testament compared to that of the Old Testament.[77]

When Calvin uses the term "law" to refer to the Jewish religion and "gospel" to refer to the Christian religion, he is not setting up an antithesis between them: "The gospel has not thus replaced the entire law so as to bring forward a different way of salvation." Rather, their relation is to be understood as variations in the degree of clarity: "Where the entire law is concerned, the gospel differs from it only in respect to its clear manifestation."[78] Consequently, Calvin rejects the association of law (Jewish religion) with justification by works. "The error of those persons is refuted," he argues, "who never compare the law to the gospel except by contrasting the merits of works with the free imputation of righteousness."[79]

There is a sense, of course, in which "law" can be used to signify a principle in opposition to the gospel with its offer of free grace; but this is not equivalent to the distinction between the Testaments or the different historical periods they represent. "The word 'gospel,' broadly construed," he asserts, "includes those testimonies of his mercy and fatherly favor that God gave to the fathers of old."[80] Abraham is the chief exemplar of the faith by which we ourselves are justified. In a comment upon Galatians 3:23, where Paul speaks of the time "before faith came," Calvin gives a clear exposition of his position:

> "Faith" signifies the full revelation of those things then hidden under
> the obscurity of the law's shadows. For Paul does not take faith away
> from the fathers who lived under the law. . . . The doctrine of faith,
> indeed, finds confirmation in Moses and all the prophets. But because
> the clarity of faith did not openly shine forth back then, the time of the
> New Testament is called the time of faith, not absolutely but in a
> comparative sense. . . . Faith was not yet revealed, not because the
> fathers lacked all light, but because they had less light than we
> have.[81]

Consequently, Calvin acknowledges a principle of progression in the
history of revelation.[82] What was present and efficacious during the old
dispensation, even if somewhat concealed under figures and shadows,
is now openly displayed to those of us who live under the new
dispensation.[83]

The notion of a progressively clearer revelation is, of course, a
reflection of Calvin's idea that God always accommodates revelation to
the human capacity to receive it. In this sense, the gospel is proclaimed
in diverse forms appropriate to the historical circumstances of those
who hear it.[84] Warding off objections to this notion, Calvin replies that
"God should not be deemed changeable simply because he
accommodated different forms to different ages, as he knew would be
advantageous for each."[85] Just as a parent speaks differently to a child
than to the same offspring as an adult, so, too, God spoke to the Jews as
to "children whose weakness could not yet bear the full knowledge of
heavenly things."[86] Consequently, Moses spoke in the manner of
common people.[87] As Calvin moves through the history of Israel, he
discerns more and more light shining forth until Jesus removes all the
shadows.

> If we come down to the later prophets, we can walk freely in our own
> field, so to speak. For if we proved our point without difficulty from
> David, Job, and Samuel, in the prophets it is much easier. The Lord
> held to this arrangement and order in administering the covenant of
> his mercy: that over the course of time, as the day of revelation drew
> nearer to a full exhibition, its brightness should increase with each
> step forward.[88]

Calvin thus reads the Old and New Testaments as one continuous
narrative of the history of true religion.

Still, if Calvin appreciates the differences in historical
circumstances that necessitate various forms for God's revelation, he is
equally aware that, within that history, individuals differ in their
capacities to appropriate the true doctrine of religion. Calvin speaks of

"implicit faith"—not to be confused with the Roman doctrine he rejects!—as a spark or "seed" of faith that is accompanied by only a small degree of understanding of doctrine.[89] Since understanding one's faith is crucial, a blind consent to the church's authority, apart from an understanding of its teachings, is ruled out. Nonetheless, there are varying degrees of *understanding* faith.

> I do not deny that in this sense there can sometimes be a kind of implicit faith (*fides implicita*) which is not accompanied by a clear and distinct knowledge of sound doctrine, provided that we hold this, that faith always springs from the word of God and takes its origin from true principles and, therefore, is always connected with some light of knowledge.[90]

Such understanding, however limited it may be, is always based on a certain knowledge of the gospel, even if dimly apprehended. And since no Christian ever has a fully adequate grasp of faith, the differences here are relative. But when seen on a continuum, the smallest seeds of faith are present in many who have only the faintest glimpse of the doctrine of true religion.[91]

In Calvin's view, there are persons whom God has illuminated apart from the ordinary means of preaching. While Calvin affirms that faith in the gospel is essential to salvation, he insists that there are those whom God calls in other ways than through the external hearing of the word:

> He has certainly used some other way in calling many, on whom he has conferred a true knowledge of himself through inward means, that is, by the illumination of the Spirit without the help of preaching.[92]

The contrary idea that God is restricted to "the ordinary arrangement and dispensation" of preaching is "not sufficiently safe" since "it would take from the Lord the ability to make himself known in any way whatsoever."[93]

Scripture narrates numerous instances of persons who stand on the brink of a true knowledge of God. Many of these are foreigners, who have not yet had the benefit of a thorough training in the doctrine of true religion. Although the distinction between true and false religion is absolute, the knowledge of true religion is relative. Yet just exactly where the line is crossed between a remnant of the knowledge of God that still shines in corrupt nature and an implicit faith that is the first fruit of regeneration is unclear to human observation. It is clear, however, to God who "alone, indeed, knows faith."[94]

The Egyptian steward who attributed the good fortune of Joseph's brothers to the graciousness of *their* God knew something of true religion. And considering the disdain with which the Egyptians viewed the gods of other nations, Calvin finds it all the more remarkable that the steward could distinguish the God of Jacob from the throng of Egyptian idols. He conjectures that "this man had been imbued with some taste of piety," probably because he had received some instruction in true religion from Joseph. "Unless he had learned something better," Calvin reasons, "he never would have deemed gods other than those of his own country worthy of such an honor." In conclusion, then, Calvin states:

> I, therefore, do not doubt that Joseph, although he was not permitted openly to correct anything in the received superstitions, tried, at least in his own house, to establish the true worship of the one God.[95]

A less ambiguous example is the case of the Ethiopian eunuch who traveled to Jerusalem in order to worship the true God. The eunuch, though having a partial knowledge that explains why he undertook his pilgrimage, was, nonetheless, aware of the extent of his ignorance and asked Philip to instruct him more fully. His request to be baptized signifies that the seed of faith planted long ago had now come to maturity: "Faith must somehow have been ripe in his heart, since he gladly moved into an external profession of it."[96]

Those Gentile "God-fearers" depicted in the book of Acts present essentially the same picture. Having tasted something of the law's teaching (i.e., Judaism), "they worshiped the God of Israel . . . and being desirous to learn, did not reject those things [taught by Paul] that they knew were taken out of Moses and the prophets." Once again, we find an example of persons with some "taste" of true religion on their way to a complete embrace of that which they do not yet fully understand. Scripture thus calls them "religious."

> Since such teachableness was an entrance to faith, indeed, it was actually a certain beginning of faith, the Spirit bestowed an *honorable title* on those who, though sprinkled ever so slightly with merely the first rudiments, drew nearer unto God; for they are called *religious* (*religiosi*).[97]

Though there are distinctions with respect to the degrees of knowledge, the distinction between true and false religion remains absolute. That is why scripture refers to the "God-fearers" as "religious":

> But let us remember that they are distinguished from others by this mark in order that all the religion of the world may be reduced to

nothing: they are called the worshipers of God who gave their name
to the God of Israel. To them alone is religion attributed. As for the
rest, therefore, there is nothing else except the disgrace of atheism,
however they might torture themselves anxiously in superstitions.
And justly so: for whatever excellence the idolators exhibit, if their
inward affection is scrutinized, nothing shall be found there except a
horrible contempt for God; and it shall turn out to be pure pretence
that they flatter themselves with idols.[98]

Calvin calls idolaters "atheists," not because there is a lack of belief in
deity but because, apart from piety, they do not adhere to "the religion
of the one God."[99]

Just as the true worshippers of God are sometimes found outside of
the visible church, it is no less true that idolaters can be found within it.
For that reason, the principles of true religion are to be used for
criticizing the doctrines and practices of the visible church. This means
that the cause of true religion is never identical with a particular
institution since all concrete embodiments of religion are subject to
perversion. For Calvin, the Reformation of the sixteenth century is the
latest incident in the monumental struggle against false religion that can
be traced all the way back to the Old Testament.

In Calvin's judgment, the religion taught by the papacy is
characterized by idolatry, superstition, and hypocrisy. "Just as today,"
he explains, "the papists boast with great pride that they worship God,
when they are trifling with their foolish pageants."[100] They are overly
concerned with the external observances while they neglect the
weightier matters of the inward affections. Unlike their heathen
neighbors, the patriarchs established external modes of worship within
the bounds of what God had instructed. By contrast, the papists do not
stay within the divinely prescribed bounds: "Whence, indeed, it appears
what kind of religion is that of the papacy: where, instead of the word
of God, the fictions of human beings are bragged about."[101] Calvin
speaks of the papacy in the same terms with which he condemns
paganism. Indeed, he often moves rather swiftly from a discussion of
one to a comment upon the other.[102] Like the heathen, the papists are
not satisfied with the religion God prescribes.

Calvin also sees an important parallel between the contemporary
condition of Christendom and ancient Israel's temptations to idolatry.

Not content with God alone, [the papists] are carried away with their
own devices and amass for themselves, as I have said, a great throng
of gods. Therefore, since this sort of thing is done under the papacy in
our day, we do not marvel that the same thing was done in former
times and that the Jews fell under reproach.[103]

And given that the papacy teaches sinners to deny God's grace by relying on their own merits, it is clear that it has fabricated a religion of its own making. Though the papists have a penitential system by which to obtain God's forgiveness, Calvin insists that this does not distinguish the papists in any respect from "Turks, Jews, and other nations."[104] Indeed, the denial of the sufficiency of faith alone in God's grace eradicates the crucial distinction between the gospel and false religion since the true God may be distinguished from all idols by the fact that he "kindly forgives the sins of his people and bears their infirmities." And in spite of the fact that the pagans appealed to their gods for mercy, "they could have no solid conviction . . . that the gods would be gracious to sinners." Calvin explains: "We know that they prayed with doubt, because they had no certain promise."[105] But this certain promise of God's mercy is precisely that upon which faith leans and which piety requires.

Calvin concludes, therefore, that the papacy leaves people in the same uncertainty with respect to God's grace as do the pagan religions:

> Hence, it appears what sort of religion is that of the papacy. For they always hesitate, being perplexed and doubtful, and they never dare to think that God will be gracious to them. Although they understand something (I know not what!) of his grace, they nevertheless consider it vain presumption and rashness if any one is persuaded of God's mercy. They thus keep consciences in suspense, indeed, they leave them doubtful and wavering. Since there is no certitude of God's grace, it follows that their entire worship is fictitious.[106]

As a result, their religion is without solid foundation. It is "a dreadful abyss," since "no one can stand firm there."[107] This confusion comes from refusing to adhere to scripture, which is the only rule of true religion:

> For unless we give this authority to the Word as to believe that, as soon as God has spoken through his ministers, our sins are forgiven and we are restored to life, all confidence of salvation withers.[108]

Calvin thus criticizes the papal reliance on the human authority of tradition. "God is robbed of his right and honor," he argues, "when mortals usurp for themselves the authority to teach, for the prerogative to teach his people properly belongs to God alone."[109]

There is no substantial difference, then, between the criticisms Calvin gives of the papacy and those he gives of false religion.[110] Calvin believed that the certainty of God's grace was the hallmark distinguishing Christian from non-Christian religion.

> In short, this is the only way in which we differ from the pagans and
> infidels: we have a religion which is assured and founded in the
> infallible truth of God instead of all the others which allow
> themselves to be led about by doubtful opinions or to become
> hardened with perverse obstinacy without any certitude.[111]

And Calvin explains that this is the difference between "the Christian
philosophy" and pagan philosophy:

> Chiefly in this respect does the gospel differ from profane philosophy,
> because it makes the salvation of the human person to consist in the
> free forgiveness of sins.[112]

Once the doctrine of faith is clearly grasped, the scripture as a whole
can be studied with profit in order to discover the principles that
illuminate the dynamics in the history of religion. When Calvin
proceeds to interpret his own historical situation in the light of these
principles, it is clear to him that the corruption of the Roman church is
of a piece with false religion generally.

Summary

The results of this study of Calvin's theology can be summarized
by reiterating the four major points advanced and substantiated by
exegesis in these two chapters. First, Calvin believes that piety ought to
have been the fitting response to the abundant testimonies of God's
goodness found in the natural order. Second, the evident human need to
worship bears witness to an innate sense of obligation toward God that
cannot be eradicated from the human heart. Third, faith in the gospel is
the instrument by which true religion is restored after humanity's fall
into false religion. Finally, the Protestant Reformation represents the
cause of true religion after the perversion of Christendom itself by false
religion.

When Calvin was converted to the Protestant camp, he brought to
his new vocation as a reformer and theologian the legacy of
Renaissance humanism in which he had been trained. As a Protestant,
Calvin was decisively shaped by Luther's reformulation of the Catholic
doctrinal tradition. As a humanist, he shared the anti-scholastic polemic
of reform-minded Catholic humanists such as Erasmus. Calvin's
distinctive contribution to the Reformation cannot be properly
appreciated apart from recognizing how he wove these two strands of

tradition together in his *summa pietatis*. Thereby, he adapted the humanist ideal of a practical and experiential theology for the purpose of teaching the Protestant doctrine. What philosophy had been to medieval scholasticism ("the handmaid of theology"), the liberal arts became for Protestant theology.[113]

In Calvin's theology, the concepts "religion" (or "piety") and "faith" are not antithetical. Moreover, human religion is not pitted against divine revelation in the manner characteristic of neo-orthodoxy. Calvin's polemic is against "speculation" since this does not receive God as he gives himself to be known, first, in the natural order and, then, in the scriptures. A knowledge of God framed by piety is based on the assurance of God's goodness, and precisely this is what the gospel restores to Adam's children. Apart from this assurance, there can be no genuine religion.

NOTES

1. B. B. Warfield says: "The definition of religion to which Calvin thus attains is exceedingly interesting, and that not merely because of its vital relation to the fundamental thought of these introductory chapters, but also because of its careful adjustment to the state of the controversy in which he was engaged as a leader of the Reformation." "Calvin's Doctrine of the Knowledge of God," in *Calvin and Augustine*, ed. Samuel G. Craig (Philadelphia: Presbyterian and Reformed Publishing House, 1956), p. 38.

2. Reinhold Seeberg says of Calvin's theology in this regard: "[S]ince Christianity is 'the true religion,' all the characteristics that make up the essence of religion are found in it." *Lehrbuch der Dogmengeschichte*, 4th ed. (Basel: Benno Schwabe and Company, 1954), 4:564.

3. Luther stood in the conservative Augustinian lineage that goes back to Gregory of Rimini (d. 1358), who accused Ockham of Pelagianism. The immediate target of Luther's polemic was the nominalist doctrine that "God does not deny grace to those who do what is in them" (*facientibus quod in se est Deus non denegat gratiam*), taught by Robert Holcot and Gabriel Biel. McGrath writes that Luther and Gregory of Rimini adopted "radically Augustinian positions" whereas the positions of Ockham, Holcot, and Biel "approach, although do not strictly constitute, Pelagianism." *Iustitia Dei: A History of the Christian Doctrine of Justification*, vol. 1, *From the Beginnings to 1500* (Cambridge: Cambridge University Press, 1986), pp. 168-69. For statements by Holcot and Biel, see Oberman, *Forerunners*, pp. 142-50, 165-74. In the same volume one may observe how the conservative Augustinian position was defended by Thomas Bradwardine and Johann von Staupitz (Luther's mentor), pp. 151-64, 175-203. Lest there be any ambiguity about what he thought of the nominalist doctrine, Bradwardine entitled his piece "The Cause of God Against the Pelagians." Oberman's essay is an excellent introduction to these late medieval controversies that set the stage for the Reformation (pp.

123-41). Oberman's classic study of nominalism is, of course, *The Harvest of Medieval Theology: Gabriel Biel and Late Medieval Nominalism* (Cambridge: Harvard University Press, 1963). Luther's many-sided relation to nominalism is explored by Gerrish, *Grace and Reason: A Study in Luther's Theology* (Oxford: Oxford University Press, 1962), pp. 43-56.

4. Roland H. Bainton, *Here I Stand: A Life of Martin Luther* (New York and Nashville: Abingdon Press, 1950), pp. 68-83. Also, *Inst.*, 3.5.1-5.

5. "The Protestant Reformation was not only concerned with the means of correcting abuses in the Church; to understand it we must realize that it was also rooted in a new emphasis on certain attitudes to religion based on particular and personal religious experience." Basil Hall, *John Calvin: Humanist and Theologian* (London: George Philip and Son, 1956), p. 19. Oberman writes: "Luther criticizes Wyclif and Hus for having directed their attacks at the moral sins of the pope. He calls for a true reformation, and this has to be not primarily a *reform* of morals but rather a *reformation* of doctrine." "The Tridentine Decree on Justification in the Light of Late Medieval Theology," in *Distinctive Protestant and Catholic Themes Reconsidered*, ed. Robert W. Funk, vol. 3 of *Journal for Theology and the Church* (New York: Harper and Row, 1967), pp. 28-29.

6. "'The righteousness of God' (*iustitia Dei*) must not be understood as that righteousness by which he is righteous (*iustus*) in himself, but as that righteousness by which we are made righteous (*iustificamur*) by Him, and this happens through faith in the gospel." *Comm.* Rom 1:17 (*WA* 56:172), cited according to the translation of Wilhelm Pauck, *Luther: Lectures on Romans*, The Library of Christian Classics (Philadelphia: Westminster Press, 1961), p. 18.

7. For their part, Catholics saw in Protestant certainty of salvation evidence of presumption, denounced by the Council of Trent as "the vain confidence of heretics." "Decree on Justification" (1547), in Henry Denzinger, *The Sources of Catholic Dogma*, trans. Roy J. Deferrari, from the 13th ed. of *Enchiridion Symbolorum* (St. Louis: B. Herder Book Co., 1957), p. 252 (§802). Calvin argues that the Roman alternative to Protestant assurance of forgiveness is despair: "If they say that we must do what is in us (*faciendum quod in nobis est*), we are always brought back to the same point. For when will anyone assure himself that he has applied all of his powers to lament his sins? Therefore, when consciences have for a long time wrestled with themselves, and exercised themselves in long struggles, they still do not find a haven in which to rest." *Inst.*, 3.4.2 (McNeill, 1:625).

8. For that reason, many conscientious persons who were deeply troubled by the condition of the medieval church could not side with the Protestants. As Ozment says: "[I]t was clear to Erasmus that Luther did not intend a gradual reform within the old faith, but a fundamental recasting of traditional doctrines and practices." *The Age of Reform*, p. 292. On the ambivalence of Erasmus toward Luther and their eventual open conflict, see Johan Huizinga, *Erasmus and the Age of Reformation, with a selection from the letters of Erasmus*, trans. F. Hopman, previously published in English as *Erasmus of Rotterdam* (Princeton: Princeton University Press, 1984), pp. 139-50, 161-69. Paul T.

Fuhrmann says: "The Reformation, to put it clearly, had not been a 'Reformation' but a Religious Revolution." "What we call 'the Reformation' would have been a Reformation only if the changes had been made by the old established authorities, that is, the Pope and Church Council. But since the changes were brought about by a new authority . . . we should call it properly a 'Religious Revolution.'" *God-Centered Religion: An Essay Inspired by Some French and Swiss Protestant Writers* (Grand Rapids: Zondervan, 1942), pp. 46 and 230, n. 11. For discussions of the meaning of the concepts "reform" and "reformation," see the following: W. Maurer, "Reformation," in *Die Religion in Geschichte und Gegenwart: Handwörterbuch für Theologie und Religionswissenschaft*, 3d ed., ed. Kurt Galling et al. (Tübingen: J.C.B. Mohr [Paul Siebeck], 1961), 5:858-73; D. S. Schaff, "The Reformation," in *The New Schaff-Herzog Encyclopedia of Religious Knowledge*, ed. Samuel Macauley Jackson et al. (New York and London: Funk and Wagnalls Co., 1911), 9:417-25; Konrad Repgen, "Reform," Mark U. Edwards, Jr., "Reformation," and John Tonkin, "Reformation Studies," in *The Oxford Encyclopedia of the Reformation*, ed. Hans J. Hillerbrand (New York and Oxford: Oxford University Press, 1996), 3:392-95, 396-98, 398-410.

9. The Reformers' call for a return to the pure sources of Christian faith in the Bible and the patristic writers has an important analogue in the Renaissance program of going back to the classical sources of virtue and eloquence in antiquity (*ad fontes*). In both instances, Protestants and humanists viewed the Middle Ages as a period of decline which could be reversed by returning to the ancient sources for inspiration and correction. On the religious implications of the Renaissance, see the two-part study of "Humanism": William J. Bouwsma, "The Spirituality of Renaissance Humanism," and James D. Tracy, "*Ad Fontes*: The Humanist Understanding of Scripture as Nourishment for the Soul," in *Christian Spirituality: High Middle Ages and Reformation*, ed. Jill Raitt in colloboration with Bernard McGinn and John Meyendorff, vol. 17 of *World Spirituality: An Encyclopedic History of the Religious Quest* (New York: Crossroad, 1987), pp. 236-67.

10. According to Warfield, "the Reformation, inwardly considered, was just the ultimate triumph of Augustine's doctrine of grace over Augustine's doctrine of the church." "Augustine," in *Calvin and Augustine*, p. 322. Pelikan comments that Warfield's dictum "may be an exaggeration but is not a total distortion." *Reformation of Church and Dogma (1300-1700)*, vol. 4 of *The Christian Tradition: A History of the Development of Doctrine* (Chicago: The University of Chicago Press, 1984), p. 9. Calvin distinguishes the "better schoolmen" (*saniores Scholastici*) from the "more recent sophists" (*recentiores Sophistae*) by which he evidently means the nominalists. *Inst.*, 2.2.6. Nonetheless, he claims that even the doctrine of Peter Lombard (ca. 1100-1160), whose *Sentences* served as the basic textbook of medieval theology, is at odds, not only with scripture, but also with Augustine, in spite of the fact that the Master of the Sentences "had Augustine constantly on his lips." *Inst.*, 2.2.6, 3.15.7. The Protestant claim to continuity with Augustine did not, however, prevent Calvin from voicing an occasional disagreement with the *doctor gratiae* (e.g., *Inst.*, 3.3.10). See the classic work by Luchesius Smits, *Saint Augustin*

dans l'oeuvre de Jean Calvin, 2 vols. (Assen: Van Gorcum and Co., 1957-58).

11. In its decree on scripture and tradition (1546), the Council of Trent not only affirmed the authority of the scriptures (according to the Roman canon and the text of the Vulgate), but also the authority of "the traditions themselves, those that appertain both to faith and to morals, as having been dictated either by Christ's own word of mouth, or by the Holy Spirit, and preserved in the Catholic Church by a continuous succession." Denzinger, p. 244 (§783). Whereas Trent first establishes the church's authority to teach before proceeding to spell out what the church actually teaches, the Protestants based their authority to teach on the correctness of their doctrine. For a discussion of the complex issues involved in the Protestant text and canon of scripture, see Roland H. Bainton, "The Bible in the Reformation," in *The Cambridge History of the Bible*, vol. 3, *The West from the Reformation to the Present Day*, ed. S. L. Greenslade (Cambridge: Cambridge University Press, 1963), pp. 1-37.

12. Much to the consternation of Protestants, the Catholics claimed for their position the authority of Augustine who wrote: "For my part, I should not have believed the gospel except as moved by the authority of the Catholic church." *Contra epistolam Manichaei quam vocant fundamenti* v (*MPL* 42.176 [*NPNF* 4.131]). The Catholics could also point to the difficulties the Protestants had in reconciling all of scripture with their doctrine of justification by faith alone, as, for example, in the exegesis of James' epistle where the Lutheran doctrine seems to be explicitly denied (James 2:24). See Luther, "Preface to the Epistles of St. James and St. Jude," in *Martin Luther: Selections from His Writings*, edited with an introduction by John Dillenberger (Garden City, New York: Anchor Books-Doubleday, 1961), 35-37; also *Inst.*, 3.17.11.

13. *Inst.*, 1.7.1. Calvin does his best to argue that "Augustine does not teach that the faith of the pious is founded upon the authority of the church, nor that the certainty of the gospel depends upon it." *Inst.*, 1.7.3.

14. *Inst.*, 2.6.1.

15. *Inst.*, 1.6.2.

16. E. David Willis insists that the fundamental principle of Calvin's theology is not the oft-cited *finitum non capax infiniti* (the so-called *extra Calvinisticum*) but another principle: "Calvin's thought is centrally that God does indeed accommodate himself to our capacity. *Humanitas capax divinitatis per accommodationem.*" "Rhetoric and Responsibility in Calvin's Theology," in *The Context of Contemporary Theology: Essays in Honor of Paul Lehmann*, ed. Alexander J. McKelway and E. David Willis (Atlanta: John Knox Press, 1974), p. 58. In this respect, Willis finds the influence of the rhetorical tradition of Renaissance humanism "not only in Calvin's *style* but in the *content* of his theology and anthropology." Ibid., p. 44.

17. *Inst.*, 1.6.1, according to the 1845 translation of Henry Beveridge, *Institutes of the Christian Religion*, originally two volumes published in a one-volume edition (Grand Rapids: Eerdmans, 1989; repr., 1994), p. 65. In the same passage Calvin explains that his method will be to explicate scripture's teaching regarding God as creator before proceeding to an exposition of scripture's teaching regarding God as redeemer. Cf. *Inst.*, 1.2.1.

18. *Inst.*, 2.6.1.

19. *Inst.*, 1.6.2.

20. *Inst.*, 3.2.29 (McNeill, 1:575). There is a tension in Calvin's doctrine of scripture's authority. H. Jackson Forstman writes: "It is proper to say that Calvin makes a distinction within the mass of the biblical material, but not at all if we understand by that term a separation of any kind. Faith may fasten on the divine promises as distinguished from the rest of the Bible, but faith in the divine promises depends in turn on a certain persuasion of the truthfulness of God— and this is a persuasion not only that the promises are true but also of the veracity of God in all things, meaning by that the entire Bible." *Word and Spirit: Calvin's Doctrine of Biblical Authority* (Stanford: Stanford University Press, 1962), p. 44. Dowey, however, actually speaks of "a discrepancy between the so-called formal and material principles of the Reformation: the authority of Scripture and justification by faith in Christ." *Knowledge of God*, p. 161. Gerrish points out that the ambiguity here accounts for both the orthodox notion of a verbally-inspired text and the liberal notion that scripture's authority is subordinated to the gospel which it contains. "The Word of God and the Words of Scripture: Luther and Calvin on Biblical Authority," in *The Old Protestantism and the New*, pp. 51-68. David H. Kelsey argues (persuasively, in my judgment) that "a theologian's decision to construe the scripture to which he appeals in a certain way rather than another" is based on a prior theological decision regarding the meaning and character of scripture's subject-matter or "how best to characterize the basic nature of Christianity, what it is 'all about.'" *The Uses of Scripture in Recent Theology* (Philadelphia: Fortress Press, 1975), pp. 167, 177. In Calvin's case, this means that he exegetes the entire canon of scripture in the light of his Lutheran construal of what the gospel is all about.

21. The promise contained in scripture has to be proclaimed in order that it may be heard and believed (Rom 10:17): "[T]he church is built up solely by outward preaching." *Inst.*, 4.1.5 (McNeill, 2:1019). Yet apart from the work of God's Spirit in the heart, what is heard does not evoke faith: "Faith is the principal work of the Holy Spirit. . . . Paul shows the Spirit to be the inner teacher by whose effort the promise of salvation penetrates into our minds, a promise that would otherwise only strike the air or beat upon our ears." *Inst.*, 3.1.4 (McNeill, 1:541). "To sum up, the Holy Spirit is the bond by which Christ effectually unites us to himself." *Inst.*, 3.1.1 (McNeill, 1:538). As Parker succinctly puts it: "The Word of God is never to be separated from the Spirit." *Calvin's Preaching* (Louisville: Westminster/John Knox Press, 1992), p. 29. On Calvin's doctrine of preaching, see Parker, *The Oracles of God: An Introduction to the Preaching of John Calvin* (London: Lutterworth Press, 1947), pp. 45-64; see also Erwin Mühlhaupt, *Die Predigt Calvins, ihre Geschichte, ihre Form und ihre religiösen Grundgedanken* (Berlin and Leipzig: Walter de Gruyter, 1931), pp. 24-38. On the relations of Word and Spirit to faith, see Forstman, *Word and Spirit*, pp. 66-85, 124-37. Dennis E. Tamburello has explored Calvin's affinities with Bernard of Clairvaux (1090-1153) with respect to their notions of a "mystical union" with Christ. *Union with Christ: John Calvin and the Mysticism of St. Bernard*, Columbia Series in Reformed Theology (Louisville: Westminster/ John Knox Press, 1994).

22. *Inst.*, 3.2.7. Cf. the substantially similar definition in the *Genevan*

Catechism: "a certain and unwavering knowledge of God's fatherly goodness toward us, as he testifies through the gospel that he will be, on account of Christ, our father and savior" (*OS* 2:92). Ronald S. Wallace writes: "Man when he lays hold of the promises of God is embracing God Himself as his Father. . . . Thus this faith that comes in response to the promises of God is no mere intellectual assent to a doctrine or a fact but is nothing less than our response to the mercy of God in Jesus Christ by which we are saved." *Calvin's Doctrine of the Word and Sacrament* (Edinburgh: Oliver and Boyd, 1953), pp. 125-26.

23. *Inst.*, 3.2.29.
24. E.g., *Inst.*, 3.2.20.
25. *Inst.*, 3.19.15. Conscience is an internal revelation of the "law of nature" or, in other words, the "will of God." *Inst.*, 2.8.1. See Dowey, *Knowledge of God*, pp. 58-59.
26. The religious activity that arises from a bad conscience "cannot place the person before a gracious God; it cannot attain the certain and final judgment of conscience that makes the person saved before God. Indeed, the religion of conscience does not lead toward faith in a gracious God, but further and further away from it." Randall C. Zachman, *The Assurance of Faith: Conscience in the Theology of Martin Luther and John Calvin* (Minneapolis: Fortress Press, 1993), p. 37. Warfield makes the perceptive observation that, according to Calvin, "what we call religion is just the reaction of the human soul to what it perceives God to be. . . . [Human beings] always and everywhere frame to themselves a religion, consonant with their conceptions of God." "Calvin's Doctrine of the Knowledge of God," p. 37. Willis writes: "Conscience is the instrument of man's self-knowledge, whereby he perceives himself either destructively as one condemned by an angry judge (and thus lives and worships idolatrously) or constructively as one assured of his acceptance by a loving Father. Self-knowledge, then, stands in correlation to the knowledge of God ..." "Rhetoric and Responsibility," p. 57.
27. *Inst.*, 2.8.6; "[W]hatever appearance [our works] may have in the eyes of human beings, they are none the less evil so long as the heart, to which God chiefly looks, is depraved." *Genevan Catechism* (*OS* 2:93). Calvin also writes that, "as works have regard to human beings, so conscience refers to God." *Inst.*, 3.19.16.
28. *Inst.*, 2.1.3. Failure to recognize this distinction is to get the Delphic precept "backwards." *Inst.*, 2.1.1.
29. "The proper object of faith is the goodness of God." *Inst.*, 3.3.19.
30. *Comm.* Hos 6:6 (*CO* 42:331).
31. *Comm.* Mic 4:2 (*CO* 43:342-43).
32. *Comm.* Mic 7:18 (*CO* 43:429). Cf. *Comm.* Acts 24:14 (*CO* 48:523) where faith is said to be the "only foundation of piety" (*unicum pietatis fundamentum*).
33. *Comm.* Mic 7:19 (*CO* 43:431-32); *Comm.* Ps 78:21 (*CO* 31:729-30). The "logic" is that trust in God's goodness issues in the willing service of God: "We see not only how hateful disbelief (*incredulitas*) is to God, but also what is the true nature of faith (*fides*) and what are the fruits it brings forth. For how could it be that human beings calmly submit themselves to God unless they

were persuaded that their salvation is utterly precious to him?" Ibid.

34. Calvin can speak of faith toward God and love toward one another as the "entire sum of piety." *Comm.* 1 Thess 3:6 (*CO* 52:157). On the other hand, "faith" can also be used as a catchword for "the sum of religion and sound doctrine," otherwise referred to in the same passage as the "doctrine of piety." *Comm.* 1 Tim 6:21 (*CO* 52:336). Elsewhere he uses faith and piety as synonyms: "The Prophet . . . sets faith or piety toward God and, then, love toward our neighbors in opposition to all external ceremonies. . . . Faith and piety please God: that is to say that the legitimate worship of God has always been spiritual." *Comm.* Hos 6:6 (*CO* 42:329-30). The diversity in Calvin's terminology is a function of the diverse ways language is used in scripture. Hence, his usage reflects the text upon which he is commenting. Still, there is a coherent pattern to be discerned: "'Faith,' in Calvin's vocabulary, is simply the restoration of the original relationship of piety that existed between Adam and God. In content, *fides* and *pietas* are identical insofar as both denote the right human response to the paternal goodwill of God. They differ in that *fides* is directed to the assurance of God's goodwill in Christ. *Pietas*, true religion, and its restoration as *fides*—this is the actual theme of Calvin's *pietatis summa*." Gerrish, "From Calvin to Schleiermacher," p. 188. Lee writes: "When we consider the relation between pietas and faith, we can easily grasp that what Calvin defines as pietas and its related matters is in accord with what he says concerning faith. . . . Calvin's explanation of faith and his references to pietas are in accord in content and even in the words used." "Calvin's Understanding of *Pietas*," p. 238.

35. *Comm.* Rom 12:1-2 (*CO* 49:233).

36. "The purpose of our redemption is the restoration of the original order of man's life. . . . The work of Jesus Christ is to restore to man the image of God which was lost in Adam." Ronald S. Wallace, *Calvin's Doctrine of the Christian Life* (Grand Rapids: Eerdmans, 1959), p. 107.

37. *Inst.*, 3.11.1.

38. *Inst.*, 3.11.2. "[I]t must be stressed that in believing the *gospel* we receive in faith Jesus Christ himself who offers himself to us through the gospel." Victor A. Shepherd, *The Nature and Function of Faith in the Theology of John Calvin* (Macon: Mercer University Press, 1983), p. 6. Indeed, Calvin speaks of Christ as "clothed with his gospel." *Inst.*, 3.2.6.

39. This is to be contrasted with the Catholic doctrine that justifying faith must be "formed by love" (*fides caritate formata*) since "unformed faith" (*fides informis*) is insufficient for justification. See *Inst.*, 3.2.8-10. Of course, the meanings assigned to the terms "faith" and "grace" differ within the Protestant and Catholic frameworks. For Protestants, faith is confidence in the divine mercy (grace) whereas for Catholics grace is the love for God "poured into our hearts by the Holy Spirit" (Rom 5:5). Therefore, faith (i.e., belief in the truth of Catholic doctrine) must be complemented or perfected by the love given to us as a gift of God. See "Canons on Justification" 9, 11-12 in Denzinger, p. 259 (§819, 821-22).

40. Luther wrote: "We conclude, therefore, that a Christian lives not in himself, but in Christ and in his neighbor. . . . He lives in Christ through faith,

in his neighbor through love. By faith he is caught up beyond himself into God. By love he descends beneath himself into his neighbor. . . . Our faith in Christ does not free us from works but from false opinions concerning works, that is, from the foolish presumption that justification is acquired by works." "The Freedom of a Christian," in *Selections*, pp. 80-81. Holl contrasts Luther's "religion of conscience" based on works-righteousness with his "religion of selfless selfhood" based on faith-righteousness. *What Did Luther Understand by Religion?*, pp. 48-86.

41. *Comm.* Deut 10:12 (*CO* 24:721).

42. E.g., *Comm.* Hos 6:6 (*CO* 42:329), where he uses *pietas* and *fides* synonymously.

43. *Inst.*, 2.8.11. Calvin speaks of God's worship as primary and justice among persons—"the true proof of piety"—as its effect. *Comm.* Mic 6:8 (*CO* 43:394). "While theocentric by nature, Calvin's concept of piety also implies an outgoing movement toward others." Lucien Joseph Richard, *The Spirituality of John Calvin* (Atlanta: John Knox Press, 1974), p. 120. Elsewhere, Richard explains that "sanctification is understood as the restoration of order willed by God. Within this context Calvin describes the Christian life under two headings: piety and justice—that is, love of neighbor." Ibid., pp. 116-17.

44. Calvin appeals to Plato's authority: "Plato also correctly teaches the distinction: *hosiotēs* [holiness] lies in the worship of God and the other part of righteousness refers to human beings." *Comm.* Eph 4:24 (*CO* 51:209); cf. Plato, *Protagoras*, 331d. Partee comments: "Calvin eschews Plato as a source of his theology, but he admits that Plato knows something about holiness." *Calvin and Classical Philosophy*, p. 111. Recall that Calvin sides with the Academic philosopher against the Epicurean in Cicero's dialogue with respect to the moral implications of piety; but unlike the ancients generally, Calvin does not view piety as one of the moral virtues. Cf. Virgil, *Aeneid*, 1:305 (*LCL*, p. 262) where Aeneas is said to be "pious" on account of his veneration of the gods, fatherland, and parents. See William Chase Green, "Pietas," *Oxford Classical Dictionary*, 2d ed., ed. N. G. L. Hammond and H. H. Scullard (Oxford: Oxford University Press, 1970), p. 833. By contrast, Calvin defends the more restricted use of the term: "Properly speaking, piety is the reverence we owe to God." *Sermons sur le Deuteronome* (*CO* 26:312). See also the discussion of *pietas* in his *Commentary on Seneca's De Clementia*, pp. 226-29, where he cites Augustine: "Piety, properly speaking, is commonly understood as the worship of God, which the Greeks call *eusebeia*" (*City of God*, 10.1.3 [*NPNF* 2:181]). Indeed, *pietas* is the word used in the Vulgate to translate *eusebeia* which appears only in later writings of the New Testament (Acts 3:12; 1 Tim 2:2, 3:16; 4:7-8, 6:3, 5-6, 11; 2 Tim 3:5; Titus 1:1; 2 Pet 1:3, 6-7, 3:11). As Robert L. Wilken writes: "The term *piety*, absent from the earliest Christian literature, began to be adopted by Christians at the time when pagans charged Christianity with superstition (impiety)." *The Christians as the Romans Saw Them* (New Haven and London: Yale University Press, 1984), pp. 204-5.

45. *Inst.*, 2.8.11. Lee writes: "Calvin relates pietas to the first of the two tables of the Law, consequently distinguishing pietas from 'righteousness' or 'exercising the duties of charity towards men' that are related to the second

table. . . . In understanding the meaning of the word pietas, we should keep in mind that Calvin's intention to distinguish pietas from righteousness or charity does not mean separation from either of them. Just as two tables of the Law have facets distinct from each other but at the same time they cannot be separated, altogether constituting one entity of Law of God, and as in Christian life the love of God and the love of men cannot be separated, so 'pietas toward God' and 'righteousness and charity toward men' cannot be separated. Therefore, we should think that when Calvin distinguishes the meanings of both of them, it is not for separating the two ideas, but for emphasizing the intimate and inseparable relation between them." "Calvin's Understanding of *Pietas*," pp. 234-35.

46. *Inst.*, 2.8.7, 51. Calvin says that those who "live uprightly and innocently with their neighbors demonstrate their piety towards God." *Comm.* Gen 18:19 (*CO* 23:259). On Calvin's view of Christ as an interpreter of the Mosaic law, see Dieter Schellong, *Das evangelische Gesetz in der Auslegung Calvins*, Theologische Existenz Heute 152 (Munich: Christian Kaiser Verlag, 1968), pp. 28-41.

47. *Inst.*, 3.3.7.

48. *Inst.*, 3.3.19. Werner Krusche explains that Calvin makes a conceptual distinction between justification and sanctification, but not an actual separation in reality (*distinguenda sunt, ut ne separentur nec misceantur*). "Justification is logically prior to sanctification. . . . It is the relation of cause and consequence." Sanctification is not to be conceived, therefore, as something that follows justification in a temporal sequence (*ein zeitliches Nacheinander*). *Das Wirken des Heiligen Geistes nach Calvin* (Göttingen: Vandenhoeck und Ruprecht, 1957), pp. 276, 278. While agreeing that these are "logically distinct" and "two graces of equal value," Wendel argues against "making one the final aim of the other. Sanctification is not the purpose of justification" (pp. 256-57). I fail to see why he argues this point since it seems to contradict the plain sense of Calvin's statement in this passage.

49. "We appropriate both newness of life and free reconciliation by faith" (*Inst.*, 3.3.1). "Whatever is done in us through his kindness is ours, provided that we understand it is not of our own doing" (*Inst.*, 2.5.15).

50. "[J]ustification by faith alone is the presupposition of the Christian life. . . . The dynamic character of this doctrine is revealed in Calvin's appeal to confidence before God, the experience of forgiveness, faith, union with Christ—all factors involved in justification by faith alone—as sources of the moral life." John H. Leith, *John Calvin's Doctrine of the Christian Life*, foreword by Albert C. Outler (Louisville: Westminster/John Knox Press, 1989), pp. 105-6.

51. *Inst.*, 3.11.1 (cf. *Inst.*, 3.15.1); *Comm.* John 20:23 (*CO* 47:440). Melanchthon called justification "the chief article of Christian doctrine" (*praecipuus locus doctrinae christianae*). "Apology of the Augsburg Confession," 4.2, in *Die Bekenntnisschriften der evangelisch-lutherischen Kirche*, 4th ed. (Göttingen: Vandenhoeck und Ruprecht, 1959), p. 159.

52. When Cardinal Sadoleto, Calvin's fellow humanist in the Roman camp, tried to persuade the Genevans by appealing to their anxiety regarding

salvation, Calvin had a ready reply: "It is not very sound theology for human beings to confine their thoughts so much to themselves, and not to set before them, as the prime motive of their lives, zeal to illustrate the glory of God. For we are born, first of all, for God and not for our ourselves." "Response to Sadoleto's Letter" (*OS* 1:463 [*A Reformation Debate*, p. 58]). See the brief discussion of Calvin's letter in Tjarko Stadtland, *Rechtfertigung und Heiligung bei Calvin*, Beiträge zur Geschichte und Lehre der reformierten Kirche (Neukirchen-Vluyn: Neukirchener Verlag, 1972), pp. 74-79. Richard writes: "For Calvin the ultimate end of history was not the salvation of man, but the glory of God." "The faithful man . . . lives for the glory of God, and because he does not give first place to his own salvation he finds it." *Spirituality of John Calvin*, pp. 144-45.

53. Willis insists that "Calvin's thought is not primarily characterized by dialectical diastasis but by rhetorical correlation." Hence, those who read his theology looking for oppositions and negations will "emphasize the sharp distinction Calvin sometimes draws between the human and the divine, reason and revelation, grace and nature, and justification and sanctification. On the other hand, if we are alerted to Calvin's location in the rhetorical tradition, we can see how many of the polar elements of his thought are correlatively joined." "Rhetoric and Responsibility," pp. 44, 57. Mary Potter Engel writes: "From the perspective of justification, there is no seed of religion left. From the perspective of sanctification, however, there is a seed left." *John Calvin's Perspectival Anthropology*, p. 71, n. 90. We must view Barth's reading of Calvin as lopsided, therefore, when he concludes that "the concept of *religio* ... has no fundamental significance in Calvin's conception and exposition of Christianity" because of Calvin's statement that the seed of religion does not ripen on account of sin. *Church Dogmatics*, 1.2, p. 285.

54. Hendrik Kraemer writes: "[T]he great reformers wrestled with the problem of the relation of God's revelation in Christ to religion and religions. They wrestled with it in the full sense of the word, and laid down some capital principles of approach. For the first time in the history of the Christian church, a true *theology* of religion and religions was designed." *Religion and the Christian Faith* (Philadelphia: Westminster Press, 1957), p. 168. J. du Preez agrees, but adds that "Calvin did not provide us with a complete systematic evaluation of religion and religions." "John Calvin's Contribution to a *Theologia Religionum*," in *Missionalia* 16 (August 1988): 70. Karl Reuter writes: "Calvin was deeply concerned to understand the relations between what is universally valid in the religions and what is valid only in the one very specific religion characterized by the Reformation." *Das Grundverständnis der Theologie Calvins, unter Einbeziehung ihrer geschichtlichen Abhängigkeiten*, Beiträge zur Geschichte und Lehre der reformierten Kirche (Neukirchen-Vluyn: Neukirchener Verlag, 1963), p. 90. Tillich is wrong when he declares that Calvin "had no interest in the history of religion, which is practically condemned as a whole as being idolatrous." I suspect that Tillich is reading Barth's theology into Calvin at this point. *History of Christian Thought*, pp. 263-64.

55. *Inst.*, 1.6.2.

56. *Inst.*, 1.5.15. See du Preez, pp. 73-74.

57. *Inst.*, 1.11.8. Luther defined idolatry as a misdirected faith: "A god is that to which we look for all good and in which we find refuge in every time of need. To have a god is nothing else than to trust and believe him with our whole heart. As I have often said, the trust and faith of the heart alone make both God and an idol. If your faith and trust are right, then your God is the true God. On the other hand, if your trust is false and wrong, you have not the true God. For these two belong together, faith and God. That to which your heart clings and entrusts itself is, I say, really your God." "Large Catechism," in *Bekenntnisschriften*, p. 560; according to the translation of *The Book of Concord: The Confessions of the Evangelical Lutheran Church*, trans. and ed. Theodore G. Tappert et. al. (Philadelphia: Fortress Press, 1959), p. 365.

58. *Comm.* Acts 14:15 (*CO* 48:325).

59. *Comm.* Acts 14:15 (*CO* 48:325). Peter Brunner writes: "'False religions' are those whose god is an idol. The reason why true religion is perverted into its opposite is that human beings want to comprehend the incomprehensible, transcendent God through their senses, thereby bringing God down into the human sphere. Wherever this occurs, God is no longer the one true God but a construct that takes its rise from the human heart. The human being then becomes through a horrible reversal of the original relation between God and humanity the 'creator of God.'" *Vom Glauben bei Calvin, dargestellt auf Grund der Institutio, des Catechismus Genevensis und unter Heranziehung exegetischer und homiletischer Schriften* (Tübingen: J. C. B. Mohr [Paul Siebeck], 1925), pp. 50-51.

60. Ford Lewis Battles believes that Rom 1:21 ("although they knew God they did not honor him as God or give thanks to him") played a pivotal role in Calvin's "conversion" to Protestantism. See his article, "True Piety According to Calvin," in *Readings in Calvin's Theology*, ed. Donald K. McKim (Grand Rapids: Baker Book House, 1984), p. 197.

61. *Comm.* Gen 12:7 (*CO* 23:181). Barth's definition of "religion" ("the realm of man's attempts to justify and to sanctify himself before a capricious and arbitrary picture of God") is a good description of what Calvin means by "false religion." *Church Dogmatics*, 1.2, p. 280.

62. *Comm.* Mic 4:2 (*CO* 43:343).

63. *Comm.* Jon 2:8 (*CO* 43:244). "Calvin's theory of non-Christian religion and theology is in fact a psychology of religious experience, perverted by unhealthy emotions that have lured the soul away from the guidance of reason and sobriety. Superstition, an improper fear of God, is the root of all religion that deviates from the universal rule of the divine will." Nuovo, p. 61.

64. *Comm.* Acts 17:24 (*CO* 48:410).

65. *Inst.*, 1.5.13. For this reason, Calvin is critical of Cicero's moderated defense of tradition.

66. *Comm.* Acts 24:14 (*CO* 48:522-23). "Turks" is a reference to Muslims though, as Preus says, "Calvin was more concerned about the invasion of Europe by Turkish armies than about Islam as a religion." Preus, p. 187, n. 6. Jan Slomp writes: "It is clear that Calvin had only very casual knowledge about Islam and its teachings and had relatively little opportunity to come into contact

with Muslims." "The *Institutes* contain only a few references to the Turks. Such mention as there is clearly comes in the context of Christian theological debate and often seems to set up Islam as a foil for denigrating Christian opponents and preaching his own doctrine of Christianity." Slomp points out that "through his humanist training in classical studies . . . [Calvin] knew the religion of the ancient Greeks and Romans better than he understood the faith and practice of his contemporary, the Turkish sultan, and his coreligionists." "Calvin and the Turks," in *Christian-Muslim Encounters*, ed. Yvonne Yazbeck Haddad and Wadi Zaidan Haddad (Gainesville: University Press of Florida, 1995), pp. 127, 130, 138. George Huntston Williams writes: "Much of what has been written on this subject has dealt with the stance taken by the reformers in the presence of the military expansion of the Turks. Yet the attitude of Christians toward the Turks as Muslims was also a theological matter, particularly for the Protestants. It is instructive to see to what extent Protestant theologians recast the traditional views about the existence and significance of religions other than Christianity in the context of the theology of justification by faith alone. What they thought belongs to the history of changing Christian attitudes toward non-Christian religiosity. Within its long history an important consideration has always been whether the Christian theorists have been thinking primarily about religions of the past, presumably superseded by Christianity, or about some contemporary religion or religio-political challenger. The theologians of the patristic age, although they had to contend as apologists with a new rabbinical orthodoxy within Judaism after the destruction of the Temple in Jerusalem and with what they considered the improper religious demands of the Roman state, nevertheless generally looked backward to biblical Judaism and to pre-Christian religious philosophies when they pondered the problem of the divine economy. Their principal categories for reflection on religion, therefore, were old and new, before and after, imperfect and perfect, lost and restored. With the extraordinary rise of Islam, however, and the sudden overwhelming of three patriarchates by the new religion of Mohammed, Christian theologians were faced with an entirely different task, for they now had to cope at once with what, considered even in the best light, was surely divine chastisement for Christian failures and with what in any case, in the eyes of the challengers themselves (who both acknowledged Moses and Jesus and yet saw them as superseded), was a superior, more comprehensive—indeed, the definitive revelation of the God of Adam and Abraham. Accordingly, Christian theologians . . . labored for centuries to recast the traditional patristic thinking about pre-Christian and praeter-Christian religions in the light of the contemporary martial, political, cultural, and theological challenge of Islam, which now had the advantage Christianity had once had in any debate in terms of before and after, old and new, partial and fulfilled. Christian apologists henceforth had to work more and more in the framework of truth and falsehood, divine election and chastisement, fruits rather than roots, eternity more than time." "Erasmus and the Reformers on Non-Christian Religions and *Salus Extra Ecclesiam*," in *Action and Conviction in Early Modern Europe: Essays in Memory of E. H. Harbison*, ed. Theodore K. Rabb and Jarrold E. Seigel (Princeton: Princeton University Press, 1969), pp. 319-20. Williams points out that Calvin's printer for the 1536

Institutes, John Operin of Basel, also issued a Latin translation of the Koran, for which Luther wrote a preface (*WA* 53: 561-72). Ibid., p. 361, n. 108 and p. 349.

67. Calvin finds in religious diversity evidence that the order of nature has been subverted. "In sum, [Paul] wanted to teach that the order of nature was violated when religion was torn asunder among [the pagans] and that the diversity apparent among themselves is a testimony that piety has been overthrown." *Comm.* Acts 17:26 (*CO* 48:414).

68. *Inst.*, 1.5.11.

69. *Comm.* Mic 6:8 (*CO* 43:392). Calvin derives the etymology of "hypocrisy" from the theatre where actors assume the part of fictitious characters on the stage. Thence, he tells us, it was applied to the religious realm to describe those "who are double in heart and phony." *Comm.* Matt 6:2 (*CO* 45:191).

70. Calvin calls religious ritual "the external confession of piety" (*externa pietatis confessio*) and cites the example of Jacob as someone who "knew that human beings need assistance, as long as they are in the flesh, and that sacrifices were not instituted without cause." *Comm.* Gen 33:20 (*CO* 23:453-54).

71. *Comm.* Gen 12:7 (*CO* 23:181). Ganoczy writes of Calvin's ideal of "worship in spirit and truth": "This worship . . . gives concrete expression to the inner feelings that come from the virtues of religion and piety." *The Young Calvin*, p. 209.

72. *Comm.* Hos 6:6 (*CO* 42:331). Cf. *Comm.* 1 Tim 4:2 (*CO* 52:294) for a similar definition of hypocrisy.

73. *Inst.*, 4.2.1-12, for Calvin's discussion of the true church.

74. Wendel writes: "The comparison that Calvin draws between the two Testaments leads him, in effect, to differentiate them by their chronological position in the plan of salvation, rather than by their content." "Thus the substance or the ground of the two Testaments is identical; the differences are in the methods employed by the Holy Spirit in imparting the knowledge of the substance, first to the Jews and then to the Christians." Wendel, pp. 209, 212. See also Dowey, *Knowledge of God*, pp. 164-67. A more thorough study is found in Hans Heinrich Wolf, *Die Einheit des Bundes: Das Verhältnis von Altem und Neuem Testament bei Calvin*, Beiträge zur Geschichte und Lehre der reformierten Kirche (Neukirchen Kreis Moers: Verlag der Buchhandlung des Erziehungsvereins, 1958), pp. 19-119.

75. *Inst.*, 2.10.2. In a strictly historical sense, however, Calvin does distinguish between Judaism and Christianity and says that the Christian faith (*christiana fides*) "flowed" from the Jewish religion (*iudaica religio*). *Comm.* Acts 24:14 (*CO* 48:522).

76. "The novelty of Christianity can be no more than relative if we adopt Calvin's point of view." Paul Wernle, *Johann Calvin*, vol. 3 of *Der evangelische Glaube nach den Hauptschriften der Reformatoren* (Tübingen: J. C. B. Mohr [Paul Siebeck], 1919), p. 273. Wilhelm Niesel writes: "[I]n Calvin's opinion the Old Testament does not reflect a primitive form of religion lower in degree than that of the New." *The Theology of Calvin*, trans. Harold Knight (Philadelphia: Westminster Press, 1956; German original 1938), p. 105.

77. See the discussion in T. H. L. Parker, *Calvin's Old Testament*

Commentaries (Louisville: Westminster/John Knox Press, 1986), pp. 42-82.

78. *Inst.*, 2.9.4. The Jewish theologian Leo Baeck praised Calvinism for its positive appreciation of the Jewish elements in Christianity's heritage. "Judaism in the Church" (1925), in *Jewish Perspectives on Christianity*, ed. Fritz A. Rothschild (New York: Crossroad, 1990), pp. 92-108. For a positive assessment from a Christian theologian, see Hans-Joachim Kraus, "'Israel' in der Theologie Calvins," in *Rückkehr zu Israel: Beiträge zum christlich-jüdischen Dialog* (Neukirchen-Vluyn: Neukirchener Verlag, 1991), pp. 189-99. It needs to be added, however, that Calvin's appreciation does not include Judaism during the Christian era. For that reason, Mary Potter Engel arrives at a more cautious conclusion regarding Calvin's attitudes on the basis of her careful study of his somewhat conflicting statements about the Jews and Judaism. "Calvin and the Jews: A Textual Puzzle," in *Princeton Seminary Bulletin*, supplementary issue, no. 1 (1990): 106-123.

79. *Inst.*, 2.9.4. Wendel discerns a tension at this point between Calvin's Lutheran heritage and the broader themes of his mature theology. When explaining the difference between "law" (works) and "gospel" (faith), "Calvin reverts to distinctively Lutheran ideas. . . . But too much accentuation of the divergences between the Law and the Gospel would not . . . be in harmony with Calvin's conception as a whole. So he hastens to return to the defense of the Law" (p. 213). This freedom to revise Luther's theology was characteristic of Calvin from the start: "[H]aving chosen Luther, Calvin made his choice in Luther, that is, he did not follow him on all points but only when he found him in agreement with the Scriptures." Ganoczy, *The Young Calvin*, p. 145. Of course, the real controversy regarding Calvin's "Lutheranism" is not here, but in the eucharistic debates between the Reformed and the Lutherans who came to consider Calvin a "Zwinglian." These issues are, however, too far afield from our present concern. I refer the reader to Gerrish, *Grace and Gratitude*, pp. 139-45.

80. *Inst.*, 2.9.2.

81. *Comm.* Gal 3:23 (*CO* 50:219-20).

82. See Wendel, p. 202, n. 57, and Dowey, *Knowledge of God*, pp. 164-65.

83. "What we possess distinctly was merely sketched in outline to the fathers." *Comm.* John 4:23 (*CO* 47:89).

84. Bouwsma speaks of this aspect of Calvin's thought as reflecting the rhetor's appreciation of *decorum*: Calvin's "rhetorical Christianity is most profoundly apparent in his emphasis on Scripture as everywhere accommodated by God's decorum to human comprehension." *Calvin*, p. 124. On Calvin's periodization of history, see Heinrich Berger, *Calvins Geschichtsauffassung* (Zurich: Zwingli Verlag, 1955), pp. 92-110; also Parker, *Calvin's Old Testament Commentaries*, pp. 83-90.

85. *Inst.*, 2.11.13.

86. *Inst.*, 2.7.2.

87. *Inst.*, 1.14.3.

88. *Inst.*, 2.10.20. For a study of Calvin's depiction of David as a model of faith, see Barbara Pitkin, "Imitation of David: David as a Paradigm for Faith in Calvin's Exegesis of the Psalms," in *The Sixteenth Century Journal* 24 (Winter

1993): 843-63.

89. For a critical discussion of Calvin's objections to the scholastic doctrine of faith by a Roman Catholic scholar, see Heribert Schützeichel, *Die Glaubenstheologie Calvins*, Beiträge zur ökumenischen Theologie (Munich: Max Hueber Verlag, 1972), pp. 68-121. Schützeichel concludes that Calvin's knowledge of scholasticism is insufficient and that many of the points Calvin correctly emphasized in his own theology can be found in the scholastic doctors (pp. 120-21). Arvin Vos writes: "If one examines the *Institutes* closely, one comes to the conclusion that Calvin did not have a firsthand acquaintance with the writings of Aquinas." Vos argues that "the case [Calvin] makes against the doctrine of faith held by the Schoolmen does not meet the discussion of Aquinas." *Aquinas, Calvin, and Contemporary Protestant Thought: A Critique of Protestant Views on the Thought of Thomas Aquinas* (Grand Rapids: Christian University Press-Eerdmans, 1985), pp. 38, 40.

90. *Comm.* Matt 15:22 (*CO* 45:456-57). In the very same passage Calvin calls it "some taste of piety." Dowey says that "faith is called implicit with reference to its degree of knowledge, that is, the depth to which the mind has penetrated in understanding the mystery of Christ, which it has for its object." *Knowledge of God*, p. 167. For a discussion of some aspects of Calvin's notion of a "seed of faith," see Otto Gründler, "From Seed to Fruition: Calvin's Notion of the *semen fidei* and its Aftermath in Reformed Orthodoxy," in *Probing the Reformed Tradition: Historical Studies in Honor of Edward A. Dowey, Jr.*, ed. Elsie Anne McKee and Brian G. Armstrong (Louisville: Westminster/John Knox Press, 1989), pp. 108-15.

91. Calvin comes very close here to what Karl Rahner meant by the "anonymous Christian." "Christianity and Non-Christian Religions," in Hugo Rahner et al., *The Church: Readings in Theology* (New York: P. J. Kenedy and Sons, 1963), p. 131.

92. *Inst.*, 4.16.19. Williams says that "the central magisterial reformers . . . were more likely to have reckoned that '*extra predestinationem nulla salus*' than with Catholics and Anabaptists that '*extra ecclesiam nulla salus.*'" *The Radical Reformation*, 3d ed., Sixteenth Century Essays and Studies 15 (Kirksville, Missouri: Sixteenth Century Journal Publishers, 1992), p. 1262.

93. *Inst.*, 4.16.18-19. Brunner writes: "Calvin leaves room for the thought that some few pious men among the heathen might have known the true God and might thus have attained to that righteousness which counts before God." *Natural Theology*, p. 44.

94. *Comm.* Matt 9:11 (*CO* 45:244). Mary Potter Engel notes that, as Calvin sees it, the distinction between true and false religion is absolute from God's perspective since God alone knows whose religion is genuine, whereas there are varying shades of ignorance and knowledge from the human perspective. Regarding the "sense of divinity" she writes: "From the perspective of God as judge, the *sensus divinitatis*, the aspiration to heavenly life, is completely gone; for when the issue is human sin and the need for redemption, all piety is to be counted as nothing. However, from the perspective of humankind, one can properly speak of a remnant of piety and worship in human beings after the Fall, at least as the *sensus divinitatis*, which can never be erased in human beings."

John Calvin's Perspectival Anthropology, pp. 59-60. This view thus offers to resolve the problem that T. F. Torrance could not: "There is no doubt that the student of Calvin is faced with a difficult problem here, for in spite of taking this total view of man's corruption, Calvin can still admit that *something remains in fallen man.*" *Calvin's Doctrine of Man* (London: Lutterworth Press, 1952), p. 88.

95. *Comm.* Gen 43:23 (*CO* 23:542-43).

96. *Comm.* Acts 8:36 (*CO* 48:196).

97. *Comm.* Acts 17:17 (*CO* 48:404), with emphasis added. Recall that Calvin described the first step in his own "conversion" as a "teachable heart." (*CO* 31:21).

98. *Comm.* Acts 17:17 (*CO* 48:404). Though Calvin condemns pagan religion as idolatry, he does imply that Greek religion was superior to other forms of paganism since the Greeks represented the gods in human form: "For we know that the Persians worshipped the sun; all the stars they saw in the heavens the stupid pagans also fashioned into gods for themselves. There was almost no animal that for the Egyptians was not the figure of a god. Indeed, the Greeks seemed to be wise above the rest, because they worshiped God in human form." *Inst.*, 1.11.1 (McNeill, 1:100). See also Bouwsma, *Calvin*, p. 103.

99. *Inst.*, 3.14.3.

100. *Comm.* Gen 12:7 (*CO* 23:181). See the discussion of Calvin's criticisms of religious practices in the church of his day in Ganoczy, *The Young Calvin*, pp. 194-201.

101. *Comm.* Gen 17:4 (*CO* 23:236).

102. Preus notes the relation between the Protestant criticisms of Catholicism and the understanding of non-Christian religions: "Their horizon was mainly Europe, with only an occasional worried glance toward the impending Turks. The profoundly corrupted and disrupted state of Christendom, as they regarded it, and its renewal, provided the field of their inquiry. . . . Other men's religions were at best on the boundary between religion and 'idolatry,' or 'superstition.' And when the reformers mentioned such aberrations, they were more likely to be thinking of medieval Christendom than the religion of the Chinese or American Indians—peoples who would enter the European consciousness decisively only late in the seventeenth century. For the reformers, the false gods of Christendom were more absurd than anything the heathen had dreamed up." Preus, pp. 187-88. Williams comments: "The Protestant theologians . . . were, theoretically, obliged to rethink the whole question of non-Christian religions and their individual devotees in terms of their new ruling principle of scriptural solafideism. But these reformers seldom came directly to grips with the problem theologically; and, whenever they came even close to undertaking the task, it was almost always in the context of an immediate religio-military crisis." "Erasmus and the Reformers," p. 321.

103. *Comm.* Jer 11:12 (*CO* 38:111).

104. *Comm.* Ps 32:1 (*CO* 31:315). "In all ages it has everywhere been the prevailing opinion that, though all persons are afflicted with sin, they are, nevertheless, simultaneously adorned with merits that earn them grace before God. Although they provoke the anger of God by their offenses, they absolve

themselves by means of the sacrifices and satisfactions that lie at hand." Ibid.

105. *Comm.* Mic 7:18 (*CO* 43:428).

106. *Comm.* Mic 7:18 (*CO* 43:429).

107. *Comm.* Mic 7:19 (*CO* 43:432).

108. *Comm.* Matt 8:10 (*CO* 45:237).

109. *Comm.* Mic 4:2 (*CO* 43:343).

110. Reuter writes: "Making connection with Cicero's terminology and Augustine's use of it to combat ancient paganism, Calvin speaks of the pagan 'superstition' and the 'superstitious practices' of the papal church." *Das Grundverständnis*, p. 89.

111. "Préface des Anciennes Bibles Genevoises" (*CO* 9:823-24).

112. *Comm.* John 20:23 (*CO* 47:440).

113. The founding of the Genevan Academy, where students were immersed in the liberal arts before engaging in theological study, was the crowning achievement of Calvin's career. Williston Walker, *John Calvin: The Organiser of Reformed Protestantism* (1509-1564) (New York: Schocken Books, 1969; originally published 1906), p. 367.

Chapter 4

Schleiermacher's Interpretation of Religion

Beyond Orthodoxy and Rationalism

Schleiermacher fully shared Calvin's conviction that the human is, by definition, a religious being.[1] Unlike the Genevan reformer, however, Schleiermacher lived in an age when the meaning of "religion" (and not simply "Christian" religion) became a problem for interpretation. Whereas the Reformation had splintered Western Christendom into competing camps each of which claimed to represent the authentic Christian tradition, the Enlightenment called into question the shared medieval premises of all parties to the debate by putting natural science and historical criticism on the theological agenda, thus relativizing the distinction between Catholic and Protestant, on the one hand, and Lutheran and Reformed, on the other. The "founder of modern theology" thus faced the challenge of translating the religious substance of the Protestant heritage so as to mediate between tradition and modernity. Although his dogmatics bears a striking resemblance to that of the father of his own Reformed tradition on account of their common commitment to pursue a "theology within the limits of piety alone," Schleiermacher's effort to clarify the nature of faith by first defining religion shouldered the added burden of finding a way beyond the polarization of orthodoxy and rationalism that the Enlightenment had occasioned for the churches of the Reformation.[2]

Schleiermacher devoted an entire book to the question of religion: his famous *Speeches* of 1799 directed to the "cultured among the despisers of religion."[3] The definition of religion also plays a prominent role in the equally famous "Introduction" to *The Christian Faith*, first published in 1821-22 (revised edition, 1830-31). Much of the

controversy surrounding Schleiermacher's reception in the subsequent
history of Protestant theology revolves around the question of the
relation between these two texts, especially since some critics have
suspected that a philosophical defense of religion was the concern
dominating even his later dogmatics, much to the detriment of his
construal of the inherited faith of the church.[4]

The task of this chapter is to delineate the contours of
Schleiermacher's theory of religion as it gradually took shape from his
initial statement in the *Speeches* to his mature definition in *The
Christian Faith*. In the next chapter, attention shall be given to his
dogmatic explication of Christian faith and its relation to the concept of
religion. It will then become apparent that his exposition of Christian
faith is intended to build a bridge between the two main Protestant
confessions, just as his view of religion is designed to move the
Reformation heritage beyond the antithesis of orthodox supernaturalism
and rationalism.

The argument of this chapter is twofold: first, religion, according to
Schleiermacher, is neither assent to metaphysical doctrines nor
adherence to a moral code but something more basic than either of these
that discloses itself in the awareness of our common finitude as a feeling
of absolute dependence; second, the feeling of absolute dependence
becomes a consciousness of our relation to God when our
consciousness of living in a "world" is fully developed. Thus the
measure of piety is the extent to which our consciousness is permeated
by the awareness that the whole network of finite relations of which we
are but parts is itself absolutely dependent upon the infinite God.

The Young Schleiermacher: From Pietism to Romanticism

When Schleiermacher wrote the *Speeches* at the age of thirty, he
was serving as the Reformed chaplain at the Charité hospital in Berlin.
This early period in his life proved to be a turning point for him
intellectually on account of his participation in the salon of Henriette
Herz, the educated wife of a Jewish physician who was the favorite
pupil of Kant.[5] In her home he met Friedrich Schlegel who introduced
him to the leading figures of Germany's burgeoning romantic
movement, which opposed the rationalism and moralism of the
Enlightenment in the name of the new cultural ideal of individual self-
cultivation (*Bildung*) so compellingly expressed by Goethe in his novel
Wilhelm Meisters Lehrjahre (1796). It was in this context that
Schleiermacher sought to redefine the nature and meaning of religion in
order to move his cultured friends beyond their disdain for religion to

an appreciation of its indispensable significance for the full flowering of a human life, which was the aim of the romantic program.

The encounter with the romantic movement also gave Schleiermacher an opportunity to draw upon aspects of the experiential religion that had molded him as a child. His father, a chaplain in the Prussian army, underwent a spiritual reawakening upon his encounter with the Moravian Brethren (*Herrnhuter*) when Schleiermacher was still a boy. The parents then decided that the children were to be educated under the auspices of the Moravians. In their midst young "Fritz" first experienced his own religious stirrings. "Religion was the maternal womb," he later explained to his romantic readers, "in whose holy darkness my young life was nourished and prepared for the world still closed to it."[6] Indeed, his mature religious thought is not intelligible apart from the tremendous influence of pietism upon him.[7] In reaction to what was perceived as the dead letter of doctrine in the established churches, pietism advocated a lively religion of the heart that focused upon a personal relationship with the redeemer.[8] And the emphasis upon the religious affections would become a hallmark of Schleiermacher's approach toward the interpretation of both religion and Christian faith.

Looking back as an adult upon his upbringing among the pietists, Schleiermacher wrote to his friend Georg Reimer:

> Here my awareness of our relation to a higher world began. . . . Here first developed that basic mystic tendency that saved and suppported me during all the storms of skepticism. Then it only germinated, now it is full grown and I have again become a pietist, only of a higher order.[9]

That he speaks of himself as having become a pietist once again indicates the deep and lasting impression Moravian spirituality had made upon him. But the reference to "storms of skepticism" is an equally clear indication that his life among the pietists was not always easy. Between his initial introduction to pietism when the seed was planted and his adulthood when it came to full flower, there was a period of crisis that left its stamp upon the future theologian. At the time, he thought he had lost his faith. In retrospect, however, it is clear that what he lost was not faith but only his first understanding of it.[10]

In an anguished letter to his father, the young man indicates the nature of the crisis:

> Alas! dearest father, if you believe that, without this faith, no one can attain to salvation in the next world, nor to tranquility in this—and such, I know, is your belief—oh! then, pray to God to grant it to me, for to me it is now lost.[11]

He then goes on to explain more precisely the doubts that troubled him: he can no longer believe that Jesus was truly God or that his death was a vicarious atonement. Clearly, the supposed loss of faith consisted in an inability to accept the inherited doctrinal formulations of the church. Though the pietists had reacted against a sterile intellectualism in matters of faith, they had not rejected orthodox doctrine itself.[12] For that reason, Schleiermacher's questioning of traditional faith was no less problematic for his pietist teachers than for his concerned father.

Schleiermacher's doubts were not unlike those that assailed many of his contemporaries in the eighteenth century. And given his unusually keen intellect, it would have been surprising if the rationalist critique of orthodoxy had not affected him as well.[13] Under the weight of scientific and historical criticism, the supernaturalist edifice of his religious heritage crumbled. To be sure, deism provided many intellectuals in the eighteenth century with a ready alternative to the orthodox tradition of the church. The deists peeled away what they considered to be the superstitious accretions that had overtaken the "positive" religious traditions in order to recover the original "natural religion" of humanity that hearkened solely to the dictates of reason. Accordingly, all rational persons subscribe to a creed that consists chiefly of two articles: first, God once set the world in motion to run according to its own immanent laws; second, God has inscribed the moral law upon every conscience and will reward virtue and punish vice in the afterlife.[14] For Schleiermacher, however, the natural religion of the Enlightenment was a rationalistic and moralistic construct. After his formative experiences among the pietists, the religion of the Age of Reason left him cold.

A way beyond the conflict between orthodoxy and rationalism presented itself in the romantic movement with its concern for the cultivation of individuality, its historical sense, and, most importantly, its conviction that the depths of life could only be *felt*, not thought.[15] In all of these respects, romanticism signified a criticism of Enlightenment rationality and its bourgeois morality. And in holding to this critical estimate, Schleiermacher was no less of a romantic than his peers.[16] He shared their literary and aesthetic sensibilities as well as their great feeling for life. In one crucial respect, however, Schleiermacher was very different from his cultured friends: unlike them, he had not rejected religion. Indeed, as a minister, he was a representative of an ecclesiastical tradition considered moribund by the romantics.

Schleiermacher's early religious experience among the pietists, coupled with the crisis of faith occasioned by rationalist criticism of orthodox theology, led him to see in the romantic program the potential for a revival of religion in his time. The romantics' rejection of intellectualism and moralism in the name of feeling appealed to his pietist sensibilities according to which religion is primarily a matter of the heart.[17] Moreover, the romantic disdain for both the dogma of the established church and the natural theology that was supposed to provide an alternative to it allowed Schleiermacher to argue that, for all their mutual opposition to one another, orthodoxy and rationalism shared a common premise: religion is a matter of intellectual belief and the moral practices that follow from it. They differed, of course, regarding the warrant for religious belief: whereas the orthodox appealed to a supernaturally inspired doctrine, the rationalists appealed to the natural religion of reason alone. But they did not differ in the basic assumption that religion is a matter of the beliefs to which one assents.

In the *Speeches* Schleiermacher aligns himself with the romanticist criticism of orthodoxy and rationalism in order to clear the field for a new appreciation of religion's true role in human life and, thereby, to move the despisers beyond their simple rejection of it in the name of culture. His rhetorical strategy is, first, to correct his interlocutors' faulty notion of what religion is by showing them that it is an irrepressible expression of the human spirit; then, he proceeds to argue that the romantic ideal of *Bildung* requires cultivation of religion on its own terms so that human life may be fully developed on all sides.[18]

In addressing his well-educated friends on a topic as scorned by them as religion, Schleiermacher aims to expose their ignorance by posing "some Socratic questions."[19] Recalling the anecdote from Cicero's dialogue, he declares the purpose of his oration.

> You know how the aged Simonides, through repeated and prolonged hesitation, reduced to silence the person who had bothered him with the question, "What are the gods after all?" I should like to begin with a similar hesitation about the far greater and more comprehensive question, "What is religion?"[20]

Though freely admitting he is a clergyman, he does not wish to speak about God or to lament an ostensible decay of religion in modern times. Rather, sharing their concern for the cultivation of everything distinctively human, he wants to inquire into what it means to be human. By demonstrating that they do not understand what they so vehemently reject, he intends to extract from them the confession that religion is an essential feature of human life. Once this is conceded, they will readily see that it is not possible to despise religion without despising humanity.

Everything important in human life, Schleiermacher explains, can be seen from two distinct perspectives: from the inside as a necessary aspect of the human spirit and from the outside as a contingent phenomenon of the historical process. Unless religion, too, is examined from both sides, it cannot be properly understood.

> If one considers religion from its center according to its inner essence, it is a product of human nature, rooted in one of its necessary modes of action or drives. . . . If one considers it from its extremities, according to the definite bearing and form it has here and there assumed, it is a product of time and of history.[21]

The problem is that the despisers have formed their inadequate concept of religion solely by observing its external manifestations without asking about their source in the human spirit. Schleiermacher is far from wishing to dispute that the history of religion is filled with human folly ("from the meaningless fables of barbarous nations to the most refined deism"); nonetheless, he insists that a merely empirical view will not suffice since it stays on the surface without penetrating deeper. Only when religion is examined from the inside will its critics come to appreciate what it is about human nature that yearns to express itself here. They may then join in the endeavor "to seek out what is true and eternal in it and to free human nature from the wrong it always suffers when some part of it is misunderstood or misdirected."[22]

The failure to examine religion both in its essence and in its manifestations accounts for the faulty assumption that religion is either metaphysics or morals or, worse yet, a mixture of the two.[23] To be sure, religion's essence never appears alone since it is always accompanied in its manifestations by the doctrines and morals that interpret and express it. But doctrines and morals are not themselves religion since they arise from other functions of the human spirit, namely, the theoretical and practical functions. Metaphysics (doctrines about God and the world) is an outgrowth of our attempt to understand what is real about the world. Morality is an outgrowth of our active impulse to shape the world according to what is ideal. The systems of theology and ethics falsely identified as religion are merely its trappings; however necessary for religion's manifestation, they should not be confused with its essence which has its own domain in the human spirit.[24]

Metaphysics and morals have the same "object" as religion: the universe and humanity's relation to it.[25] But religion has its own way of apprehending this object that cannot be reduced to either of these other two.

> Thus religion maintains its own sphere and its own character only by completely removing itself from the sphere and character of speculation as well as from that of praxis. Only when it places itself

next to both of them is the common ground perfectly filled out and
human nature completed from this dimension. Religion shows itself
to you as the necessary and indispensable third next to those two, as
their natural counterpart, not slighter in worth and splendor than what
you wish of them.[26]

Whereas metaphysics explains the universe and moral practice
cultivates it, religion is "neither thinking nor acting, but intuition
(*Anschauung*) and feeling (*Gefühl*)."[27]

Religion is "intuition of the universe."[28] Unlike metaphysics and
morals, religion seeks neither to explain nor to act upon the universe but
simply to intuit it.

> It wishes to intuit the universe, wishes devoutly to overhear the
> universe's own manifestations and actions, longs to be grasped and
> filled by the universe's immediate influences in childlike passivity.[29]

Since every intuition "proceeds from an influence of the intuited on the
one who intuits," just as the emanations of light affect our eyes, religion
proceeds from the activity of the universe upon those spirits affected by
it. What is intuited is not "the nature of things" (*die Natur der Dinge*)
but "their action" (*ihr Handeln*) upon us.[30]

Specifically, religion is an intuition of the activity of the universe
as a whole that works in and through the discrete parts. It is, in other
words, the intuition of the infinite in and through the finite: "a sense and
taste for the infinite" (*Sinn und Geschmack fürs Unendliche*).[31]

> The universe exists in uninterrupted activity and reveals itself to us
> every moment. Every form that it brings forth, every being to which
> it gives a separate existence according to the fullness of life, every
> occurrence that spills forth from its rich, ever-fruitful womb, is an
> action of the same upon us. Thus to accept everything individual as a
> part of the whole and everything limited as a representation of the
> infinite is religion.[32]

The intuition of the infinite acting upon us in and through each finite
action alters our perspective on the world since everything is now seen
as part of an inclusive, encompassing whole: "To a pious mind (*einem
frommen Gemüthe*) religion makes everything holy and valuable, even
unholiness and commonness itself."[33] Religion intuits each finite
individual as a unique reflection of the infinite activity of the universe.
Each intuition, moreover, is itself individual and unique since none of
us stands in quite the same relation to the whole.

Every intuition of the universe is accompanied by a feeling.

Whereas intuition proceeds from the activity of the universe upon us, feeling is the response evoked by the reception of this influence: it is an action "brought forth" (*hervorgebracht*) in us. "In the act of intuiting it, you must necessarily be seized by various feelings."[34] Just as each intuition of the universe is individual and particular, so the feelings that accompany religious intuition vary in their degree of intensity. The stronger these feelings, the more religious we are.

> Is it really a miracle if the eternal world affects the senses of our spirit as the sun affects our eyes? Is it a miracle when the sun so blinds us that everything else disappears, not only at that moment, but even long afterward all objects we observe are imprinted with its image and bathed in its brilliance?[35]

The analogy clarifies the relation between religious intuition and its accompanying feeling: the universe affects us and we are overcome by the feelings evoked by it.

The feelings brought forth by our intuitions of the infinite in the finite are "heartfelt reverence in the face of the eternal and invisible," "unaffected humility" when we recognize our smallness in comparison with the immeasurability of the universe, "heartfelt love and affection" as well as "compassion" for our fellow human beings when we intuit each one as a representation of humanity, "gratitude" for those who have sacrificed themselves on behalf of others, "honor" for those who are conscious of their union with the whole, "remorse" over everything in us that is hostile to humanity and "the humblest desire to be reconciled." These feelings arise from our awareness of "dependence" upon the whole in common with all other mortals, from our sense that whatever we experience and do is an expression of the infinite working in and through the finite and is an activity of the whole in and through the parts.[36] "All these feelings are religion," Schleiermacher explains. "The ancients certainly knew this. They called these feelings 'piety' (*Frömmigkeit*) and referred them immediately to religion (*die Religion*), considering them its noblest part."[37]

The distinction between feeling and intuition is necessary for reflection since consciousness separates everything into subject and object and there is no way to speak about them except in this way. Yet Schleiermacher laments that he cannot treat both in their original unity since "the finest spirit of religion is thereby lost for my speech, and I can disclose its innermost secret only unsteadily and uncertainly."[38] He thus seeks, like a conjurer, "to call forth a rare spirit that does not deign to appear in any oft-seen familiar guise." It is the "first mysterious moment that occurs in every sensory perception, before intuition and feeling have separated, where sense and its objects have, as it were, flowed into one another and become one, before both turn back to their original position."[39] Since this union is "as fleeting and transparent as the first scent with which the dew gently caresses the waking flowers," it can only be suggested and indicated apart from desecration.[40] Though this immediate apprehension of the original unity of all things quite defies conceptual analysis, it is an error to believe that religion can have intuition without feeling or feeling without intuition. "Intuition without feeling is nothing," just as "feeling without intuition is also nothing."[41]

Religion is neither thinking nor acting, neither metaphysics nor morals, but intuition of and feeling for the infinite in the finite. Religion is the sense for the underlying unity of all things prior to the split within consciousness between subject and object. Yet precisely this unity ever eludes the grasp of theoretical and practical reason. Where, he asks, is the unity between the real and the ideal to be found?

> If this binding principle lies in metaphysics, you have recognized, for reasons that are related to metaphysics, a highest being as the moral lawgiver. Therefore annihilate practical philosophy, and admit that it, and with it, religion, is only a small chapter of the theoretical. If you want to assert the converse, then metaphysics and religion must be swallowed up by morality. . . .[42]

Thus religion must be appreciated as a unique mode of relating to the universe. The romantics have, after all, been "seeking for some time a highest philosophy in which these two categories unite and are always on the verge of finding it; and religion would lie so close to this!"[43]

Schleiermacher has come full circle: he has posed his "Socratic questions" and forced his interlocutors, at least, to ask whether they truly understand what they claim to despise. "I have shown you," the apologist insists, "what religion actually is. Have you found anything therein that would be unworthy of your highest human formation (*Bildung*)?"[44] Have not these educated critics, moreover, felt within their own breasts the yearning to be grapsed by the infinite of which he speaks?

> Become conscious of the call of your innermost nature, I beseech you, and follow it. Dispel the false modesty in front of an age that is not supposed to define you but that is supposed to be defined and made by you![45]

Indeed, their disdain for what commonly passes as religion testifies that the romantic vocation to shape a new cultural ideal harbors within it the possibility of a rediscovery of religion beyond its distortions and, therewith, the full flowering of humanity.

But the question cuts deeper than simply whether the romantics have misunderstood religion. If religion is, as he has argued, an inescapable feature of the human spirit demanding cultivation on its own terms, then have not the very people whose task is *Bildung* forsaken humanity in this most important concern? Or is their ignorance merely a cloak with which they wrap themselves "to make fun of a serious subject in a worldly manner"?[46] Schleiermacher's rhetorical strategy is thus more than apologetic. He criticizes the anthropocentrism and moralism of the romantic elite. "Humanity itself," he exclaims, "is actually the universe for you, and you count everything else a part of this only to the extent that it comes into connection with humanity or surrounds it."[47] Indeed, metaphysics and morals treat "humanity as the center of all relatedness."

> To want to have speculation and praxis without religion is rash arrogance. It is insolent enmity against the gods; it is the unholy sense of Prometheus, who cowardly stole what in calm certainty he would have been able to ask for and to expect.[48]

Priding ourselves on humanity's likeness to divinity is "an unjust possession" apart from the humble recognition of our finitude and contingency. The clergyman spoke to his educated friends as those who had made their lives so rich with the finer things of culture that they had lost sight of anything transcending humanity which might also relativize its importance: "You no longer need the eternal, and after having created a universe for yourselves, you are spared from thinking of that which created you."[49]

By placing such excessive value on humanity, moreover, the romantics operate with an ideal of the cultivated human being and disdain those who fail to exemplify it.

> [W]ith all your love for humanity and all your zeal for it, you are nevertheless always embroiled and at odds with it. You labor to improve and educate it . . . and you disgruntledly leave behind whatever fails to produce the desired result. I may say, this also comes from your lack of religion.[50]

Schleiermacher admits that he, too, knows how to pride himself on an excellent moral disposition. Still, religion lifts him higher to see even what is common and unrefined with new eyes.

Since the "genuis of humanity" is an artist who displays it in countless forms, we should rejoice over the unique design of each individual.

None is like the other and in the life of each there is some moment, like the silvery flash in the melting process of baser metals, when . . . it is, as it were, raised out of itself and placed on the highest pinnacle of what it can be. For this moment it was created. . . . It is a special pleasure to help small souls to attain this moment or to observe them in it; but their whole existence must indeed appear superfluous and despicable to those who have never had this experience.[51]

"Do you not sense," he urges, "that it is impossible that humanity itself can be the universe?" Humanity is to the universe what individuals are to humanity: one expression of the infinite in the finite. Thus even the authentic cultivation of a distinctively human life is possible only when religion corrects our restricted vision and we see clearly that humanity is not the center of the cosmos. Through its intimation of something beyond humanity, religion is the antidote to anthropocentrism and its consequent moralism, thereby giving significance to each individual as a part of the whole. Yet precisely this desire for that which transcends and relativizes humanity suffices to explain why religion is regarded as "folly."[52]

Although the self-confessed member of the clerical guild knows that much remains to be said about religion, he has led his interlocutors to the limit of what they can grasp at this time: "Any further word about it would be an incomprehensible speech about which you would not know whence it came or where it was going."[53] Still, if they would acknowledge their possession of these elementary religious intuitions he has outlined, it may be possible to take them further along the road; but for now he wishes neither "to arouse particular feelings" nor "to justify or dispute particular ideas." He is content simply to have shown "from what capacity of humanity religion proceeds" and that it is inextricably wrapped up with everything the romantics value as "the highest and dearest."[54]

Schleiermacher's achievement in the *Speeches* consisted in drawing upon aspects of romanticism and utilizing these to pose the question of religion in a way that transcended the polarization of orthodoxy and rationalism. In this new synthesis he also reclaimed the heritage of his pietist upbringing, putting the accent on the experiential dimensions of religion, thereby becoming, in his words, "a pietist of a higher order."[55] How successful his apology was in winning the romantics for his cause is a dubious matter, as he himself soon came to see. Beyond question, however, is the fact that the highly unorthodox way in which the youthful apologist defended religion caused some of his colleagues in the clergy to suspect that the author of the *Speeches* had forsaken the traditional faith of the church. The subsequent

revisions and modifications of his initial statement from 1799 that lead
to his mature definition in *The Christian Faith* have to be understood
against the background of this quite different discussion.

The Mature Schleiermacher: From the "Speeches" to the "Glaubenslehre"

In 1788 the Prussian minister of ecclesiastical affairs, J. C. von
Wöllner, issued an edict ordering all members of the clergy to adhere to
the official definitions of orthodoxy in their respective churches,
whether Lutheran or Reformed, on penalty of dismissal. State
censorship of the press was among the strictures of the Wöllner edict
and Schleiermacher's work had to pass the censor before appearing in
print. His mentor in the Reformed church, Chaplain F. S. G. Sack, was
appointed to inspect the *Speeches*. In spite of the fact that the book was
issued anonymously, Sack soon discovered the author's identity. And
though he gave his official approval for publication, the older man felt
obliged to reproach his younger colleague for the unorthodoxy of his
views.[56] Sack's response is a telling indication of an important line of
criticism that would accompany the theological reception of
Schleiermacher's interpretation of religion.

Besides questioning the moral propriety of a minister's association
with the likes of the romantic circle, Sack objected that
Schleiermacher's apology for religion failed to sound like biblical faith.
Actually, he is somewhat shocked that an educated man so well
acquainted with the simple purity of the Greeks could be duped by the
hollow and pompous language of his romantic friends. But Sack's
critique was more than merely formal and stylistic. He confessed to find
in the *Speeches* nothing but "a spirited defense of Pantheism, a
rhetorical presentation of the Spinozistic system." He hastened to add:

> [T]his system appears to put an end to all that religion has meant and
> been to me up to now; I consider its underlying theory to be the most
> disconsolate and the most pernicious, and I know of no way that it can
> be harmonized with either a sound mind or with the needs of the
> moral nature of the human being. Just as little can I comprehend how
> a man who subscribes to such a system can be a sincere teacher of
> Christianity, for no art of sophistry and eloquence can ever convince
> a rational person that Spinozism and Christian religion can co-exist
> with one another.[57]

True, Schleiermacher's language *was* unusual and startling. Not
even the romantics were accustomed to hearing a clergyman address

them in these terms! He had, after all, interpreted the essence of religion as an "intuition of the universe," and had spoken of "the infinite" where one might have expected to find "God." When he did invoke traditional categories, he gave them a new twist. "Miracle," as he defined it, is "only the religious name for an event." "Revelation," similarly redefined, "is every original and new intuition of the universe."[58]

But these novel turns of phrase appeared to be more than the usual concessions one might expect of a Christian apologist who seeks a "point of contact" when addressing the Athenians.[59] Some of Schleiermacher's statements could be interpreted as outright rejections of the church's faith. In drawing such a sharp distinction between religion and morality, for instance, he had employed primarily aesthetic metaphors to describe religion, likening it to a musical score ("a holy music") that accompanies our moral deeds but does not motivate them: "We should do everything with religion, nothing because of religion."[60] He thus assured his romantic readers that "religion has nothing to do" with the "commanding God."[61] Furthermore, he had criticized the traditional aspiration for personal immortality as "completely irreligious" and "contrary to the spirit of religion" since it seeks to secure the everlasting survival of the finite individual.[62] But most offensive of all, no doubt, was his declaration that religion does not require any particular idea of God because concepts of deity depend upon the direction of the imagination that construes our intuitions.[63] Since everything in religion is a matter of intuiting the universe, a religion without God may even be better than one with God.[64] Compared with pagan Rome which was "truly pious and religious in a lofty style" and thus hospitable to many gods, Christian Rome with its excommunications and anathemas is godless indeed![65]

The charge of pantheism was a serious one. What began as a disagreement between Jacobi and Mendelssohn over the question whether Lessing (1729-81) had gone to his grave as a secret admirer of Spinoza (1632-1677) soon became a public occasion for Germany's philosophical minds to discuss the merits of Spinoza's philosophy.[66] While Spinozism was viewed with suspicion by the ecclesiastical authorities for whom its rejection of a personal deity was tantamount to atheism, for romantic and idealist thinkers it provided an attractive alternative to deism's conception of God as the extra-mundane artificer of the cosmic machine. In place of a deity who relates to the world from *outside* the law-governed system of nature, the latter-day friends of Spinoza described the world as a living organism and interpreted God as the creative activity at work *within* nature. Thus their alleged "pantheism" signaled a shift in the dominant images of God and the world for those who already rejected the orthodox assumption of periodic divine interventions in the system of nature: from a mechanistic analogy (the world is like a watch and God is like a watchmaker) to an organic analogy (the world is like an organism and God is like the soul that animates a body). But to orthodox and rationalist theologians alike, the Spinozist refusal to ascribe personality to the deity amounted to nothing other than an atheistic denial of God's existence.[67]

In the *Speeches* Schleiermacher had, indeed, lavished praise on the Jewish philosopher who was expelled from the synagogue in Amsterdam on account of his heretical views.

> Respectfully offer up with me a lock of hair to the manes of the holy rejected Spinoza! The high world spirit permeated him, the infinite was his beginning and end, the universe his only and eternal love; in holy innocence and deep humility he was reflected in the eternal world and saw how he too was its most lovable mirror; he was full of religion and full of holy spirit; for this reason, he also stands there alone and unequaled, master in his art but elevated above the profane guild, without disciples and without rights of citizenship.[68]

Yet in response to Sack, Schleiermacher denied that the book was an apology for Spinozism: "Something spoken of only parenthetically on a few pages is supposed to be the main point?" And regarding the charge that his view deprecated belief in a personal God, he explained:

> [R]eligion does not depend upon whether or not in abstract thought a person attributes to the infinite, supersensual Cause of the world the predicate of personality. . . . Though I am as little a Spinozist as anyone, I introduced Spinoza as an example, because throughout his *Ethics* a sensibility prevails that one can only call piety. From the fact that some people attribute personality to God while others do not, I have shown that the ground lies in differing tendencies of mind and heart, and at the same time that neither of these tendencies hinders religion.[69]

Amid "the present-day storm of philosophical opinions" his goal has ever been, he insists, "to establish the independence of religion from every metaphysics."[70] He is fully convinced, moreover, of his inward possession of the religion he is called to preach so that there is no dissimulation on his part when he stands in the pulpit. Indeed, the thought of a conflict between his religion and Christianity on account of a philosophical idea had never occurred to him. If his *Speeches* gave offense, the fault lies with those who are "not in a position to separate their metaphysics and their religion."[71]

The real innovation of the young Schleiermacher is that he believed it possible to speak of religion's essence apart from metaphysical doctrines and moral precepts. Thus in an important respect the accusation that the author of the *Speeches* was a Spinozist is simply beside the point, as is the counter-argument that he did not identify God with the world in pantheistic fashion. Van Harvey writes:

> The radicality of Schleiermacher's early position does not consist in his pantheism or, indeed, in any view he articulated regarding the relation of God to the universe. It consists, rather, in his view that the entire dispute—pantheism versus theism—is irrelevant for religion as he conceives it because religion neither posits nor requires any such relationship.[72]

Indeed, Schleiermacher's aim was to talk about "religion," not about "God." He had said as much when he compared his endeavor to that of "old Simonides" who hesitated to give his opinion on the nature of the gods. Inquiry into the nature of religion, by contrast, is "the greater and more comprehensive question" than that about the deity.[73] Yet to those for whom religion is a matter of assenting to certain doctrines (whether of the orthodox or rationalist variety), an investigation into the essence of religion that brackets the theistic question may as well be atheism! The critical question thus raised by Sack is the relation of religion in Schleiermacher's sense to a concept of God.

As a mature theologian, Schleiermacher never repudiated what he had written in the *Speeches*. Although the book underwent two important revisions (1806, 1821), he claimed the changes were made simply to clarify the basic argument in light of the controversies that had been evoked. In spite of his affirmation of continuity, however, it remains a debated question among scholars just how much of the original position from 1799 is retained after he had assumed the responsibilities of a professor of Protestant theology.[74]

The first revision from 1806 is the most significant. Schleiermacher engaged in extensive rewriting, especially of the second speech on the essence of religion. Two changes, in particular, are of import for the further development of the theory of religion. First, the role of "intuition" as a description for the religious mode of relating to the world is greatly diminished and, for the most part, replaced by "feeling" alone. Previously "intuition and feeling" had been said to be mutually indispensable elements for appreciating the integrity of religion next to metaphysics and morals.[75] Second, the exposition is given a decidedly theistic cast and the word "God" is inserted into the text in many places where "universe" had originally appeared as the object of religious experience.

In 1799 Schleiermacher had attempted to point his audience to that elusive moment at the origin of every experience wherein our fundamental unity with all things is sensed before consciousness divides it into an intuition of the universe (object) and feeling (subject). Precisely this underlying unity is that to which religion, unlike theoretical and practical reason, has immediate access. But in 1806 "intuition" becomes associated with the knowing function of the human spirit, thus assuming connotations of theorizing that belong to metaphysical inquiry. Whereas Schleiermacher had written in 1799, "Praxis is art, speculation is science, religion is sense and taste for the infinite," in 1806 he altered this to read: "True science is perfected intuition (*Anschauung*), true praxis is self-generated cultivation (*Bildung*) and art, true religion is feeling and taste for the infinite."[76] For whatever reason, Schleiermacher dropped the pair "intuition and feeling" (*Anschauung und Gefühl*), thereby allowing "feeling" (*Gefühl*) to stand by itself as the designation for that function whence religion takes its rise.[77]

The other significant revision is that religious experience is explicitly interpreted as a relation to God. In 1799 "intuition of the universe" was said to be "the highest and most universal formula" for determining religion's essence.[78] In 1806, however, not only is feeling given as religion's domain in the human spirit, but feeling is said to relate us immediately to God.

> Your feeling, insofar as it expresses the being and life common to you
> and to the universe in the manner described, is your piety, that is,
> insofar as you receive the individual moments of this being and life as
> the work of God in you through the universe.[79]

The statement of Schleiermacher's position in 1806 is now modified in a dual manner: first, religion takes its rise from feeling alone and, second, religious feeling is the operation of God upon us through the world's activity.

The new formulation points toward the classic definition that first appears in the "Introduction" to the dogmatics in 1821. There the essence of piety is identified as the "feeling of absolute dependence," which is further specified as a "consciousness of being in relation with God."[80] The revision also shows how Schleiermacher responded to the charge of pantheism (atheism) which his 1799 statement had called forth.

> Seeing then that I have presented nothing but just this immediate and

original existence of God in us through feeling (*das unmittelbare und ursprüngliche Sein Gottes in uns durch das Gefühl*), how can anyone say that I have depicted a religion without God? Is not God the highest, the only unity? Is it not God alone before whom and in whom all particular things disappear? And if you see the world as a Whole, a Universe, can you do it otherwise than in God? . . . Otherwise than by the emotions produced in us by the world we do not claim to have God in our feeling, and consequently I have not said more of Him.[81]

What remains unchanged in 1806 and ever after is the sharp distinction of religion from metaphysics (including theological doctrine) and morals. But clearly the revised text has taken on a new character since its author is concerned to clarify the relation of religious experience to a concept of God.[82] The modifications in the text reflect a new context in which Schleiermacher did his thinking and a new audience to which he addressed himself.

In 1804 Schleiermacher had been appointed as the first Reformed professor to what had hitherto been an exclusively Lutheran theological faculty at Halle.[83] His context was no longer the literary salon but the academic lecture hall where a crisp conceptual distinction carried more weight than a suggestive figure of speech. And his new circle consisted of the theologians and philosophers who were once the target of his biting polemic. The erstwhile romantic who had previously railed against dogmatic and metaphysical "systems" that enslave the free spirit of religion now made the problems of academic theology his own.[84]

Moreover, by 1806 the young professor had become somewhat disillusioned with the romantic movement to which he had once looked for a revival of religion beyond orthodoxy and rationalism. What could not have been forseen in 1799 is that romanticism would give rise to an interest in Catholicism. Surely the most unexpected occurence of all was the conversion to the Roman church of his former associate Schlegel and his wife Dorothea Veit. If Schleiermacher had ever harbored the hope that a new appreciation for religion would lead his cultured friends into the doors of the Protestant church, seeing them head for Rome gave him second thoughts.[85]

The text of 1806 can thus be seen as a transitional document from the early phase of Schleiermacher's career to its mature development. In 1821 when Schleiermacher issued the first edition of his *Glaubenslehre*, he was at the height of his influence as one of the foremost preachers and theologians of his day. The explanatory notes appended to the third edition of the *Speeches* indicate that he sought to connect the earlier formulations with those found in the dogmatic theology.[86] Moreover, it is apparent that the intellectual matrix had shifted somewhat as well, demanding that he defend his position on two fronts. On one side were the speculative theologians captivated by the genius of Hegel, Schleiermacher's colleague in the philosophical faculty at the University of Berlin. For this group theology represented the highest form of philosophical knowledge. On the other side were the pietistic biblicists and confessionalists whom Schleiermacher described as "sanctimonious" (*Frömmelnde*), "slaves to the letter," "ignorant, loveless, and condemning," "superstitious and credulous" (*Aber- und Übergläubige*).[87] The antipathy of these two groups would have a significant impact upon Schleiermacher's reception in the subsequent history of Protestant theology in the nineteenth century.[88]

In his "Introduction" Schleiermacher discusses the essence of piety (*das Wesen der Frömmigkeit*), not to commend religion as in the *Speeches*, but simply to place the language of Christian dogmatics on the broader map of human experience.[89] The reason for delineating the religious domain before clarifying "faith" is to secure the independence of theology's discourse about God from speculative approaches. Since dogmatics is an activity of the Christian church which is, above all, a religious community (and not a political or a scientific community), understanding what makes religion "religious" is a necessary (though not a sufficient) step toward discerning what makes Christian religion "Christian." Thereby a methodological rule for dogmatics is established that safeguards the *religious* integrity of the church's language against alien intrusions from logically distinct "language games" that speak of God for other purposes.[90]

As he did in the *Speeches*, Schleiermacher makes known both where we may discover the religious element within human experience and what it is. First, piety is "neither a knowing nor a doing but a determination (*Bestimmtheit*) of feeling or of immediate self-consciousness." Second, the distinguishing feature of piety is the feeling of absolute dependence or, in other words, a consciousness of being related to God.[91] The connection between "feeling" (*Gefühl*) and "consciousness" (*Bewußtsein*) indicates how Schleiermacher thinks the independence of religion from metaphysics can be maintained, all the while affirming that the religious texture of experience discloses a relation to God constitutive of the human being.[92]

Although "feeling," the former pietist explains, has long been a common term in religious discourse, it requires more conceptual precision within academic theology.[93] To give it the necessary precision, Schleiermacher employs the phrase "immediate self-consciousness" (*unmittelbares Selbstbewußtsein*)—not as a synonym for "feeling" but as a clarification of it—to indicate that the religious feeling of which he speaks is a conscious awareness and does not refer to unconscious states of mind.[94] Furthermore, the adjective "immediate" modifies "self-consciousness" to distinguish it from mediated forms of self-consciousness, in which the self is made the object of its own reflection and judgment.[95]

Unlike knowing and doing, feeling alone is completely receptive. Whereas "doing" (*Tun*) is intrinsically active, knowing (*Wissen*) has both a receptive and an active aspect. As the state of knowing something, of course, knowledge is receptive since the self is at rest; but as the process of coming to know something, the self is active in its "going-forth beyond itself" (*Aussichheraustreten*) into the world. On the map of human consciousness, therefore, feeling alone stands in antithetical relation to knowing and doing as thoroughly receptive. Feeling, moreover, is the mediating link between moments in which either knowing or doing predominates. This is not to say that feeling can never become the object of knowledge or lead to an action designed to represent it externally. But feeling is neither of these; it is, rather, the determination of self-consciousness that underlies them.

Receptivity (*Empfänglichkeit*) is expressed in self-consciousness as a feeling of dependence and presupposes the presence of an "other" (*ein Anderes*) alongside the self. Without the other there would be no awareness of receptivity, only of activity (*Selbsttätigkeit*). Activity is expressed as a feeling of freedom. Yet even activity presupposes receptivity since it, too, requires an other to be the recipient of our free actions. Our consciousness is characterized by this polar tension between receptivity and activity. We are passive as well as active creatures in a web of mutually conditioning relationships. Corresponding to these poles of passivity and activity, we feel ourselves to be relatively dependent and relatively free.

Consequently, self-consciousness has two elements posited for it: the subject in its existence for itself and its co-existence with that which is not the self. If we consider both together (the totality of all others and ourselves along with it), we have a "world." The world is constituted by this entire network of relationships wherein we are acted upon (hence our feeling of dependence) and wherein we in turn act (hence our feeling of freedom). Awareness of ourselves is thus inextricably bound up with cognizance of a world of active and passive relations in which we are partially free and partially dependent.[96]

Within the world there cannot arise a feeling of absolute freedom since this would presuppose that the objects over which we exercise an active influence had come into existence through our own activity, but this is never the case in an unconditional sense.[97] There is, however, in self-consciousness a feeling of absolute dependence that negates the feeling of absolute freedom. Our sense of relative freedom (presupposed by our activity) implies a sense of dependence since we are aware that our very existence has not proceeded from our own activity. Thus our consciousness of being part of a world of relative freedom and dependence, while ruling out a feeling of absolute freedom, presupposes a feeling of absolute dependence.

This feeling of absolute dependence cannot be aroused in us by any object within the world (since we could exercise an active influence upon it which would give us a feeling of partial freedom in relation to it). Neither can it be stimulated by the world as a whole since this is the total system of reciprocal relations of dependence and freedom and our free actions may, indeed, have an influence upon the whole, however insignificant and minute.[98] Thus the feeling of absolute dependence does not belong to the "objective" consciousness at all; it is, rather, the highest grade of the self-consciousness.[99]

Once the feeling of absolute dependence is identified, the religious meaning of the word "God" becomes clear. "God" signifies the "Whence" (*das Woher*) of our feeling of absolute dependence.[100] Since dependence presupposes receptivity to influence from an other, absolute dependence points to the source of our active and passive existence in relation to which we are completely receptive.

> When, however, absolute dependence and relation with God are said to be equivalent in our proposition, this is to be understood in the precise sense that the expression "God" designates that "Whence" of our receptive and active existence that is co-posited in our self-consciousness. This is for us the truly original meaning of the term.[101]

Apart from considerations of theoretical and practical philosophy, the word "God" arises simply as a designation of the absolute "Other" upon whom we and the whole world of finite relations depend without qualification.[102]

The "consciousness" of our relation to God is a matter of giving language to the Whence of finite existence.[103] This emergence into consciousness is what it means to say that God is "revealed" in an original way in human feeling.

> When one speaks of an original revelation (*ursprüngliche Offenbarung*) of God to the human being or in the human being, this will always be the precise meaning: that to the human being is given, along with the absolute dependence that characterizes all finite being no less than humanity, an immediate self-consciousness of this dependence that becomes a consciousness of God. To whatever extent during the course of a person's life this actually appears, precisely to that extent do we ascribe piety to the individual.[104]

The feeling of absolute dependence is a necessary feature of self-consciousness that qualifies human experience as religious and discloses our relation to God. Schleiermacher thus brings together the two ideas of religiousness and revelation: all persons have a propensity toward religion on account of a revelation of God originally given within consciousness. Indeed, to deny that human nature is essentially religious is "genuine atheism."[105]

Monotheism represents the highest stage in the development of religion (not, however, the historically "original" religion of humanity as in classical theology or deism) because only here is the consciousness of living in a world completely developed. Without a fully developed consciousness of ourselves as parts of a unitary nexus of finite relations, the feeling of absolute dependence is falsely attributed either to an object within the world (as in "idolatry" or "fetishism") or to the manifold diversity present within our sensible self-consciousness (as in "polytheism").[106] In the pre-monotheistic stages of religion the consciousness of the world is less perfectly developed, thereby leading to a confusion between God and the world within self-consciousness.

The idol worshiper ascribes to the idol only so much power and influence as is necessary to satisfy the concerns of a limited domain of interests. And one idol is hardly monotheism just as the accumulation of idols is not yet polytheism. Polytheism emerges with the development of a notion of "totality" as a result of which an attempt is made to relate the various gods to one another by means of a comprehensive system that aims to cover the whole of reality. Genuine polytheism is found only where the local attachments of the gods recede into the background and their interrelations, spiritually interpreted, are depicted as an ordered and unitary plurality.[107] The more any one of these deities is identified with the whole system of reality, the more the absolute dependence of all finite existence is expressed, not yet upon a highest being but upon the totality. But precisely in this consciousness of the absolute dependence of finitude upon the whole lies the impulse toward monotheism, where it is suspected that behind the manifold plurality is a highest being who is infinite and upon whom the whole depends.[108]

In monotheism the consciousness of ourselves in the world becomes a consciousness of finite being in general.

> [I]n so far as we are constituent parts of the world, and therefore in so far as we take up the world into our self-consciousness, and expand the latter into a general consciousness of finitude, we are conscious of ourselves as absolutely dependent. Now this self-consciousness can only be described in terms of Monotheism. . . . For if we are conscious

of ourselves, as such and such in our finitude, as absolutely dependent, the same holds true of all finite existence, and in this connexion we take up the whole world along with ourselves into the unity of our self-consciousness.[109]

Absolute dependence is the "fundamental relation" inclusive of all others. If we are conscious of ourselves *qua* finite as absolutely dependent, the same applies across the board to all finite reality. World-consciousness and God-consciousness thus belong together and cannot be separated.

The question whether "pantheism" is an adequate conceptual vehicle for interpreting the relation of God to the world can only be addressed in the light of this clarification that we have no consciousness of God, in the strict sense, apart from a fully developed consciousness of the world. Of course, if pantheism is taken to mean that no distinction is drawn between God and the world, it is obviously inadequate. But, provided the distinction is properly made, it becomes difficult to distinguish this position from many theological interpretations of the church's doctrine, e.g., those found in the patristic writings where the attribution of "personality" to God is carefully qualified.[110] The crucial point is that God and the world belong together in consciousness so that we cannot have one without the other.[111] An adequate monotheistic doctrine of God must reflect this togetherness: neither is God to be conceived as "outside" the world (as in supernaturalism and deism) nor is God to be simply identified with the world (as in the vulgar version of pantheism).[112]

When the mature statement is compared with the earlier definition from 1799, a theme recurs throughout all phases of the evolution of Schleiermacher's thought: religion concerns our sense of belonging to the whole. What later becomes explicit (though it was clearly implied in 1799) is that this unity is only to be found in the finitude we share with all things, in our identity as "creatures" who must rely utterly upon a reality that transcends finitude as its source and support. It is this to which religious persons point when they speak of "God."[113]

The affirmation that our feeling of absolute dependence becomes a consciousness of God when our consciousness of living in a world is fully developed is not a retreat from the insistence that religion is independent of a knowledge of metaphysics. It is, rather, the attempt to make good on the suggestion in the *Speeches* that the concepts employed in religious discourse can truly be appreciated only when the religious domain of human experience has first been clarified.[114] While philosophy may be driven to speak about God on account of the internal logic of its own inquiry, there is a distinctively religious reason for speaking of God quite independent of philosophical argumentation.

Schleiermacher has thus found a religious route to language about God that has its own autonomy with respect to metaphysical and moral approaches, such as those proposed by Hegel and Kant. To speak of God as "the Whence" of our absolute dependence is neither a metaphysical knowledge of the infinite (Hegel) nor a postulate of the practical reason (Kant).[115] But this is *not* to deny that there may well be avenues to God through the theoretical and practical concerns of philosophy (and, indeed, Schleiermacher happens to believe that there are!).[116] His point is simply that such knowledge as a philosopher might possess is not what is meant by piety.[117] Religion is not a second-hand version of philosophy for the masses! Whatever "knowledge" a religious person may be said to have is knowledge of what is mediated through *feeling*.[118] Religion does not depend upon proofs since the word "God" emerges in consciousness to express that total receptivity implied by our active and passive existence which makes us one with the world.[119]

Summary

Schleiermacher's pioneering effort to examine anew the nature of religion grew out of his own early crisis of faith in the face of rationalist criticism. As a result of his encounter with the romantic movement, he redefined religion as "feeling," thereby distinguishing the underlying religious experience from the theological doctrines that seek to express it intellectually. Moreover, he identified a distinctively religious path to language about God that does not rely on the fortunes of philosophical inquiry. The mature theologian thus believed it to be a grievous error when an ostensible conflict between religion and science arises, since religion is a matter of the heart's feeling whereas science represents the mind's quest for knowledge.

This is what Schleiermacher tried to explain to old Jacobi (d. 1819) who had described himself as "a pagan with the intellect (*Verstand*)" though "a Christian with the heart (*Gemüth*)."[120] This meant, as Jacobi painfully knew, that the conflicting claims of mind and heart could never be harmonized.[121] But to Schleiermacher's way of thinking, such a chasm between heart and mind was intolerable and rested, moreover, on a misunderstanding of the relation between religion and philosophy. In his response to Jacobi (1818), Schleiermacher gave his view that paganism and Christianity can conflict only as one religious feeling against another; thus the idea of a Christian heart and a pagan mind is a confusion of categories.

> Religiosity is a matter of feeling. . . . If your feeling is Christian, how
> can your mind interpret it in a pagan fashion? I can't understand that
> at all.[122]

By contrast, Schleiermacher described himself as a "philosopher with
the intellect," since philosophizing is the activity proper to the intellect.
But with his feeling he is completely a Christian in whom paganism has
never found a home.[123]

Schleiermacher did affirm, however, Jacobi's resolve to pursue
philosophical inquiry unhampered by dogmatic concerns, and he would
not allow this freedom to be taken away from himself, either. But if the
philosophical perspective with which the mind operates is not able to
make sense of the religious affections of a Christian heart, then the
philosophy must be re-examined. Still, it is not to be replaced in
arbitrary fashion by a dogmatics that claims for itself to be a better
philosophy. That, Schleiermacher believed, is the error of Catholicism,
which demands the surrender of free inquiry for the sake of possessing
faith![124] As a Protestant he is convinced that theology *and* philosophy
should be independent of one another and determined not to conflict
with each other, even if, for that very reason, both tasks remain open-
ended inquiries that never attain perfect completion.[125]

In Schleiermacher's view, the historic entanglements of theology
and philosophy (e.g., medieval scholasticism) have long been a source
of problems for the full development of both theology and philosophy.
From the start, Protestantism sought to liberate theology from its
"Babylonian captivity" to philosophy by returning it to its own proper
sources in the Christian religious affections.[126] For its part, the
Enlightenment freed philosophy from its ecclesiastical tutelage as "the
handmaid of theology." The Reformation thus initiated an "eternal
covenant" between theology and free inquiry that allows each to pursue
its course apart from external interference.

> Unless the Reformation from which our church first emerged
> endeavors to establish an eternal covenant between the living
> Christian faith and completely free, independent scientific inquiry, so
> that faith does not hinder science and science does not exclude faith,
> it fails to meet adequately the needs of our time and we need another
> one, no matter what it takes to establish it. Yet it is my firm conviction
> that the basis for such a covenant was already established in the
> Reformation.[127]

There is, thus, no reason for science to become identified with irreligion
and religion with barbarism.

In securing the independence of religion from philosophy and defining theology in strict relation to the religious affections, the first liberal Protestant saw himself standing in the tradition of the first Protestant.

> Was not even our Luther such a person, and did he not begin to reflect about his piety only when he was hard pressed to strengthen his possession of it, so that his theology is plainly a daughter of his religion?[128]

Schleiermacher's theology, like that of Luther, was born of a personal struggle to understand his own religious experience.[129] In that sense, theology is "a daughter of religion" since it does not proceed from the disinterested philosophical quest for knowledge.

The real revolution in theology that Schleiermacher initiated should not be seen, however, in his redefinition of religion as feeling but in how that interpretation enabled him to develop a fully historical understanding of theology as a "positive" discipline.[130] If religion is not to be identified with doctrines, whether these are derived from a supernatural revelation or from the dictates of reason alone, then the doctrines of a religious tradition are to be understood as intellectual expressions of the particular modification of religious feeling that distinguishes this religious community from all others. And like Luther's, the religion Schleiermacher sought to understand was the concrete experience of sin and grace that he had known so vividly among the Brethren. While the doctrines that interpret this religious experience participate in the flux of historical change and development, the underlying experience is the same. Indeed, the point of subjecting doctrines to theological criticism, then and now, is to find the most adequate statement of this experience of Christ's redemption that constitutes the Christian church as a distinct religious community.

To be sure, Schleiermacher believed it possible to give a general definition of the nature of religion in abstraction from any particular religion since a definition aims simply to identify the religious element in the religions. But clarity about the nature of religion, while necessary, is not sufficient in and of itself for understanding distinctively Christian religion. "Faith" in Christ can only be defined with reference to the historic religious community that proclaims him as the redeemer. Human experience as such has a religious dimension by virtue of a relation to God as the source of our feeling of absolute dependence; nonetheless, Christian experience is constituted by a relation to the redeemer who so transforms our consciousness of God that we are aware, not merely of our absolute dependence, but that we are absolutely dependent upon God's love and wisdom. To discuss this specifically Christian religious experience, Schleiermacher has to turn from the concept of religion to its history.

NOTES

1. Niebuhr writes: "In fact, like Calvin before him, Schleiermacher freely exploits the conception of man as a being in whom his creator has sown the seed of piety." *Schleiermacher on Christ and Religion*, p. 174.

2. See the discussion of Schleiermacher in Christoph Senft, *Wahrhaftigkeit und Wahrheit: Die Theologie des 19. Jahrhunderts zwischen Orthodoxie und Aufklärung* (Tübingen: J.C.B. Mohr [Paul Siebeck], 1956), pp. 1-46.

3. The speeches were first issued anonymously under the title *Über die Religion. Reden an die Gebildeten unter ihren Verächtern* (Berlin: Johann Friedrich Unger, 1799), reprinted in *KGA* 1.2, pp. 183-326.

4. There are those, however, who argue precisely the opposite thesis by defending the *Speeches* as an apology for specifically Christian faith, i.e., as "theology," not "philosophy." For examples, see Paul Seifert, *Die Theologie des jungen Schleiermacher*, Beiträge zur Förderung christlicher Theologie (Gütersloh: Gütersloher Verlagshaus Gerd Mohn, 1960); Friedrich Hertel, *Das theologische Denken Schleiermachers untersucht an der ersten Auflage seiner Reden "Über die Religion,"* Studien zur Dogmengeschichte und systematischen Theologie (Zurich: Zwingli Verlag, 1965). In this vein is the older work by Otto Ritschl, *Schleiermachers Stellung zum Christentum in seinen Reden über die Religion: Ein Beitrag zur Ehrenrettung Schleiermachers* (Gotha: Friedrich Andreas Perthes, 1888). Hans-Joachim Birkner argues that this line of defense, besides obscuring the difference between "dogmatic" and "philosophical" theology within Schleiermacher's own frame of reference, presupposes the same formulation of the crucial question (philosophy or theology?) used by the critics. Birkner believes that the question must be reformulated to take into account important distinctions in order to move the discussion beyond the usual impasse. *Theologie und Philosophie: Einführung in Probleme der Schleiermacher-Interpretation*, Theologische Existenz Heute 178 (Munich: Christian Kaiser Verlag, 1974), pp. 22-25.

5. Redeker, *Schleiermacher*, pp. 25-33.

6. *Reden*, 1:11 (Crouter, p. 8).

7. See the biographical study by Wilhelm Dilthey, *Leben Schleiermachers*, vol. 13 of *Gesammelte Schriften* (Göttingen: Vandenhoeck und Ruprecht, and Berlin: Walter de Gruyter, 1970; originally published 1870), especially first half-volume, pp. 3-52; also the richly detailed study by James David Nelson, *Herrnhut: Friedrich Schleiermacher's Spiritual Homeland* (Ph.D. diss., The University of Chicago, 1963), esp. pp. 456-592; Erwin H. U. Quapp, *Christus im Leben Schleiermachers: Vom Herrnhuter zum Spinozisten*, Studien zur Theologie und Geistesgeschichte des neunzehnten Jahrhunderts 6 (Göttingen: Vandenhoeck und Ruprecht, 1972) traces the developments from 1778 to 1796; Georg Wehrung, *Schleiermacher in der Zeit seines Werdens* (Gütersloh: C. Bertelsmann, 1927) follows him until 1806.

8. On the history of pietism, see Kurt Dietrich Schmidt, *Grundriß der Kirchengeschichte* (Göttingen: Vandenhoeck und Ruprecht, 1954), pp. 420-38.

9. Letter of 30 April, 1802, in Ludwig Jonas and Wilhelm Dilthey, eds., *Aus Schleiermacher's Leben. In Briefen*, 4 vols. (Berlin: Georg Reimer, 1860-1863; repr. ed. Berlin: Walter de Gruyter, 1974), 1:294-95.

10. Gerrish, *A Prince of the Church*, p. 26.

11. Letter of 21 January, 1787, Jonas and Dilthey, 1:42; according to the translation of Frederica Rowan, *The Life of Schleiermacher as Unfolded in His Autobiography and Letters*, 2 vols. (London: Smith, Elder and Co., 1860), 1:46.

12. Nelson says that the relation between the pietist emphasis upon "feeling" and orthodox doctrine was "the basic problem for Brethren theology." *Herrnhut*, p. 428.

13. For an account of German theology in the 18th century, see Friedrich Wilhelm Kantzenbach, *Protestantisches Christentum im Zeitalter der Aufklärung* (Gütersloh: Gütersloher Verlagshaus Gerd Mohn, 1965); also relevant here is the study by Peter Hans Reill, *The German Enlightenment and the Rise of Historicism* (Berkeley and Los Angeles: University of California Press, 1975).

14. Schmidt, *Grundriß*, pp. 438-57, esp. 447-49. It should be noted that "deism" is a rather broad term that encompasses a number of different theological positions, including those that accepted "revelation" as being in some sense compatible with the demands of natural religion as well as those that rejected revelation altogether. See Allen Wood, "Deism," in *The Encyclopedia of Religion*, ed. Mircea Eliade (New York: Macmillan, 1987), 4:262-64, and the more extensive discussion in Ernest Campbell Mossner, "Deism," in *The Encyclopedia of Philosophy*, 2:326-36.

15. Crane Brinton, "Romanticism," in *The Encyclopedia of Philosophy*, 7:206-9; Marshall Brown, *The Shape of German Romanticism* (Ithaca and London: Cornell University Press, 1979).

16. Jack Forstman, *A Romantic Triangle: Schleiermacher and Early German Romanticism*, American Academy of Religion Studies in Religion 13 (Missoula: Scholars Press, 1977) studies him in relation to Schlegel and Novalis.

17. "For the Herrnhuter, 'feeling' (*Gefühl*) was the key to religious experience." Nelson, *Herrnhut*, p. 556.

18. See the important study by Terry Hancock Foreman, *Religion as the Heart of Humanistic Culture: Schleiermacher as Exponent of Bildung in the Speeches on Religion of 1799* (Ph.D. diss., Yale University, 1975; Ann Arbor, Mich.: University Microfilms, 1980), especially pp. 22-58 for discussion of the 18th-century concept of *Bildung* in relation to "religion"; also the detailed study by Kurt Nowak, *Schleiermacher und die Frühromantik: Eine literaturgeschichtliche Studie zum romantischen Religionsverständnis und Menschenbild am Ende des 18. Jahrhunderts in Deutschland* (Göttingen: Vandenhoeck und Ruprecht, and Weimar: Hermann Böhlaus Nachfolger, 1986); and Gerhard Ebeling, "Frömmigkeit und Bildung," in *Wort und Glaube*, 3:60-95, esp. 75-90.

19. *Reden*, 1:40 (Crouter, p. 20). He warns readers not to be duped by the

"sophistical disputations" of those who defend false views of religion. *Reden*, 1:115 (Crouter, p. 48). Schleiermacher was a serious student of Plato. At Schlegel's suggestion, he translated the Platonic dialogues into German. See *Schleiermacher's Introductions to the Dialogues of Plato*, trans. William Dobson (London: J. and J. J. Deighton, 1836; repr. ed.: New York: Arno Press, 1973). After he became a professor, one of his students (Börne) even said of him that "he taught theology the way Socrates would have taught it had he been a Christian." Cited by Redeker, p. 79. See also Werner Schultz, "Das griechische Ethos in Schleiermachers Reden und Monologen," *Neue Zeitschrift für systematische Theologie und Religionsphilosophie* 10 (1968): 260-88.

20. *Reden*, 1:32 (Crouter, p. 18); Cicero, *De natura deorum*, 1.22.60; cf. Calvin, *Inst.*, 1.5.12.

21. *Reden*, 1:17 (Crouter, p. 12). On the "inner-outer dialectic" in Schleiermacher's thought, see Terrence N. Tice, "Schleiermacher's Conception of Religion: 1799 to 1831," in *Archivio di Filosofia* 52 (1984): 334-35.

22. *Reden*, 1:17-18 (Crouter, p. 12).

23. "This mixture of opinions about the highest being or the world and of precepts for a human life (or even for two) you call religion!" *Reden*, 1:39 (Crouter, p. 20).

24. "Religion must indeed be something integral that could have arisen in the human heart, something thinkable from which a concept can be formulated about which one can speak and argue." *Reden*, 1:42-43 (Crouter, p. 21).

25. "This similarity has long since been a basis of manifold aberrations; metaphysics and morals have therefore invaded religion on many occasions, and much that belongs to religion has concealed itself in metaphysics or morals under an unseemly form." *Reden*, 1:35 (Crouter, p. 19).

26. *Reden*, 1:49 (Crouter, p. 23).

27. *Reden*, 1:46 (Crouter, p. 22).

28. He says this is "the hinge" of his speech defining religion's nature since "it is the highest and most universal formula of religion on the basis of which you should be able to find every place in religion, from which you may determine its essence and its limits." *Reden*, 1:52 (Crouter, p. 24).

29. *Reden*, 1:46-47 (Crouter, p. 22).

30. "What you know or believe about the nature of things lies far beyond the realm of intuition." *Reden*, 1:55 (Crouter, p. 25).

31. *Reden*, 1:49 (Crouter, p. 23, where *Sinn* is translated as "sensibility").

32. *Reden*, 1:55-57 (Crouter, p. 25). Cf. Calvin's view that the created order consists of "mirrors" reflecting God's goodness. *Inst.*, 1.14.21.

33. *Reden*, 1:68 (Crouter, p. 29). Cf. 1 Tim 4:4.

34. *Reden*, 1:69-70 (Crouter, p. 29).

35. *Reden*, 1:70 (Crouter, p. 29). "Just as the particular manner in which the universe presents itself to you in your intuitions . . . determines the uniqueness of your individual religion, so the strength of these feelings determines the degree of your religiousness (*Religiosität*). . . . [I]ts feelings are supposed to possess us, and we should express, maintain, and portray them." *Reden*, 1:70-71 (Crouter, p. 29).

36. *Reden*, 1:109-10 (Crouter, pp. 45-46). This is the sole reference to

"dependence" (*Abhängigkeit*) so central to the mature definition (Crouter, p. 46, n. 37). Yet, as Rudolf Otto points out, the seeds of the later formulation are to be discerned in the early work: "This sense and humble consciousness of one's own dependence within the mysterious whole is the root from which, in later years, his famous definition developed: 'Religion is the feeling of absolute dependence.'" "How Schleiermacher Re-discovered the Sensus Numinis," in *Religious Essays: A Supplement to "The Idea of the Holy,"* trans. Brian Lunn (Oxford: Oxford University Press, 1931), p. 76.

37. *Reden*, 1:110 (Crouter, p. 46). In the third edition (1821) Schleiermacher added the Latin derivative *Pietät* as a supplement to *Frömmigkeit*, thereby connecting the German expression to its Latin equivalent *pietas*.

38. *Reden*, 1:75 (Crouter, p. 31).

39. *Reden*, 1:32 and 77 (Crouter, pp. 18 and 31).

40. *Reden*, 1:78 (Crouter, p. 32).

41. *Reden*, 1:76-77 (Crouter, p. 31). Crouter points out that this sentence plays on Kant's dictum: "Thoughts without content are empty, intuitions without concepts are blind" (Crouter, p. 31, n. 16). Immanuel Kant, *Critique of Pure Reason*, unabridged ed., trans. Norman Kemp Smith (New York: St. Martin's Press, 1965), p. 93.

42. *Reden*, 1:41 (Crouter, p. 21).

43. *Reden*, 1:42 (Crouter, p. 21). On Schleiermacher's concern to delineate a concept of religion that does justice to the way religion actually relates us to reality, see Ebeling, "Zum Religionsbegriff Schleiermachers," in *Wort und Glaube*, 4:61.

44. *Reden*, 1:119 (Crouter, p. 50).

45. *Reden*, 1:120 (Crouter, p. 50).

46. *Reden*, 1:40 (Crouter, p. 20).

47. *Reden*, 1:94 (Crouter, p. 38).

48. *Reden*, 1:47, 49 (Crouter, p. 23). On the figure of "Prometheus" in romantic literature and Schleiermacher's critique of anthropocentrism, see Nowak, pp. 192-93; also, Forstman's discussion of the theme of "deification" through the poetic imagination in Novalis, *A Romantic Triangle*, pp. 38-39.

49. *Reden*, 1:2 (Crouter, pp. 3-4).

50. *Reden*, 1:94-95 (Crouter, p. 38).

51. *Reden*, 1:97-98 (Crouter, p. 39). Is this a reference to Schleiermacher's pastoral work in the hospital?

52. *Reden*, 1:106 (Crouter, p. 44); cf. 1 Cor 1:23.

53. *Reden*, 1:107 (Crouter, p. 44).

54. *Reden*, 1:15 (Crouter, pp. 10-11). Otto Piper says that "the *Speeches* are not an example of the philosophy of religion but are sermons about religion." Their purpose is "to clarify the nature of religion among religious people or those who are at least receptive to religion. One understands, therefore, why Schleiermacher appeals to the despisers as those who are already traveling down the road of religion. . . ." *Das religiöse Erlebnis: Eine kritische Analyse der Schleiermacherschen Reden über die Religion* (Göttingen: Vandenhoeck und Ruprecht, 1920), p. 15.

55. "The young Schleiermacher humanized pietistic spirituality and

inwardness" *("... ins Humane übertragen")*. Redeker, p. 41 (German original: *Friedrich Schleiermacher: Leben und Werk*, Sammlung Göschen [Berlin: Walter de Gruyter, 1968], p. 61); also Nelson, *Herrnhut*, pp. 556-57, who writes: "Schleiermacher broadened his concept of religious feeling and experience from a specific emotional reliving of the life, death, and resurrection of Jesus Christ to a general psychological realm which was the seat and source of 'the religious' as such. Thus in his intellectual biography do we see how Schleiermacher transformed the Brethren concept of *Gefühl* and made it the keystone of his philosophy of religion" (p. 557).

56. The circumstances surrounding Sack's reception of the *Speeches* and Schleiermacher's response are well documented by Albert L. Blackwell, "The Antagonistic Correspondence of 1801 between Chaplain Sack and his Protégé Schleiermacher," in *Harvard Theological Review* 74 (January 1981): 101-21. Blackwell's article provides the text of this correspondence (pp. 112-21), which is also found in Jonas and Dilthey, 3:275-86.

57. Jonas and Dilthey, 3:276-77; also Blackwell, p. 113.

58. *Reden*, 1:115-16 (Crouter, pp. 48-49).

59. The early romantic movement found its outlet in Schlegel's literary journal *Athenaeum*. Cf. Acts 17:16-34.

60. *Reden*, 1:71 (Crouter, p. 30).

61. *Reden*, 1:129-30 (Crouter, p. 53).

62. *Reden*, 1:131-32 (Crouter, pp. 53-54), though he cites Matt 10:39 (and parallels) in support of his view: "Whoever loses his life for my sake, will find it, and whoever would save it will lose it."

63. "You will not consider it blasphemy, I hope, that belief in God depends on the direction of the imagination." *Reden*, 1:128 (Crouter, p. 53).

64. "Now if you cannot deny that the idea of God adapts itself to each intuition of the universe, you must also admit that one religion without God can be better than another with God." *Reden*, 1:125 (Crouter, p. 52).

65. *Reden*, 1:68 (Crouter, p. 28).

66. For the origins and development of the debate see Gerrish, "The Secret Religion of Germany: Christian Piety and the Pantheism Controversy," in *Continuing the Reformation*, pp. 109-26; also, Reinhard Schwarz, "Lessings 'Spinozismus,'" in *Zeitschrift für Theologie und Kirche* 65 (1968): 271-90; also the discussion of Spinoza and Lessing in Otto Pfleiderer, *Geschichte der Religionsphilosophie von Spinoza bis auf die Gegenwart*, vol. 1 of *Religionsphilosophie auf geschichtlicher Grundlage*, 2d expanded ed. (Berlin: G. Reimer, 1883), pp. 31-68 and 132-44, esp. pp. 142-44. See, moreover, the discussion by George F. Thomas, "Pantheism: Spinoza," in *Religious Philosophies of the West* (New York: Charles Scribner's Sons, 1965), pp. 170-96.

67. The seriousness of the "atheism" controversy can be seen in the 1799 dismissal of Fichte from his professorship at Jena on account of his refusal to ascribe personality to the deity, albeit on Kantian, not Spinozist, grounds. See Emanuel Hirsch, *Geschichte der neuern evangelischen Theologie im Zusammenhang mit den allgemeinen Bewegungen des europäischen Denkens*, 3d ed. (Gütersloh: Gütersloher Verlagshaus Gerd Mohn, 1964; originally

published C. Bertelsmann Verlag, 1949), 4:337-407.

68. *Reden*, 1:52 (Crouter, p. 24).

69. Blackwell, p. 118 (Jonas and Dilthey, 3:283). In an explanatory note added to the second speech in 1821, Schleiermacher wrote: "How was I to expect that, because I ascribed piety to Spinoza, I would myself be taken for a Spinozist?" *Reden*, p. 136 (Oman, p. 104). But Schleiermacher had been engaged in studies of Spinoza for quite some time. See his "Kurze Darstellung des Spinozistischen Systems" (1793/94), in *KGA* 1,1:561-82; this volume of the *KGA* contains other writings by Schleiermacher that pertain to Spinoza: pp. 511-58, 583-97. For analysis of the relevant texts, see Julia A. Lamm, *The Living God: Schleiermacher's Theological Appropriation of Spinoza* (University Park, Pennsylvania: The Pennsylvania State University Press, 1996), pp. 13-56. For discussions of Schleiermacher's relation to Spinoza, see Dilthey, *Leben Schleiermachers*, 1:166-79, 332-41; also Quapp, pp. 229-63; and the detailed study by Günter Meckenstock, *Deterministische Ethik und kritische Theologie: Die Auseinandersetzung des frühen Schleiermacher mit Kant und Spinoza 1789-1794*, Schleiermacher-Archiv 5 (Berlin and New York: Walter de Gruyter, 1988). Spinoza was important in Schleiermacher's attempt to overcome what he saw as the excessive formalism of Kant's ethical theory; in Schleiermacher's view, Kant sacrificed the individuality of the moral agent to the universal law of practical reason. Meckenstock, pp. 220-21.

70. Blackwell, p. 119 (Jonas and Dilthey, 3:284).

71. Blackwell, p. 120 (Jonas and Dilthey, 3:285-86).

72. Van A. Harvey, "On the New Edition of Schleiermacher's *Addresses on Religion*," in *Journal of the American Academy of Religion* (December 1971): 504. "From my standpoint . . . the belief 'No God, no religion' cannot occur." *Reden*, 1:121 (Crouter, p. 51).

73. *Reden*, 1:32 (Crouter, p. 18).

74. Louis Dupré writes: "[T]here may have been an evolution in Schleiermacher's thought, but no break. . . . [T]hese variations are to be seen as an attempt to clarify his original meaning, rather than as a real change in ideas." "Toward a Revaluation of Schleiermacher's Philosophy of Religion," in *The Journal of Religion* 44 (April 1964): 97-98. For a somewhat different evaluation of the changes, see Harvey, "On the New Edition," pp. 488-512. Regarding the relation between the *Reden* and the *Glaubenlehre*, see James K. Graby, "The Question of Development in Schleiermacher's Theology," in *Canadian Journal of Theology* 10 (January 1964): 75-87. Graby concludes: "[T]he bald statement of great change in Schleiermacher is misleading if not false. To be sure, he modified certain statements as he matured, but what man does not do this?" (p. 87). Eugen Huber, *Die Entwicklung des Religionsbegriffs bei Schleiermacher* (Leipzig: Dietrichsche Verlags-Buchhandlung, 1901), affirms continuity in the interpretation of religion from the *Speeches* to the dogmatics (p. 313).

75. Emil Fuchs, *Schleiermachers Religionsbegriff und religiöse Stellung zur Zeit der ersten Ausgabe der Reden (1799-1806)* (Giessen: J. Ricker'sche Verlagsbuchhandlung [Alfred Töpelmann], 1901), p. 6.

76. *Reden*, 1:49 (cf. Crouter, p. 23, who renders this sentence: "Praxis is an art, speculation is a science, religion is the sensibility and taste for the

infinite."), *Reden*, 2:50-51 (Oman, p. 39). "Intuition no longer counts as a characteristic of religion, but rather as a central feature of the theoretical realm distinguished from it: science." Friedrich Wilhelm Graf, "Ursprüngliches Gefühl unmittelbarer Koinzidenz des Differenten: Zur Modifikation des Religionsbegriffs in den verschiedenen Auflagen von Schleiermachers *Reden über die Religion*," in *Zeitschrift für Theologie und Kirche* 75 (1978): 169.

77. Scholars differ regarding the reasons why Schleiermacher made this change. Brandt suggested that "intuition" was minimized because the term had come to be connected with the idealism of Schelling: "[W]hat Schleiermacher called the 'intuition' of or 'sense' for the whole is strikingly similar to what Schelling seems to have meant by the phrase 'intellectual intuition.' Both men referred by this word to the becoming aware of the interrelation of finite objects in the Infinite. . . . " "[I]t is very likely that Schleiermacher was anxious not to have his view of religion associated with Schelling, who had now pre-empted 'intuition' for his own purposes. So it is not surprising that he felt it necessary to redefine religion." Richard B. Brandt, *The Philosophy of Schleiermacher: The Development of His Theory of Scientific and Religious Knowledge* (New York and London: Harper and Brothers, 1941), pp. 154, 166. By contrast, Hirsch attributes the shift to Fichte's influence. *Geschichte*, 4:564. Against attempts to correlate this change with influences from other thinkers, Graf believes that the revisions of the *Speeches* are best accounted for simply on immanent grounds as clarifications on the way to the mature definition in the "Introduction" to his dogmatics. "Ursprüngliches Gefühl," p. 150.

78. *Reden*, 1:52 (Crouter, p. 24). But in 1821 Schleiermacher inserted that the assigning of religion to the domain of feeling is the "chief point" of his second speech. *Reden*, 2:57 (Oman, p. 45).

79. *Reden*, 2:57. Oman translates the third edition which was further clarified to read: "Your feeling is piety in so far as it is the result of the operation of God in you by means of the operation of the world upon you" (p. 45).

80. In 1821 piety's essence is said to be that "we are conscious of ourselves as absolutely dependent, which means that we feel ourselves dependent on God." *Gl.¹*, §9. In 1831 this is slightly modified: "We are conscious of ourselves as absolutely dependent or—which is to say the same thing—we are conscious of being in relation with God." *Gl.*, §4. Crouter argues that, in general, the altered formulations in the second edition serve to clarify the basic intention of the first edition. "Rhetoric and Substance in Schleiermacher's Revision of *The Christian Faith* (1820-21)," in *The Journal of Religion* 60 (July 1980): 285-306. Maureen Junker provides a detailed analysis of the modifications in the concept of piety from the first to the second editions undertaken by Schleiermacher for the sake of making his argument more precise. See her study *Das Urbild des Gottesbewußtseins: Zur Entwicklung der Religionstheorie und Christologie Schleiermachers von der ersten zur zweiten Auflage der Glaubenslehre*, Schleiermacher-Archiv 8 (Berlin and New York: Walter de Gruyter, 1990), pp. 39-71.

81. *Reden*, 2:122 (Oman, p. 94). "[W]hat about such primary religious ideas as God and immortality? Schleiermacher admits that for most people these are the very roots of religion, and claims that he has presupposed them in all that he

has said; only he does not, and we must not, hold them in the sense in which they are usually understood. In this sense they are no more than ideas, and ideas do not make men religious. Our feelings only become emotions of piety in so far as they are to us revelations of God. Feeling affects and calls forth the divine which is in us, and in us as a whole, not in any part or parts of our being. It is through feeling that the immediate and original existence of God is presented to us. So we cannot see the world as a whole save in God. . . . " W. B. Selbie, *Schleiermacher: A Critical and Historical Study* (London: Chapman and Hall, 1913), pp. 46-47; also Pfleiderer, p. 302.

82. Philosophical criticism of Schleiermacher's thought tends to focus precisely on the relation between his *description* of religious experience as feeling and his *explanation* of this feeling as an experience of God. The most extensive recent critique of which I am aware is that of Wayne Proudfoot, *Religious Experience* (Berkeley: University of California Press, 1985), pp. 1-40. Proudfoot argues that Schleiermacher is guilty of confusing "the relation between descriptive and theoretical accounts of religious experience" (p. 8). "Schleiermacher is trying to have it both ways. The religious consciousness is said to have the immediacy and independence from thought which are characteristic of sensations, and yet to include an intuitive component whose object is the infinite. It is both intentional, in that it is directed toward the infinite as its object, and immediate. It is not dependent on concepts or beliefs, yet it can be specified only by reference to the concept of the whole or the infinite" (p. 11). "To summarize, the account of piety as an affective state which Schleiermacher offers in *On Religion* contains two components. First, he contends that ideas and principles are foreign to religion and that piety is a matter of feeling, sense, or taste distinct from and prior to concepts and beliefs. Second, he identifies piety as a sense and taste for the infinite, an identification that requires not only reference to God or the infinite as the object of the feeling but also a judgment that this feeling is the result of divine operation. Both of these components are required by Schleiermacher's program, and they are incompatible" (p. 15). A differing estimate of the issues is given by John E. Smith in his book, *Experience and God* (London and New York: Oxford University Press, 1968). Smith writes: "Interpreting religion as a dimension of experience is not the same as interpreting God and religion by means of the concept 'religious experience.' . . . But certain problems are raised by the appeal to 'religious experience' that need to be brought forth and considered in a critical light. For it is likely that the proper contribution of experience to an understanding of God and the religious life may be obscured by the supposition that this contribution must be found only in the special doctrine of 'religious experience'" (p. 46). "More than one critic has raised a question about the justification by which one can claim to have the 'existence' of God, for example, by appeal to the 'facts' of religious experience" (p. 47). Smith proposes a general understanding of experience as "encounter": "If experience is understood as encounter, there is no difficulty whatever in supposing that a reality can be ingredient in experience while also transcending—in the sense of not being identical with—that experience" (p. 49). "The realities we encounter and the dimensions of experience in and through which they are interpreted are

not the creations of the philosophical intelligence. In this sense the philosopher is not called upon to produce, but rather to understand, what experience affords. Philosophical interpretation does mean transformation of what is interpreted, and therefore we cannot say that the philosopher merely 'analyzes' or clears up a content given to him. But the transformation does not *constitute* what he is interpreting. . . . For the idea of a divine disclosure belongs essentially to religion as something that is constituted apart from the interpreting mind" (p. 50). "With regard to the charge that approaching religion through religious experience means reducing God to human experience, it is necessary only to repeat what has been said about the need for encounter. Concentration upon religious consciousness as something confined to the individual consciousness has been responsible for the widespread belief that if one begins with experience, it will be impossible to allow for the disclosure of God from beyond the limits of the self. But if experience always means encounter of some sort, then the possibility of revelation or divine disclosure remains open and constitutes a matter for further discussion. This is all that is required for an experiential approach—namely, that it not entail the impossibility of revelation at the outset" (p. 51).

83. Halle was thus the first "united" theological faculty in Prussia, portending the Prussian union of Lutheran and Reformed churches formed in 1817. Redeker, p. 76; Dilthey, *Leben Schleiermachers*, 2:97-109.

84. 2 Cor. 3:6 ("For the letter kills, but the spirit gives life") is the most frequently cited biblical text in the *Speeches* (Crouter, p. 9, n. 15).

85. In the "epilogue" added in 1806, he discusses the romantic attraction to Catholicism and attempts to distance himself from his original audience: "At present there are some who appear to rescue themselves from the Protestant into the Catholic Church . . . some to whom I myself have formerly drawn your attention who are somewhat-able poets and artists who are worthy of honour. ... The reason given is that in Catholicism alone there is religion, and in Protestantism only irreligiousness, a godlessness growing out of Christianity itself. . . . What they are really in search of is idolatry. The Protestant Church, alas! has also to contend with idolatry, but in a less gorgeous, and therefore less seductive form. And because it is not pronounced and colossal enough here, they seek it beyond the Alps." *Reden*, p. 302 (Oman, pp. 268-69).

86. In the 1821 edition Schleiermacher asked his readers to consider the *Speeches* in the light of his dogmatics. "For understanding my whole view I could desire nothing better than that my readers should compare these *Speeches* with my Christian *Glaubenslehre*. In form they are very different and their points of departure lie far apart, yet in matter they are quite parallel." *Reden*, p. 136 (Oman, p. 105).

87. "Preface to the Third Edition," *Reden*, p. xiii. Hengstenberg, who joined the theological faculty in 1826, represented the conservative view.

88. Hermann Mulert made a detailed study of the reception of the 1821 dogmatics by contemporaries that includes extensive citation from reviews many of which are no longer readily accessible: "Die Aufnahme der *Glaubenslehre* Schleiermachers," in *Zeitschrift für Theologie und Kirche* (1908):107-39. See also the two supplements issued in the same journal, the

first by Mulert in 1909 ("Nachlese zu dem Artikel: Die Aufnahme der *Glaubenslehre* Schleiermachers," pp. 243-46) and the second by Heinrich Scholz in 1911 ("Analekta zu Schleiermacher," pp. 293-314). The latter article contains a discussion of Schleiermacher's reception by Hengstenberg's *Evangelische Kirchenzeitung* (pp. 305-11). See also the important study by Karl Dunkmann, *Die Nachwirkungen der theologischen Prinzipienlehre Schleiermachers*, Beiträge zur Förderung christlicher Theologie (Gütersloh: C. Bertelsmann, 1915), esp. pp. 36-74 for discussion of the supernaturalists and pp. 62-79 for discussion of the speculative (Hegelian) theologians.

89. Schleiermacher calls this "placement" an *Ortsbestimmung. Gl.*, § 3.1. Cf. the discussion of an *Ortsbestimmung* in his *Sendschreiben*, p. 55; also *KD*, §21. The task of clarifying "piety" is not intended as a *Begründung* of Christian faith. "We entirely renounce the attempt to prove the truth or necessity of Christianity and assume that all Christians, prior to entering upon inquiries of this kind, have the inner certainty that their piety can only assume this form." *Gl.*, §11.5.

90. "Since Dogmatics is a theological discipline, and thus pertains solely to the Christian Church, we can only explain what it is when we have become clear as to the conception of the Christian church." *Gl.*, §2 (*CF*, p. 3); "That a Church is nothing but a communion or association relating to religion or piety, is beyond all doubt for us Evangelical (Protestant) Christians, since we regard it as equivalent to degeneration in a Church when it begins to occupy itself with other matters as well, whether the affairs of science or of outward organization." *Gl.*, §2.1 (*CF*, p. 5).

91. *Gl.¹*, §§8-9; *Gl.*, §3-4.

92. Proudfoot writes: "The conception of piety proposed in the introduction to *The Christian Faith* is developed from that in *On Religion*, but it is more carefully formulated. The care can be seen in the manner in which Schleiermacher's dual thesis, that piety is independent of thought and practice and that it has an intentional object, is made more precise. . . . The edifying language of *On Religion* has been supplanted by a careful analysis of the religious self-consciousness" (p. 17). Nonetheless, Proudfoot detects the same inconsistency in Schleiermacher's identification of the essence of piety as a feeling of absolute dependence that he finds in the earlier work: "Piety so defined, however, is certainly not independent of concepts and beliefs. To say that the religious person is conscious of being absolutely dependent is to attribute to him or her the concept of dependence and that of complete dependence" (p. 19). Proudfoot is attempting to correct a simplistic view that language merely expresses an experience that is in no way formed by the language used to interpret it. He writes: "The recognition that religious language is often expressive remains one of Schleiermacher's contributions to the study of religion, though the affections that are expressed are not independent of concepts and beliefs. Although religious language is expressive and thus shaped by certain affections, it is also formative and shapes emotions and experiences. It can be highly evocative and can prepare the conditions under which a person will attend to a particular moment and identify that moment as an experience of a certain kind" (pp. 39-40). In other words: "The

most important ambiguity in the concept of religious experience emerges not from the term *religious* but from *experience*" (p. xviii). This explicitly philosophical line of argument has played an important role in the recent theological criticism of Schleiermacher's "experiential-expressivist" model of religion given by Lindbeck, *The Nature of Doctrine*. Tracy, in his response to Lindbeck, questions the assumption that this type of *philosophical* criticism is sufficient as a warrant for the *theological* criticism of the tradition of liberal theology that takes Schleiermacher's achievement as its point of departure. Tracy writes: "The first issue is Lindbeck's analysis of what he calls the 'dominant' liberal theological paradigm since Schleiermacher. . . . In sum, the theologians in this dominant tradition understand inner-pre-reflective experience as 'foundational' and all language and culture as merely 'expressive' of that foundational, non-discursive experience. They possess a 'unilateral' understanding of the relationship of experience and language as well as of experience and culture when what we need is a 'dialectical' understanding of these complex relationships. The problem with Lindbeck's descriptions of the 'dominant' theological model is not that his analyses do not point to real problems within the tradition from Schleiermacher to Tillich, Eliade, Rahner, Lonergan, et al. The problem is that Lindbeck is apparently unaware that thinkers in this very tradition he targets for criticism have addressed precisely these issues as their own major questions for at least fifteen years. . . . Indeed, anyone who has read modern hermeneutics in either philosophy or theology can discover that the major claim . . . has been to rethink the dialectical (not unilateral) relationship between experience and language. . . . In fact, the major argument of the hermeneutical tradition since Gadamer has been against Romantic 'expressivist' understandings of language's relationship to 'experience.' This work, in turn, has been what has allowed a major transformation of the Schleiermacher-Tillich-Rahner-Lonergan experiential paradigm into an explicitly hermeneutical one. Moreover, this hermeneutical transformation has been continuous with the major 'correlation' schema of the liberal theological tradition, and with its discovery of a non-empiricist notion of 'experience.'" "Lindbeck's New Program for Theology: A Reflection," in *The Thomist* 49 (July 1985): 462-63. Proudfoot says: "Schleiermacher's program cannot be carried through *as he envisioned it*" (p. xvi; emphasis added). As Tracy points out, this does mean that Schleiermacher's program cannot be carried out at all!

93. Tillich faults Schleiermacher for employing the term "feeling" to describe religion since it is vulnerable to the charge of subjectivism; nonetheless, he defends Schleiermacher's intention: "This was a very questionable term, because immediately the psychologists came along and interpreted Schleiermacher's concept of feeling as a psychological function. But 'feeling' in Schleiermacher should not really be understood as subjective emotion. . . . [T]he best evidence that when Schleiermacher spoke of feeling he did not mean subjective emotion is the fact that in his systematic theology . . . he uses the expression 'feeling of unconditional dependence.' In the moment that these words are combined, the feeling of unconditional dependence, the psychological realm has been transcended. For everything in our feeling,

understood in the psychological sense, is conditioned. . . . On the other hand, the element of the unconditional, wherever it appears, is quite different from subjective feeling." *History of Christian Thought*, pp. 392-93. Louis Roy writes: "For [Schleiermacher], *Gefühl* has a meaning different from ordinary feelings such as sensations, emotions, sentiments, or unconscious states, which are often subjectivistic. It is a *Zustand*, a 'mental state,' that consists in 'self-consciousness.' . . . In the inner life of the human self, this stable feeling is by no means merely subjective, since it has to do as much with the general (*allgemeine*) as with the individual self-consciousness. . . . Several commentators have pointed out that Schleiermacher's feeling of absolute dependence is not an emotion. . . . But *Gefühl* was bound to be mistaken by careless readers, who would hear its usual psychological ring (as in William James) and be lured by the Siren's seductive sound." "Consciousness according to Schleiermacher," in *The Journal of Religion* 77 (April 1997): 217-19.

94. Roy continues: "Anyone familiar with the intricate hermeneutical problems created by Schleiermacher's vocabulary cannot but sympathize with Paul Tillich's judgment that 'Schleiermacher made a great mistake' when he used the term *Gefühl* to refer to a profound religious experience that lies beyond the realm of human emotions. . . . [T]he author of *The Christian Faith* has recourse to an expression that explicates what 'feeling' is supposed to convey: 'immediate self-consciousness.' This phrase does not carry the ambiguity of 'feeling' and should have replaced it rather than coexisted with it." Ibid., p. 220.

95. The difference, for example, between states of joy and sorrow, on the one hand, and self-approval and self-reproach, on the other, is an instance of the distinction between immediate self-consciousness and mediated self-consciousness. What makes approval and reproach "mediated" is that the self becomes an object to itself. *Gl.*, §3.2.

96. *Gl.*, §4.1-2.
97. *Gl.*, §4.3.
98. *Gl.*, §4.3.
99. *Gl.*, §5.1-3.

100. Tracy's distinction between a "limit-to" and a "limit-of" as a key to identifying the religious dimension of human experience seems applicable here. *Blessed Rage*, pp. 92-94, 105-9.

101. *Gl.*, §4.4. The feeling of absolute dependence is "the original expression of an immediate existential relationship." *Sendschr.*, p. 15. Aside from Proudfoot's work, other studies that take issue with Schleiermacher's account of religious experience as disclosing a relation to God are: Charles E. Scott, "Schleiermacher and the Problem of Divine Immediacy," in *Religious Studies* 3 (April 1968): 499-512; Robert Roberts, "The Feeling of Absolute Dependence," in *The Journal of Religion* 57 (July 1977): 252-66; Jan Rohls, "Frömmigkeit als Gefühl schlechthinniger Abhängigkeit: Zu Schleiermachers Religionstheorie in der '*Glaubenslehre*,'" in *Internationaler Schleiermacher-Kongreß*, 1:221-52. For an alternative view of Schleiermacher's understanding of the relation between religious experience and the concept of "God," see Robert R. Williams, *Schleiermacher the Theologian: The Construction of the Doctrine of God* (Philadelphia: Fortress Press, 1978), pp. 23-56. Williams

illuminates Schleiermacher's affinities to the later phenomenological tradition
of philosophy.

102. "Within the experience of self-consciousness, the self is always
necessarily related to an 'Other' in 'reciprocity'—sometimes acting upon the
latter in freedom, sometimes receiving the action of the other in dependence.
But Schleiermacher regarded receptivity as always prior and 'primary.' . . .
Moreover, an important distinction was to be maintained between the relation
of the self to the other, as *reciprocity*, and the relation of the self to God, as
receptivity. . . . Hence, in the feeling of absolute dependence, God is not to be
objectified as the Other—neither as 'the world' nor as 'any single part' thereof,
but is to be recognised as the '*Whence*' (*Woher*) of the subject-object
relationship." Robert F. Streetman, "Romanticism and the *Sensus Numinis* in
Schleiermacher," in *The Interpretation of Belief: Coleridge, Schleiermacher
and Romanticism*, ed. David Jasper (New York: St. Martin's Press, 1986), p.
119. Georg Wobbermin writes: "The feeling of absolute dependence . . . takes
us beyond the phenomenal world in its entirety and in its widest possible
conception. It brings us in relation to a reality on which the finite world as a
whole is dependent. That 'Other, presupposed' in the feeling of absolute
dependence by the relation of dependence is neither a special aspect of the
phenomenal world nor the totality of all its phenomena; no! it is a reality which
transcends the entire phenomenal world, and upon which that world is itself just
as dependent as is the particular consciousness which has the feeling of
dependence." *The Nature of Religion*, trans. Theophil Menzel and Daniel
Sommer Robinson, with an introduction by Douglas Clyde Macintosh (New
York: Thomas Y. Crowell Co., 1933), p. 78.

103. On the role of the word "God" in the transition from feeling to
consciousness, Ebeling writes: "The movement of the feeling of absolute
dependence to God-consciousness is a matter of its becoming language. . . .
Insofar as Schleiermacher understands piety as a determination of feeling or
immediate self-consciousness, he does not therefore separate piety from
language, but rather traces the path of its original movement into language. Of
course, he thereby fights against the mistaken notion that piety emerges out of
the mere repetition of language that has been spoken before. But he therewith
secures the correct use of the language that has been handed down."
"*Schlechthinniges Abhängigkeitsgefühl als Gottesbewußtsein*," in *Wort und
Glaube*, 3:133. Ebeling correctly understands Schleiermacher's intention,
especially in his clarification of the relation of experience to language.
Schleiermacher himself disclaimed any suggestion that this was a "proof" for
God in the traditional sense. *Gl.*, §33. Richard R. Niebuhr unpacks
Schleiermacher's definition of religion and finds four steps that should be
distinguished for the sake of clarity: "First of all, then, the use of the term *self-
consciousness* points to the fact that in Schleiermacher's mind religion has to do
with the way in which the self is present to itself. . . . Secondly, the self that is
present to the self in this mode of consciousness is the underived self. . . . In the
third place, and again as the choice of the phrase *absolute dependence* indicates,
the self that is so apprehended is, in effect, apprehended as having been posited.
. . . Finally, the reader must take note of the fourth and all-important facet of

Schleiermacher's apprehension of this phenomenon: religion is located first of all in feeling and not in an idea." "That which is immediate to the self is simply and solely the self as dependent. Therefore Schleiermacher believed himself to be under no obligation to prove that that upon which the self feels dependent is God. This necessity does not arise, because the name *God* obtains its first denotation precisely from this feeling. . . . If the reader insists that the word *God* cannot be dissociated from some idea, then Schleiermacher's reply is to say that the idea which underlies the word is simply the expression of the feeling of absolute dependence and the first and most direct reflection upon it." *Schleiermacher on Christ and Religion*, pp. 182-85.

104. *Gl.*, §4.4. "What made [Schleiermacher] consider feeling to be the essence of the religious experience? The answer lies in the fact that the feeling of dependence reveals the transcendent ground of self-consciousness, the point where consciousness is no longer opposed to, but coincides with, reality. . . . It follows, then, that religion for Schleiermacher is not merely a subjective experience, as many people have thought, but a revelation of the ultimate ground of reality and consciousness. . . . Even though the immediate consciousness has no object, as thinking and willing do, it still has an intentionality of its own, for it reveals the subject-object totality." Dupré, p. 107. Again, from Niebuhr's pen: "With Augustine and Calvin, whom he cited as his particular mentors in theology, and, we may add, with Jonathan Edwards who represents on American soil the same theological tradition and spirit, Schleiermacher conceived the central religious reality to be the situation of the creature who finds himself as a being whose existence at every level is implicated in a God-relationship. . . . Religion as a universal, human phenomenon symbolizing the inextricable relatedness of personal existence led Schleiermacher to take his stand in the tradition that is constrained to begin its thinking with a God who is already in relation to man and with a human nature already in relation to God, because personal existence is given in and through that relation. . . . The antithesis between religion and revelation, which dominates so much of post-Hegelian theology, is lacking in *The Christian Faith* simply because religion stands for man in the totality of his being and not simply or primarily for man the knower." *Schleiermacher on Christ and Religion*, pp. 192-95.

105. "If religious communities are not to be viewed as aberrations, then it must be possible to demonstrate that the existence of such associations is a necessary element for the development of the human spirit. . . . To view piety itself in that way [i.e., as an aberration] is the real atheism." *KD*, §22.

106. *Gl.*, §8.2. Schleiermacher speaks of the "sensible self-consciousness" to indicate the awareness of ourselves under the antithesis of relative freedom and relative dependence characteristic of finite being, whereas the "higher self-consciousness" (i.e., the feeling of absolute dependence) transcends this antithesis. *Gl.*, §5.1.

107. Examples of the transition to polytheism are the religions of Greece and India. *Gl.*, §7.1.

108. *Gl.*, §8.1.

109. *Gl.*, §8.2 (*CF*, p. 35).

110. *Reden*, p. 144, n. 19 (Oman, p. 116).

111. *Gl.*, §32.

112. *Gl.*, §51.

113. Hegel thought that Schleiermacher's definition of religion as the "feeling of absolute dependence" debased the human being. "If religion in man is based only on a feeling, then the nature of that feeling can be none other than the *feeling of his dependence*, and so a dog would be the best Christian for it possesses this in the highest degree and lives mainly in this feeling. The dog also has feelings of deliverance when its hunger is satisfied by a bone. The human spirit on the contrary has its liberation and the feeling of its divine freedom in religion." "Hegel's Foreword to H. Fr. W. Hinrichs' *Die Religion im inneren Verhältnisse zur Wissenschaft*," in *Beyond Epistemology: New Studies in the Philosophy of Hegel*, ed. Frederick G. Weiss (The Hague: Martinus Nijhoff, 1974), p. 238. As Crouter points out, "[T]here are no texts by Schleiermacher in which a critical review (and thus a potential refutation) of Hegel's work is given. . . . In thirteen years of association at the same university (1818-31) neither figure engaged the other in public debate or wrote a major critical review which names the other figure directly." "Hegel and Schleiermacher at Berlin: A Many-Sided Debate," in *Journal of the American Academy of Religion* 48 (March 1980): 20. Crouter gives a balanced interpretation of Hegel's criticism of Schleiermacher: "To compare the consciousness of absolute dependence to an animal feeling seems manifestly unfair as an interpretation of the introductory paragraphs of *The Christian Faith*. Any careful reader of Schleiermacher knows that the feeling in question presupposes a capacity for self-consciousness that is possessed only by humans. No matter how dependent a dog may feel, it is doubtful whether the ultimacy or finality of any dependence is felt. . . . [Hegel's] point is that reason cannot be systematically excluded from the deepest and holiest moments of our experience. If it is, we are indeed reducing ourselves to something less than human; and the remark about the dog (from the Hinrichs preface) is not then inappropriate." Ibid., pp. 36-37. Crouter cites a letter from Schleiermacher to de Wette (1823) in which Hegel is mentioned: "For his part Hegel continues to grumble about my animal-like ignorance of God, just as he already did in the preface of Hinrich's [sic] philosophy of religion and in his lectures, while recommending Marheineke's theology exclusively. I pay no attention to it, but still it is not exactly pleasant." Philipp Marheineke (1780-1846), of course, was a Hegelian! Cited from G. Nicolin, ed., *Hegel in Berichten seiner Zeitgenossen* (Hamburg: Meiner, 1970), p. 391.

114. The religious concepts (e.g., miracle, grace, revelation, inspiration) are "the first and most essential ones, if religion must indeed have some concepts. They indicate in a most characteristic manner human consciousness of religion; they are all the more important because they identify not only something that may be in religion universally, but precisely what must be in it universally." *Reden*, 1:117 (Crouter, p. 49).

115. Ebeling, "Zum Religionsbegriff," p. 64.

116. Schleiermacher thinks that an adequate metaphysics must work with a concept of God in order to be comprehensive. But metaphysical knowledge

(i.e., knowledge of God attained via metaphysical argument) is not a prerequisite for a religious approach to God. See his clarifications in *Gl.*, §16: "Postscript," 1:111, §33: "Postscript," 1:180; on conscience as an "original revelation" of God, see §83.1. So there is, in Schleiermacher's view, both a philosophical and an ethical basis for speaking of God; what interests him, however, is the distinctively religious basis for speaking of God. Schleiermacher's philosophical lectures are published as *Dialektik, aus Schleiermachers handschriftlichem Nachlasse*, ed. Ludwig Jonas, *SW*, 3/4, 2. An English translation is found in *Dialectic or, The Art of Doing Philosophy: A Study Edition of the 1811 Notes*, translated with introduction and notes by Terrence N. Tice, American Academy of Religion Texts and Translations Series (Atlanta: Scholars Press, 1996). The relation between the doctrine of God in Schleiermacher's philosophical lectures and in his dogmatics has been explored by John E. Thiel, *God and World in Schleiermacher's Dialektik and Glaubenslehre: Criticism and the Methodology of Dogmatics*, Basler und Berner Studien zur historischen und systematischen Theologie 43 (Bern and Frankfurt: Peter Lang, 1981). The question of faith and reason has recently been analyzed by Christian Albrecht, *Schleiermachers Theorie der Frömmigkeit: Ihr wissenschaftlicher Ort und ihr systematischer Gehalt in den Reden, in der Glaubenslehre und in der Dialektik*, Schleiermacher-Archiv 15 (Berlin and New York: Walter de Gruyter, 1994).

117. "[T]he religious attitude is basically different from the speculative. Almost every philosopher uses the idea of God in his speculation, but that does not make him a religious person." Dupré, p. 101.

118. "The usual position is the reverse [of mine], namely, that the feeling of absolute dependence first arises from a knowledge of God that is found elsewhere. This, however, is false. For if we ascribe to the philosophers such a knowledge, the God-consciousness of the masses does not come from there. Wherefore, all attempts to popularize the speculative God-consciousness (proofs for the existence of God) are a failure. If we accept this, then we may not think of both being divorced, so that some only have piety, because they are not capable of speculation, whereas others either have never had piety or they were required to forget it, because they came to the speculative consciousness. On the contrary, both are equally original and, therefore, can co-exist with one another." *Gl.*, §4.4a. Cf. *Reden*, 2:46.

119. *Gl.¹*, §9.3: "Postscript," 1:32-33. When interest in Schleiermacher was being eclipsed by the neo-orthodox repudiation of him, Hermann Mulert suggested that it would be a valuable contribution to historical scholarship to explore the extent to which Schleiermacher's expression "dependence upon God" can be traced back to Calvin's influence. "Neuere Deutsche Schleiermacher-Literatur," in *Zeitschrift für Theologie und Kirche* 15 (1934): 81. Important in this regard is the statement of Heinrich Heppe: "Schleiermacher was the first able to give conceptual determination to the thoughts which were expressed by the earlier dogmaticians descriptively and in a scattered way." *Reformed Dogmatics, Set Out and Illustrated from the Sources*, revised and edited by Ernst Bizer, trans. G. T. Thomson (George Allen and Unwin Ltd., 1950; repr., Grand Rapids: Baker Book House, 1978), p. 6.

120. In a letter to Karl Leonhard Reinhold, professor of philosophy at Kiel (8 Oct. 1817); cited by Martin Cordes, "Der Brief Schleiermachers an Jacobi: Ein Beitrag zu seiner Entstehung und Überlieferung," in *Zeitschrift für Theologie und Kirche* 68 (June 1971): 206.

121. See the discussion in Pfleiderer, pp. 218-224, who speaks of Jacobi's *Verstandesheidenthum* (p. 224).

122. Cordes, p. 208.

123. Cordes, pp. 208-209.

124. Cordes, p. 209.

125. Schleiermacher is thus committed to the independence of dogmatics from philosophy and, at the same time, the mutual compatibility of theology and philosophical inquiry. See Thomas Curran, "Schleiermacher wider die Spekulation," in *Internationaler Schleiermacher Kongreß*, 2:997-1001. Curran argues that Schleiermacher failed to hold these two commitments together and he cites the criticisms of F. C. Baur to corroborate his point (p. 1001). Baur's criticisms can be found in his *Die christliche Gnosis, oder die christliche Religions-Philosophie in ihrer geschichtlichen Entwicklung* (Tübingen: C. F. Osiander, 1835; repr., Darmstadt: Wissenschaftliche Buchgesellschaft, 1965), pp. 628-68. Hans Liebling gives a glimpse into the complexity of Baur's relation to Schleiermacher. See "Ferdinand Christian Baurs Kritik an Schleiermachers *Glaubenslehre*," in *Zeitschrift für Theologie und Kirche* 54 (1957): 225-43. David Friedrich Strauß accused Schleiermacher of a "double betrayal": betraying theology into the hands of philosophy and betraying philosophy into the hands of theology. *Die christliche Glaubenslehre in ihrer geschichtlichen Entwicklung und im Kampfe mit der modernen Wissenschaft dargestellt*, 2 vols. (Tübingen and Stuttgart: 1840-41), 2:176f. Both Baur and Strauß were Hegelians. The various critical interpretations of the relation of theology to philosophy in Schleiermacher's thought have been systematically explored by Felix Flückiger, *Philosophie und Theologie bei Schleiermacher* (Zollikon-Zurich: Evangelischer Verlag, 1947). Flückiger distinguishes Brunner's criticism from that of Barth by saying that the former sees in Schleiermacher's dogmatic language only a thinly disguised philosophy whereas Barth acknowledges Schleiermacher's intention to distinguish theology from philosophy but suspects that he has sacrificed much of the traditional content of dogmatics in order to make it compatible with philosophy. Ibid., pp. 13-17, 184-85. Like Flückiger, Frei finds himself in sympathy with Barth who recognizes Schleiermacher's intention but doubts whether he has pulled it off. Frei gives this description of Schleiermacher's position: "Theology is not founded on philosophy. The two are quite autonomous. Schleiermacher thinks that both moral philosophy and metaphysical philosophy lead to an idea of a transcendent ground of all being and action. But like Kant, he also believes that this inevitable idea never becomes an item for real knowledge. But we are immediately related to that same ground that is elsewhere elusive, in the experience or immediate self-consciousness of ourselves as absolutely dependent, which is the heart of religion. Thus, there is a real reciprocal relationship between philosophy and theology. At the same time, Schleiermacher insisted on the autonomy of theology from philosophy, which

cannot serve as a foundational discipline for theology." But: "Does he succeed? I'm not sure." *Types of Christian Theology*, pp. 38, 36.

126. *Gl.*, §16: "Postscript." Schleiermacher saw himself as a "dilettante" in philosophical matters and explained: "I am not at all inclined to philosophize in dogmatics." *Sendschr.*, p. 21 (*OtGl.*, p. 45). In his view, philosophy may contribute to the definiteness of the form of a dogmatic proposition, but it must not influence the content of dogmatics. *Gl.*, §17:2. He cited as his maxim the line from Virgil: *timeo Danaos et dona ferentes* ("I fear the Greeks even when they are bearing gifts"). *Sendschr.*, p. 66 (*OtGl.*, p. 87); *Aeneid* 2:49 (*LCL*, p. 296).

127. *Sendschr.*, p. 40 (*OtGl.*, p. 64). See Gerhard Spiegler, *The Eternal Covenant: Schleiermacher's Experiment in Cultural Theology* (New York: Harper and Row, 1967), who criticizes Schleiermacher's execution of his self-appointed task yet affirms the validity of his formulation of the problem. Similarly, John Clayton argues that Schleiermacher's enduring legacy is not to be sought in his own solution but, rather, in his posing of the real dilemma for a "theology of mediation": "to establish the relation between religion and culture so that genuine reciprocity exists which does not endanger the autonomy of either one." "Theologie als Vermittlung—Das Beispiel Schleiermachers," in *Internationaler Schleiermacher Kongreß*, 2:913-14. Van Harvey calls for "a refinement and extension of Schleiermacher's method" so that we should view his program for theology as "*an unfulfilled possibility* and not as an accomplishment forever witnessing to the errors following from his methodological starting point." "A Word in Defense of Schleiermacher's Theological Method," in *The Journal of Religion* 42 (July 1962): 153.

128. *Sendschr.*, p. 16 (*OtGl.*, pp. 40-41).

129. H. Richard Niebuhr has some perceptive comments about Schleiermacher's similarity to Luther in this regard. *The Meaning of Revelation* (New York: Macmillan, 1941), p. 17f. Barth asks "whether and to what extent Luther's well-known question in the cloister . . . contributed if only by way of temptation" to "an intolerable truncation of the Christian message" which "Schleiermacher's genius was to bring to its logical conclusion." *The Doctrine of Reconciliation*, vol. 4.1 of *Church Dogmatics*, trans. G. W. Bromiley (Edinburgh: T. and T. Clark, 1956), pp. 150, 153.

130. "Theology is a positive science, whose parts join into a cohesive whole only through their common relation to a particular mode of faith, i.e., a particular way of being conscious of God. Thus, the various parts of Christian theology belong together only by virtue of their relation to 'Christianity.'" *KD*, §1 (*BO*, p. 19). Heinrich Scholz explains the relation between the "ecclesial" and the "academic" elements in Schleiermacher's understanding of theology and defends Schleiermacher's practice in the light of his stated intention. *Christentum und Wissenschaft in Schleiermachers Glaubenslehre: Ein Beitrag zum Verständnis der Schleiermacherschen Theologie*, 2d ed. (Leipzig: J. C. Hinrichs'sche Buchhandlung, 1911), pp. 122-23.

Chapter 5

Schleiermacher on the Christian Faith

The Positivity of Religion

Although Schleiermacher is most often remembered for his definition of religion as the feeling of absolute dependence, it is sometimes forgotten that his efforts to clarify the *essence* of religion were intended to set the stage for a new appreciation of the concrete *manifestations* of religion in history. By itself, the essence of religion is a conceptual abstraction that allows us to identify the religious element in the religions. But, as we are told already in 1799, religion never appears alone in its essence.[1] Not only is it accompanied by the doctrines and practices with which its essence is easily confused, but each historical manifestation of religion is a distinct "individual" with a defining essence of its own. It is necessary, therefore, to identify the spirit animating a given religious community so that it may be appreciated in its uniqueness in relation to all the others. One has not interpreted Christianity, for example, simply by explaining what makes it religious; yet a further step is required to indicate what makes it distinctly Christian.

If each positive religion has an essential character of its own that distinguishes it as an individual among others, then that individuating quality can only be discerned through a method of historical study involving a comparison of one religion with another. Once the essence of a particular religious community is identified, the doctrines and morals found within it can properly be appreciated as expressing the unique spirit or idea that constitutes the core of this positive tradition. Whereas the task of identifying a religion's essence is necessarily comparative and requires that one adopt a standpoint *external* to the religious community, the task of interpreting a community's doctrines and morals as living expressions of its unique essence presupposes personal participation in that tradition and implies a standpoint *internal* to the community. The former task is the job of the comparative philosophy of religion; the latter task is the job of dogmatic theology.[2]

The assignment of this chapter is to investigate Schleiermacher's understanding of these two tasks and their relation to one another as he develops his thoughts in the *Speeches* and *The Christian Faith.* In the course of the exposition it will become apparent how Schleiermacher addresses the question of religious plurality both within the Christian church and beyond its borders. Just as his attempt at a new definition of the essence of religion sought to find a way out of the polarization of orthodoxy and rationalism, his endeavor to find a method whereby the essence of a positive religion can be identified is intended to respect the individuality of every religious tradition and to affirm the uniqueness of Christianity.

The argument of this chapter is twofold: first, Christianity, according to Schleiermacher, is an "individual" among the religions and can only be grasped as such by *historical* study that identifies its defining essence; second, Christian faith is a historically concrete way of being related to God that is available only through participation in the redemptive fellowship established by Christ. Though Christianity is one religion among several, for the Christian whose consciousness of God is formed by the redemptive influence of Jesus, piety becomes the determining factor of personal life only through faith in the gospel.

Identifying the Place of Christianity among the Religions

The fifth and final speech, entitled "On the Religions," is an unambiguous signal indicating the real direction of Schleiermacher's thought about religion.[3] There he tells his romantic readers of the new task he has to carry out: to show them "religion as it has divested itself of its infinity and appeared, often in paltry form, among human beings." This is, so to speak, religion's incarnation. He would move his readers beyond the incomplete knowledge of "a general concept of religion" to the fullness of insight when religion is understood "in its reality and in its manifestations."[4] Since religion is a mere abstraction until it assumes concrete historical form, Schleiermacher points his readers to the positive religious traditions as the place where living religion is to be found: "In the religions, you are to discover religion."[5]

The appreciation for the positivity of religion set Schleiermacher against the "natural religion" that was so popular among intellectuals in the eighteenth century. Though the romantics were engaged in a revolt against the rationalism and moralism of the age, they were more impressed with the natural religion of the Enlightenment than with the inherited ecclesiastical traditions. But to Schleiermacher's mind, so-called "natural religion" is an artificial intellectual construct through which "little of the actual character of religion shines through."[6]

> You call these existing determinate religious manifestations "positive religions," and under this name they have long been the object of a quite exquisite hatred. But in spite of all your aversion to religion generally, you have always endured ever more easily and have even spoken with esteem of something else, which is called "natural religion." I shall not hesitate to allow you a glimpse of my inner convictions on this matter, since I for my part protest most vehemently against this preference.[7]

Though the positive religions are despised by the romantics, Schleiermacher insists that they take a second look. But for some, that was asking too much. Goethe enjoyed the *Speeches* until he got to the fifth speech, whereupon he quit reading and cast the book aside in disdain.[8]

Schleiermacher's appreciation of the positivity of religions goes hand in hand with his respect for religious plurality. One of the first things that strikes a reader of the *Speeches* is the celebration of diversity in religion. Unlike Calvin, Schleiermacher does not attribute this diversity to human sinfulness; rather, he finds it to be an inescapable feature of historical existence. In this respect, the Enlightenment's assumption that the differences evident among the positive religions are the result of superstition stands in a line of continuity with the classical Protestant viewpoint: in both cases, historical diversity is regarded as a sign that the religion originally possessed by humanity has been corrupted. By contrast, Schleiermacher affirms that the multiplicity of religions is "rooted in the essence of religion."[9]

Given the myriad ways people are shaped by varying historical circumstances, it takes different forms of religion to awaken "the dormant seed" that lies in each person.[10] Religion, Schleiermacher explains, "must therefore have in itself a principle of individualization, for otherwise it could not exist at all and be perceived."[11] The whole of religion (*die ganze Religion*) can only be expressed through the totality of its manifestations.[12]

> And if religion is exhibited only in and through such determinate forms, then only the person who settles down in such a form with his own religion really establishes a firm abode and, might I say, an active citizenship in the religious world; only he can boast of contributing something to the existence and growth of the whole; only he is a truly

religious person with a character and fixed and definite traits.[13]

The positivity of religion is not the source of religion's corruption but the possibility of its concrete actualization in historical life.[14]

Yet once religious diversity is no longer seen in a negative light, a new basis has to be found for conceiving the critical factors that differentiate the religions from one another and, perhaps, even justify a claim for the relative superiority of one religion over the others. Since it is of the essence of religion to individualize itself in multiple forms, each positive religion must be approached with the question: In what form has *this* particular religion individualized itself? For that reason, the essence that defines a positive religion cannot be deduced from the essence of religion in general any more than a concrete fact can be deduced from an abstract idea. The determination of the individual character of a given religious community is a matter for comparative historical study that isolates what is distinctive in a religion from the common element it shares with others.

In seeking to uncover the essence of a positive religion, we ought to look for two things: the historical event that gave it birth and its fundamental "intuition" or way of being related to the deity.

> If a specific religion is not supposed to begin with a fact, it cannot begin at all; for there must be a basis, and it can only be a subjective one for why something is brought forth and placed at the center; and if a religion is not supposed to be a specific one, then it is not a religion at all, but merely loose, unrelated material.[15]

Along with the contingent fact of its origin, each religion emerges only "by making a particular intuition of the universe the center of the whole of religion and relating everything therein to it."

> It cannot happen otherwise, since every single intuition would have similar claims to be established. Thereby the whole suddenly takes on a determinate spirit; everything that was previously ambiguous and indeterminate is fixed. . . . [16]

The essence of a positive religion is found in the interplay of these two elements: its originating event and its central intuition. But this entails that the only way for an individual religion to arise is through free choice since there is nothing necessary either about its commencement in history or the particularity of its religious vision.

As a consequence, each positive religion is a "heresy" ("a word that should again be brought to honor") in the same sense that ancient philosophical schools were so called: "because something highly voluntary is the cause of its having arisen."[17] From the idea of religion itself, the decision to elevate one way of being religious is arbitrary; but from the perspective of those whose religion is determined by that intuition of the universe, it is a most natural expression of their being and character.

Christianity's fundamental intuition is that "of the universal straining of everything finite against the unity of the whole, and of the way in which the deity handles this striving."[18]

> Corruption and redemption, enmity and mediation, are two sides of this intuition that are inseparably bound to each other, and the shape of all religious material in Christianity and its whole form are determined through them.[19]

Seen through this lens, the world is "fallen" (*abgewichen*) from its perfection. All evil is "a consequence of the will, of the self-seeking endeavor of individual nature that everywhere tears itself loose from relationship with the whole in order to be something for itself."[20] The center of Christian concern is

> how [the deity] reconciles the enmity directed against it and sets bounds to the ever-greater distance by scattering over the whole individual points that are at once finite and infinite (*zugleich Endliches und Unendliches*), at once human and divine (*zugleich Menschliches und Göttliches*).[21]

Christianity's originating event is found in the activity of its central figure, Jesus. Of greatest importance to Schleiermacher is not the ethical teaching of Jesus ("which only expressed what all persons who have become aware of their spiritual nature have in common with him"), but the fact that he exemplified in his own soul the religious truth he proclaimed to others: "the idea that everything finite requires higher mediation in order to be connected with the divine."[22] This was the "truly divine" element (*das wahrhaft Göttliche*) in him.

> This consciousness of the uniqueness of his religiousness, of the originality of his view, and of its power to communicate itself and arouse religion was at the same time the consciousness of his office as mediator and of his divinity.[23]

That which mediates the infinite to the finite, however, cannot itself stand in need of such mediation.

> It must belong to both; it must be a part of the divine nature just as

much as and in the same sense in which it is part of the finite.[24]

Thus Jesus is "the sublime originator of what has been the most majestic in religion even to now."[25]

The Christian ideal is a complete permeation of life by religion so that "from everything finite we are to look upon the infinite." Religion should combine with every thought and every action. Thus Christianity's highest demand is that "religiousness shall be a continuum in human life." As a consequence, it is dissatisfied "even with the strongest expressions of religiousness as soon as it is supposed to pertain to and govern only certain parts of life."[26] Yet precisely the absolute character of its religious ideal allows it to detect the deep and pervasive resistance of the finite to the revelation of the infinite in its midst.

> In each moment when the religious principle cannot be perceived in the mind, the irreligious principle (*das Irreligiöse*) is thought to be dominant, for only through opposition can that which is be canceled and brought to naught. Every interruption of religion is irreligion; the mind cannot for a moment feel devoid of intuitions and feeling of the universe without at once becoming conscious of enmity and distance from it.[27]

From the perspective of this religious ideal, Christianity turns its attention to the world of religion and judges the various efforts at mediation found therein to be futile. "Every revelation is in vain," declares Schleiermacher. "Everything is swallowed up by earthly sense, everything is carried away by the indwelling irreligious principle."[28]

Christianity's insight into the resistance of the finite to the infinite accounts for its polemical nature in the common field occupied by the positive religions.

> Precisely because it presupposes an irreligious principle as widespread, and because this forms an essential part of the intuition to which everything else is related, it is thoroughly polemical. . . . Without mercy it therefore unmasks every false morality, every inferior religion, every unfortunate mixture of the two whereby their mutual nakedness is supposed to be covered; it penetrates into the innermost secrets of the corrupted heart and illuminates every evil that lurks in the darkness with the holy torch of its own experience.[29]

Since Christianity "treats religion itself as material for religion" and therein finds its most distinctive character, "it is raised to a higher power of religion."[30] Its polemical relations to non-Christian religions as well as the reformatory zeal to purify its own household result from the exacting nature of its religious ideal.

> Nowhere is religion so completely idealized as it is in Christianity by means of its original presupposition; and just for that reason continuous polemicizing against everything real in religion is simultaneously posed as a task that can never be fully and adequately achieved.[31]

Though Schleiermacher insists that "nothing is more unchristian than to seek uniformity in religion," thereby abjuring any attempt to establish Christianity as the only religion, he speaks of it, nonetheless, as "the religion of religions" (*die Religion der Religionen*) on account of its commission to pursue "an infinite holiness" (*eine unendliche Heiligkeit*) in religion itself.[32]

Far from asserting its hegemony over the other religions, Christianity has, from the start, acknowledged its transitoriness as a vehicle for mediating the infinite to the finite: "There will come a time, it declares, when there will be no more talk of a mediator, but the Father will be all in all."[33] Should the need for mediation cease, Schleiermacher confesses that he would be glad to stand on the ruins of the religion he so honors.[34] Indeed, Jesus himself understood the difference between his religion and the "school" of disciples he founded: "He never confused his school (*seine Schule*) with his religion (*mit seiner Religion*)."[35] Thus all persons are "Christians" whose religion proceeds from the same principle as his.

> People who make the same intuition the basis of their religion are Christians without regard to the school, whether their religion be derived historically from themselves or from someone else.[36]

The disciples never set limits to the work of the Holy Spirit and the holy writings of Christianity "prohibit no other book from also being or becoming Scripture (*Bibel*)" since they would gladly acknowledge their kinship with those expressing the same religion as theirs.[37]

The fifth speech closes on a note celebrating the diversity of religion, reminding readers that each religion is too limited a vehicle to become the only way in which everyone should worship the deity. To be sure, the emphasis upon the necessity of religion's positivity leads Schleiermacher to a strong affirmation of religious pluralism, since the essence of religion can never be exhausted by its finite manifestations. Still, his pluralism does not entail the consequence of relativism in religious matters. In this early work, Schleiermacher has given a description of the essence of Christianity as a positive religion that puts it in a most favorable light in relation to its contenders in the religious field.[38] If the essence of religion is defined as "sense and taste for the infinite," then the religion of Jesus mediates the infinite in spite of finite opposition. Schleiermacher's early judgment of Christianity's superiority is based on his estimate of its excellence as a vehicle for religion.

The method for clarifying the essence of a positive religious tradition is articulated with greater precision in the "Introduction" to *The Christian Faith.* The task involves four steps: first, locating a religion with respect to its *stage of development*; second, classifying a religion *typologically*; third, identifying a religion's *central idea*; and, fourth, specifying its *originating historical event.* Taken together, these four components provide the concept by means of which the distinctive element in a positive religion can be formulated. If a general definition of religion's essence is necessary for specifying what makes Christian religion "religious," the definition of Christianity's essence as a positive religion is sufficient to identify what makes Christian religion "Christian."

Schleiermacher writes:

> The various religious communities which have appeared in history
> with clearly defined limits are related to one another in two ways: as
> different stages of development and as different types.[39]

We have seen that Schleiermacher discerns three stages in the historical development of religion: idolatry (fetishism), polytheism, and monotheism. These stages represent differing attainments of a consciousness of the world as a whole. When the awareness of living in a world is fully developed, monotheism emerges as the consciousness that the totality of finite reality is absolutely dependent upon the infinite God. Thus the feeling of absolute dependence, which is the essential hallmark of piety, can only come to full clarity in monotheism. As a result, monotheism is the highest stage in the evolutionary development of religion.[40]

Just as Schleiermacher refused to identify religion with doctrines, he sought to preclude its identification with morality and he argued against the utilitarian notion that religion is important to the extent it furthers moral sensibility. Nonetheless, Schleiermacher makes a fundamental distinction between two types of positive religions: those that take the moral impulse as constitutive of their communal form of piety and those that do not. He calls the former type "teleological" because the consciousness of our absolute dependence upon God leads to an awareness of a moral responsibility in the world. The latter type he calls "aesthetic" because the consciousness of absolute dependence induces a passive posture of contemplating one's place in the world apart from an active impulse to reform the world (e.g., fatalism).[41] Unlike the aesthetic type, the teleological type of religion combines the distinctively religious element (consciousness of absolute dependence upon God) with the distinctively moral element (responsibility to shape the historical world of human society and culture).[42] Thus the feeling of absolute dependence does not negate the sense of relative freedom but, rather, enhances it.[43]

In addition to specifying a given religion according to its stage of development and its type, it is necessary to identify its originating event and its central idea.

> Each particular form of communal piety has both an outward unity, as a historical constant that proceeds from a definite beginning, and an inward unity, as a peculiar modification of that which also appears in every form of faith of the same type and at the same stage of development; and it is from both of these together that the actual essence of any given form is to be discerned.[44]

In the case of Christianity, its "outward unity" is provided by the fact that it began with the ministry of Jesus. Its "inward unity" is given by the fact that all religious elements in Christianity are related to the experience of redemption: the antithesis of sin and grace.

When these four elements are combined, it is possible to give a precise definition of the essence of Christianity as a positive religion:

> Christianity is a monotheistic mode of faith, belonging to the teleological type of piety, and essentially distinguishes itself from other such modes of faith in that everything in it is related to the redemption accomplished by Jesus of Nazareth.[45]

Christianity is thus a *monotheistic* religion with respect to its stage of development and a *teleological* religion with respect to its type, and it has *Jesus of Nazareth* as its originating event and *redemption* as its central idea.[46]

Once the essence of a postive religion has been identified by means of this fourfold scheme, it becomes possible to indicate the relations of Christianity to the other religious traditions with greater precision. This is so because Schleiermacher has indicated that, in addition to the "outward unity" provided by its originating historical event, a positive religion (or "mode of faith") receives its "inward unity" as a "peculiar modification of that which also appears in every form of faith of the same type and at the same stage of development."[47] To get at the unique element that distinguishes Christianity among the religions, therefore, it is best to compare it with other religions at the monotheistic stage and of the teleological type.

Judaism, Christianity, and Islam share the honor of standing at the highest stage of religious development as the three great monotheistic traditions. Nonetheless, Schleiermacher judges that only in Christianity is monotheism pure. Judaism exhibits an affinity with fetishism inasmuch as it is the religion of a particular nation. Islam, for its part, exhibits an affinity with polytheism inasmuch as the passionate character and the sensuous content of its religious ideas betray the influence of the sensual forces upon the religious affections that otherwise keep persons at the stage of polytheism. Since, however, Christianity avoids these failings, it is "superior to those other two forms and asserts itself as the purest form of monotheism ever to appear in history."[48]

While religions may stand on the same level developmentally, they can differ with respect to type. Thus Schleiermacher classifies Islam under the aesthetic type of religion whereas Judaism and Christianity belong to the teleological type.[49] Consequently, Christianity is most to be compared with Judaism, since both religions share in the ethical character of the teleological type whereby the monotheistic consciousness of absolute dependence leads necessarily to the consciousness of the moral task implied by our sense of relative freedom to shape the world.[50]

Two things need to be said about the monotheistic and teleological character of Christian religion. First, since Christian piety could never arise apart from a fully developed monotheistic consciousness, it was necessary that the redeemer come from a monotheistic people.[51] Moreover, the fact that Christianity's central idea is redemption presupposes the teleological type of religion since there can be no consciousness of sin apart from a consciousness of freedom. Freedom implies responsibility for the use of freedom; therefore, the inability to combine the feeling of absolute dependence with every moment of our world-consciousness is viewed as a failing for which we are held accountable. Hence, a teleological type of religion has freedom of activity as its premise and finds "guilt in all arrestments of the disposition to the God-consciousness, and merit in every progression of it."[52] By contrast, the aesthetic type of religion can dispense with the ideas of merit and guilt since it reduces every change in our experience to passive states. Therefore, all hindrances to the God-consciousness are represented as the effects of circumstances for which we are not responsible. Thus, apart from the monotheistic stage of development and the teleological type of religion, Christian faith in the redemption offered by Jesus of Nazareth is not conceivable.

Although Judaism is also a monotheistic religion of the teleological type, its defining essence is not constituted by the idea of redemption. In the *Speeches* Schleiermacher says that Judaism's basic religious intuition is that of "a universal immediate retribution, of the infinite's own reaction against every individual finite form that proceeds from free choice by acting through another finite element."

> Everything is considered this way; origin and passing away, fortune and misfortune; even within the human soul an expression of freedom and choice and an immediate influence of the deity always alternate. . . . The deity is thus portrayed throughout as rewarding, chastising, and punishing what is singled out in the individual person. . . . This whole idea is highly childlike, intended only for a small arena without complications where, in a simple entity, the natural consequences of actions are neither disturbed nor hindered.[53]

In *The Christian Faith* Schleiermacher indicates how Judaism and Christianity differ from one another in their otherwise common character as teleological religions:

> As for Judaism, then, though it relates the passive states to the active rather in the form of divine punishments and rewards than in the form of moral challenge and influence (*Aufforderungen und Bildungsmitteln*), nevertheless the predominating form of God-consciousness is that of the commanding Will; and thus, even when it proceeds from passive states, it necessarily turns to the active.[54]

Whereas Christianity expresses its teleological character through incitements to moral improvement, Judaism expresses it in the legal form of commands and rewards or punishments for obeying or disobeying its commands.[55]

Schleiermacher argues that Christianity, as a distinct religion in its own right, stands in the same relation, religiously speaking, to paganism as to Judaism, even though its historical origins are bound up with the latter. What he means is that, in both instances, the transition to Christianity is a passage to another religion. To be sure, the conversion to Christianity from paganism appears to be greater on account of the latter's polytheism; but this consideration obscures the fact that monotheism was already anticipated in much Graeco-Roman philosophy and that embracing the gospel was for pagans simultaneously a conversion to monotheism. And, of course, it must be remembered that conversion to Christianity required of Jews an abrogation of the Mosaic legislation and a reinterpretation of the Jewish scriptures so that Abraham's faith is now understood as a prototype of distinctively Christian faith (e.g., Rom 4:1f., Gal 3:6-9).[56]

Indeed, the apostle Paul represents the relations of Jews and pagans to Christ as being exactly the same: "in Christ" each one becomes "a new creation" as regards religion (e.g., Rom 2:11-12, 3:21-24, 2 Cor 5:16-17). This means that the "nobler and purer" pagan philosophy stands in an analogous relation to Judaism as far as Christianity is concerned: as preparation for and anticipation of something new in the religious realm that cannot be derived solely from its historical antecedents. "If [Christianity] stands in the same relation to Judaism as to Paganism, then it can no more be regarded as a continuation of Judaism than of Paganism."[57] With respect to both, Christianity represents a new religious formation with its own distinctive essence.

These judgments are a continuation of thoughts Schleiermacher developed in the fifth speech, where he said that with respect to the two original historical contexts (Judaism and paganism) in which it made its first appearance, the Christian religion worked polemically to restore a purer religion among people. Hence, he can say that the first Christians offended their Jewish contemporaries by insisting that the only restoration they should expect is that of a purer religion. As far as the pagans are concerned, Christianity led them out of the separation they had made between the world of the gods and the world of human beings. It recovered the inner consciousness of "living, moving, and having one's being" in the being of God, a consciousness that had been buried under a mass of sensible impressions and desires.[58] In both instances, Christianity worked for a purer religion.

In the "Introduction," however, Schleiermacher goes beyond what he had said in the fifth speech about Christianity's essence.[59] Previously he had distinguished the religion of Jesus from his "school." But now the redeemer and redemption are indissolubly linked together: "Only through Jesus, and thus only in Christianity, has redemption become the central point of religion."[60]

> Our proposition sets forth two points in this regard that distinguish Christianity from all other religious communities. First, that these two, the incapacity and the redemption, together constitute not merely one religious element among others but rather that all the religious affections are related to these. Therefore, these two are posited in all the others as the very thing which makes them truly Christian. Second, redemption is posited as something that has universally and perfectly been brought about by Jesus. And these two points are not to be separated but rather essentially belong together.[61]

Christianity is thus distinguished from every other religion in that the redemption accomplished by Christ is the central fact to which all religious affections are referred.

The comparative philosophy of religion allows one to make some judgments regarding the relative superiority of Christianity as a religion among others.[62] As a monotheistic religion, it stands at the highest stage of development. With respect to its competitors at this highest developmental stage, however, it is superior to both Judaism and Islam because monotheism is not pure in these two religions. Moreover, the fact that Christianity is constituted by the idea of "redemption" makes the concern for purity of religion central, which accounts for its polemical nature with respect to other religious traditions and its reformatory zeal within Christendom itself.

Christian Faith according to the Principles of the Protestant Church

Since the essence of a positive religion cannot be deduced from the essence of religion in general any more than a concrete fact can be deduced from an abstract idea, the determination of the individual character of a given religious community is a matter for comparative historical study that isolates what is distinctive in a religion from the common element it shares with others. The task of defining the essence of Christianity, therefore, is a "critical" endeavor since it is neither purely speculative (i.e., working with concepts in abstraction from empirical realities) nor purely empirical (i.e., working with facts apart from any concern for conceptual analysis).[63]

Unlike the critical task of defining the essence which requires that one adopt a standpoint "above" Christianity, the dogmatic task presupposes personal participation in that religious community since its task is the description of a fact of inward experience.[64] Dogmatics discerns the coherence between the Christian religious affections and their intellectual expression in doctrine and their practical expression in morals. Although religion itself is feeling and should not, therefore, be confused with doctrines and morals, these can be properly appreciated as giving expression in knowledge and praxis to the particular way religious feeling has constituted itself in a positive religious community.[65] Dogmatic theology thus has two parts: *Glaubenslehre* is disciplined reflection upon Christian doctrine and *Sittenlehre* is disciplined reflection upon Christian ethics.[66]

Doctrines (*Glaubenssätze*) are "accounts of the Christian religious affections set forth in speech."[67] The one source of Christian doctrine is the preaching of Jesus himself as this is communicated through the church's proclamation.[68] Dogmatics has reference to this preaching and presupposes faith in the redeemer that this preaching evokes. Dogmatics works with the doctrinal expressions of the religious affections produced by the religious community itself and aims to discern their logical coherence with one another by identifying their origins in the Christian religious affections. As the final part of historical theology, dogmatics is disciplined inquiry into the "coherence" (*Zusammenhang*) of a church's doctrine in the present time.[69]

Since dogmatics works only with doctrines arising from the Christian religious affections, the purpose of setting forth a clear statement of the essence of Christian piety is to safeguard the genuinely ecclesiastical material by excluding the "heretical" (in the negative sense).[70] There are four "natural heresies" that contradict the essence of Christianity: the Docetic and the Nazarean, the Manichean and the Pelagian.

> If, in truth, the distinctive essence of Christianity consists in the fact that all religious emotions are related to the redemption accomplished by Jesus of Nazareth, then there will be two ways for heresy to arise. . . . [E]ither human nature will be defined in such a way that a redemption in the strict sense is not possible or the redeemer will be so defined that he cannot accomplish redemption.[71]

With respect to redemption, it must be posited that human beings both stand in need of redemption and are capable of receiving it; with respect to the redeemer, it must be posited that he is both absolutely superior to all other persons by virtue of his God-consciousness and that there is, nonetheless, an essential likeness between him and those to whom he imparts redemption. With respect to redemption, therefore, heresy can assume one of two forms: the denial that human beings stand in need of redemption is "Pelagian," whereas the denial that they are capable of receiving it is "Manichean." With respect to the redeemer, heresy can also assume one of two forms: the denial that Jesus is absolutely superior to all others with respect to his God-consciousness is "Nazarean," whereas the denial that there is an essential likeness between him and other persons is "Docetic."

Within the boundaries of the genuinely ecclesiastical established by the essence of Christianity, there are two questions to be answered before Schleiermacher can give a dogmatic description of "the Christian faith according to the fundamental principles of the Protestant church."[72] First, what is the distinctive essence of Protestantism? And, second, what is the relation between the two major branches of the Reformation (the Lutheran and the Reformed)?

Modern Protestants must take account of the fact that, contrary to the intentions of the Reformers themselves, the Reformation created yet another ecclesiastical tradition in the West next to Catholicism. For Schleiermacher, this means that the Reformation cannot be understood simply as a purification of abuses in the church. It must also be viewed as having brought into being a "distinctive form" of the Christian communion. Hence, not everything that differentiates Catholicism from Protestantism is the result of corruption; it has to be admitted that some things alien to Protestants but not to Catholics are simply the expression of a different form of Christian faith. But "difference" in this sense need not call forth a polemical response.

The actual antithesis between Catholicism and Protestantism is important for Schleiermacher only as it pertains to doctrine and this antithesis, he believes, has not affected the whole range of Christian teaching. He gives this provisional formulation of the antithesis:

> [Protestantism] makes the individual's relation to the church dependent on his relation to Christ, while [Catholicism] reverses the relation and makes the relation of the individual to Christ dependent on his relation to the church.[73]

Note that the antithesis focuses on the doctrine of the church. Whereas Catholics charge Protestants with undermining the communal foundations of Christianity in favor of a religious individualism, Protestants charge Catholics with putting the church in Christ's proper place. But in neither case is the extreme reached, so that Schleiermacher considers both churches to be genuine, albeit different, expressions of the essence of Christianity.[74] To be sure, this view of the antithesis between the two Western churches is very irenic in its ecumenism and Schleiermacher looks forward to the day when the antithesis will disappear, as he is certain it must.[75] But in the meantime there can be no general *Christian* dogmatics that does not pitch its tent in one of the two camps.[76]

Schleiermacher has a "progressive" view of the Reformation. He rejects the idea that there was some pure period in the apostolic age to which Protestantism might return, even if such a thing were possible. But such a return is never possible, since "that which once was never returns at a later time in quite the same form as previously." The apostolic age cannot be recovered, in part, because the political and religious conditions (e.g., relations to Judaism and paganism) no longer exist; moreover, Protestantism has achieved a precision in its dogmatic formulations that was not the case in earlier periods of Christianity. There may, indeed, be analogues to Protestantism in earlier phases of the church's history, but as a phenomenon with its own form it did not exist.

All of which is to say that Schleiermacher's view of history is forward-looking, not backward-looking. As an individual formation of the common Christian spirit, the unique essence of Protestantism cannot be deduced from the general essence of Christianity any more than the essence of Christianity can be deduced from the general essence of religion. History produces individuals and a genuinely historical approach to theology must take account of these with due appreciation.[77] But this means, as was mentioned earlier, that, from the perspective of hindsight, the Reformation was not simply an attempt at a purification of abuses. It must also be understood and appreciated as bringing forth a distinctive formation of the common essence of Christianity shared by both Western churches.[78]

The confessional issue was posed anew when the Reformed King Friedrich Wilhelm III announced to the Prussian church authorities in 1817 that he wished to receive the sacrament of the Lord's Supper together with his Lutheran wife during the service marking the three-hundredth anniversary of the Reformation. As a result the Prussian "Union" of Lutheran and Reformed churches was born. Schleiermacher enthusiastically endorsed the Union and did his part to facilitate mutual understanding between the confessions. In this spirit he wrote his *Glaubenslehre*, intending it as a dogmatics for the united church that would express the common faith of Protestants and not merely the viewpoint of his own Reformed tradition.[79] As he put it:

> Thus it starts from the presupposition that the division of both [viz., Lutherans and Reformed] is not well-founded insofar as their doctrinal differences can in no way be traced back to a difference in the religious affections themselves, and both churches do not diverge from one another either in their morals and moral doctrine or in their constitution in any way that reflects those doctrinal differences.[80]

As a result, Schleiermacher looks upon these divergences in doctrine as "a matter of school" (*eine Sache der Schule*), i.e., Reformed versus Lutheran *school*.[81]

When Schleiermacher wrote his dogmatics, there was much confusion regarding doctrinal matters within the Protestant church of the union. Not only was there the older confessional divide between the two major branches of the Reformation but also the more recent confrontation between rationalists and supernaturalists. Moreover, the conflict between supernaturalists and rationalists cut across confessional lines, so that each church was rent by the issues raised for

Protestant theology by the Enlightenment.

Schleiermacher uses the word "revelation" with great circumspection because of its many misleading associations, chief among these being the idea that doctrines themselves are revealed.[82] Nonetheless, he affirms that Jesus, in his perfect God-consciousness, is a "revelation" of God. Schleiermacher understands the revelation in Christ to be, simultaneously, a natural act, insofar as the natural process is not abrogated, as well as a supernatural act, insofar as Christ's perfect God-consciousness is not explicable by antecedent historical factors. He declares that "special revelation does not need to be absolutely supernatural."[83] Furthermore, "The appearance of the redeemer in history is, as divine revelation, neither something absolutely supernatural nor something absolutely supra-rational."[84] In other words, while the appearance of Christ transcends the realms of nature and reason, it does not violate them. This perfect God-consciousness is what distinguishes Jesus from all other human beings and it is this distinctive feature that was "an actual being of God in him" (*ein eigentliches Sein Gottes in ihm*).[85]

Redemption is brought about through the communication of Jesus' sinless perfection.[86] This communication occurs through participation in the new community he established. Consequently, the relation betweeen Christ and the church is a most intimate one, since in the church Christ continues his historical activity in the present. In the church, in place of the personal encounter with him that the original disciples had, we have the portrait (*Bild*) of Jesus that his early followers transmitted to us through the scriptures. Nonetheless, the faith evoked in us through the church's preaching of the biblical portrait of Christ is the same faith evoked in the original disciples by means of his personal activity among them.[87]

Christ is the "second Adam" since he completes human nature and, in this way, introduces a "new creation."[88]

> For this second Adam is just like all those who are descended from the first, except for the fact that he has been endowed with an absolutely powerful God-consciousness. As such, he enters into the existing historical process of human nature by virtue of a creative divine causality. And according to the law of this process, his perfection must work in a stimulating and communicative way upon the same [human] nature: first, so that by comparison it may bring the consciousness of sinfulness to perfection, and, second, that by assimilation it may then overturn our misery.[89]

Just as the "first Adam" constituted the physical life of the human race, so the "second Adam" constitutes the new spiritual life of the race.[90]

Redemption is thus the completion of human nature.[91] Through Christ the divine causality is directed toward the creation and preservation of free persons in whom the God-consciousness becomes the determining principle of all their relations to the world.[92]

Schleiermacher's dogmatics is divided in two parts: the description of the antithesis of sin and grace (Part Two) and the description of the God-consciousness presupposed by and contained in the experience of redemption through Christ (Part One).

> The distinctive feature of Christian piety lies in the fact that whatever alienation from God there is in the phases of our experience, we are conscious of it as an action originating in ourselves, which we call sin; but whatever fellowship with God there is, we are conscious of it as resting upon a communication from the Redeemer, which we call Grace.[93]

But, as Schleiermacher explains, "the antithesis between the inability to combine all moments of life with the feeling of absolute dependence and the ability to do so communicated to us by the redeemer already presupposes that feeling itself and a knowledge of the same."[94]

> Therefore the condition that precedes the communicated ability can be neither absolute God-forgetfulness nor even the mere empty striving after God-consciousness, but rather [God-consciousness] must somehow be given in self-consciousness.[95]

The ideal of human existence is that there be an "absolute ease in the development of the God-consciousness from every given stimulus and in every condition" or, in other words, "constant communion with God."[96] The ideal, however, never constitutes by itself a moment of actual experience in the life of a Christian. Actual experience is constituted either by the painful awareness of our inability to feel absolutely dependent in each moment or by pleasure at the redeemer's communication of this ability to us.[97]

> [I]n the reality of the Christian life, both are always linked to one another: there is no general consciousness of God apart from a relation to Christ, and there is no relationship with the Redeemer which has no relation to the general consciousness of God.[98]

In the Christian religious experience, the generally human relation to God and the specifically Christian relation to Christ are inextricably bound up with one another.

In Schleiermacher's account, the doctrines of creation and

preservation give expression to the consciousness that "the totality of finite being exists only in dependence upon the Infinite."[99] Schleiermacher develops his doctrines of creation and preservation as elaborations of the feeling of absolute dependence given in human self-consciousness itself.[100] Abstracted from the pleasure-pain continuum of actual experience, the doctrines of creation and preservation present the bare outlines of the religious consciousness apart from the issue of hindrance to or facility of the God-consciousness to combine with every moment of our world-consciousness. By themselves, they are "empty frames" waiting to be filled in by the content of Part Two.[101]

Schleiermacher states that we ought not to seek the characteristic element of sin except in relation to the God-consciousness.[102] Consequently, we may define sin as everything "that has hindered the free development of the God-consciousness." A sinful God-consciousness does not belong to the *essence* of human nature but is, rather, a *disturbance (Störung)* of that nature. The fact that guilt accompanies the sinful self-consciousness is a confirmation of this claim that a perfect God-consciousness is not incompatible with the essence of human nature.[103] If we had an absolutely perfect God-consciousness, then in every moment wherein we are conscious of ourselves as either acting upon the world or being acted upon by the world, we would always be conscious simultaneously of our and the world's absolute dependence upon God. Sin is the inability to be conscious of our absolute dependence in every moment, an inability for which the human being is responsible and, hence, guilty.[104] As such, sin is a derangement of our nature.[105] Hence, the consciousness of sin is itself "a bad conscience" since we know of the demand to conform all moments to the God-consciousness.[106]

In connection with the disruption of the God-consciousness, the human being looks out upon the world and finds many hindrances to life. These external hindrances are perceived as evils, whether they be "natural" evils or "social" (i.e., moral) evils that arise from human actions. Without sin, nothing in the world would, properly speaking, be considered an evil, including the inevitable features of finite existence. Hence, it is not death itself but, rather, the fear of death that keeps us in bondage.[107] "The world appears differently to the human being," Schleiermacher writes, "than it otherwise would if there were no sin."[108] Accordingly, the extent to which the world appears evil is the extent to which we are sinful. In this view, sin is the original fact and evil is the derived perception of the world by a sinful self-consciousness. Misfortune is experienced by the sinful self-consciousness as punishment for sin; but without sin, not even the so-called natural "evils" would appear to be such. They would be seen merely as hindrances to our life in the world. But the fact that we experience them as punishments is the result of our sin. Hence, evil does not give rise to sin but, rather, sin gives rise to evil.[109]

On the basis of our consciousness of sin, God is perceived as holy and just. We perceive God as holy because our conscience testifies that all actions emanating from the God-consciousness confront us as moral demands.[110] The conscience respects God's will, expressed in the moral demand, as absolutely holy. We are conscious of God as holy when we experience our absolute dependence upon God in the emergence of conscience. We say that God is just in virtue of the connection that exists between sin and evil. Justice is the attribute of God by which we understand our absolute dependence on God in the perception of the world's evil as a punishment for our sin. The connection between sin and evil, therefore, is the consciousness of punishment and this is the result of God's justice, even as conscience is the result of God's holiness.[111]

The work of Christ consists in his activity as redeemer and reconciler. Whereas Christ's redemptive activity is his assumption of believers into the power of his own God-consciousness, his reconciling activity consists in assuming us into the fellowship of his blessedness.[112] This means, principally, that the hindrances we experience in the realms of our social and natural life are no longer perceived as punishments for our sin. "Being received into living fellowship with Christ," Schleiermacher explains, "dissolves the connection between evil and sin, inasmuch as the two are no longer morally related to each other, even if, naturally considered, the one is a consequence of the other."[113] Hence, the reconciliation Christ brings does away with the consciousness of deserving God's punishment and precisely this is the blessedness of Christ in which believers share.

Since the essence of redemption consists in a new power of the God-consciousness through the activity of Christ, the believer may be said to be a "new person." Schleiermacher takes the term "regeneration" to indicate the turning-point whereby the new life may properly be said to have come into being. "Sanctification," on the other hand, expresses the growing strength of the new God-consciousness in relation to the "old life" of the enfeebled God-consciousness. Regeneration points to the act of union with Christ whereas sanctification points to the state of union with Christ.[114]

Regeneration includes within itself the notions of conversion and justification. Conversion is the origin of faith, whereas faith as an enduring state of mind (*Gemütszustand*) is the basis of the new life. Schleiermacher defines "faith" as an "appropriation" (*Aneignung*) or as a "taking possession" (*Besitzergreifung*) of Christ.[115] Schleiermacher begins by defining "conversion" as "the start of the new life in fellowship with Christ" and he states that it "makes itself known in each individual through repentance, which consists in the bond of regret and change of heart and through faith, which consists in the appropriation of the perfection and blessedness of Christ."[116]

Justification is both the remission of sins and the recognition of the believer as a child of God.[117] Justification is a consciousness of forgiveness; as faith apprehends Christ, one is conscious of being a child of God. "Forgiveness of sins," Schleiermacher writes, "expresses the end of the old state, as does repentance, just as being a child of God expresses the character of the new, as does faith."[118] In the sinful self-consciousness, the individual has no relation to God except as one who is guilty. But when fellowship with Christ begins, the consciousness of sin disappears and is replaced by a consciousness of forgiveness. We cannot, moreover, embrace Christ through faith without inheriting his own sonship in relation to God along with him.[119]

Sanctification expresses the new life of the believer in fellowship with Christ, whereby "the natural powers of the regenerate are put at [Christ's] disposal, whence a life similar to his perfection and blessedness constitutes itself."[120] Sanctification is a process through time, stretching from the moment of regeneration and aiming at a purer harmony with Christ. Schleiermacher suggests that "regeneration is to be regarded as the divine act of union with human nature and sanctification as the state of that union."[121] And although there remain in the life of believers battles with the old sinful nature, the decisive victory has already been won. Still, the difference between Christ and ourselves remains unaltered: whereas Christ's God-consciousness developed in an uninterrupted progression in unison with his lower faculties, in our case sin has already had, so to speak, a life of its own.

In the light of redemption, the divine causality upon which we are absolutely dependent presents itself to us as love and wisdom. In the state of redemption, believers understand themselves as the object of the divine love, just as they understand the development and extension of the church as the object of the divine government.[122] The *telos* of the Christian church is to effect recognition of the world as a good place, thereby making the entire world an organ for the divine Spirit.

> The divine wisdom, as the unfolding of love, leads us into the realm of Christian ethics, for we are presented with the task of gaining ever more recognition of the world as a good world and of making all things into an organ of the divine Spirit in accordance with the divine idea originally underlying the world-order, thereby bringing it into relation with the system of redemption.[123]

Schleiermacher speaks of the world as a "theatre of redemption" and as a revelation of God, wherein lies its goodness.[124] In traditional terms, redemption effects the recognition that the world shows forth God's glory. This recognition leads to the ethical task of Christian faith since Christian ethics, in his view, is based upon the consciousness of being redeemed.[125] On this basis, the ethical task of the Christian is to promote the Kingdom of God so that all persons may participate in Christ's redemption.

From the perspective of redemption, God may be spoken of either as "loving omnipotence" or as "omnipotent love." There is, moreover, no other attribute that can be so thoroughly equated with the being of God as love.[126] Wisdom, too, can claim to express the divine essence itself, although it is never used in quite the same way as is love to describe God's being. Wisdom, as an attribute, is based on God's love since "wisdom is the perfection of love."[127] Where one posits omnipotent love, there one must also speak of divine wisdom. The divine wisdom is the way God orders the world so as to bring about redemption, which is the aim of God's wisdom.[128] Apart from redemption, the divine causality upon which we are absolutely dependent cannot be seen either as wise or loving. In this precise sense, then, the doctrines of creation and preservation are "empty frames" waiting to be filled with content.

> To be sure, an omnipotence, whose aim and motive I do not know, an omniscience about which I do not know how it considers and values the objects of its knowledge, an omnipresence, of which I do not know what it radiates and attracts to itself, are unspecific and barely living representations. It is quite different, however, when omnipotence makes itself known in the consciousness of the new spiritual creation, when omnipresence makes itself known in the activity of the divine Spirit, and when omniscience makes itself known in the consciousness of divine grace and goodwill.[129]

Redemption, in other words, effects a change in our perception whereby we become conscious of the world as a divine revelation of God's love and wisdom that sustain and redeem us.

Summary

The results of this study of Schleiermacher's theology can be summarized by reiterating the four major points advanced and substantiated by exegesis in these two chapters. First, for Schleiermacher, the essence of religion is neither assent to metaphysical doctrines nor adherence to a moral code but, rather, the feeling of absolute dependence. Second, the feeling of absolute dependence becomes a consciousness of being in relation to God as the infinite "Whence" of finite existence when our consciousness of living in a world of relative freedom and relative dependence is fully developed. Third, Christianity is an individual formation among the positive religions which can only be appreciated as such by historical study that identifies its defining essence by comparison with that of the other positive religions. Finally, Christian faith is a historically concrete way of being related to God that is available only through participation in Jesus' perfect consciousness of God which is mediated through the church's preaching.

Schleiermacher's early crisis of faith led to a new formulation of the experiential understanding of religion he had first learned among the pietists. After the dramatic confrontation with Enlightenment rationalism had called into question the adequacy of the orthodox doctrinal apparatus of his youth, Schleiermacher's encounter with romanticism gave him the categories with which to reframe the problem of religion and modern knowledge. His reformulation of religion as feeling, moreover, enabled him to develop an understanding of Christian theology as a positive discipline whose task is to reflect critically upon a historically particular religious experience.

Schleiermacher's interpretation of religion and theology moved decisively beyond the stalemate of orthodox supernaturalism and enlightened rationalism that had occasioned his efforts to set a new course for Protestant theology in the modern world.[130] In particular, his appreciation for the necessary plurality of religions broke with the older view, shared by orthodox and rationalist alike, that diversity in religion is a sign of religion's degeneration from its original purity. Nonetheless, Schleiermacher was firmly convinced, as he believed every Christian believer must be, that faith in Christ empowers the otherwise feeble God-consciousness with a new vitality that comes as a gift of divine grace. As such, the revelation in Christ actualizes the possibility of piety originally given with human self-consciousness, thereby completing the creation of human nature.

NOTES

1. *Reden*, 1:43 (Crouter, p. 21).
2. "Philosophy of religion" (*Religionsphilosophie*) is a non-theological discipline that properly belongs within the humanistic curriculum of the university. When this discipline is employed in connection with theology, it

pertains to what Schleiermacher calls "philosophical theology," the task of which is to define the "essence of Christianity." *Gl.* §2; *KD* §6, 23-24, 43.

3. "If one wants to arrive at an understanding of the *Speeches* at all, one must proceed from its last part." Albrecht Ritschl, *Schleiermachers Reden über die Religion und ihre Nachwirkungen auf die evangelische Kirche Deutschlands* (Bonn: Adolph Markus, 1974), p. 4.

4. *Reden*, 1:239, 242-43 (Crouter, pp. 96-97). The allusion is to John 1:14 which Schleiermacher later described as "the basic text for all dogmatics." *Sendschr.*, p. 34 (*OtGl.*, p. 59). On the Johannine character of the *Speeches*, see Giovanni Moretto, "Angezogen und belehrt von Gott: Der Johannismus in Schleiermachers *Reden über die Religion*," in *Theologische Zeitschrift* 37 (September/October 1981): 267-91.

5. *Reden*, 1:239 (Crouter, p. 96).

6. *Reden*, 1:244 (cf. Crouter, p. 98, who translates *eigenthümlich* as "unique."). See Forstman's discussion in *A Romantic Triangle*, pp. 75-78.

7. *Reden*, 1:243 (Crouter, p. 98).

8. Redeker, p. 49. "Schleiermacher has come full circle returning to one of the major objections of his readers, for the cultured despisers were alienated from the visible forms of religion and from institutional Christianity in particular." Forstman, p. 75.

9. *Reden*, 1:241 (Crouter, p. 97).

10. Diversity insures "that each person may seek out religion in a form that is congenial to the slumbering bud *(dem schlummernden Keim)* that lies in him." *Reden*, 1:240 (Crouter, p. 96).

11. *Reden*, 1:242 (Crouter, p. 97).

12. *Reden*, 1:256 (Crouter, p. 104); also *Reden*, 1:247 (Crouter, p. 100). This does not mean, as Piper points out, that the essence of religion is to be understood as the sum of all the concrete religions: "The religions of the fifth speech are not parts of one never-to-be-completed religion, but are individual formations of the one principle that must always be fully present in all of them." *Das religiöse Erlebnis*, p. 17.

13. *Reden*, 1:257 (Crouter, p. 104).

14. An appreciation for religion's positivity was also expressed, in differing ways, by both Kant and Hegel. See Kant, *Religion Within the Limits of Reason Alone*, pp. 91-114; also Hegel, *On Christianity: Early Theological Writings*, trans. T. M. Knox (Chicago: The University of Chicago Press, 1948; repr., New York: Harper and Row, 1961), pp. 67-181.

15. *Reden*, 1:271 (Crouter, p. 110).

16. *Reden*, 1:256 (Crouter, p. 104). This lack of a determinate character is at the heart of Schleiermacher's criticism of natural religion: "If you boast that natural religion accords its adherents more freedom to form themselves *(sich bilden)* religiously according to their own inclinations, then I can imagine your boast meaning nothing else than . . . the freedom to remain unformed *(ungebildet)*." *Reden*, 1:267 (Crouter, p. 108); "Thus natural religion is also the worthy product of an age whose hobbyhorse was a lamentable generality and an empty sobriety, which, more than anything else, works against true cultivation *(Bildung)* in all things." *Reden*, 1:270 (Crouter, p. 110). Hence, his subsequent

argument for the positivity of religion is based on the same premise with which
he initially asked his interlocutors to reconsider religion's essence: the romantic
ideal of individual self-cultivation in all things pertaining to humanity. Just as
individual persons are always unique in their concrete specificity, so too are
individual religions!

17. *Reden*, 1:257 (Crouter, p. 104). In Greek a *hairesis* originally meant a
"sect" or a "philosophical school" before acquiring its Christian connotation as
a departure from the truth. In 1821 he clarified the analogy: "It must be a bad
philosophical system indeed that has not caught some truly philosophic
element, and in some way sought to refer to it all other elements. The same
holds of the positive religions, and we may conclude that if they were all
developed there would be contained in the sum of them the whole religion of
the human race." *Reden*, p. 294, n. 7 (Oman, p. 257). See Peter L. Berger, *The
Heretical Imperative: Contemporary Possibilities of Religious Affirmation*
(Garden City: Anchor Press/Doubleday, 1979), esp. pp. 125-56, for a creative
development of this aspect of Schleiermacher's thought.

18. *Reden*, 1:278 (Crouter, p. 115).
19. *Reden*, 1:278 (Crouter, p. 115).
20. *Reden*, 1:278 (Crouter, p. 116).
21. *Reden*, 1:278 (Crouter, p. 115).
22. *Reden*, 1:283-84 (Crouter, pp. 119-20).
23. *Reden*, 1:284 (Crouter, p. 120). The Johannine character of
Schleiermacher's christology is already apparent in the *Speeches*, since John's
gospel, for Schleiermacher, is the only source from which a coherent picture of
the inner life of Jesus can be formed. The historical veracity of John is defended
in a note added in 1821: *Reden*, pp. 297-98 (Oman, pp. 262-63). New Testament
scholarship would eventually move in a direction contrary to that of
Schleiermacher, however. On the difference between John and the Synoptics as
sources for understanding the life of Jesus, he wrote: "There is only *one* real
difference in kind. The Gospel of John is, namely, in quite a different sense a
continuous narrative; the three others are far more aggregations of individual
narratives." *The Life of Jesus*, trans. S. Maclean Gilmour, edited with an
introduction by Jack C. Verheyden, Lives of Jesus Series, ed. Leander E. Keck
(Philadelphia: Fortress Press, 1975), p. 37; originally published as *Das Leben
Jesu. Vorlesungen an der Universität zu Berlin im Jahr 1832*, ed. K. A. Rütenik
(Berlin: Georg Reimer, 1864). Albert Schweitzer says that the value of
"Schleiermacher's Life of Jesus . . . lies in the sphere of dogmatics, not of
history. Nowhere, indeed, is it so clear that the great dialectician had not really
a historical mind than precisely in his treatment of the history of Jesus. . . .
Scheiermacher is not in search of the historical Jesus, but of the Jesus Christ of
his own system of theology; that is to say, of the historic figure which seems to
him appropriate to the self-consciousness of the redeemer as he represents it."
"What is chiefly fatal to a sound historical view is his one-sided preference for
the Fourth Gospel. It is, according to him, only in this Gospel that the
consciousness of Jesus is truly reflected." *The Quest of the Historical Jesus*,
with a new introduction by James M. Robinson (New York: Macmillan, 1968),
pp. 62, 66. For a very good critical analysis of the problematic relation of the

dogmatic and the historical elements in Schleiermacher's christology, see Brent
W. Sockness, "The Ideal and the Historical in the Christology of Wilhelm
Hermann: The Promise and the Perils of Revisionary Christology," in *The
Journal of Religion* 72 (July 1992): 372-77.

24. *Reden*, 1:284 (Crouter, p. 120).

25. *Reden*, 1:283 (Crouter, p. 119).

26. *Reden*, 1:282 (Crouter, p. 118). "[A]n uninterrupted sequence of
religious emotions can be required of us, as indeed Scripture actually requires
it." *Gl.*, §5.5 (*CF*, p. 24).

27. *Reden*, 1:282 (Crouter, p. 118): "Religion is never supposed to rest, and
nothing is to be so absolutely opposed to it that it cannot also exist with it
concurrently."

28. *Reden*, 1:279 (Crouter, p. 116).

29. *Reden*, 1:279-80 (Crouter, pp. 116-17). Schleiermacher paints a grim
picture of the religious situation: "The moral world is progressing from bad to
worse; being incapable of producing something in which the spirit of the
universe really would live, it darkens the understanding; having departed from
the truth, it corrupts the heart; and being devoid of any praise before God, it has
extinguished the image (*das Ebenbild*) of the infinite in every part of finite
nature." *Reden*, 1:278 (Crouter, p. 116).

30. *Reden*, 1:279 (Crouter, p. 116).

31. *Reden*, 1:280-81 (Crouter, p. 117). Polemics toward other religions does
not, however, prevent Christianity from acknowledging "in all distortions and
degenerations . . . the heavenly seed of religion (*den himmlischen Keim der
Religion*)." *Reden*, 1:280 (Crouter, p. 117). Even the contentious internal history
of Christianity is "rooted in its nature." *Reden*, 1:281 (Crouter, p. 118).

32. *Reden*, 1:290, 281 (Crouter, pp. 123, 117). This idea approximates
Tillich's notion of the "Protestant principle" which he interprets as "an
expression of the conquest of religion by the Spiritual Presence and
consequently an expression of the victory over the ambiguities of religion, its
profanization, and its demonization. . . . It is the expression of the victory of the
Spirit over religion." *Systematic Theology*, 3:245. In his own way, Barth makes
the same point by insisting that human religion must be judged and redeemed
by divine revelation: "The abolishing of religion by revelation need not mean
only its negation: the judgment that religion is unbelief. Religion can just as
well be exalted in revelation, even though the judgment still stands. It can be
upheld by it and concealed in it. It can be justified by it, and—we must at once
add—sanctified. Revelation can adopt religion and mark it off as true religion.
And it not only can. How do we come to assert that it can, if it has not already
done so? There is a true religion: just as there are justified sinners. If we abide
strictly by that analogy . . . we need have no hesitation in saying that the
Christian religion is the true religion." *Church Dogmatics*, 1.2, p. 326.

33. *Reden*, 1:288-89 (Crouter, p. 122); 1 Cor 15:28.

34. *Reden*, 1:289 (Crouter, p. 122).

35. *Reden*, 1:285 (cf. Crouter, p. 121: "[H]e never confused his school with
a religion.").

36. *Reden*, 1:286 (Crouter, p. 121).

37. *Reden*, 1:286 (Crouter, p. 121).

38. Hermann Süskind writes: "There is no doubt that with all these statements Schleiermacher gives more (and intends to give more) than just an analysis of the essence of Christianity; they contain at the same time a historical-philosophical demonstration of the superiority of Christianity in relation to all other religions by means of a comparative investigation of the history of religions." *Christentum und Geschichte bei Schleiermacher. Die geschichtsphilosophischen Grundlagen der Schleiermacherschen Theologie, Erster Teil: Die Absolutheit des Christentums und die Religionsphilosophie* (Tübingen: J. C. B. Mohr [Paul Siebeck], 1911), p. 25. In response to Brunner's charge that a non-Christian concept of religion determines Schleiermacher's theology, Gerrish replies: "Naturally, a great many problems remain even if we decline to veto in advance, like Brunner, any attempt to place Christianity among the religions; for the theologian will still inquire whether, in practice, Schleiermacher holds the Word in bondage to a general theory of religion, while the historian of religion may suspect that actually it is Schleiermacher's Christian faith that determines his concept of religion." "Continuity and Change," p. 196f., n. 61.

39. *Gl.*, §7.

40. "Those forms of piety in which all pious affections express the dependence of everything finite upon a highest and infinite being, that is, the monotheistic forms, occupy the highest level, and all others are related to them as subordinate, from which the human being is destined to move over into those higher ones." *Gl.*, §8. Whereas idolatry, polytheism, and monotheism are distinct stages of religious development on account of their differing attainments of self-consciousness, the same cannot be said of theism, deism, and pantheism which are different modes of "representation" of the monotheistic consciousness. Thus the decision to be made between these three forms of representation is: Which best represents the feeling of absolute dependence as a consciousness of God? *Gl.*, §8.2 and "Postscript" 2.

41. The crucial difference is whether the natural or passive states are subordinated to the moral or active states (teleological) or whether the moral or active states are subordinated to the natural or passive states (aesthetic). *Gl.*, §9.

42. Süskind says that, although Schleiermacher does not explicitly claim that the teleological type is superior to the aesthetic type, it is implied in his philosophical position. *Christentum und Geschichte*, 1:2-3, 54-59.

43. A contemporary analogue to this distinction is found in the recent constructive theology of Gordon D. Kaufman who writes: "[T]here has been a great divide among human civilizations between these two fundamentally distinct perspectives: those which have taken structure/order/being as primary, an emphasis characteristic of most of human religious history (including especially 'eastern' religious traditions, but also Greece); and those which have taken history/change/process/development as primary, essentially the descendants of ancient Israel (Judaism, Christianity, Islam, but also Marxism, and modern secular humanism with its confidence in historical progress). . . . In the one case, thus, the movement through time is a threat and an evil, something to be avoided and, if possible, overcome. In the other, the movement through

time is positively valued, a good, because through it the kingdom of God and thus the final fulfillment for humanity (and, indeed, creation as a whole) is being ushered in. These two conceptions of the significance of time imply two radically different understandings of human existence, two quite different proposals about how humans should orient themselves in life. They are based on sharply different assessments of the nature of the world in which we live and of what is going on in that world." *In Face of Mystery: A Constructive Theology* (Cambridge, Mass. and London: Harvard University Press, 1993), pp. 252-54.

44. *Gl.*, §10.

45. *Gl.*, §11. See also the discussion in *Gl.*, §10 (1:64-68). Note the change in terminology from "a religion" to a "mode of faith." The need to speak of religion in its positive manifestations led Schleiermacher to employ the word "church" as a generic sociological concept for a religious community in place of the more ambiguous term "religion." "Each such relatively circumscribed pious community . . . we designate through the expression 'church.'" *Gl.*, §6.4. In the first edition of the *Brief Outline* (1811), he spoke of "religion" (*Religion*) in the sense of a definite religious community, but in the second edition (1830) he dropped this term in favor of "way of believing" or "mode of faith" (*Glaubensweise*). *KD*, §1 (see note 1). Part of the problem with the term "religion," he explains, is its equivocal meaning: it cannot be used in the same sense when speaking of "natural religion" and "Islamic religion" since there is no living community where "natural religion" is embodied. Hence, he declines to use the word "religion" because its usage is ambiguous and its application to Christianity is relatively new, even if he himself used the term in the *Speeches*. *Gl.*, §6: "Postscript," 1:47. Should one insist on retaining the word "religion," its meaning should be nothing other than "the directionality of the human spirit generally to bring forth pious emotions, always thought of in connection with their expression and the aspiration for community, that is, the possibility of individual religions. . . . That directionality by itself, that is, the capacity for piety (*die fromme Erregbarkeit*) in the individual soul, would be 'religiosity' in general. These expressions, however, are seldom properly distinguished in actual practice." *Gl.*, §6: "Postscript," 1:46.

46. Thiemann is thus wrong when he charges Schleiermacher with "discovering the essence of Christianity in a self-authenticating feeling of absolute dependence." For Schleiermacher, the essence of religion is not the essence of any positive religion. "On Speaking of God—the Divisive Issue for Schleiermacher and Barth: A Response to Frei and Sykes," in *Beyond the Impasse?*, p. 111.

47. *Gl.*, §10.

48. *Gl.*, §8.4: "[T]his comparison of Christianity with other similar religions is in itself a sufficient warrant for saying that Christianity is, in fact, the most perfect among the most highly-developed religions."

49. "Islam . . . in no way shows this subordination of the passive to the active. Rather does this form of piety come to complete rest in the consciousness of immutable divine appointments, and even the consciousness of spontaneous activity is only united with the feeling of absolute dependence in the sense that its determination is supposed to rest upon those appointments.

And this fatalistic character reveals in the clearest manner a subordination of the moral to the natural." *Gl.*, §9.2 (*CF*, pp. 43-44). Still, the best example of an aesthetic religion that Schleiermacher can find is not Islam but Greek polytheism which, however, is not on the same developmental level as Christianity. "In this [religion] the teleological direction falls entirely into the background. Neither in their religious symbols nor even in their Mysteries is there any considerable trace of the idea of a totality of moral ends and of a relation of human states generally to these ends. . . . Now no one can well deny that Christianity, even apart from the fact that it belongs to a higher level, is sharply opposed to this type. In the realm of Christianity the consciousness of God is always related to the totality of active states in the idea of a Kingdom of God." *Gl.*, §9.2 (cf. *CF*, p. 43). See the helpful visual schema for charting the relations between development and type in the history of religions provided by Carl Clemen, *Schleiermachers Glaubenslehre in ihrer Bedeutung für Vergangenheit und Zukunft* (Giessen: J. Ricker'sche Verlagsbuchhandlung [Alfred Töpelmann], 1905), p. 9.

50. *Gl.*, §9.2: "That figure of a Kingdom of God, which is so important and indeed all-inclusive for Christianity, is simply the general expression of the fact that in Christianity all pain and all joy are religious only in so far as they are related to activity in the Kingdom of God, and that every religious emotion which proceeds from a passive state ends in the consciousness of a transition to activity" (*CF*, p. 43). This delineation of the teleological character of Christianity was implied in Schleiermacher's response to Chaplain Sack who accused him of defining religion in aesthetic rather than moral categories. "[J]ust because I declare that religion is not necessarily in the service of morality, I do not therefore hold religion to be something empty. I have said clearly enough that I consider our church as presently constituted to be a double institution, dedicated in part to religion and in part to morality. Thus I believe I am doing neither something contrary to my conviction nor something insignificant when I speak to people of religion as to those who should at the same time be moral, and of morality as to those who at the same time support religion—and of both, according to the relation I find appropriate at the time." Blackwell, p. 119 (Jonas and Dilthey, 3:284). See in this connection the essay by Dietz Lange, "Das fromme Selbstbewußtsein als Subjekt teleologischer Religion bei Schleiermacher," in *Schleiermacher und die wissenschaftliche Kultur des Christentums*, ed. Günter Meckenstock in connection with Joachim Ringleben (Berlin and New York: Walter de Gruyter, 1991), pp. 187-205. Albrecht Ritschl criticized Schleiermacher for failing to do justice to the teleological nature of Christian faith and attributed this failure to the "aesthetic" character of Schleiermacher's concept of religion; for that reason, Ritschl believed it necessary for Protestant theology to learn from Kant as well as from Schleiermacher. See James K. Graby, "The Problem of Ritschl's Relationship to Schleiermacher," in *Scottish Journal of Theology* 19 (September 1966): 264. James M. Brandt responds to Ritschl's characterization in his article "Ritschl's Critique of Schleiermacher's Theological Ethics," in *Journal of Religious Ethics* 17 (Fall 1989): 51-72. Brandt's essay clarifies the relation of the teleological character of Christian piety to the idea of piety itself as a non-moral

category. He writes: "Schleiermacher's is a theology of piety, and the status of the ethical is defined by piety. . . . Seen in his own terms, his grasp of the ethical is as firm as it should be" (p. 69). Gustafson points out that the priority of the religious response in the theological ethics of Schleiermacher is characteristic of the Reformed tradition in general. *Ethics from a Theocentric Perspective*, 1:183.

   51. *Gl.*, §12.1: "A universal redeemer could scarcely spring from any other than a monotheistic people."

   52. *Gl.*, §63.1 (*CF*, pp. 262-63).

   53. *Reden*, 1:276-77 (Crouter, pp. 114-15); cf. *Inst.*, 2.7.2. In the same passage Schleiermacher interprets the incident narrated in John 9:1-3 as exemplifying the religious spirit of Judaism and Jesus' polemic against it. Further, Schleiermacher judges that "Judaism is long since a dead religion (*eine todte Religion*), and those who at present still bear its colors are actually sitting and mourning beside the undecaying mummy and weeping over its demise and its sad legacy." *Reden*, 1:275 (Crouter, pp. 113-14). In the *Glaubenslehre*, he speaks of Judaism as "almost in process of extinction." *Gl.*, §8.4. See Joseph W. Pickle, "Schleiermacher on Judaism," in *The Journal of Religion* 60 (April 1980): 115-37. Pickle argues that Schleiermacher's view of Judaism is both "appreciative" and "ambivalent." "Schleiermacher's appreciative assessment of Judaism recognizes the uniqueness of Judaism and rejects attempts to treat it or the Old Testament as a *preparatio evangelii*." This appreciation of Judaism as a religion that has to be understood on its own terms follows from his "defense of positivity in religion as the necessary expression of piety, emphasizing individuality and diversity of religious communion." His negative depiction is to be explained by the fact that "his own contact with Judaism was through members of a *Haskalah* influenced community whose own interpretations of Judaism were grounded in natural religion perspectives. Thus, the specific criticisms he makes reflect the enlightened Judaism with which he is familiar." Ibid., pp. 115-16. Henriette Herz, in whose home Schleiermacher first met the Romantic circle, was a Jew who eventually converted to Christianity. Pickle writes: "For most of these [modern Jews], Judaism had been corrupted by the accretions of legalism, mysticism, and superstition. . . . Moreover, the peculiar insistence on the special relation of the Jews as such to God is denounced as nationalistic and incompatible with either a realistic assessment of history or a morally acceptable idea of God" (p. 122). The irony here, Pickle concludes, is that "[t]he advocate of historical-critical understanding accepts a view of Judaism that is utterly ahistorical" (p. 137). For a discussion of *Haskalah* Judaism and the modern emancipation of the Jews, see Robert M. Seltzer, *Jewish People, Jewish Thought: The Jewish Experience in History* (New York: Macmillan, 1980), pp. 541-70. See the brief discussion in Hermann Bleek, *Die Grundlagen der Christologie Schleiermachers: Die Entwicklung der Anschauungsweise Schleiermachers bis zur Glaubenslehre mit besonderer Rücksicht auf seine Christologie* (Freiburg: J. C. B. Mohr [Paul Siebeck], 1898), pp. 151-55. For an assessment of Schleiermacher's views that differs from that given by Pickle, see Amy Newman, "The Death of Judaism in German Protestant Thought from Luther to Hegel," in *Journal of the American Academy*

of Religion 61 (Fall 1993): 462-63.

54. *Gl.*, §9.2 (*CF*, p. 43).

55. Schleiermacher did not make theological use of the concept "law," either in its function of condemning sin or in its function of instructing the redeemed. He explicitly repudiated Calvin's "third use" of the law (the pedagogical use) which was, for Calvin, its primary function. *Gl.*, §112.5; cf. *Inst.*, 2.7.12. This deviation from Calvin's practice follows from Schleiermacher's view that law is not in its origin a Christian term. *Gl.*, §66.2.

56. Schleiermacher's view of the Old Testament as the scriptures of Judaism has implications for its use in Christian dogmatics: "Everyone must admit that if a doctrine finds neither direct nor indirect confirmation in the New Testament, but only in the Old Testament, no one could have assurance that it is truly Christian. If a doctrine finds confirmation only in the New Testament, however, no one will object that it is not to be found in the Old Testament. For that reason, the Old Testament is a superfluous authority for dogmatics." *Gl.*, 27.3. See Hans-Joachim Kraus, *Geschichte der historisch-kritischen Erforschung des Alten Testaments von der Reformation bis zur Gegenwart* (Neukirchen Kreis Moers: Verlag der Buchhandlung des Erziehungsvereins, 1956), pp. 176-77. In light of the growing influence of the natural sciences, coupled with the recent historical studies of the Bible, Schleiermacher did not want the truth of Christian dogmatics to depend upon the outcome of scientific and historical criticism of the Old Testament. *Sendschr.*, pp. 41-42 (*OtGl.*, pp. 65-66). This did not, however, prevent him from preaching on texts from the Old Testament. See Wolfgang Trillhaas, "Schleiermachers Predigten über alttestamentliche Texte," in *Schleiermacher und die wissenschaftliche Kultur des Christentums*, pp. 279-89.

57. *Gl.*, §12.2.

58. *Reden*, 1:280 (Crouter, p. 117): "To the one who does not live, move, and have his being in the eternal, God is completely unknown" (Acts 17:28). Seifert finds support for his argument that the *Speeches* should be viewed, not as "philosophy," but as an apology for specifically Christian faith in the fact that Judaism is the only other positive religion to receive more than passing treatment in the fifth speech. Moreover, Seifert argues that, besides the polemical description of Judaism designed to present Christianity in a favorable light, Schleiermacher had little actual acquaintance with religious traditions other than that recorded in the Old Testament, with the result that his references to these traditions are superficial. "What appears in the *Speeches* as a broad perspective surveying the history of religions is only rhetorical decoration. In fact, the field of vision is quite narrow with respect to the historical manifestation of religion." *Die Theologie des jungen Schleiermacher*, p. 163. One should add that Schleiermacher knew the literary sources of ancient paganism just as well as he knew the Bible. Seifert's point, I take it, is that he didn't have first-hand knowledge of living non-Christian religious communities. By contrast to Seifert, Werner Schultz detects in the *Speeches* a tension between the concerns of the theologian and the historian of religions; nonetheless, he concludes: "There can be no question that in the *Speeches* it is the historian of religion in Schleiermacher who dominates over the theologian."

184   *Christian Faith as Religion*

"Schleiermachers Deutung der Religionsgeschichte," in *Zeitschrift für Theologie und Kirche* 56 (1959): 60. Joseph M. Kitagawa identifies Scheiermacher as an early contributor to what eventually became the discipline of the historical study of religion. See his essay, "The History of Religions (Religionswissenschaft) Then and Now," in *The History of Religions: Retrospect and Prospect*, ed. Joseph M. Kitagawa (New York: Macmillan, 1985), pp. 130-31. The full truth is that Schleiermacher finds the historical study of religion to be theologically important. Schultz writes: "Inasmuch as he recognized . . . the historically conditioned character of every attempt to establish norms, he was the precursor of that great argument between theology and historicism which still characterizes the central struggle in the theology and philosophy of religion of our day" (p. 82). For a treatment of this latter theme, see Trutz Rendtorff, "The Modern Age as a Chapter in the History of Christianity; or, The Legacy of Historical Consciousness in Present Theology," in *The Journal of Religion* 65 (October 1985): 478-99.

59. The suggestion made in the *Speeches* of "the possibility of a more perfect religion than Christianity Schleiermacher afterwards limited to a continuous development within Christianity itself, just as in his later *Glaubenslehre* he no longer regarded Christ as one mediator among several, but as the only one whose consciousness of God was perfect and of unceasing efficacy for the whole race." Otto Pfleiderer, *The Development of Theology in Germany since Kant and its Progress in Great Britain since 1825*, trans. J. Frederick Smith, 3d ed. (London: Swan Sonnenschein and Co., 1909), p. 54.

60. *Gl.*, §11.4. The shift toward a new christological formulation is to be discerned in Schleiermacher's *Die Weihnachtsfeier: Ein Gespräch*, Sonderausgabe (Darmstadt: Wissenschaftliche Buchhandlung, 1953). It has been translated by Terrence N. Tice as *Christmas Eve: Dialogue on the Incarnation* (Richmond: John Knox Press, 1967). The dialogue was first published in 1806, the same year in which the *Speeches* were radically revised. In this second edition, Schleiermacher added an important sentence to the fifth speech that qualifies his original distinction between Jesus' "school" and his "religion": "It will naturally follow that when Christ with His whole efficacy is shown (to the person whose religion is the same as Jesus') he must acknowledge Him, who has become historically the centre of all mediation, the true Founder of redemption and reconciliation." *Reden*, 2:286 (Oman, p. 248). In the explanatory note added in 1821, Schleiermacher wrote: "At that time the distinction between the teaching of Christ and the teaching about Christ was hailed as a great discovery. . . . Our teaching about Christ is nothing but the ratification and application of that teaching of Christ as it is fashioned by faith and sealed by history. And if I distinguish His school from His religion it is only, as the conclusion quite clearly shows, a different consideration of the same matter from different points of view." *Reden*, pp. 298-99, n. 16 (Oman, p. 264). See the discussion in Johannes Wendland, *Die religiöse Entwicklung Schleiermachers* (Tübingen: J. C. B. Mohr [Paul Siebeck], 1915), p. 150f. Gerrish says: "Schleiermacher tries in the *Speeches on Religion* to commend religion first, then Christianity, and I think the result is that he has great difficulty doing Christianity justice." *A Prince of the Church*, p. 46. Graby

writes: "The *Reden* is an apology for religion, *per se*, and its motivating principle is the defence of the thesis that religion, *per se*, is a valid part of life and that it is concretized in the various positive religions. Religion, not Christianity, is the hero of this tale. . . . But the *Glaubenslehre* is intent upon expounding Christianity and not religion." "The Question of Development," pp. 83-84.

61. *Gl.*, §11.3.

62. "[E]ven this could not properly be called a proof of Christianity, since even the Philosophy of Religion could not establish any necessity . . . to recognize a particular Fact as redemptive. . . . Moreover, it is obvious that an adherent of some other faith might perhaps be completely convinced by the above account that what we have set forth is really the peculiar essence of Christianity, without being thereby convinced that Christianity is actually the truth, as to feel compelled to accept it." *Gl.*, §11.5 (*CF*, pp. 59-60).

63. A "critical inquiry" seeks the constant element in a historical phenomenon. See *Sendschr.*, pp. 33-34; and *KD*, §32. Troeltsch wrote: "The definition of the essence does not involve only an imaginative abstraction, but also . . . a criticism grounded in personal, ethical judgment, which measures the manifestations against the essence. For this reason it is only possible for Protestantism, which is based precisely upon the principle that personal insight into what is essential in Christianity is able to evaluate selectively the mass of actual historical manifestations." "What Does 'Essence of Christianity' Mean?," in *Ernst Troeltsch: Writings on Theology and Religion*, trans. and ed. Robert Morgan and Michael Pye (Atlanta: John Knox Press, 1977), p. 145. See the important study by Stephen Sykes, *The Identity of Christianity: Theologians and the Essence of Christianity from Schleiermacher to Barth* (Philadelphia: Fortress Press, 1984), pp. 81-101. Sykes writes: "Schleiermacher stumbles on a theological tool, namely that of the critical definition of the essence of Christianity, which meets the future exigencies of the impact of the biblical-critical movement on doctrinal theology. Not merely does he make essence definition central to his theology. . . . [H]e seeks to establish a permanent relationship with the non-theological disciplines, and he expects the theologian's definition to be subject to a process of continuous checking against the whole history of Christianity, as presented by contemporary historical research." Ibid., p. 99. What Schleiermacher means by "philosophical theology" is the discernment of the essence of Christianity, which requires a point of departure "above" Christianity. *KD*, §33. In the revised "Introduction" to the second edition of the dogmatics, Schleiermacher speaks of propositions "borrowed" from other disciplines (*Lehnsätze*) but which are not themselves dogmatic statements. *Gl.*, §2, and "Postscript" 1 and 2, and *Gl.*, §7; cf. *Gl.¹*, §6. In this case the propositions are borrowed from the comparative study of religions (*Religionsphilosophie*) since this is the relevant non-theological discipline engaged in the same historical-critical endeavor. See the study by Doris Offermann, *Schleiermachers Einleitung in die Glaubenslehre: Eine Untersuchung der "Lehnsätze"* (Berlin: Walter de Gruyter, 1969), especially pp. 139-234.

64. *Gl.*, §11.5, §28.2.

65. In this respect, Lindbeck is correct to describe Schleiermacher's understanding of the relation between religion and doctrine as "experiential-expressivist": theological doctrines seek to give intellectual expression to a religious experience which is the direct object of interpretation; therefore, it is improper to say religion arises in response to doctrines understood as intellectual propositions. But given Schleiermacher's insistence upon the positivity of religion and the abstract character of the definition of religion's essence, his view of the religion-doctrine relation could fit just as well into Lindbeck's "cultural-linguistic" model. Lindbeck himself acknowledges that the relation between a positive religion (understood after the analogy of a "culture" with its own peculiar language) and experience "is not unilateral but dialectical. It is simplistic to say . . . merely that religions produce experiences, for the causality is reciprocal." *The Nature of Doctrine*, p. 33. Even a cultural-linguistic model for religion does not escape the necessity of defining what makes a given cultural-linguistic system "religious," as Lindbeck recognizes. His own view comes very close to that of Tillich's definition of religion as "ultimate concern" or, as he puts it, "the maximally important." Ibid., pp. 33-34. For a recent defense of Schleiermacher's theology that addresses itself to this question, see Jacqueline Mariña, "Schleiermacher's Christology Revisited: A Reply to His Critics," in *Scottish Journal of Theology* 49 (April 1996): 177-200. Mariña explains Schleiermacher's use of "experience" in relation to Lindbeck's critique. "[T]he founding of dogmatics upon experience can more adequately be understood as the result of a profound reflection which goes back to the classical Christian tradition of Augustine and is a correct account of the only way that the contents of faith can be apprehended, that is, through experience. . . . The experience of redemption does not occur in a vacuum; it is mediated by the community of faith through the Word. Since all language is already an interpretation of the experience it mediates, it thus follows that this experience does not occur uninterpreted. . . . If experience is reduced to raw feelings bereft of thought-content interpreting them, then Schleiermacher is not an 'experiential-expressivist.' Indeed, we would probably be hard pressed to find an example of *this* version of experiential-expressivism." Ibid., pp. 182-84.

66. "It should be clear that, taken together, both *Glaubenslehre* and *Sittenlehre* represent the whole reality of the Christian life. For it is inconceivable that a person, whose self-consciousness is everywhere and always determined by the religious emotions expressed in Christian doctrine, should not also everywhere and always act in the ways described by Christian ethics." *Gl.*, §26.2. Theological ethics is thus a descriptive, not a prescriptive, discipline in Schleiermacher's thought. *Die christliche Sitte nach den Grundsätzen der evangelischen Kirche im Zusammenhange dargestellt*, 2d ed., ed. L. Jonas, *SW* 1:12. A small portion of this work has been made available in English as Schleiermacher's *Introduction to Christian Ethics*, trans. John Shelley (Nashville: Abingdon Press, 1989).

67. *Gl.* §15 (*CF*, p. 76). Schleiermacher interprets each doctrine in the threefold form of statements about self, world, and God. He understands doctrinal statements about the world and God to be elucidations of what is already given in the fundamental form which is the direct description of the

religious self-consciousness itself. *Gl.*, §30-31. The point of this method is to insure the non-speculative character of dogmatics: "The Protestant church is unanimous in its consciousness that the form of dogmatic propositions proper to it does not depend on any form or school of philosophy, and has not proceeded from a speculative interest, but simply from the interest of satisfying the immediate self-consciousness solely through the genuine and uncorrupted means ordained by Christ." *Gl.*, §16: "Postscript," 1:112.

68. "There is only *one* source from which all Christian doctrine is derived, namely, the self-proclamation of Christ, and only *one* way, whether more or less perfectly, for doctrine to arise out of the pious self-consciousness and the immediate expression of the same." *Gl.*, §19: "Postscript," 1:124.

69. *Gl.*, §19. Unfortunately, the translators have rendered this sentence: "Dogmatic theology is the science which *systematizes* the doctrine. . . . " This gives the misleading impression that the logical coherence of doctrine with which dogmatics is concerned is imposed by the theologian, but this is not Schleiermacher's meaning. "Dogmatic propositions arise only from logically ordered reflection (*logisch geordnete Reflexion*) upon the immediate utterances of the religious self-consciousness." *Gl.*, §16: "Postscript," 1:110. The coherence of doctrine is discerned, not imposed, contra Thiemann, "On Speaking of God," p. 111. In German one could say (though Schleiermacher does not) that the coherence (*Zusammenhang*) of doctrines is demonstrated by showing how they all "hang together" (*zusammen hängen*). Placher says that "Christian theology should focus primarily on describing the *internal* logic of Christian faith—how Christian beliefs relate to each other and function within the life of a Christian community." *Unapologetic Theology*, p. 18. In his next paragraph, it becomes clear that Placher proposes this job-description of theology as an alternative to that of the tradition of Schleiermacher. Yet this seems a perfectly good description of Schleiermacher's view of the properly "dogmatic" task. But this is not the *only* task of theology, according to Schleiermacher, since dogmatics is simply one part of historical theology, and the other tasks of philosophical and practical theology must not be forgotten, either. *KD*, §24-31.

70. For a detailed, though critical, study, see Klaus-Martin Beckmann, *Der Begriff der Häresie bei Schleiermacher*, Forschungen zur Geschichte und Lehre des Protestantismus 16 (Munich: Christian Kaiser Verlag, 1959). Thiemann is guilty of a misreading when he writes: "Schleiermacher's position is ambiguous on the question whether that essence is located *within* those diverse first-order utterances or in a deeper universal and pre-linguistic substratum. Insofar as Schleiermacher asserts the former, his method is supportive of descriptive theology. Insofar as he supports the latter, he gives aid and comfort to foundational theology." *Revelation and Theology*, p. 172, n. 5. Thiemann's entire case against Schleiermacher as a "foundationalist" rests upon this basic confusion of categories. There is absolutely no ambiguity in Schleiermacher's text regarding his position: "faith," not "religion," is the norm of Christian doctrine.

71. *Gl.*, §22.2; Beckmann, pp. 36-46, 49-62.

72. The full title of the dogmatics is: *Der christliche Glaube nach den*

Grundsätzen der evangelischen Kirche im Zusammenhange dargestellt. The full
title has not been rendered in the English translation. Also omitted is the citation
from Anselm that Schleiermacher placed on the title page: "I do not seek to
understand in order that I may believe, but I believe in order that I might
understand." "For whoever has not believed, does not experience (*experietur*),
and whoever has not experienced, does not understand." *Proslogion* (*MSL* 158,
227) and *De fide trin.* (*MSL* 158, 264).

73. *Gl.*, §24.

74. *Gl.*, §24.3.

75. Johann Sebastian Drey (1777-1853), the founder of the Catholic
theological faculty at Tübingen, had read Schleiermacher and was engaged in a
similar revisionist project from his own Roman Catholic perspective. Bradford
E. Hinze has done a major comparative study investigating their views of
history in relation to the question of doctrinal development. *Narrating History,
Developing Doctrine: Friedrich Schleiermacher and Johann Sebastian Drey*,
American Academy of Religion Academy Series (Atlanta: Scholars Press,
1993).

76. Just as the definition of Christianity's essence requires a standpoint
"above" Christianity since it is a critical endeavor necessarily involving
comparison with other positive religious communities, so the definition of the
essence of Protestantism is not itself a part of the descriptive task of dogmatics
since it, too, is a critical inquiry requiring a standpoint "above" the antithesis
between Protestantism and Catholicism. Thus Schleiermacher speaks of the
need for a "Protestant philosophical theology." *KD*, §36 and 39. See also
Birkner, *Theologie und Philosophie*, pp. 25-27. Schleiermacher opposes a false
ecumenism that would step back from the controversies between Protestant and
Catholic by adopting older formulae held in common since that would entail a
less definite formulation of a church's doctrine. *Gl.*, §23.3.

77. See the essay by Wilhelm Pauck, "Schleiermacher's Conception of
History and Church History," in *From Luther to Tillich: The Reformers and
Their Heirs*, ed. Marion Pauck with an introduction by Jaroslav Pelikan (San
Francisco: Harper and Row, 1984), pp. 66-79. See also Hermann Mulert,
*Schleiermachers geschichtsphilosophische Ansichten in ihrer Bedeutung für
seine Theologie*, Studien zur Geschichte des neueren Protestantismus (Giessen:
Verlag von Alred Töpelmann, 1907), pp. 25-46. Schleiermacher's lectures on
church history are published as *Geschichte der christlichen Kirche*, ed. E.
Bonnell, in *SW*, 1.11.

78. Schleiermacher does not deny that Eastern Orthodoxy is also a
formation of the common essence of Christianity; his focus on the Western
churches is intended to show that they have more in common with one another
than either does with the East, in spite of the anti-papal character of the latter.
Gl., §23.1.

79. "Since I have attempted to present the essence of the Protestant view of
faith and life within its own boundaries as being the same in both confessions
and since I have attempted to identify the differing opinions of both confessions
within this common terrain, it is clear that these differences in teaching within
our two confessions can and perhaps must co-exist just as in the larger unity of

Christendom a whole host of differences co-exist one with another." *Gl.¹*, 1:6. See the study by Martin Stiewe, *Das Unionsverständnis Friedrich Schleiermachers: Der Protestantismus als Konfession in der Glaubenslehre* (Witten: Luther-Verlag, 1969).

80. *Gl.*, §24: "Postscript," 1:142.

81. *Gl.*, §24: "Postscript." The Protestant character of a dogmatic presentation must be demonstrated by appeal to the confessional documents of the Reformation era. By itself, citing the New Testament cannot guarantee the distinctively *Protestant* character of a dogmatic proposition but can only secure its generally *Christian* character. His point is that a Roman Catholic or Eastern Orthodox presentation of doctrine can also make legitimate appeal to the New Testament. *Gl.*, §27. Schleiermacher's view anticipated the argument made in this century by Ernst Käsemann who writes: "The time when it was possible to set up Scripture in its totality in opposition to Catholicism has gone beyond recall. Protestantism today can no longer employ the so-called Formal Principle without rendering itself unworthy of credence in the eyes of historical analysis. . . . [T]he New Testament canon does not, as such, constitute the foundation of the unity of the Church. On the contrary, as such (that is, in its accessibility to the historian) it provides the basis for the multiplicity of the confessions. . . . It is thus quite comprehensible that the confessions which exist today all appeal to the New Testament canon. Fundamentally, the exegete cannot dispute their methodological or their material right to do this. If the canon as such is binding in its totality, the various confessions may, with differing degrees of historical justification, claim as their own larger or smaller tracts of it, better or lesser known New Testament writers." See his essay, "The Canon of the New Testament and the Unity of the Church," in *Essays on New Testament Themes*, trans. W. J. Montague (Philadelphia: Fortress Press, 1982), pp. 103-4. Schleiermacher's approach to the confessions illustrated a new historical-critical appreciation of these documents. Unlike conservative confessionalists, Schleiermacher was not willing to exempt these symbolic standards from historical and theological criticism; but unlike rationalist theologians, he was convinced that the identity of Protestantism as a distinct form of Christian faith could only be discerned through a serious and respectful engagement with these historic confessions. See Martin Ohst, *Schleiermacher und die Bekenntnisschriften: Eine Untersuchung zu seiner Reformations- und Protestantismusdeutung*, Beiträge zur historischen Theologie 77 (Tübingen: J. C. B. Mohr [Paul Siebeck], 1989). I have reviewed this book in *The Journal of Religion* 72 (July 1992): 437-38. Further, there is the essay by Hans Graß, "Schleiermacher und das Bekenntnis," in *Internationaler Schleiermacher-Kongreß*, 2:1053-60. Schleiermacher did not believe the church of the union needed a new confessional standard. "Vorrede," *Gl.*, 1:4-5 (*CF*, p. viii). Thus both the Lutheran and Reformed confessions are employed within his ecumenical dogmatics.

82. *Gl.*, §10: "Postscript."

83. *Gl.*, §13.1, note b (1:87).

84. *Gl.*, §13. Schleiermacher's procedure in the dogmatics is to consider the orthodox doctrinal formulations as well as the rationalist criticisms of them and

to seek a resolution of the tension that gives to each side its due.

85. *Gl.*, §94. "To ascribe to Christ an absolutely powerful God-consciousness and to posit an existence of God in him are one and the same." §94.1. See also his introductory discussion of christology under §13.

86. *Gl.*, §87-88.

87. *Gl.*, §88.2. On the importance of preaching for the emergence of faith, Schleiermacher writes: "Thus this communication is, on the one hand, something different from piety itself, though the latter cannot, any more than anything else which is human, be conceived as entirely separated from all communication. But, on the other hand, all forms of doctrine have their ultimate ground so exclusively in the affections of the religious self-consciousness that, where these do not exist, the doctrines cannot arise." *Gl.*, §15.2. Since it is through the continuation of Christ's self-proclamation in the church's preaching that the distinctively Christian religious affections are evoked, the object of Schleiermacher's dogmatics may appropriately be designated "existence under the Word." Seen in this light, the characterization of Schleiermacher's dogmatic method given by H. R. Mackintosh misses the point: "Schleiermacher's failure to take Revelation seriously creates all kinds of perplexity for the student of his system, and gives rise to the natural accusation that for him theology is less concerned with God than with man's consciousness of God. . . . On page after page of his main work, his regular method is to proceed by introspection rather than listen to the voice of God speaking in His Word." *Types of Modern Theology: Schleiermacher to Barth* (1937; repr., London: Nisbet and Co., 1962), pp. 94-95. Richard R. Niebuhr says it better: "Theological thinking is, according to Schleiermacher, reflection upon and clarification of believing experience." *Schleiermacher on Christ and Religion*, p. 139. For a discussion of the role of preaching in Schleiermacher's theology and ministry, see the introduction by Dawn DeVries to her translation of his sermons in *Servant of the Word: Selected Sermons of Friedrich Schleiermacher*, Fortress Texts in Modern Theology (Philadelphia: Fortress Press, 1987), pp. 1-17. DeVries has recently published a major study comparing Schleiermacher's preaching with that of Calvin: *Jesus Christ in the Preaching of Calvin and Schleiermacher*, Columbia Series in Reformed Theology (Louisville: Westminster/John Knox Press, 1996).

88. *Gl.*, §89.1, with reference to 2 Cor 5:17 ("If any one is in Christ, he is a new creation"). Niebuhr writes: "[I]nasmuch as Schleiermacher believes that every man is an 'Adam' in his own right, the problem of relating Christianity to religion is also the problem of relating Christ to 'Adam'; it is the problem of relating the author of Christianity to the man whose religion Christianity becomes." *Schleiermacher on Christ and Religion*, p. 211.

89. *Gl.*, §89.2.

90. *Gl.*, §94.3. Of course, Schleiermacher does not believe that Adam was a historical person. See *Gl.*, §61.

91. *Gl.*, §89.

92. *Gl.*, §100.2. Schleiermacher describes a "pious personality" as one in which all passive and active elements are produced by the impulse of the God-consciousness. *Gl.*, §106.1.

93. *Gl.*, §63 (*CF*, p. 262).

94. *Gl.*, §29.1.

95. Ibid.

96. *Gl.*, §62.2; see also *Gl.*, §62.1 for a description of the ideal.

97. Schleiermacher insists that all consciousness takes place on a continuum of pleasure and pain, including our consciousness of being absolutely dependent (*Gl.*, §5). "The God-consciousness described in the previous section [i.e., in Part One] occurs as the actual content of a moment of experience only under the general form of self-consciousness, namely, the antithesis of pleasure and pain." *Gl.*, §62. For that matter, the feeling of absolute dependence is never simply the actual content of a moment of experience in any other historically determinate form of piety either, since there is always an arrested development of its facility in human life. But the peculiarly Christian way of articulating the antithesis is always connected to a claim about the redeemer. *Gl.*, §62.2-3.

98. *Gl.*, §62.3.

99. *Gl.*, §36.1. In his own way Calvin also wishes to understand creation and providence ("preservation" in Schleiermacher's scheme) as inextricably bound up with one another: "unless we cross over to his providence, we do not yet properly grasp what it means that God is the creator." *Inst.*, 1.16.1.

100. "All attributes which we ascribe to God are to be taken as denoting not something special in God, but only something special in the manner in which the feeling of absolute dependence is to be related to him." *Gl.*, §50 (*CF*, p. 194). Schleiermacher's doctrine of God is, therefore, distributed throughout his dogmatics and is not to be found in one place. Schleiermacher postponed consideration of the doctrine of the Trinity to the conclusion of his dogmatics "since this doctrine itself, as ecclesiastically framed, is not an immediate utterance concerning the Christian self-consciousness, but only a combination of several such utterances." *Gl.*, §170 (*CF*, p. 738). In other words, his non-speculative method precludes an independent treatment of this doctrine. Ebeling detects in this procedure a departure from the traditional order of dogmatics: "Whereas in the traditional outline the doctrine of God, including of course the doctrine of the divine attributes, stands as a completed whole at the beginning of dogmatics, at the beginning of Schleiermacher's *Glaubenslehre* there is— *cum grano salis*—no doctrine of God at all. Instead, the doctrine of the divine attributes is distributed in three sections over the whole *Glaubenslehre* and the doctrine of the Trinity is dealt with in a concluding section." "Schleiermacher's Doctrine of the Divine Attributes," in *Schleiermacher as Contemporary*, p. 149. Gerrish questions Ebeling's assessment of a departure from traditional dogmatics on Schleiermacher's part by pointing to Calvin's example and asking "must we not also affirm, even without the pinch of salt, that the *Institutes* nowhere contain a doctrine of God but *are* a doctrine of God? There is no *locus de deo* because the entire work presents the knowledge of God as creator and redeemer." "Theology within the Limits of Piety Alone," p. 199. Zachman, however, argues that any attempt to move from these obvious formal similiarites to a material comparison of Calvin and Schleiermacher must ultimately come to naught on account of the differing status of the doctrine of the Trinity in the two theologies. "The material difference between

Schleiermacher and Calvin . . . is ultimately rooted in the difference of their understanding of who the true God is." Whereas in Schleiermacher "[t]he pious consciousnesss . . . excludes thinking about God as the eternal relation of Father, Son, and Holy Spirit . . . [f]or Calvin, God is the Father even apart from God's relationship to the world. . . . Ultimately, it is the doctrine of the Trinity, attesting the self-revealing and self-bestowing love of the Father in the Son through the Holy Spirit, that distinguishes Calvin from Schleiermacher." "The Awareness of Divinity and the Knowledge of God in the Theology of Calvin and Schleiermacher," in *Revisioning the Past: Prospects in Historical Theology*, ed. Mary Potter Engel and Walter E. Wyman, Jr. (Minneapolis: Fortress Press, 1992), pp. 144-46. By contrast, Tillich writes: "As a follower of Calvin, [Schleiermacher] said that we cannot say anything about the *essentia dei*, God in his true essence. We can say something only on the basis of his relation to us which is manifest through revelatory experiences. This has implications for the doctrine of the trinity. A doctrine of an objective trinity as a transcendent object is impossible. The doctrine of the trinity is the fullest expression of man's relation to God." *History of Christian Thought*, pp. 407-8. In this connection it seems important to mention that chapter 13 of Book One in the 1559 edition of the *Institutes*, which explicates the trinitarian doctrine, has no organic relation to what precedes it in chapter 12 or to what follows it in chapter 14, thereby suggesting that, perhaps, Calvin himself didn't quite know what to do with the patristic formulae within his new order of arrangement. At the Lausanne Disputation in 1537 Calvin had found it necessary to defend himself against the accusation of anti-trinitarianism brought forward by Pierre Caroli. On this matter Karl Barth writes: "Calvin was inclined to regard the Greek dogma as idle speculation in contrast to the practical knowledge that he himself thought he could gain from scripture, and it was only to the extent that the doctrine of the Trinity could be understood as practical knowledge that it seemed to him to be scriptural and acceptable. . . . I would advise you to treat [Calvin's evaluation of the Greek dogma] with caution. . . . It should be noted in this regard that had Caroli been more acute he would have had to accuse Calvin and his party of Sabellianism rather than Arianism. . . . The reformers undoubtedly tended to stress the unity rather than the distinction in God, as we see plainly in Calvin. You are probably aware that on the last pages of his *Christian faith* Schleiermacher counsels a serious weighing of the Sabellian solution in contrast to the Athanasian. Calvin did not go that far, but a more perspicacious adversary who advocated the Greek dogma could certainly have found it necessary to attack him on this side. . . . If he was an antitrinitarian—and if there are any who feel confident enough to take this view in spite of his assurances, let them do so!—then it was certainly not as an Arian." *The Theology of John Calvin*, trans. Geoffrey W. Bromiley (Grand Rapids, Michigan and Cambridge, England: Eerdmans, 1995; original German, 1922), pp. 326-28. See the good article by Robert F. Streetman, "Some Questions Schleiermacher Might Ask about Barth's Trinitarian Criticisms," in *Beyond the Impasse?*, pp. 114-37.

101. *Sendschr.*, p. 32. Since they are not themselves expressions of the antithesis, Schleiermacher fears lest his interpreters misunderstand the doctrines of creation and preservation developed in Part One as a "natural theology" in

contrast to the actual Christian theology of Part Two. But the fact that the doctrines of creation and preservation are less distinctively Christian than the doctrines of sin and grace does not mean that they are any less essential for a complete description of Christian piety. In fact, there is a nice symmetry in the way the two parts balance each other: "Those doctrines are in no way the reflection of a sorry monotheistic God-consciousness. Rather, they are abstracted (*abstrahiert*) from that consciousness of God which has developed in relation to the redeemer. In the same manner, all doctrines which express a relation to Christ are truly Christian insofar as they recognize no other standard for the relation to the redeemer except the constancy of that God-consciousness brought about by him. Hence, a relation to Christ in which consciousness of God were pushed to the background or made obsolete, because only Christ and not God were present in self-consciousness, might be very intimate but in the strict sense of the term it would no longer belong in the realm of piety." *Gl.*, §62.3.

102. *Gl.*, §66.1. That is to say: sin is not primarily a moral category but a religious one because it concerns our relationship with God.

103. *Gl.*, §94.1.

104. Schleiermacher confesses that, although this interpretation coheres with traditional views that depict sin as a turning away from the creator, it is nevertheless difficult to reconcile his view with the notion of sin as a violation of God's law. It is more properly Christian to say that sin is that which Christ disparages since Christ is the embodiment of our "original perfection." *Gl.*, §66.2. Cf. *Gl.*, §61.5 and 68.3. He appeals to Augustine's statement that "no sin can be committed unless, of course, either those things are sought after which he has disdained or those things are avoided which he has upheld." *Gl.*, §66.2, n. 1, from *De vera religione* 31 (*MPL* 34, 135). Wyman discusses Schleiermacher's doctrine of sin in relation to Augustine's legacy. "Schleiermacher's terminology is distinctive, even peculiar. Yet striking continuities with the Augustinian tradition are clearly present. Schleiermacher affirms the reality of original sin, the distinction between original sin and actual sin, and total depravity. Still, one might ask whether Schleiermacher's differing terminology points to a material difference from Augustine's understanding of sin. It would seem on the face of it that the location of sin has shifted. For Augustine, sin lies in the defection of the will from God and the consequent misdirection of one's love from love of the eternal to love of the temporal and mutable (and the self). . . . For Schleiermacher, the root of the problem lies neither in the will nor in the direction of one's love, but at a prior level (prior to willing or sensible feelings), in the inability to integrate one's consciousness of the divine with the rest of one's conscious life." "Rethinking the Christian Doctrine of Sin: Friedrich Schleiermacher and Hick's 'Irenaean Type,'" in *The Journal of Religion* 72 (April 1994): 206. Following a suggestion made by John Hick, Wyman presents a strong case for understanding Schleiermacher's doctrine of sin as an immanent criticism of the Augustinian tradition that moves in the direction of Irenaeus. "Schleiermacher develops a convincing critique of the Augustinian understanding of sin by demonstrating its internal incoherence. But he does not simply jettison the doctrine of sin or fail to take it seriously;

rather, he provides a critical reconstruction which, while maintaining continuity with some aspects of the Augustinian tradition, finally shatters the Augustinian framework. Understanding Schleiermacher as an 'Irenaean' rather than as a failed 'Augustinian' makes a considerable difference to the critical evaluation of his position." Ibid., p. 201.

105. *Gl.*, §68.
106. *Gl.*, §68.2.
107. *Gl.*, §75.1, with reference to Heb 2:15, where Christ is said to "deliver those who through fear of death were subject to lifelong bondage."
108. Ibid.
109. *Gl.*, §76.1.
110. *Gl.*, §83.1.
111. *Gl.*, §84.2.
112. *Gl.*, §100; *Gl.*, §101.
113. *Gl.*, §101.2.
114. *Gl.*, §106.1.
115. *Gl.*, §108.1. Schleiermacher cites Melanchthon's statement from the *Loci Theologici* (1543) that "faith (*fides*) is trust (*fiducia*) that applies the benefit of Christ to ourselves." Ibid. (*Corpus Reformatorum*, 21:749). He says that faith is the certainty that our relation to Christ puts an end to our need for redemption and leads to blessedness: "This certainty is precisely faith in Christ." He goes on to say that this faith is "a purely factual certainty, but a certainty of a fact which is entirely inward." That is to say, it cannot be demonstrated either that we need redemption or that Christ is the redeemer. *Gl.*, §14.1-2. "This exposition is based entirely on the inner experience of the believer; its only purpose is to describe and elucidate that experience. Naturally, therefore, it can make no claim to be a proof that things must have been so. . . . We must seek to bring doubters to the same experience as we have had." *Gl.*, §100.3 (*CF*, p. 428).
116. *Gl.*, §108.
117. *Gl.*, §109.
118. *Gl.*, §109.2.
119. *Gl.*, §109.4. Schleiermacher cites with approval Calvin's statement: "[I]t is beyond controversy that no one is loved by God apart from Christ." *Inst.*, 3.2.32. Schleiermacher affirms: "[I]t is certain that the God-consciousness which (along with the self-consciousness) belongs to human nature originally, before the Redeemer and apart from all connexion with Him, cannot fittingly be called an existence of God in us, not only because it was not a pure God-consciousness (either in polytheism or even in Jewish monotheism, which was everywhere tinctured with materialistic conceptions, whether cruder or finer), but also because, such as it was, it did not assert itself as activity, but in these religions was always dominated by the sensuous self-consciousness." *Gl.*, §94.2 (*CF*, p. 387). "[W]e must now say, if it is only through [Christ] that the human God-consciousness becomes an existence of God in human nature . . . that in truth He alone mediates all existence of God in the world and all revelation of God through the world. . . ." Ibid. (*CF*, p. 388). This affirmation seems, at first glance, to stand in tension with Schleiermacher's historical appreciation of

religious diversity. But he insists that the recognition of other religions does not contradict "the conviction, which we assume every Christian to possess, of the exclusive superiority of Christianity." *Gl.*, §7.3 (*CF*, p. 33).

120. *Gl.*, §110.

121. *Gl.*, §110.3.

122. *Gl.*, §164-67. From this standpoint, Schleiermacher looks forward to a time when the other religions will be subsumed by Christianity since this would signify the consummation of the church. *Gl.*, §157.1.

123. *Gl.*, §169.3.

124. *Gl.*, §169: "The divine wisdom is the ground in virtue of which the world, as a theatre of redemption, is also the absolute revelation of the Supreme Being, and is therefore good."

125. See the discussion of Schleiermacher's "ethics of sanctification" in Gustafson's *Christ and the Moral Life* (Chicago and London: The University of Chicago Press, 1968), pp. 61-115, where Schleiermacher is compared with another pietist, John Wesley. Gustafson writes: "Like Wesley, but in very different terms, Schleiermacher makes a case for the moral efficacy of the work of Christ made known in the religious experience of men" (p. 92).

126. *Gl.*, §167.1; see 1 John 4:8.

127. *Gl.*, §167.2.

128. *Gl.*, §168.2.

129. *Sendschr.*, p. 32. See also *Gl.*, §64.2. In Part One omnipotence, omniscience, and omnipresence are delineated as attributes to be predicated of God on the basis of the religious self-consciousness abstracted from the antithesis of sin and grace. *Gl.*, §53-55. It is important that Schleiermacher thought he could have reversed the two parts of his dogmatic system without injury to his meaning, thereby beginning with the concrete description of the religious self-consciousness as it is determined by the antithesis of sin and grace. He pointed to the Heidelberg Catechism as an example of this mode of arrangement since it begins with the question: "What is thy only comfort in life and in death?" to which answer is made: "That I, with body and soul, both in life and in death, am not my own, but belong to my faithful Saviour Jesus Christ. . . ." The Catechism is found in Philip Schaff, *The Creeds of Christendom, with a History and Critical Notes*, 6th ed., revised by David S. Schaff (Harper and Row, 1931; repr., Grand Rapids: Baker Book House, 1990), 3:307-55. Schleiermacher asked: "Would it not have been quite natural and appropriate for a theologian who comes from the Reformed school and who does not believe that this ought to be denied even in the present state of union if I had followed more closely the Heidelberg Catechism in this regard?" *Sendschr.*, p. 30. Barth said of the Heidelberg Catechism: "One may say that it is distinctively a theology of the third article, a theology of the Holy Spirit, constructed from the particular point of view of the work of God in relation to man. A theology so oriented stands in danger of anthropocentricity, that is, of slipping into a one-sided interest in man so that God and the things of God become only an exponent of human experience. The Heidelberg Catechism has often been reproached for a certain tendency in this direction. Is it a forerunner of Schleiermacher?" *Learning Jesus Christ Through the Heidelberg Catechism,*

trans. Shirley C. Guthrie, Jr., originally published in English under the title *The Heidelberg Catechism for Today* (Richmond: John Knox Press, 1964; repr., Eerdmans), p. 25. Barth returned to this theme in his last published words on his old adversary: "[I]nterpreting everything and everyone *in optimam partem*, I would like to reckon with the possibility of a theology of the Holy Spirit, a theology of which Schleiermacher was scarcely conscious, but which might actually have been the legitimate concern dominating even his theological activity." "Concluding Unscientific Postscript," p. 278. Barth made a similar comment about Bultmann's theology with reference to Schleiermacher. See their *Letters*, p. 108 (letter of 24 December, 1952).

130. With respect to Schleiermacher's "apologetic agenda . . . to offer some guarantee of a harmony between authentic Christian doctrine on the one hand, and the presuppositions and results of natural and historical science on the other," Georg Behrens writes: "He is enough of a Calvinist to think 'that the recognition of creation leads to the consciousness of God' and he considers it highly implausible to suppose that 'the love of piety' should be at war with the 'drive to research and to the expansion of our knowledge of nature.'" "The Order of Nature in Pious Self-Consciousness: Schleiermacher's Apologetic Argument," in *Religious Studies* 32 (March 1996): 94-95, with reference to *Gl.*, §46.1.

Chapter 6

Christian Faith and Religion: From Calvin to Schleiermacher

The Comparison of Classical and Liberal Protestant Theology

When the neo-orthodox theologians rejected the liberal theology of the nineteenth century in the name of a return to Reformation principles, they were unable to explain what was to them a historical riddle: how the Reformation of the sixteenth century could issue in its own antithesis in the theology of the modern period. The alleged discovery of radical discontinuity in the history of Protestant theology resulted from setting up a false antithesis between liberal "religionism" and biblical-Reformation faith in the revealed Word of God. By inquiring of Calvin and Schleiermacher regarding their understanding of the nature of religion and of Christianity as a religion, a new framework for comparison offers the possibility of an alternative historical description of the development of Protestant theology from its classical to its liberal form.

The object of this comparison is the *systematic function* of the concept "religion" in the dogmatic theologies of Calvin and Schleiermacher. It is only when the question of function is addressed that the possibility of genuine theological differences between Calvin and Schleiermacher can be honestly appraised. For this reason, the exegetical comparison of these two theologians demands that the regulative assumptions of the neo-orthodox theologians be set aside in favor of a new conceptual framework.

Brunner argued against the "Protestant" character of Schleiermacher's theology on two counts. First, the theology of Schleiermacher is focused upon a concern with the nature of religion in general whereas Calvin's theology is concerned to explicate biblical faith. Second, the particular definition of religion to which Schleiermacher attains is incompatible with faith in the biblical sense. According to Brunner, Schleiermacher's definition of religion is "mystical" and, therefore, cannot be brought into harmony with the biblical notion of faith as an obedient hearing of the Word of God.

This study acknowledges that the dogmatics of Schleiermacher can readily be compared with that of Calvin since both theologians preface their carefully structured systematic presentations of the meaning of specifically Christian faith with a consideration of the nature of religion in general. Instead of measuring Schleiermacher's concept of religion against Calvin's concept of faith, it makes more sense to compare what Schleiermacher says about religion with what Calvin says about it and to compare Schleiermacher's exposition of faith with Calvin's account of it.

Only when the comparison has been conducted along these lines does it then become possible to pose two important questions suggested by Brunner's criticism. First, if Calvin and Schleiermacher differ in their interpretations of religion, does it necessarily follow that their differences in this respect are to be understood as indicating mutual opposition between them? Second, is Schleiermacher's definition of religion, in fact, incompatible with a Protestant doctrine of faith?

This second question can only be answered once we have gained clarity regarding Schleiermacher's interpretation of Christian faith and compared it to that of Calvin. If the result of this comparison should demonstrate that Schleiermacher and Calvin are remarkably similar in their accounts of the nature of Christian faith, then one of two conclusions must follow: either Brunner is wrong when he argues that Schleiermacher's definition of religion precludes the possibility that his doctrine of faith could stand in material continuity with the Reformation heritage, or Brunner is right about the unchristian character of Schleiermacher's concept of religion, in which case there is a striking internal inconsistency at the heart of Schleiermacher's dogmatic system. For this reason, the comparison of Calvin and Schleiermacher examines the concept of "faith" in the two theologies before moving to a consideration of the concept of "religion."

Barth argued that Schleiermacher's theology is anthropocentric and subjectivistic since it interprets Christian faith as a form of human religious experience. By contrast, Calvin's theology is based upon God's self-revelation in Jesus Christ and, therefore, is neither anthropocentric nor subjectivistic. "Religion," in Barth's sense of the term, is the sinful aspiration of the human being to justify itself before God. "Faith" is the antithesis of religion since it obediently accepts the revelation of God's judgment upon all human works and lives by grace alone. A theology that interprets Christian faith by means of the category "religion" thus betrays the gospel since God's revelation is opposed to human religion just as justification by faith is opposed to works righteousness.

Barth's definitions of the terms "revelation" and "religion" are idiosyncratic and, while they can be employed with internal consistency within Barth's own dogmatics, they cannot be applied to the analysis of either Calvin's or Schleiermacher's dogmatics. Since Barth claimed that his theology in this respect was a more faithful interpretation of the Reformation heritage than that of Schleiermacher, two observations must be made about the way in which Barth's use of terms represents a substantial departure from their employment within the context of Calvin's theology. First, Barth's negative definition of "religion" as a synonym for justification by works finds its counterpart only in Calvin's definition of "false religion," but not in his definition of "religion" itself. Second, Barth defines "revelation" in a strictly christocentric sense that cannot be read back into Calvin's theology. Calvin's theology can be interpreted adequately only when it is acknowledged that "revelation" has to be understood in two senses: first, as the "original revelation" of God as the creator given to human awareness simply as such and, second, as the "decisive revelation" of God as creator and redeemer presented to the hearer of the Christian message. When Barth's categories are employed as the analytical tools for the interpretation of Calvin's theology, it becomes impossible to understand how Calvin correlates the two senses of revelation and how he interprets Christian faith as the fruition of a "seed of religion" universally present in human experience.[1]

It is precisely on account of these ways in which Barth's theology differs from Calvin's that the comparison with Schleiermacher recommends itself as the more obvious and natural one. Schleiermacher's dogmatics is divided into two parts corresponding to the distinction in Calvin's theology between the knowledge of God as creator and the knowledge of God as redeemer. Moreover, like Calvin, Schleiermacher interprets Christian faith as bringing to fruition the potential for religion in every human consciousness. Indeed, for both Calvin and Schleiermacher, the two issues are systematically interrelated. First, there would be no religion at all were it not for the presence of an awareness of God woven into the created texture of human experience itself. Second, the redemptive message of Christian faith can be interpreted aright only when it is recognized that human existence is at odds with itself precisely to the extent that the appropriate religious response to this immediate sense of God's reality is wanting. The theological interpretation of religion and Christian faith as religion is thus bound up with the question of understanding the relation between the original revelation of God in common human experience and the decisive revelation of God in the gospel of Jesus Christ.

From Barth's christocentric viewpoint, the notion of an original revelation of God given with the created structure of human existence to which all religion is a response, however inadequate, is an instance of "natural theology." Here again, it has to be remembered that Barth's definition of terms is suited to their peculiar use within his own systematic framework.[2] For this reason Barth's definition of "natural theology" cannot be extracted from that framework and employed as the standard for measuring what is genuinely Protestant in classical or liberal theology. For one thing, we then lose sight of the ways in which Schleiermacher saw himself as standing in continuity with the Reformation heritage precisely on account of his rejection of "speculation" in theology in favor of a descriptive account of the Christian religious self-consciousness.[3] Furthermore, as the debate with Brunner regarding natural theology illustrates, Calvin's theology cannot be invoked as it stands to support Barth's position; Barth himself admits that he must go beyond the explicit statements of the Reformers in order to say what needs to be said in 1934. And, ironically, while Brunner appeals to Calvin to defend his own position against Barth's criticisms, Brunner concedes that Calvin's actual statements in this respect veer further in the direction of liberal Protestantism than he himself is willing to go.

This comparative study of Calvin and Schleiermacher with respect to their interpretations of religion and Christian faith thus proceeds from a different set of conceptual categories than that employed by the neo-orthodox when they accused the liberal tradition of a betrayal of the Reformation heritage. Contrary to the view of Brunner, Calvin is a theologian at one with Schleiermacher in his concern to define the essence of religion as a preliminary step toward defining the essence of Christian faith. Contrary to the view of Barth, Calvin is in agreement with Schleiermacher in portraying the human person as an essentially religious being whose true self-understanding demands the acknowledgment of its inescapable relatedness to God. If, therefore, we wish to ask regarding the degrees of continuity and discontinuity between Schleiermacher and the classical Protestant tradition, the proper comparison can only be conducted on the basis of a different set of conceptual categories than that employed by the neo-orthodox theologians themselves.

To be sure, an alternative set of comparative categories does not necessarily invalidate the concerns of the neo-orthodox theologians altogether. In other words, there may still be good reasons for criticizing the tradition of Schleiermacher in the name of fidelity to the Reformation. But this type of theological criticism would have to proceed on the basis of an adequate historical comparison of classical and liberal theology which neither prejudices the outcome in advance by applying misleading categories nor fails to take seriously the systematic function of the concept "religion" within the dogmatic interpretations of Christian faith given by the preeminent representatives of the classical and liberal paradigms. But, in any case, the question of the relation between the two epochs of Protestant theology will have to be reconceived in order for contemporary theologians to ask, as did the neo-orthodox theologians in an earlier day, whether and, if so, how the liberal tradition of Schleiermacher should be judged inadequate in certain respects in the light of our present theological situation.

What is Christian Faith?

The two epochs of Protestant theology must be understood as responses to distinct religious crises in the theological tradition of Augustine: the Reformation and the Enlightenment. From the Reformation to the Enlightenment there was a shift in the religious question itself from a concern with personal salvation from sin and guilt to a concern with the place and significance of human life within the comprehensive order of nature. In response to their respective historical contexts, Calvin and Schleiermacher interpret the meaning of Christian faith in such a way as to provide an answer to these differing formulations of the religious question.

In addition to this transformation of the religious question from the Reformation to the Enlightenment, there was a corresponding shift in the criteria for criticizing inherited religious traditions: from a novel interpretation of scripture that shook the foundations of the church's doctrinal heritage to a new way of looking at the world opened up by scientific and historical modes of inquiry that demanded of received traditions a rational account of the meaning of theological discourse. Hence, Reformation and Enlightenment can be spoken of as religious crises in the West that, in each instance, occasioned critical reflection upon the meaning and truth of inherited religious traditions. The efforts of Calvin and Schleiermacher to define the authentic essence of Christian religion reflect these shifts in the criteria by which theological traditions from the past are critically evaluated.

Following Luther, Calvin diagnosed the religious problem of the sixteenth century as stemming from a faulty theology that encouraged sinners to rely upon their own abilities to cooperate in the process of salvation. According to this interpretation, such a theology expressed a lack of wholehearted trust in the utter sufficiency of God's grace for salvation. It also led to the various abusive practices of the late medieval church that had been criticized by reform-minded humanists such as Erasmus. But from the Protestant viewpoint, these abuses of the church signified far more than mere moral lapses resulting from a poorly educated clergy and a corrupt ecclesiastical administration in Rome. They illustrated in very practical terms the theology taught by the church itself, which the Protestants did not hesitate to denounce as "Pelagian" works-righteousness. Thus the cause of reform demanded a reform of the church's theology and not simply a reform of its practice.

According to Calvin, a religion of "works" results from "speculation" in matters of theology. Speculation is the attempt to invent a religion for ourselves instead of adhering to the religion God has revealed. Its consequence is that God is no longer the sole object of our ultimate trust, gratitude, and obedience. In place of the true God who alone is the benevolent source of life and its good gifts, human beings worship false gods fabricated out of their own perverse imagination. This false religion is characterized by idolatry, superstition, and hypocrisy. Whereas piety is the proper religious response to the revelation of God's goodness, false religion is the zealous attempt to placate idols resulting in a deluded sense of our own goodness.

Faith in the gospel is "the root of true piety" because Jesus Christ reveals God's goodness anew in the form of a promise of forgiveness to sinners who have turned away from the overflowing fountain of all good gifts.[4] When God is trusted as a merciful father who forgives his wayward children, our hearts are once again disposed to obey him in all things. Since piety consists in genuine service of God arising out of love and reverence in response to his goodness, faith in God's mercy re-establishes for guilt-stricken sinners the proper foundation for true religion.

Faith in the promise of forgiveness unites us with Christ so that we share in his righteousness before God, along with all its benefits. By participating in Christ, we undergo a shift in perception regarding how God considers us: instead of viewing God as angry with us on account of our sin, we see God as graciously disposed to us for the sake of Christ. Now we are freed of the guilt that made us see God's curse wherever we looked and that led us to our vain efforts to placate his wrath by means of works. Justified by faith alone in the gospel, we are enabled to stand before the heavenly judge with a good conscience.

Nonetheless, the gospel's demonstration of God's mercy leads to a new zeal to serve God out of gratitude for the gift of salvation. Thus, the gospel offers a "double grace": justification (forgiveness) and sanctification (a new life based on forgiveness). In the process of sanctification, the law serves as a model of piety toward God and love toward our neighbors. Sanctification restores human existence to its original vocation: to live in constant and wholehearted praise of God.

In an age when modern science had shattered the medieval picture of the world and of humanity's place in it, Schleiermacher saw the problem of his day to lie, not in an attempt to rely upon our own merits for salvation, but in a confusion regarding the meaning of religious "faith." Amid the rationalistic ethos of the Enlightenment, faith had come to be associated with intellectual assent to the doctrines supernaturally revealed in scripture and summarized by the church's confessional standards. As an alternative to the orthodox doctrine, enlightened intellectuals proposed a religion based on metaphysics (speculation) or practical philosophy (morals) that would provide an answer to the question of the meaning and purpose of human life within the natural order. Hence, the modern person was confronted with a choice between the orthodox substance of the Protestant tradition or a rational religion that harmonized with the new scientific interpretations of the world. From Schleiermacher's perspective, however, both orthodoxy (with its rejection of the Enlightenment) and rationalism (with its rejection of inherited tradition) were equally inadequate because they operated with a similar definition of religious faith as intellectual assent to theoretical propositions accompanied by the appropriate moral consequences of such belief. While orthodoxy and rationalism differed in the content of the doctrines to be affirmed and the reasons given for affirming them, they nonetheless shared a faulty premise.

Schleiermacher's indebtedness to pietism and romanticism must be appreciated in light of his efforts to reframe the problem. Although the pietists of the eighteenth century did not reject orthodox doctrine, they insisted that faith consists not in mere assent to doctrines but in a personal relationship with the redeemer. For their part, the romantics, though despising the ecclesiastical tradition, criticized the intellectualism and moralism of the Enlightenment in the name of the individual cultivation of feeling. Drawing upon both pietism and romanticism, Schleiermacher believed that the way forward beyond the conflict between orthodox supernaturalism and Enlightenment rationalism lay in an interpretation of the inherited doctrines of the Protestant church as giving intellectual and moral expression to the distinctive configuration of religious affections resulting from a

Christian's redemptive experience with Christ.

Redemption, in Schleiermacher's theology, occurs through participation in the sinless God-consciousness of Jesus wherein we share his relationship with God and its attendant benefits. In the proclaimed Word Jesus presents himself not only as the ideal exemplar of piety but as one who assumes believers into the power of his own relationship with God. Indeed, in his perfect God-consciousness Jesus is a revelation of God. Through his activity, continued in the ministry of the church, Jesus introduces a "new creation" that completes the old by virtue of his perfect mediation of God. The redemption effected by Jesus is nothing less than the fulfillment of nature's design through the creation of free persons whose every active and passive relation to the world is permeated by the consciousness of their absolute dependence upon the infinite God.

The inability to feel one's absolute dependence upon God in every moment of relative dependence and relative freedom leads to a distorted perception of reality and of one's relation to it. Sin is a "disturbance" of nature, not in the sense that nature itself is distorted but, rather, because the human subject no longer sees it correctly. "The world appears differently to the human being," Schleiermacher writes, "than it otherwise would if there were no sin."[5] By setting ourselves against the comprehensive and inclusive whole of reality, we wrongly perceive the whole to be pitted against us. Thus, the "evils" that encounter us, whether they be the inevitable result of natural process (e.g., sickness and death) or the result of other people's actions, are experienced by us as punishments for our sin. In truth, the sense of punishment arises from our own actual guilt in relation to God. What cannot, however, be perceived in the sinful state is that the world, as a whole and in all its parts, is an "organ" for the divine self-manifestation.[6]

Through his office as redeemer, Christ assumes us into the power of his own God-consciousness. Through his office as reconciler, Christ assumes us into the fellowship of his blessedness. That is to say, we no longer experience the hindrances that life in the world presents to us as divine punishments of our sin. Fellowship with Christ, therefore, not only gives us a new power in relation to our consciousness of God but also dissolves the connection between sin and evil that is the result of the guilt-ridden consciousness of sin.

The life of believers in Christ may appropriately be described as consisting in regeneration and sanctification: from Christ we receive a new power with respect to the God-consciousness as well as the strength to increase in piety. Regeneration points to the act of union with Christ whereas sanctification points to the state of union with him.[7] Faith, in Schleiermacher's theology, is the means by which we appropriate Christ for ourselves.[8] It consists in the dual consciousness of the forgiveness of sin and of adoption as a child of God.[9]

As those who are redeemed and reconciled by participation in Christ we are conscious of God's love and wisdom. The creative power that sustains the world is now perceived by the believer as "loving omnipotence" or "omnipotent love."[10] The world, accordingly, is understood to be a "theatre of redemption" through which God is revealed.[11] The world is, therefore, finally to be recognized as a good place on account of its absolute dependence upon God's loving and wise power. It is the lens of redemption that enables believers correctly to perceive the world and their apppropriate place within it.

When Calvin and Schleiermacher are compared with respect to their understandings of the content of Christian faith, their material agreement is striking. For both, sinners are unable to perceive the truth about the world and their place within it. We are unable to see the world as the realm of God's providential care and concern. In Calvin's terms, we are unable to see the world as the object of God's fatherly solicitude and, consequently, we fail to bring to God the appropriate trust, obedience, and gratitude. In Schleiermacher's terms, we are unable to perceive our absolute dependence upon God in every moment of our lives. As a result, we live under the illusion of a self-sufficiency of the finite in relation to the infinite God.

Luther's new religious answer to the anxiety regarding personal salvation shattered the premises of medieval theology that gave rise to this anxiety in the first place. It is not insignificant that Calvin does not consider personal salvation to be the primary goal of a life of faith; rather, it is the glory of God for which the faithful live. Whereas Luther's initial quest was to find a gracious God who forgives sin, Calvin's theology has its point of departure in Luther's answer, which gave birth to the Protestant alternative to Catholicism: the sinner is justified by faith alone in the assurance of God's mercy revealed in the gospel of Jesus Christ. We might even say that the driving concern of Calvin's theology is what it means to serve the God whose graciousness has been revealed in the gospel and rediscovered by Luther.

Schleiermacher's theology adapts the inherited Protestant tradition to answer a modern formulation of the religious question: What is the place and significance of human life within the whole system of nature? Though Calvin's theology was not explicitly intended as an answer to that question, it is easy to see how his theology of grateful service in response to God's graciousness can be reshaped for the purposes of a different historical circumstance in which the religious question assumes a new form. Just as Luther's answer provided the point of departure for Calvin's theology, in the hands of Schleiermacher Calvin's theology of service to God proved itself adaptable to the modern situation in which the question of the meaning and purpose of human life was being asked in a radically new form.[12] There is, then, an important similarity in the material content of their interpretations of Christian faith in spite of the difference in the formulation of the religious question in response to which Calvin and Schleiermacher addressed their theologies.

For both theologians, the *Protestant* character of the dogmatic task necessarily involves a critical sifting of received theological traditions for the sake of defining the authentic essence of Christian faith. It is in relation to this critical task that each theologian confronts the problem of religious diversity, both within Christianity itself and between Christianity and the non-Christian religions. When Calvin and Schleiermacher are compared regarding the question of religious diversity, it becomes apparent to what extent Protestant theology has undergone a shift from its classical to its liberal form with respect to the critical criteria employed for evaluating the validity of inherited religious traditions.

For Calvin, the question of religious diversity was primarily, though not exclusively, a matter of competing interpretations of Christian faith within Christendom. Calvin's purpose in composing his *pietatis summa* was to provide a discussion of true religion amid cultural confusion about religious matters. At the time of the Reformation, "true religion" meant the correct theological understanding of apostolic Christianity as opposed to Roman Catholicism. In this controversy, Calvin saw nothing less than a continuation of the ancient struggle between true and false religion recorded in the scriptures. Using the biblical writings to criticize the subsequent doctrinal tradition of the church, Calvin compared the Roman doctrine to the false doctrines taught by the pagans, on the one hand, and by the Jews, on the other. Whereas the religious folly of the pagans is chiefly to be discerned in their polytheistic idolatry, the monotheism of the Jews did not prevent them from rejecting the gospel. In both cases, the crucial thing to note is that false religion is based upon a refusal to admit our absolute dependence upon God's grace for salvation. According to Calvin, the Roman Catholics are no less guilty of false religion than the pagans and Jews of antiquity. Protestantism, therefore, has to be interpreted as the contemporary restoration of true religion in an era when Christendom itself has fallen victim to false religion.

It is crucial to note that Calvin's discussion of religious diversity does not identify the historic Christian tradition unambiguously with true religion. To be sure, Calvin is no pluralist. In one sense, of course, only Christianity can be said to be the true religion of humanity. But Calvin is aware that even those who claim to profess allegiance to the Christian religion can, in fact, be practicing false religion. In this respect, these Christians are no better off, religiously speaking, than pagans, Jews, or Muslims. This means that rigorous theological judgment must be exercised in order to determine which form of Christianity can lay claim to being the true religion of humanity. Nonetheless, Calvin does not exclude the possibility that those who are not in any empirical sense within the Christian fold can be devotees of true religion. Among the pagans there have always been those whom God has illuminated directly through the internal agency of the Holy Spirit apart from the ordinary means of preaching.

Moreover, Calvin discerns a progressive revelation in the history of religion that requires us to interpret Christian faith as standing in fundamental continuity with what preceded it in Judaism. Instead of viewing Christianity as an absolutely unique phenomenon that emerged only in the apostolic period, the Christian gospel is simply a clearer, less ambiguous presentation of the message taught by the Old Testament prophets regarding faith in the utter sufficiency of God's grace for salvation. In this sense, it can be affirmed that the Old Testament teaches the Christian religion. And even though paganism as a whole is to be condemned as a departure from the one true religion of humankind, Calvin notes distinctions among the pagans themselves with respect to religious matters so that he can make relative judgments regarding the degrees in their apprehension of truth. In Calvin's interpretation, there is and always has been only one true religion which is identical with the Christian religion, correctly understood; all other religions are the spoiled fruits of the seed of religion. Nonetheless, among persons living within the orbit of these other religions, one can discern differing levels of knowledge of this one true religion.

From Calvin's perspective, the truth of religion does not depend upon the ambiguities of received religious tradition since human traditions, including Christianity, can be distorted by false religion. In its original criticism of Catholicism, therefore, Protestantism gave evidence of a deep ambivalence regarding "tradition" and its authority in matters religious. On the one hand, Protestants criticized the received tradition of the church according to the norm of a more ancient standard (*sola scriptura*); on the other hand, they construed the meaning of this ancient standard in a way that posited discontinuity in the history of its reception (*sola fide*). The Protestant position thus involved a tense relation to the received Christian tradition. The Reformers' view of history, similar to that of Renaissance humanists, looked upon the Middle Ages as a decline from—indeed, a perversion of—the original purity of the church. Their concept of "reformation," accordingly, was backward-looking. They did not seek to revise the old tradition according to a new norm but, rather, they sought to restore the tradition to its pristine character as this could be discerned through a proper interpretation of the scriptures. It must be remembered that, within this classical Protestant paradigm, the scriptures are not understood as the product of human traditions. As a consequence, the scriptures provide an unambiguous rule by which true religion can be measured amid the ambiguities of human traditions.

The question of religious diversity assumes quite a different form in Schleiermacher's reflections upon the essence of Christian faith. For one thing, Schleiermacher does not adopt the classical Protestant view that looks upon the Reformation as the restoration of a lost purity that had characterized the apostolic age. Unlike Calvin, Schleiermacher views both Protestantism and Catholicism as representing genuine modifications of the authentic essence of Christianity, so that the cause of reforming the church of abuses is not to be equated with Protestantism and opposed to Catholicism. In Schleiermacher's perspective, history moves forward, not backwards, ever generating more specific historical individuals. Thus, the essence of Protestantism, for Schleiermacher, is not identical with the essence of authentic Christianity, as it was for Calvin. For this reason, both Catholics and Protestants can make legitimate appeal to the New Testament; the appeal to scripture can only serve as a warrant that a doctrine is genuinely Christian, not that it is genuinely Protestant. But scripture is not elevated above the flux of the historical process; its unique authority resides in the fact that it contains the original apostolic witness to the message of Jesus.[13]

By contrast with Calvin, then, Schleiermacher exhibits a very appreciative attitude toward the meaning of "tradition" within Christian history since he does not posit a radical break between the purity of the apostolic age and the subsequent history of Christendom before the Reformation. And, of course, for a modern Protestant like Schleiermacher, this essentially positive attitude toward tradition is applied to what has since the sixteenth century become the *tradition* of the Reformation!

Within this Protestant tradition, Schleiermacher clearly identifies himself with the Reformed heritage of Calvin. But, in accord with the ecumenical spirit of the church of the Prussian "union," Schleiermacher does not pit his own Reformed tradition against the Lutheran tradition since he views both as participating equally in the distinctive essence of Protestantism. Nonetheless, this ecumenism within Protestantism does not lead him to dismiss the confessional differences between the

Lutherans and the Reformed; he simply believes that a proper historical understanding of these differences can show how they admit of doctrinal reconciliation as interpretations of the religious affections shared in common by Protestants. Indeed, the contemporary task of theology is to bring this distinctive Protestant spirit, shared by the Lutherans and Reformed alike, into sharper focus by extending the scope of its theological criticism to include those doctrines not reworked by the original Reformers.[14] Thus Schleiermacher adopts a "progressive" view of the Reformation that looks forward, not backward. The Reformation did not end with the sixteenth century but remains a never-ending task for Protestant theology itself.

Aside from the question of religious diversity within Christianity, differences between Calvin and Schleiermacher can be observed with respect to the question of religious diversity beyond Christendom. To Calvin's way of thinking, religious diversity is a certain sign of the perversion of nature's design, since it is the result of human fabrication in religious matters. Unlike Calvin, Schleiermacher does not evaluate religious diversity negatively as the outgrowth of sin. He looks upon diversity, rather, as the inevitable result of the historical character of human life. The fact of religious diversity, then, is not a problem to be overcome, but a reality to be accepted and appreciated.

This is a shift of enormous magnitude from the classical to the liberal Protestant assessment of religious diversity. But precisely this shift entails that the question of the "truth" of Christian faith be radically reconceived. According to Schleiermacher, the difference between Christianity and the other religions is not that between true and false religion. In accordance with a truly historical perspective, each religion must be evaluated with respect to the developmental stages of human self-consciousness. Since the progression of our consciousness of God goes hand in hand with the furtherance of our consciousness of the world of which we are parts, we attain to a fully developed consciousness of the infinite reality upon which the finite world is absolutely dependent only in relation to a fully developed consciousness of the world as a system of reciprocal relations. Such a consciousness of God emerges only in the monotheistic religions and, for that reason, they are to be judged superior to the non-monotheistic religions.

In Schleiermacher's view, Christianity is a unique religious formation among others and its defining essence can only be discerned by historical comparison with the non-Christian religions. As a monotheistic religion, Christianity stands with Judaism and Islam at the highest stage of religious development. Unlike these other two religions, however, monotheism in Christianity is not tainted by vestiges from the lower forms of religious development. Seen in this light, Christianity is properly judged by the historian of religions to be the highest religion.

Still, Christianity is not defined solely by its monotheistic stage of development; like Judaism, it is also a teleological religion in which our consciousness of God as the infinite reality upon which we are absolutely dependent is a matter for personal responsibility. The teleological type of religion is thus a necessary presupposition of Christianity's central idea of redemption from sin. But Christianity is not to be viewed as a continuation of Jewish religion, even though its historical origins are bound up with Judaism. Christianity is a new formation in the history of religion and, as such, it stands in the same relation, religiously speaking, to Judaism as to paganism. As a unique individual among the religions Christianity is properly defined as a monotheistic religion of the teleological type wherein our consciousness of God is traced to the redemption from sin made possible by Jesus of Nazareth. Apart from this explicit relation to Jesus as the redeemer, no person may be called a "Christian" in Schleiermacher's sense. Given this insistence upon the historical particularity of the individual positive religions, Schleiermacher considers the Old Testament as the product of Jewish, not Christian, religion.

To be sure, Schleiermacher believes that Christianity's central idea of redemption gives it a radical concern for purity of religion that suffices to explain its polemical history as a religious tradition. With regard to other positive religions as well as within its own house, the drive toward a pure piety makes Christianity "the religion of religions."[15] But this is not the distinction between true and false religion. When Schleiermacher considers the positive religions from the perspective of the comparative study of religions, he concludes that Christianity represents the purest expression of the highest stage in the development of religion. From the perspective of the dogmatic theologian, however, who pitches his tent within the religious community established by Christ, the God-consciousness has no real power over sin apart from Christ's redemptive activity.

Hence, Schleiermacher presents us with a paradox: on the one hand, he is a pluralist with respect to his historical-comparative approach to the positive religions, though not a relativist since he evaluates religions according to their placement on the trajectory of religious development; on the other hand, he takes his stand among the religions as a Christian who confesses with his religious community that Christ communicates a power with respect to the God-consciousness that is not available in the other positive religions. Here we witness the beginnings of the distinctively modern attempt to integrate the non-theological study of the history of religions with a theological evaluation of Christianity in relation to the other religious traditions.[16]

In Protestant theology in both the classical and liberal paradigms the systematic attempt to define the authentic essence of Christian faith has necessarily involved addressing the question of religious diversity. In classical Protestantism the problem of religious diversity was primarily a question of competing theological interpretations of Christian faith itself. Nonetheless, what was at stake for Protestants during the Reformation was the question of "true religion" and, for that reason, Calvin defended the Protestant interpretation of Christian faith by setting the sixteenth-century conflict within the larger context of his understanding of the history of religion.

In the modern period, the question of religious diversity did not mean only or even primarily theological diversity within Christianity itself. Of course, diversity with respect to traditional divisions within the Christian tradition remained important, but this type of diversity (Catholic and Protestant, Lutheran and Reformed) was not the most fundamental challenge. The Enlightenment's criticism of theological traditions forged in the Middle Ages relativized to an important extent these classical divisions within Christianity itself. In the modern context, the problem of religious diversity became primarily the question of understanding Christianity as one religious tradition among others. And the historical approach to the interpretation of religious traditions, including the Christian tradition, required that the critical criteria by which inherited religious traditions are evaluated be consistent with the methods employed in the modern study of history. Schleiermacher's attempt to define and to interpret the Christian tradition thus represents the historicization of Protestant dogmatics.

When it comes to comparing Calvin and Schleiermacher regarding their dogmatic expositions of Christian faith, what strikes the careful reader is the material similarity in their interpretations. Though the two theologians are articulating the meaning of Christian faith so as to provide answers to differing cultural formulations of the religious concern, the continuity of theological substance is evident. Thus it becomes necessary for the historical student to reject Brunner's assessment that Schleiermacher's theology is deficient as a Protestant interpretation of faith if Calvin's theology is taken as the measure of what is genuinely Protestant (as Brunner has acknowledged he does).

In their attempts to give an appropriate theological definition of the authentic character of distinctively Christian faith, both theologians are required to grapple with the questions of theological and religious diversity. The most important differences between Calvin and Schleiermacher are to be discerned in the critical criteria employed in the two epochs of Protestant theology for evaluating inherited religious and theological traditions.

The next step is to compare the elemental definitions of religion given by Calvin and Schleiermacher.

What is Religion?

When we consider the definitions of religion given by Calvin and Schleiermacher, we must remember the reason why such an initial definition is deemed necessary for Protestant theology. Each theologian views the polemical character of Protestantism as issuing from a concern for the religious integrity of the church's faith in Jesus Christ. If Calvin and Schleiermacher can be said to be committed, precisely as Protestants, to upholding the religious integrity of the Christian message and, as a consequence, to criticizing Christian theology to the extent it confuses the gospel with either irreligious concerns (e.g., for Calvin, with "speculation" leading to "works") or non-religious concerns (e.g., for Schleiermacher, with the theoretical concerns of metaphysics and the practical concerns of moral philosophy), this requires of them not only a statement of the essence of *Christian* religion but, also, a statement of the essence of *religion*.

The place to begin is with the observation of the experiential character of the definitions of religion given by both Calvin and Schleiermacher. The designation of their interpretations of religion as "experiential" allows for sufficient flexibility in specifying more closely the differences that can be identified. The most important difference to be addressed in this respect is that Calvin typically speaks of religion as born of a knowledge of God whereas Schleiermacher repudiates the idea that religion is knowledge and argues, instead, that its proper location on the map of human experience is feeling. This difference suggests, at first glance, that Calvin's definition of religion should be described as "cognitive" since it arises in response to knowledge. By contrast, Schleiermacher's location of religion in the realm of feeling has often been characterized as "subjectivistic" and, therefore, lacking in cognitive content.

There are two major difficulties that confront anyone who seeks to compare Calvin and Schleiermacher on this question. First, Calvin did not provide the kind of crisp, dialectically precise definitions sought by Schleiermacher (at least in *The Christian Faith*, if not in the *Speeches*). In humanist fashion, Calvin works with metaphors such as "the seed of religion" implanted in all persons that it might blossom into piety toward God. The acknowledgment of the metaphorical and, indeed, rhetorical use of language in the *Institutes* makes it advisable not to press for a degree of conceptual clarity that would be foreign to the anti-scholastic character of Calvin's humanist model for a *summa pietatis*.[17] Having said that, however, we may nonetheless assume that a humanist scholar trained in the rhetorical traditions of the Renaissance knew precisely what he was doing when he used a metaphor and that it is completely appropriate, therefore, for readers to take it seriously as a clue to the interpretation of his text. Moreover, it would be wrong to assume that a metaphor has no cognitive significance in serious intellectual discourse.[18]

More difficult, perhaps, is the fact that Calvin and Schleiermacher develop their interpretations of religion on different sides of Kant's "Copernican Revolution" in philosophy. Schleiermacher made his conceptual distinctions in an effort to clarify his experiential definition of religion in the light of Kant's critique of traditional metaphysics. Furthermore, Schleiermacher's definition is intended as an alternative to Kant's grounding of religion in the postulates of practical reason after he had removed it from the realm of theoretical reason. Calvin was not responding to Kant's epistemology and we have no way of translating Calvin's terminology directly into a post-Kantian philosophical framework. What we do know, however, is that Calvin polemicized against an intellectualized approach to the knowledge of God which he, like other humanists of his day, thought was characteristic of the scholastic theology that needed to be replaced by a new approach emphasizing the affective and practical dimensions of religious knowledge.

The best question to ask, given these obstacles to direct comparison, may simply be: What is the relation between cognitive, moral, and affective elements in the definitions of religion given by Calvin and Schleiermacher?

It is true of Calvin that he posits a certain knowledge of God to be the indispensable foundation of true religion (piety). In this respect, he is at one with the ancient philosophers in conversation with whom he hammers out his own definition of religion. But it is also the case that Calvin insists upon the proper religious response as the necessary condition for the subjective appropriation of the knowledge of God. There is, then, this tension in Calvin's theology: apart from certain knowledge of God there is no true religion, yet apart from genuine religion there is no adequate appropriation of the knowledge of God. For this reason, Calvin insists that the knowledge of God with which piety is concerned dare not, like speculation, merely tickle the mind since it must sink its roots deep within the heart.[19] In his definition of religion, therefore, Calvin stresses the affective aspects of the knowledge of God.[20] Indeed, Calvin asserts that the seat of religion is in the "heart," not the intellect.[21] Apart from an appropriate knowledge of self, any knowledge of God is useless and, indeed, pernicious since it can yield only the worst fruit.

For Calvin, human nature is intrinsically religious on account of a "sense of divinity" originally given to all persons as a constitutive aspect of their experience. This is not to be understood as a propositional sort of knowledge. It is, rather, an awareness or a feeling (*sensus*) of the numinous and holy which evokes our worship and commitment. When the seed of religion comes to fruition in a pious heart and mind, this sense of God's reality imbues our perception of the natural order with awe and respect so that we understand all things as gifts of the creator to be received with appreciation and thanksgiving.[22] When this is not our response to nature's witness, we are afflicted with a bad conscience which convicts us of denying what we know to be true.[23] What is undeniable is that, for Calvin, the religious relation is not primarily intellectual since, apart from its affective and moral components, the knowledge of God that shines within us and outside of us is of no use at all.

By locating religion in feeling, Schleiermacher makes two fundamental distinctions: first, he distinguishes religion from knowledge and, second, he distinguishes religion from morality. First, with respect to knowledge, Schleiermacher's central concern is to deny that religion arises in response to a metaphysical knowledge attained either through philosophical argument (natural theology) or through a set of revealed propositions about God contained in the Bible and summarized in the church's confessions (orthodox supernaturalism). Such a procedure, in Schleiermacher's view, renders the religious life dependent upon the intellectual faculty. Furthermore, it gives pride of place to intellectuals, whether philosophers or theologians, who make the mastery of such knowledge their special vocation. In his protest against defining piety as a form of knowledge, therefore, Schleiermacher sounds a radically egalitarian note in assuring us that religion is not a "second-hand" version for lay people of a more academically refined product of the intelligentsia. By locating religion in its own sphere, so to speak, he intends to grant an integrity to religious experience which is logically independent of the fortunes of natural theology in the face of the critical philosophy and which does not, moreover, require that the doctrinal traditions of the church be exempted from historical investigation. The deep experiential emphasis of his definition of religion certainly reflects his roots in the pietist movement. Indeed, it is entirely appropriate that in his relocation of religion from the domain of knowledge to that of feeling he understood himself as a pietist "of a higher order." The knowledge that is of concern to theology is knowledge of the religious affections, which find intellectual expression in the doctrines of a particular religious community.

Aside from distinguishing religion from knowledge, Schleiermacher also distinguishes religion sharply from morality, locating them in different domains of the human person. Whereas religion is a modification of feeling and essentially consists in a consciousness of absolute dependence, moral obligation is an active impulse leading to a certain praxis and presupposes an awareness of our partial freedom to shape the world in which we live. Thus, in contrast to Kant, Schleiermacher distances himself from a moral approach to the interpretation of religion. The question here is whether, in so doing, he distances himself from Calvin as well, for whom moral considerations play an important role in his interpretation of the nature of religion.

Unlike Schleiermacher, Calvin does invoke the sense of moral obligation in order to make his case on behalf of the essentially religious character of human life. In addition to the "seed of religion" that gives rise to the religious practices of human beings, Calvin adduces conscience as a further testimony of God's claim upon human life.[24] In this respect, Calvin's approach seems, at first glance, to have more affinities with Kant than does Schleiermacher's strictly "religious" approach. Once again, however, it is important to note that Schleiermacher does not doubt that there is a moral avenue to God any more than he doubts that there is a philosophical avenue to God. Schleiermacher, too, argues that God is the source of moral obligation.[25] Indeed, he even speaks of the conscience as an "original revelation" of God to the human being.[26] Schleiermacher's concern is simply to identify the distinctively religious element and to build his theological house on this foundation alone so as not to confuse religion with knowledge or morality.[27]

Calvin, on the other hand, does argue that the only true foundation of morality is religious and he opposes any interpretation of religion that would leave the moral life untouched. This is a large part of his polemic with Epicureanism. Still, Calvin is concerned to distinguish religion from morality in order to argue against the Pelagianizing tendencies of late scholastic theology, which led to a moralistic interpretation of Christian faith. For that reason, he is intent upon explaining the distinctions between piety and justice or, as he also says, faith and love.[28] The former element in each pair pertains to our relation with God whereas the latter element pertains to our relation with the neighbor. Hence, Calvin distinguishes his own definition of piety from that which he finds typical among the ancients whereby piety is directed not only to the gods but also to parents and rulers. So while he insists that our ethical obligations are grounded in our relation to God and that there is no genuine piety apart from an appropriate moral response to our neighbor, Calvin does, nevertheless, distinguish between religion and morality.

Still, it has been argued by some critics that Schleiermacher's theology is insufficiently concerned with the problems of the moral life and that this deficiency has its root in his non-moral definition of religion.[29] As a result, an adequate definition of religion for the purposes of Protestant theology must, following Kant, include reference to the teleological or moral dimension within the elemental definition of religion itself.[30] Three observations seem pertinent in this regard when comparing Schleiermacher with Calvin.

First, it may well be that Calvin's theology differs from Schleiermacher's in the relative weight given to reflection upon the religious dimension of the moral life. The prominence of this feature in Calvin's theology can be explained by recalling that the original Protestant alternative to Roman Catholic theology was to suggest that the sixteenth-century crisis in the church is fundamentally a religious, not a moral, problem. From that perspective, it was thus necessary to expose the religious problematics inherent in any moralistic approach to the problem of church reform.

Second, Schleiermacher distinguished two distinct tasks for Protestant dogmatics: the interpretation of doctrine (*Glaubenslehre*) and the interpretation of morals (*Sittenlehre*).[31] There is no such corresponding division of labor in Calvin's view of the dogmatic task of Protestant theology. One would, therefore, have to pay sufficient attention to Schleiermacher's theological ethics before deciding that the teleological dimension of Schleiermacher's theology is inadequately developed.[32]

Third, there are differing ways to develop theological ethics within the context of a Christian theology. If Calvin and Schleiermacher take different approaches to theological ethics, this does not mean that Calvin works with a "moral" definition of religion by contrast with Schleiermacher.[33]

We may cautiously conclude, therefore, that it is inaccurate to think of Calvin's definition of religion as having more affinities with Kant's approach than with Schleiermacher's. Like Schleiermacher, Calvin distinguishes the religious from the moral dimension of experience, even as he gives a great deal of attention to understanding the religious aspect of the moral life.[34]

So where does this leave us with respect to the question of the relation between the intellectual, moral, and affective elements in the two definitions of religion we are seeking to compare? Schleiermacher makes a sharp distinction between the realm of religion (feeling) and the realms of knowledge (intellect) and morality (activity). This is a conceptual distinction in thought, not a separation in experience. The importance of this clarification is that Schleiermacher does not, as is commonly assumed, isolate religion from either the cognitive or the moral functions of the human person. Indeed, for him, religious feeling issues in an appropriate knowledge (expressed in doctrines) and a corresponding conduct (expressed in morals). To be sure, this distinction is foreign to Calvin in the strict sense, yet analogues can be found in his thought that suggest important commonalities.

For Calvin, unlike Schleiermacher, religion begins with a knowledge of God, though this is not to be understood as a propositional knowledge but, rather, as an immediate awareness of being related to God. Knowledge of self thus leads inescapably to knowledge of God. Still, this knowledge is useless if it does not sink its roots in the heart and give birth to piety. Piety, therefore, is an affective response to the knowledge of God which necessarily brings with it an appropriate moral response to our circumstances. Calvin distinguishes between heart, head, and deed; when disconnected from a pious heart, the head's knowledge is "speculation" just as when disconnected from a pious heart our good deeds are "works."

For the sake of gaining clarity regarding the essential nature of religion, Schleiermacher began his discussion by bracketing the question of the concept or idea of "God." This led his critics to suppose that he was advocating a "religion without God." But his point is that "God" is a religious word; if you don't understand what "religion" means, you can't understand what a religious person means by the word "God." Defining "religion" thus serves as a rule for monitoring theology's discourse about God by distinguishing it from other uses of the word in theoretical and practical philosophy. While Calvin insists that true religion is based on knowledge of God's character, his tireless polemic against "speculation" requires that all authentic speech about God be immediately connected with its existential and practical implications. In Calvin's vocabulary, "God" is the referent of a properly defined "piety."[35]

When the definitions of religion given by Calvin and Schleiermacher are set side by side, there are important similarities to be discerned. Calvin defines religion as "reverence joined with love of God which the knowledge of his benefits induces."[36] Schleiermacher defines the essence of religion as "the feeling of absolute dependence" which, in turn, is said to be a "consciousness of being in relation to God."[37] While different from one another, these two definitions of religion are by no means incompatible. In each case, the definition of religion includes a reference to the human being who is the subject of religion and to God who is the object of religion.

The fundamental similarity in the material definitions of the essence of religion lies in the view shared by Calvin and Schleiermacher that the religious character of human existence arises in response to a revelation of God mediated through an awareness of the finitude we share in common with all created things. What distinguishes the human being from other creatures is that it can become conscious of this finite structure of our existence. Moreover, this consciousness discloses to us that finite being is essentially constituted by a relation to God as the infinite source and sustenance of finite being. The religious aspect or dimension of our common human experience leads to the recognition that the meaning and purpose of human existence is finally defined by its relatedness to God.

Furthermore, according to both theologians, God is known only through his effects in the order of finite being, never *a se*. This is what Calvin means when he speaks of God's accommodation of himself to the capacity of finite minds and what Schleiermacher means when he says that we have no experience of God apart from our experience of the world. It is this commonality, by the way, that gives to their theologies what some critics may call a "pantheistic" tinge, though, as we have seen, each theologian is careful to distinguish the creator from the creation, even as they both acknowledge that finite creatures have no direct access to God apart from the mediation of the creation. For this reason, therefore, religion has its own "field" of discourse, so to speak, in the illumination of the finite character of existence and its peculiar meaning for the human being which lies in the explicit consciousness of our relation to the infinite God.

In spite of this material similarity in the definition of religion, there is an important difference to be noted in the function of the concept "piety" in the two theologies. This difference becomes evident when we reflect upon the fact that Schleiermacher's definition is relatively abstract in comparison with Calvin's.

When Calvin speaks of "piety" (*pietas*), he is simultaneously defining a normative concept and describing a concrete instantiation of the norm that characterized the first human beings before their fall into sin (false religion). Not only is true religion to be defined as love and reverence in appreciation of God's bounty, but Adam actually embodied these defining characteristics of true religion before his fall. Indeed, Calvin obtains his definition by considering what humanity was like before its knowledge of God's goodness was clouded by sin. Nonetheless, this is not merely a historical fact to be recounted by Calvin, but the acknowledgment of a normative claim upon human existence even after the fall. In other words, Calvin's definition of piety is both a description of humanity in the beginning of history (*in principio*) and a statement of the human ideal which still exercises a normative claim upon Adam's children in the present moment (*prinzipiell*). For that reason, faith in the gospel is understood as the *restoration* of piety.

When Schleiermacher defines the essence of "piety" (*Frömmigkeit*), he is isolating the abstract feature common to all concrete manifestations of religion that suffices to identify them as "religious." Of course, the correct definition of religion's essence has a normative import. Since religion is defined as a "feeling of absolute dependence," it is possible to sift out the non-religious elements that are often confused with religion (e.g., knowledge and morality which have to do with matters of relative dependence and relative freedom). And since the perfect development of the feeling of absolute dependence requires a consciousness of God as the infinite reality upon which we are absolutely dependent, monotheism can be judged the highest form of religion since only in monotheism does the religious self-consciousness come fully into its own.

But Schleiermacher does not believe that the earliest history of human religion was characterized by a monotheistic consciousness of God. For that reason, Schleiermacher is not able to arrive at a definition of piety by seeking to describe what Adam was like before the fall. Thus Schleiermacher's definition is not in any sense a description of a concrete state of affairs, even of one from the distant past. Hence, he seeks to define piety in the abstract in order to be able to identify the religious element which appropriately claims our attention (*prinzipiell*). It is also for that reason that Christian faith in Schleiermacher's theology cannot be understood as a restoration of the piety lost by Adam. Whereas Christian faith is fully concrete, piety is abstract since, in and of itself, it is never actualized apart from the other factors that go into the making of a positive religion. It is, therefore, only in relation to the redeemer that Christians know that the divine reality upon which they are absolutely dependent has the character of omnipotent love and wisdom. Nonetheless, he affirms that the world is designed as a "good" world by virtue of its ideal structure. Accordingly, there is no reason why the human being should not know a constant communion with God.[38] What for Calvin is both historically original and normative in the present moment is for Schleiermacher normative, though not historically original.[39] Given these differences, it seems more accurate to suggest that Schleiermacher's concept of *Frömmigkeit* finds its direct counterpart, not in Calvin's concept of *pietas*, but rather in his notions of a *semen religionis* or a *sensus divinitatis*.

It may be concluded, therefore, that there is an important similarity in the material content of the definitions of religion given by Calvin and Schleiermacher, in spite of a shift in the way these definitions are employed within their respective theological systems in order to argue for the intrinsically religious character of human existence. But this shift does not detract from the fundamental agreement between them as to why a concept of religion is systematically important in a Christian dogmatics. The delineation of an inescapable religious dimension to human existence leads them to affirm that, apart from the full flowering of piety, the human being can never be authentically human.[40] This argument is not, however, anthropocentric, as if the value of religion were its utility for merely human purposes. On the contrary, this is a radically anti-anthropocentric polemic which emphasizes that we can only become fully human when we acknowledge that humanity is not the center of reality and that God is.[41] Both Calvin and Schleiermacher believe that, in the final analysis, the hallmark of our humanity is to be found in the religious dimension of our lives. And it is here that the systematic explication of distinctively Christian religion finds its "point of contact" with common human experience.

The dogmatic theologies of Calvin and Schleiermacher are more or less internally coherent presentations of the meaning of Christian faith. To be sure, there are differences between Calvin and Schleiermacher regarding the interpretation of religion and Christian faith as religion. But these differences can be properly evaluated only when seen within the broader systematic context of their respective theologies and in light of the questions being posed in their respective historical contexts with which Calvin and Schleiermacher are engaged.

From the perspective of this revised comparative framework, however, what stands out as decisive is the crucial role assigned by both the classical and the liberal Protestant theologian to the concept "religion" as a conceptual tool for the systematic interpretation of Christian faith. In both cases, dogmatics is understood as a descriptive enterprise that has as its immediate object of inquiry the faith of Protestant Christians. But "faith," according to Calvin and Schleiermacher, can be properly defined in its specificity only when clarity has first been gained regarding the definition of "religion" in general. If this means that "theology within the limits of piety alone" has an anthropological starting-point, it does not mean that the faith upon which theology reflects is anthropocentric or subjectivistic.

When Calvin and Schleiermacher are compared with respect to

their definitions of religion, it is evident that both Reformed theologians define "religion" in a way that fits their larger systematic purposes. In neither case can it be said that the definition of religion stands in tension with the definition of faith given by each theologian. And since, as we have seen, there is a significant material similarity in the interpretations of faith given by Calvin and Schleiermacher in spite of differences in the formulation of the religious question to which their theologies seek to respond, we must conclude that Brunner is wrong when he judges Schleiermacher's definition of religion to be antithetical to a doctrine of faith in material continuity with the Reformation. Therefore, when the attempt is made to chart the course of the Reformation heritage from its classical to its modern form, it is misleading to posit a radical break in the Protestant theological tradition on account of Schleiermacher's systematic interpretation of Christian faith as religion.

Calvin and Schleiermacher are most appropriately compared as theologians within a common tradition of theological reflection when their interpretations of Christian faith and religion are examined in light of the shared formal structure that their theologies exhibit. For both, the phenomenon of human religiousness is a response to an original revelation of God given immediately to all persons, just as Christian faith is a response to the decisive revelation of God proclaimed in the gospel of Jesus Christ. When the exemplars of the classical and liberal Protestant paradigms are analyzed from the perspective opened up by this revised posing of the comparative question, it becomes apparent that there are significant affinities in the ways they interpret Christian faith and religion amid important shifts both in the formulation of the religious question and in the critical criteria employed for evaluating inherited religious traditions.

Conclusion

It is difficult to avoid the conclusion that the neo-orthodox historiography is distorted by its employment of a misleading comparative framework that pits the concept of "religion" against the concepts of "faith" and "revelation." By applying these categories in a lopsided fashion, Barth and Brunner were able to make their case for a radical discontinuity between classical and liberal Protestant theology, thereby vindicating their own claims to be in continuity with the Reformation. But close exegetical analysis of the dogmatic theologies of Calvin and Schleiermacher with respect to this question proves that the neo-orthodox thesis of radical discontinuity rests upon a caricature of classical and liberal Protestant theology.

As an example of historical argument based upon such caricature, we may cite the statement of Barth's pupil, Wilhelm Niesel, who decided to investigate the question of Schleiermacher's claim to continuity with the Reformed tradition of Calvin. Niesel concludes:

> It is not surprising that, in response to our question concerning the relations of Schleiermacher's doctrine and the Reformed tradition, we have received a completely negative answer. For can the doctrine about the religious human being stand in any other relation to the theology of the Word? The one excludes the other.[42]

Of course, it comes as no surprise that Niesel received "a completely negative answer" given the way he set up the terms for comparison. But that is the crux of the issue: How can the Reformed tradition's concern for "the theology of the Word" be pitted against its attempt to formulate "the doctrine about the religious human being"? The recognition that the neo-orthodox criticism of Schleiermacher makes use of an inadequate historical framework raises two issues.

First, scholarly integrity requires that we give a fair description of any theology, whether classical or liberal, on its own terms. When, for instance, Calvin's statements are exegeted through the lens of Barth's theological commitments, it is virtually impossible to make sense of the internal logic of Calvin's own position. Consequently, Niesel is constrained both to affirm and to deny the importance of a "seed of religion" in Calvin's theology.

> [Calvin] asserts that there is implanted in man a natural religious disposition. . . . Calvin does not say all this somewhat vaguely on the edge of his theological arguments; he teaches it quite consciously and decisively. . . . Were we to overlook these considerations in an interpretation of Calvin's theology we should be omitting something essential. But we should equally be distorting the doctrine of the Reformer if we were to go no further. . . . For Calvin assigns to this religious disposition of man no importance whatsoever as a link with the proclamation of the Christian verities.[43]

On strictly historical grounds, it may be questioned whether Niesel has given an accurate description of the systematic interrelation within Calvin's theology between his assertion of "a natural religious disposition" (which Niesel concedes is "something essential" to Calvin) and "the proclamation of the Christian verities."

Second, there is the hermeneutical question: What exactly does it mean for modern theologians to claim continuity with the Reformation? As we have seen, Barth and Brunner argued that it was precisely

Schleiermacher's effort to interpret the Protestant faith in positive relation to the Enlightenment ("apologetics") that occasioned his alleged betrayal of the Reformation heritage. Although the neo-orthodox theologians protested against liberal theology's relation to the Enlightenment, these theologians were just as modern in their fundamental philosophical presuppositions. Like the liberals, they fully accepted the historical-critical methods of investigating the Bible and the doctrinal tradition of the church and they embraced without reservation the results of scientific inquiry into the natural world. In these respects, the neo-orthodox had more in common with the liberals of the nineteenth century than with the Reformers of the sixteenth century.

But unlike the liberal theologians who lived in an era of great confidence in the modern culture of the Western world, the neo-orthodox were modern theologians at the very moment when the modern West was experiencing its greatest crisis of self-confidence. If liberal theology was, by definition, an effort to bring the Christian message into a critical correlation with modern self-understanding, neo-orthodox theology was an exemplary attempt to relate that message to the crisis of modern self-understanding. But in both instances, the theology in question was thoroughly modern in its basic presuppositions and procedures.[44]

The power of Barth's initial theological protest has to be understood and appreciated in the light of its ability to speak to the crisis of the modern world without ceasing to participate in that world intellectually. Langdon Gilkey writes of Barth:

> He understood modernity long before most philosophers and other theologians did; he saw its intellectual and moral dilemmas, the collapse of confidence in rationality and goodness, even its sense of helplessness and fatedness, with great clarity while most were still dreaming of civilization's control over its destiny and so of progress.[45]

When Barth told his contemporaries that Christian faith was the antithesis of human religion, his message struck a responsive chord in those who had witnessed the collapse of liberal civilization in the trenches of World War I. It was this same crisis of culture, of course, that made it possible for the hermeneutics of suspicion to emerge into the light of day after having been furtively nourished by the pessimistic undercurrents of the intellectual life of the nineteenth century. Interestingly, theologians agreed with the secular thinkers who argued that religion is "illusion." The message that, according to both the Bible and the Reformation, Christian faith is opposed to the pretensions of religion was thus a powerful idea for a generation in crisis that had experienced a violent break with its own immediate past.[46]

Any fair-minded evaluation of the neo-orthodox era in theology must take this historical situation with utter seriousness. The neo-orthodox theologians were immensely creative in their response to the crisis of modern European civilization signified by the two world wars. The critical question before us is not whether their theologies are responsible interpretations of Christian faith when measured according to their own criteria of theological excellence. The issue is whether the anti-liberal rhetoric of the neo-orthodox theologians, by which they sought to portray their theologies as modern restatements of the Reformation, makes it impossible to grasp the real historical relations between liberal theology and its Reformation roots.[47]

When the neo-orthodox consensus in theology was being radically challenged by a younger generation of Protestant theologians, it is not surprising that the neo-orthodox historiography began to be re-examined as well. In 1964, for instance, Richard R. Niebuhr wrote:

> Something very nearly approaching a Barthian captivity of the history of modern Christian thought reigns in theology outside of ultra-orthodox circles. It manifests itself in the efforts, sometimes rather strained, to interpret the theology of the Reformation in conformity with the canons of Barth's *Church Dogmatics*, and it also appears in the evident preconceptions with which the nineteenth century and Schleiermacher are interpreted by those who have fallen under the sway of this captivity.[48]

Niebuhr goes on to write:

> I suspect the time to be not far away, when the Barthian reading of the history of Christian thought will be corrected in a fashion comparable to that in which the last generation veered away from the theological presuppositions of Adolf von Harnack's history of dogma. In any case, it is this phenomenon, I believe, that does much to explain the character of Schleiermacher research, in the present, and the general lack of esteem for his theology.[49]

Although these lines were written over thirty years ago, much historical work remains to be done. At the end of the twentieth century when there is no longer any consensus regarding how the task of Protestant theology is to be understood and implemented, it is imperative that we seek to get a sense of historical orientation that will clarify both the relation of modern theology to its classical roots and the relations between liberalism and neo-orthodoxy within modern theology itself.[50]

Once the inadequate historiography of the neo-orthodox theologians is laid to rest and replaced by a more accurate account of the complex relations between classical and modern theology, contemporary theologians must still grapple with the hermeneutical question: What exactly does it mean for a modern Protestant theologian to stand in the line of continuity with the Reformation? Since Barth and Brunner understood themselves as the rightful heirs to Calvin's legacy when they challenged Schleiermacher's claim to a share in the Reformed inheritance, this study has employed Calvin's theology as the standard for measuring what is classically "Reformed." This must not, however, be construed as implying that the theological disagreements between Schleiermacher, Barth, and Brunner should be adjudicated only on the basis of their respective degree of conformity to Calvin's explicit statements.[51] Interestingly, all three of these modern theologians feel free, precisely as Reformed theologians, to disagree with Calvin when necessary. And this is surely in keeping with Calvin's own judgment that no single theologian, not even Luther himself, should be accepted as an authority beyond question. But these observations only serve to disclose the complicated nature of the hermeneutical problem since the question of fidelity to the Reformation involves more than strictly historical considerations. It also involves a *theological* judgment about what it means to be a Protestant Christian.

This acknowledgment prevents us from concluding this historical study by claiming that Schleiermacher is the sole legitimate heir to the heritage of the Reformation. To maintain that Calvin would have endorsed Schleiermacher's theology as a completely faithful re-statement of his own position in the modern world is just as simplistic and naive as is the counter claim that he would have been forced to oppose it as a complete distortion of his theological intention. Who's to say how Calvin himself would have answered Schleiermacher's questions?[52] Nonetheless, from a strictly historical point of view it cannot be denied that Schleiermacher's theology represents a creative revision of prominent elements in Calvin's theology in the light of new questions and challenges. In this sense, there is every reason to speak of Schleiermacher's theology as a further development of the Reformed heritage.

In conclusion, therefore, while this study has demonstrated the necessity of abandoning the neo-orthodox historiography, it leaves open the systematic possibility that Schleiermacher's theology can still be criticized in the name of fidelity to the Reformation heritage. But a crucial distinction has to be made between two forms that such theological criticism could assume. First, it is possible to take issue with his notion of what it means to stand in the line of continuity with Luther and Calvin, in which case one must propose a different theological standard for measuring what is genuinely "Protestant" in place of the standard to which Schleiermacher understood himself beholden. Such disagreement would necessarily represent an *external* criticism of Schleiermacher since it proceeds from a different theological judgment regarding what it means to be faithful to the Reformation.[53] Second, one can share Schleiermacher's theological construal of what it means to be genuinely Protestant and yet criticize his achievement according to the norms of theological excellence he himself recognized. Such a position would necessarily represent an *internal* criticism since it takes issue with Schleiermacher's theology for the sake of furthering his own theological intentions. It is important not to confuse the two distinct types of criticism since any hope for real progress in contemporary theology depends upon the logical clarity of the various proposals being debated.

In the first half of the twentieth century when the crisis of the modern world was breaking upon the European mind with urgency, theologians who stood in the tradition of Calvin responded to their religious situation by emphasizing the need to make a radical break with the theology that had grown up in relation to the modern world. As all theologians do, they looked at the past through the lens of their own present needs and circumstances. The question is not whether they were faithful to their own circumstances but whether their view of the past can be our own given that Protestant theology must respond to a different set of historical circumstances at the end of the twentieth century. Of course, in and of itself, a revised reading of the historical record that seeks to be responsive to a new set of theological challenges, such as those arising from the respectful encounter of Christianity with non-Christian religions or from the non-theological study of religion, does not answer the normative question of constructive theology regarding how to articulate the meaning of Christian faith for today in a way that is faithful to the Protestant heritage. At best, historical theology can offer alternative ways of reading the past so that constructive theology can make an informed judgment regarding the resources latent within the tradition which is to be handed on to future generations. But this task of "handing on" a tradition received from the past requires a discernment on the part of the constructive theologian as to how that tradition can serve most effectively to bear witness to the gospel in today's world. As Calvin once said, "Our constant endeavor, day and night, is not just to transmit the tradition faithfully, but also to put it in the form we think will prove best."[54]

NOTES

1. Gerrish writes: "Calvin distinguishes sharply between natural and saving knowledge of God. . . . But it seems clear that the saving knowledge, when it comes, attaches itself to a remnant of the natural knowledge of God; otherwise, Calvin's famous comparison of Scripture to a pair of spectacles, which brings to clear focus a *confusa alioqui Dei notitia*, would make no sense (*Inst.*, 1.6.1; cf. 14.1). Consequently, I do not see how those for whom a 'christocentric' theology entails denial of a point of contact for the gospel can cite Calvin in their support." "From Calvin to Schleiermacher," p. 187, n. 37.

2. "To [Barth] a term like *revelation* could mean only one thing, that is, the true revelation, or in other words what he himself meant by the term. . . . [A]ny deviation from that one meaning would be a departure from revelation: as such, it was therefore a resort to natural theology." Barr, *Biblical Faith and Natural Theology*, p. 114. Barr goes on to speak of "the difficulty in making an ultimate distinction between natural and revealed theology. If one believes that God has revealed himself in his creation and continues to do so, why is that 'natural' theology and not 'revealed'? . . . If one believes that God was revealing himself in ancient Israel, why is this not 'natural'? Perhaps all theology is both 'natural' and 'revealed'?" Ibid., p. 115. Tillich suggests: "Perhaps the conception 'natural theology' is itself the product of a faulty supernaturalism." "What is Wrong with the 'Dialectic' Theology?," in *The Journal of Religion* 15 (April 1935): 140.

3. "In identifying Roman Catholicism as involving 'a compromise with' natural theology, indeed, Barth had an arguable case, and that opposition to Roman tradition gave the appearance of validating the claim of his own theological position to be a truly Reformational one. But in saying that 'Modern Protestantism' was likewise based on a compromise with natural theology he was somewhat misleading his hearers. For one of the main features of Modern Protestantism—let us say, since the mid-eighteenth century—was its departure from the tradition of natural theology which had, in fact, been highly influential in Protestantism. Schleiermacher, for instance, had already emphasized the futility of natural theology. Ritschl had polemicized furiously against 'metaphysics' as an element within theology. . . . Thus, contrary to the impression that was deliberately made, the denial of natural theology was one of the aspects in which Barthianism was *continuing* the line which Modern Protestantism had initiated, and was alienating itself from the older religious world in which the Reformers and the Fathers had lived. The attraction of the Barthian position lay precisely in the fact that it seemed to fit with the experience of a generation in which science on the one hand and war on the other had seemed to make the world empty of God." Barr, pp. 105-6.

4. *Comm.* Ps 78:21 (*CO* 31:729-30).
5. *Gl.*, §75.1.
6. *Gl.*, §169.
7. *Gl.*, §106.1.
8. *Gl.*, §108.1.
9. *Gl.*, §109.
10. *Gl.*, §167.1.

11. *Gl.*, §169.

12. "To find a niche for humanity in the cosmos may sound like an obvious enough formulation of the religious quest. But it was not the quest of the dominant form of piety in . . . Germany. Protestant pietism had nurtured an intensely inward, private, emotional religiousness, centered on the ever-repeated experience of guilt and forgiveness. . . . Even within traditional Protestantism, there had been one reformer for whom the primary religious question was not 'How can I get a gracious God?' but 'What is the chief end of human life?' . . . John Calvin answers that God has placed humans in the cosmos to be glorified in them; in this their chief end and their highest good alike consist." Gerrish, "The Secret Religion of Germany," p. 126. Similarly, Gustafson notes that the shift of religious concern away from a focus on the salvation of the individual to the appropriate relation of the individual to the whole of reality is implicit in Calvin's theology: "The key . . . lies within the Reformed tradition itself; the chief end of man is to glorify God, to relate to all things in a manner appropriate to their relations to God, in recognition of the dependence of all things upon him, and in gratitude for all things." *Ethics*, 1:184.

13. "The authority of Holy Scripture cannot be the foundation of faith in Christ; rather must the latter be presupposed before a peculiar authority can be granted to Holy Scripture." "The Holy Scriptures of the New Testament are, on the one hand, the first member in the series, ever since continued, of presentations of the Christian Faith; on the other hand, they are the norm for all succeeding presentations." *Gl.*, §128, 129 (*CF*, pp. 591, 594).

14. "[Protestantism's] distinctive character has not yet become fully manifest in doctrine. . . . [T]he Reformation itself did not transform the whole tenor of doctrine, but allowed much to be simply taken over unaltered from earlier definitions. . . . " *Gl.*, §25.2 (*CF*, p. 109).

15. *Reden*, 1:279-81, 290.

16. It should be added that this correlation also subjects Christian theology to criticism from the perspective of the historian of religions precisely to the extent that the theologian's description of non-Christian religions is inadequate on strictly historical grounds. While this observation applies particularly to Schleiermacher's theology wherein there is a self-conscious attempt to relate Christian theology to a non-theological study of the history of religions, Calvin's theology is not exempt from this kind of criticism since he, too, makes judgments about non-Christian religions that are, in principle, subject to the empirical testing of the historian.

17. For example, it should be recognized that Calvin speaks of the "sense of divinity" (*divinitatis sensus*) and the "seed of religion" (*religionis semen*) to emphasize differing aspects of the same reality: there is within each human breast an immediate awareness of God's reality that inescapably gives rise to some religious response. *Inst.*, 1.3.1, 1.4.1. Note how Calvin can vary his language and speak of the "seed of divinity" (*divinitatis semen*) and the "seed of the knowledge of God" (*semen notitiae Dei*) which is prevented from blossoming into a "good fruit" (*ad frugem bonam*). *Inst.*, 1.5.4, 1.5.15.

18. By contrast, however, Jones argues: "Instead of carefully laying out his

position in a style that invites a close philosophical or theological analysis, Calvin uses a language and an argumentative form that resist textual closure." For that reason, she rejects "contemporary readings [that] attempt to get at Calvin's meaning by penetrating his figurative images in search of the propositional truth that lies buried beneath them. This type of approach is evidenced clearly in the readings given by Brunner, Barth, and Tillich. In their quest for Calvin's 'cleaner' meaning, each of these theologians wants to dig beneath the text's rhetoric and uncover the truth it hides." *Calvin and the Rhetoric of Piety*, p. 94. Clearly, I do not believe that an appreciation of Calvin's rhetoric precludes a logical analysis of his theological ideas. This judgment reflects my belief that Calvin is a systematic thinker. Partee argues: "The recent discussion of Calvin as rhetorician rather than dialectician permits interpreters to understand his theology more as persuasion than demonstration. However, the need remains to identify Calvin's foundational convictions as well as his fundamental doctrines—and their relationships." After all, he goes on to say, "a 'pious mind' is still a mind." "Calvin's Polemic: Foundational Convictions in the Service of God's Truth," in *Calvinus Sincerioris Religionis Vindex*, p. 98, n. 5 and p. 120, n. 121.

19. The following two citations from Calvin can be taken as methodological rules for his dogmatics: "[W]e are called to a knowledge of God: not that knowledge which, content with empty speculation, merely flits in the brain, but that which will be sound and fruitful if we duly perceive it, and if it takes root in the heart." *Inst.*, 1.5.9 (McNeill, 1:61-62). "Now, the knowledge of God, as I understand it, is that by which we not only conceive that there is a God but also grasp what befits us and is proper to his glory, in fine, what is to our advantage to know of him. Indeed, we shall not say that, properly speaking, God is known where there is no religion or piety." *Inst.*, 1.2.1 (McNeill, 1:39).

20. "I call 'piety' that reverence joined with love of God which the knowledge of his benefits induces." *Inst.*, 1.2.1 (McNeill, 1:41). The affective emphasis is true of his definition of faith as well: "Now we shall possess a right definition of faith if we call it a firm and certain knowledge of God's benevolence toward us, founded upon the truth of the freely given promise in Christ, both revealed to our minds and sealed upon our hearts through the Holy Spirit." *Inst.*, 3.2.7 (McNeill, 1:551). Calvin becomes more explicit about what he means by faith as a sort of knowledge: "When we call faith 'knowledge' we do not mean comprehension of the sort that is commonly concerned with those things which fall under human sense perception. . . . Even where the mind has attained, it does not comprehend what it feels. But while it is persuaded of what it does not grasp, by the very certainty of its persuasion it understands more than if it perceived anything human by its own capacity. . . . From this we conclude that *the knowledge of faith consists in assurance rather than in comprehension.*" *Inst.*, 3.2.14 (McNeill, 1:559-60; emphasis added). Calvin also says that the "assent" contained in faith "is more of the heart than of the brain, and more of the disposition than of the understanding." *Inst.*, 3.2.8 (McNeill, 1:552). Given that Calvin defines piety as "reverence joined with love" and faith as "assurance" and, moreover, that he does not believe it possible for the finite mind to know God *a se*, there is much to suggest that Calvin would not be

caught completely offguard by Kant's critique of reason.

21. "Religion has truly its proper seat in the heart." *Comm.* Gen 12:7 (*CO* 23:181); Calvin also says that it is "in the heart where faith dwells. . . . " *Inst.*, 3.2.21 (McNeill, 1:567). Calvin affirms that doctrine has its seat in the heart: "[I]t is a doctrine not of the tongue but of life. It is not apprehended by the understanding and memory alone, as other disciplines are, but it is received only when it possesses the whole soul, and finds a seat and resting place in the inmost affection of the heart. . . . [The Gospel] ought to penetrate the inmost affections of the heart, take its seat in the soul, and affect the whole person a hundred times more deeply than the cold exhortations of the philosophers!" *Inst.*, 3.6.4 (McNeill, 1:688).

22. Calvin does, following the Stoics, avail himself of the argument for God's existence based on evidence of design that Hume and Kant criticized. In this respect, Calvin is simply a person of his times since he assumes that the validity of the logical structure of this argument is non-controversial. His point, rather, is that this kind of knowledge is not sufficient apart from piety. For that reason, Calvin's polemic with the so-called "atheists" of his day does not require him to give a theoretical proof of God's existence (since this question is not up for dispute); he seeks, rather, to show that the real atheism consists in a denial of the affective and practical implications of theistic belief. *Inst.*, 1.4.2, and *Comm.* Ps 14:1 (*CO* 31:136). See also Febvre, *The Problem of Unbelief in the Sixteenth Century*.

23. Calvin defines conscience as a "sense of divine judgment" (*sensus divini iudicii*) that accuses the human being of living in contradiction with itself. *Inst.*, 3.19.15.

24. *Comm.* John 1:5 (*CO* 47:6).

25. *Gl.*, §83.2.

26. *Gl.*, §83.1.

27. Jack Verheyden makes a very interesting argument about the transformation of Protestant theology from the classical to the modern period. Starting from the observation that Calvin, in his doctrine of the knowledge of God the creator, draws upon three distinct sources (the "sense of divinity," the design of the universe, and the conscience), Verheyden points out that modern theologians have tended to select one of these sources and to give it the primacy in their theologies. He cites Schleiermacher as an instance of the "religious" approach, Samuel Clarke (1675-1729) as an instance of the "aesthetic" approach, and Kant as an instance of the "moral" approach. By rejecting all three sources, Barth makes Calvin's doctrine of the knowledge of God the redeemer bear the burden of the knowledge of God's existence traditionally dealt with under the rubric of God as creator. "In sum, Barth has taken that element which Calvin included under knowledge of God the Redeemer and radically contrasted such apprehension with that knowledge of God the Creator elaborated by a Clarke, a Kant, and a Schleiermacher. But for all his disagreement with what they represent, Barth has one deep-lying agreement with them. He joins with them in maintaining that knowledge of God has a single and exclusive function. The lamp may shed a redemptive light but it still shines all alone." By contrast, for Calvin "[t]here are a variety of lamps which

light one's way to God and they appear to possess a definite independence from one another." "The Knowledge of the Existence of God in Protestant Theology," *Dialogue and Alliance* 1 (Spring 1987): 38, 28.

28. He makes these distinctions most consistently whenever he discusses the two tables of the law, e.g., *Inst.*, 2.8.11. Dowey speaks of the distinction between "worship and obedience" or, in other words, "the numinous and the moral." *Knowledge of God*, p. 50. Dowey also suggests, however, that Calvin is vulnerable to the charge of "moralizing" religion. Ibid., p. 55, n. 33.

29. E.g., Albrecht Ritschl, *A Critical History of the Christian Doctrine of Justification and Reconciliation*, vol. 1, trans. by John S. Black (Edinburgh: Edmonston and Douglas, 1872), pp. 440-511.

30. Ritschl "does not see Schleiermacher by himself as inaugurating a new epoch in Protestant theology. And this conclusion is based on Ritschl's judgment regarding the status of the ethical moment in Schleiermacher's theology. For Ritschl's historical and constructive purposes the new epoch in theology opens up only when Schleiermacher is taken together with Kant. Kant provides the ethical impetus which Ritschl finds to be inadequate in Schleiermacher. By combining Schleiermacher with Kant, Ritschl creates an historical precedent for his own elliptical theology in which the 'religious' and 'ethical' moments stand as two foci." Brandt, "Ritschl's Critique of Schleiermacher's Theological Ethics," p. 53. Outlining the direction of his own constructive development of the Reformed tradition, Gerrish makes this criticism of Schleiermacher: "[I]n defining the faith that corresponds to revelation as 'discernment,' 'recognition,' or 'insight,' I am working with *cognitive* categories such as Schleiermacher deliberately avoided in specifying the content of general revelation, which, for him, was given in the 'feeling' of absolute dependence. And I must also dissent when he excludes *moral* categories as well from this 'original revelation,' as he calls it. The exclusion seems all the more remarkable when he tells us later—much later!—that conscience, too, is an original revelation of God. In any case, I have sought in my own dogmatic efforts to keep the idea of general revelation closer to the moral understanding of it in the older dogmatic tradition, including Calvin. I have argued that this awareness, which I call 'elemental faith' and take to be the counterpart of an elemental concept of God, is 'secure' insofar as *order* is the presupposition of all scientific inquiry and *moral* order is presupposed in all our everyday discourse about right and wrong." "Errors and Insights in the Understanding of Revelation: A Provisional Response," in *The Journal of Religion* 78 (January 1998): 73. Notice that Gerrish is not concerned as a dogmatic theologian to define "the essence of religion." In its place, he works with a notion of "elemental faith" that allows him to hold together the religious and the moral dimensions. This notion performs the same function as Schleiermacher's *Ortsbestimmung* by getting the language of dogmatics on the "map" of human experience. As Gerrish says elsewhere, this is "an alternative, but structurally similar, approach to Christian theology." "Friedrich Schleiermacher on the Task of Theology," in *Tradition and the Modern World*, p. 36. H. Richard Niebuhr made a similar suggestion, namely, that we move away from the attempt to analyze the essence of "religion" and ask, instead,

about the abstract nature of "faith" which he defines in a twofold way as "confidence" and "fidelity." *Radical Monotheism and Western Culture, with Supplementary Essays* (New York: Harper and Row, 1960), pp. 11, 16. Niebuhr's shift of emphasis reflects his own attempt to answer the question: "How has monotheistic faith affected human religion as piety?" Ibid., p. 50.

31. *Gl.*, §26.

32. Brandt faults Ritschl here: "[B]ecause Ritschl overlooks the *Sittenlehre*, his judgment as to the status of the ethical within Schleiermacher's theological system is suspect. Exclusive attention to the *Glaubenslehre* leaves a one-legged creature which cannot walk. But Schleiermacher conceives of theology as a two-legged creature, walking by steps taken alternatively on dogmatic and ethical legs." Brandt, p. 55.

33. Indeed, Schleiermacher does adopt a different approach to theological ethics than that developed by Calvin in spite of their agreement on the necessary religious qualification of morality within a Christian theology. For Schleiermacher, theological ethics is a *descriptive* discipline, not a *prescriptive* one; his rejection of Calvin's "third use" of the law indicates the important difference in the way these theologians frame the ethical task within their theologies of piety. While Gustafson defends Schleiermacher's place in the Reformed tradition on account of his defining theology in relation to the religious affections or piety, he notes a difference between Schleiermacher and other Reformed theologians regarding the way the task of theological ethics is construed: "My reading of Schleiermacher's ethics . . . suggests that he takes a different turn from the others. His Christian ethical thought is focused on the agent and the actions that are forthcoming from the Christian God-consciousness far more than on a conformation of action to the objective ordering of life in the world." *Ethics*, 1:176.

34. For this reason, I would qualify Verheyden's statement that, for Calvin, the religious, the aesthetic, and the moral approaches "possess a definite independence from one another" (p. 28). The argument from design and the testimony of conscience are used by Calvin as confirmations of his basic point about the innate "sense of divinity" that gives rise to religion.

35. Gerrish, *Grace and Gratitude*, p. 25.

36. *Inst.*, 1.2.1 (McNeill, 1:41).

37. *Gl.*, §3-4.

38. *Gl.*, §59, 57.2. Gerrish explains: "Even the universal consciousness of God, though its presence can be verified by anyone who has acquired the art of introspection, becomes what Schleiermacher calls an *actual* consciousness of God in Christians only through their relation to Christ." "From Calvin to Schleiermacher," p. 193.

39. In Schleiermacher's definition of the term "original revelation" (*ursprüngliche Offenbarung*), it is clear that he does not mean "historically original." *Gl.*, §4.4.

40. In Tillich's terms, the interpretations of religion given by Calvin and Schleiermacher would belong to the "ontological" type of the philosophy of religion in contrast to the "cosmological" type. Tillich writes: "One can distinguish two ways of approaching God: the way of overcoming estrangement

and the way of meeting a stranger. In the first way man discovers *himself* when he discovers God; he discovers something that is identical with himself although it transcends him infinitely, something from which he is estranged, but from which he never has been and never can be separated. In the second way man meets a *stranger* when he meets God. The meeting is accidental. Essentially they do not belong to each other. They may become friends on a tentative and conjectural basis. But there is no certainty about the stranger man has met. He may disappear, and only *probable* statements can be made about his nature. The two ways symbolize the two possible types of philosophy of religion: the ontological type and the cosmological type. The way of overcoming estrangement symbolizes the ontological method in the philosophy of religion. The way of meeting a stranger symbolizes the cosmological method." "The Two Types of Philosophy of Religion," in *Theology of Culture* (London: Oxford University Press, 1959), p. 10.

41. Gustafson brings out the theocentric character of Schleiermacher's understanding of piety and locates him in this regard squarely in the tradition of Augustine, Calvin, and Edwards. *Ethics*, 1:176-78. Gustafson, moreover, criticizes Barth's theology in a way that would not apply to Schleiermacher's theology: "Barth says vividly and categorically: 'God is for man.' I do not say that God is against man. But the sense in which God is for man must be spelled out in a carefully qualified way." Ibid., 1:181.

42. Wilhelm Niesel, "Schleiermachers Verhältnis zur reformierten Tradition," *Zwischen den Zeiten* 8 (1930): 524.

43. *Theology of Calvin*, pp. 44-46.

44. Gilkey writes: "[Neo-orthodox] theology . . . was by no means a simple return to an unworldly orthodoxy. On the contrary, despite its antipathy to much of the humanism that characterized the modern mind, it accepted a great deal of its own liberal inheritance and so many of the basic assumptions of the modern world view. It was at least half secular and naturalistic in its attitudes, and was thus genuinely neoorthodox. First of all, it accepted for the purposes of rational understanding—if not for 'faith'—the naturalistic account of all space-time events as being caused by other preceding finite factors (natural or human) and not by miraculous divine interventions. It accepted, moreover, the concept of historical relativity, with regard even to its own scriptural writings and doctrines. . . . Surprisingly, no neoorthodox ever criticized either in principle or in practice the biological theory of evolution or the liberal practice of Biblical criticism, although theologically they tended to ignore both these products of scientific inquiry on which, at least in part, liberal theology had been founded. No more for them than for the liberals did the Bible communicate information about 'matters of fact'—as the orthodox had surely thought, and as fundamentalists still believe." *Naming the Whirlwind*, pp. 82-83.

45. "An Appreciation of Karl Barth," in *How Karl Barth Changed My Mind*, ed. Donald K. McKim (Grand Rapids: Eerdmans, 1986), p. 153. McCormack writes: "[T]o the extent that Barth concerned himself with philosophical epistemology at all, he was an idealist (and more specifically, a Kantian). All of his efforts in theology may be considered, from one point of view, as an attempt to overcome Kant by means of Kant; not retreating behind him and seeking to

go around him, but going through him. . . . But if all this be true, then it also means that Barth still had a very strong foot in the nineteenth century. . . . [H]owever critical Barth may have been of modern theology, it is of the utmost importance—if we are to have a more accurate understanding of the history of theology in the last two centuries—to see that dialectical theology in the form in which it was taught by Barth was a thoroughly modern option." *Karl Barth's Critically Realistic Dialectical Theology: Its Genesis and Development (1909-1936)* (Oxford and New York: The Clarendon Press of Oxford University, 1995), pp. 465-66. Paul Löffler compares Schleiermacher's notion of "self-consciousness" with Bultmann's "self-understanding" and traces both of them back to the influence of Kant. "Selbstbewußtsein und Selbstverständnis als theologische Prinzipien bei Schleiermacher und Bultmann," in *Kerygma und Dogma* 2 (1956): 313. Any reconsideration of the history of modern theology, including the place of both Schleiermacher and Barth within it, will have to examine anew Kant's decisive role in setting the agenda of modern religious thought.

46. It is not surprising that, with the collapse of the neo-orthodox synthesis in the 1960's, Protestant theologians joined in proclaiming the "death of God." In his historical analysis of the rise of the radical "secular" theologies, Gilkey shows how the brilliant neo-orthodox synthesis of modern secularity and Reformation theology ultimately led to its own demise. "Neoorthodoxy was ... on two counts in tune with the contemporary 'secular' mind: (1) it agreed that God was not revealed in ordinary secular life, and (2) it accepted the naturalistic account of the system of space-time events. On the other hand, it was 'orthodox' in the sense that for it the *religious* meanings of this naturalistically interpreted life, its 'ultimate concerns' and ultimate questions of faith, meaning, and hope, were not to be resolved by man's wisdom alone on the level of either nature or history, but to be resolved only by a faith attendant to the transcendent Word. It attempted to accept the secular world *secularly*, but to retain the Biblical and orthodox worlds *religiously*. . . . [T]his dual posture, while the source of its very considerable power, proved its undoing in the end." *Naming the Whirlwind*, p. 84.

47. Richard Crouter writes: "It is disquieting to see how frequently the discussion of Karl Barth and Friedrich Schleiermacher is dominated by sets of theological concerns that are legitimate but that minimize the historical-contextual side of each figure's work. It is especially appropriate for historians of Christianity to recognize and give weight to the fact that both Schleiermacher and Barth belong to historical theology. The sooner we recognize this, the better our chances will be of getting clear on what the debate between them is all about. The point is that, strictly speaking, neither thinker belongs to contemporary systematic theology. . . . [I]n addition to determining the 'correctness' of Barth's critique, we need to ask, assuming for the moment that Barth does go astray in his view of Schleiermacher, why this is the case. What are those problems and horizons of thought in Barth's world that lead him to his view of Schleiermacher? How do those factors—social, political, intellectual—relate to similar factors operating in the climate of theological work of Schleiermacher's own time and place? The task of comparison needs to be

contextualized at both ends of the spectrum. I am not sure we really get to the bottom of these issues by a judgment merely that Barth may be wrong in the case of Schleiermacher." "A Historical Demurral," in *Barth and Schleiermacher: Beyond the Impasse?*, pp. 165-66.

48. *Schleiermacher on Christ and Religion*, p. 11. James Barr (who also cites this passasge from Niebuhr) writes: "Barthianism moulded past intellectual history in its own image, and its efficiency in doing this was one of the reasons for its great influence." *Biblical Faith and Natural Theology*, p. 105.

49. Niebuhr, p. 11.

50. McCormack also insists upon this point: "Perhaps the most pressing need in contemporary theology is a historical one. It is high time that we subject the dominant historiography of nineteenth- and twentieth-century theology to critical scrutiny. The pattern—liberal, neo-orthodox, postliberal (and whatever other 'posts' one might wish to throw in)—is much too simplistic. It fails to grasp adequately the complex relationship of theology in the early half of the twentieth century—and, I would say, of theology in our day as well—to nineteenth-century antecedents and serves all too often as an ideological crutch to justify whatever theological programme a particular theologian would have advocated without its help. I personally would regard it as a most hopeful sign that theology today is becoming self-critical, if the celebration of our 'postmodernity' were restrained long enough to ask the crucial question: precisely what is this 'modernity' that we think ourselves now to have transcended?" *Karl Barth's Critically Realistic Dialectical Theology*, pp. 466-67.

51. George Hasson Thomas asks: "Does Calvin's theology then include a basis for both Schleiermacher and Barth?" He concludes that this is, indeed, the case and that a contemporary Reformed theology needs "to transcend differences between Calvin, Schleiermacher, and Barth." "Revelation, Faith, and Doctrine: A Study Based on the Theology of John Calvin, Friedrich Schleiermacher, and Karl Barth" (Ph.D. diss., Vanderbilt University, 1961), pp. 52, 326.

52. Gerhard Ebeling writes: "[T]his very task of carrying on the heritage of the Reformation in a way that genuinely moves with the times necessarily led to the point where in regard to the general principles of thought certain problems that had very rightly remained untouched at the Reformation arose and demanded a decision such as was not to be gained from the utterances of the Reformers and from the Confessions. To these problems that necessarily emerged sooner or later there belonged, however, first and foremost the hermeneutic problem, which as a result of the Reformation had already in actual fact—though how far that was recognized is another question—been made central and set on a new theological basis, but only hestitatingly come to grips with in all its implications." "The Significance of the Critical Historical Method for Church and Theology in Protestantism," in *Word and Faith*, trans. James W. Leitch (Philadelphia: Fortress Press, 1963), pp. 41-42.

53. The neo-orthodox theologian, for instance, differs from the liberal on the meaning of history, a difference which has tremendous consequences for the theological evaluation of "tradition." Comparing Brunner and Schleiermacher,

Gerrish writes: "The contrast is not that between religious mysticism and historical revelation, but between history as finality and history as change. For Brunner, the Word of God in history means the 'once-for-allness' of God's revelation in Jesus Christ, an event with which I am somehow linked contemporaneously in faith. . . . For Schleiermacher, by contrast, although the ideal became historical in Christ, this unrepeatable revelation is the beginning of a wholly new historical development, the church, through which alone I have access to the original event. While the wish for a direct access to Christ, unmediated through the corporate life he has founded, is characterized by Schleiermacher as 'magical,' *his* view is judged by Brunner, equally disapprovingly, to be romanticist, historicist, and catholicizing; for if Christ is merely the first cause of a historical development, then my immediate relationship is not to Christ, but to the church and the historical tradition. And with these two starkly opposed views of the way the grace of Christ is communicated goes an equally sharp difference over the status of Christian doctrines. In the densely packed aphorisms of the *Brief Outline*, a theological revolution is quietly taking place in exactly this respect. Doctrines, like the church (or rather *with* the church), are also in constant movement and change. The old absolutes of Protestant orthodoxy give way before a thoroughly historicized conception of the church's teaching." "Continuity and Change," pp. 42-43. Gerrish goes on to contrast Schleiermacher's view that continuity with the tradition consists in a *development* of its doctrine with Barth's quite different view that the theologian's proper task is to hand on the gospel unspoiled, much as a letter-carrier delivers the mail without tampering with it (p. 44).

54. *Defensio contra Pighium* (*CO* 6:250), cited by Gerrish in "Continuity and Change," p. 13.

Afterword

This comparative analysis of the theologies of Calvin and Schleiermacher observes the limits proper to a strictly historical mode of inquiry. The reason for this limitation is readily apparent: exegeting the dogmatic texts of Calvin and Schleiermacher through the lens of our revised comparative framework sheds an important light upon their material and formal affinities with respect to the question of Christian faith as religion. By making a case for Schleiermacher's continuity with Calvin in this regard, it is possible for the historical question raised by the neo-orthodox theologians to be decided on its own merits regardless of one's constructive theological commitments in the present situation.

Nonetheless, the delineation of a trajectory moving from Calvin through Schleiermacher provides a historical warrant for the hermeneutical decision that the questions and concerns of the liberal tradition represent an appropriate way of continuing the Reformation heritage in a post-Enlightenment world. But an evaluative assessment of this kind shifts the discussion from a strictly historical inquiry to the constructive problem of contemporary theology. It further requires that the methodological questions of constructive theology be addressed, including the knotty problem of theology's relation to philosophy.

Throughout this comparative study the issues of theological method have been subordinated to the substantive questions of theological interpretation. This decision reflects my conviction that the formal criteria of theological method are in each case abstracted from the concrete material concerns of the theological system in question. The formal and the material concerns of a theological system can (and should) be logically distinguished for clarity's sake but they can never be entirely separated from one another. If this general observation regarding the relation between theological method and theological system is valid, then it is self-defeating for theologians to discuss the formal questions of method as if these were neutral with respect to the substantive questions of theological interpretation. In order for the controverted issues of theological method to be clarified, their relation to the material concerns of Christian theology must be illuminated.

The dogmatic theologies of Calvin and Schleiermacher share a similar formal structure inasmuch as both systematic presentations of Christian doctrine begin with a consideration of the nature of *homo religiosus*. This formal move results from their substantive theological decision to interpret "revelation" in two distinct senses of the word: an "original revelation" of God to human beings simply as such and God's "decisive revelation" in Jesus Christ. In the classical and liberal paradigms of Reformed dogmatics, faith in Jesus Christ is understood as the one redemptive possibility for human existence which is constituted by a religious dimension that refers the human being to God as its creator.[1] Both theological systems, therefore, require for their internal coherence a "point of contact" with common human experience.

From Barth's point of view, of course, a theology that makes a "point of contact" with common human experience is no longer properly "dogmatic" but "apologetic." Yet for Barth as well, this is not a purely formal issue of theological method; it is, fundamentally, a material issue regarding the proper interpretation of the meaning of the gospel. Barth's christocentric doctrine of revelation necessarily leads him to reject as "natural theology" any suggestion that God is universally revealed within human experience which would, in turn, justify the important methodological role assigned to the topic "religion" as we encounter it in the theologies of Calvin and Schleiermacher. Hence, the question regarding theological method before which Barth places us may not be adjudicated apart from a decision regarding the substantive question of an "original revelation" of God to which the religious character of human existence bears witness. As this historical investigation has argued, it is Barth, not Schleiermacher, who has departed from Calvin with respect to this issue.

Clearly, this is not to question whether Barth's christocentric construal of Christian faith is a viable option for a contemporary Protestant theology. In my reading of it, Barth's theology is a more or less internally coherent interpretation of Christian doctrine in the same sense that this judgment applies to the theologies of Calvin and Schleiermacher. Criticism of Barth's theology must address his concerns within the framework of the systematic position he developed.[2] But it is to call into question the assumption that the formal decisions regarding method made by other Protestant theologians are to be evaluated through the lens of Barth's material theological commitments. If Barth deems Schleiermacher's method to be problematic, he does so on account of a very different reading of how the gospel is best interpreted.[3] The debates among contemporary Protestant theologians would be greatly clarified if it were generally acknowledged that there is no theologically neutral place from which the formal questions of method can be adjudicated.[4]

Such an acknowledgment would require that the issue between Barth and Schleiermacher not be framed as that of the antithesis between dogmatics and apologetics or, in other words, the decision between theology and philosophy.[5] The issue, rather, is that of contrasting construals of the Protestant heritage with differing consequences for theological method. But assuming that the liberal model for theology is an appropriate formal expression of a more fundamental material decision regarding how Christian faith is to be construed on the basis of its sources in scripture and tradition, the question of liberal theology's relation to philosophy can be posed in a way that does not prejudice the outcome of the investigation. Like Barth, Schleiermacher is convinced that theology has its own integrity as disciplined interpretation of Christian faith and that this integrity must not be compromised by confusing the line between theology and philosophy. Nonetheless, what this means within his own frame of reference is quite different from what it means for Barth.[6]

Schleiermacher's contributions to philosophical inquiry, especially in the area of philosophical hermeneutics, are well known.[7] For some critics this fact is proof of their contention that Schleiermacher was really a philosopher, not a theologian. While no one, to my knowledge, has ever leveled this charge at Calvin, Calvin's theology clearly gives evidence of an engagement with, as well as an indebtedness to, certain philosophical perspectives. For scholars with Barthian theological commitments, of course, this aspect of Calvin's work has constituted a problem for interpretation, giving rise to rather strained attempts to explain Calvin's relation to the philosophers in such a way that he cannot be accused of "natural theology." According to this line of defense, Calvin was only formally influenced by Renaissance humanism with its roots in antiquity unlike Schleiermacher who was materially influenced by romanticism or idealism.[8] But as this study has shown, such an artificial distinction does not do justice to the complex relations of either theologian to the philosophical perspectives with which they are engaged in debate.

Yet if philosophical influences can be detected in the theologies of Calvin and Schleiermacher, the question arises whether they have violated their own methodological ideal of a "theology within the limits of piety alone." An answer to this question depends on whether one judges that Calvin and Schleiermacher would have been troubled by evidence of philosophical indebtedness in their theological work.[9]

Would they have understood their own methodological ideal to have precluded borrowing from philosophy? I think not. Since both theologians find evidence in non-theological sources of insight that lend support to their arguments for a religious dimension of human experience, it seems that the ideal of a theology framed by piety does not require that there be no contact with philosophy but only that the theological explication of Christian faith not be determined by considerations alien to piety's proper domain.[10] "Theology within the limits of piety alone" should thus be understood as a hermeneutical ideal that aims to keep theology focused on its proper subject-matter: Christian faith's understanding of human existence in its religious dimension.

In evaluating Schleiermacher's theological method, it is important to keep his own ideal for theology before us, even if the contemporary theologian should decide to adopt another formulation of the methodological ideal. For Schleiermacher, the crucial issue is not to sever theology altogether from philosophy but, rather, to distinguish between them in such a way that each discipline may go about its own work unhampered by interference from the other. On the side of theology, this means allowing the Christian religion to come to appropriate intellectual expression in the system of doctrine apart from a dilution of its distinctiveness and integrity as a historically particular way of being religious. Accordingly, he articulated a model for theology that he hoped would be responsible to both ecclesial and academic norms.

In his day this meant an alternative to the standard ecclesial model represented by orthodox Protestant dogmatics, on the one hand, and the usual academic model represented by Enlightenment natural theology, on the other. In the orthodox model, theology is ecclesial but at the cost of its academic character since Christian doctrines are exempted from scientific and historical criticism. In the Enlightenment model, theology is academic but at the cost of its ecclesial character since the philosophical doctrines of "reason alone" have no organic relation to the historical particularity of the church's distinctive tradition. Both options, in Schleiermacher's view, approach their subject-matter in an ahistorical manner, albeit for quite different reasons. As an alternative, Schleiermacher proposed a "historicized" approach to theology that would respect the integrity of the church's distinctive way of being religious while allowing for the continual development of Christian doctrine as the church's ongoing interpretation of its faith. In this way, he believed, theology could embody the twin criteria of academic and ecclesial excellence.[11]

Schleiermacher defined theology as a "positive discipline" (*eine positive Wissenschaft*) in which the various parts cohere insofar as they are necessary for the sake of carrying out the practical task of training leaders for the church.[12] In other words, theology can be spoken of as a single field of study only if we understand this to mean a "field-encompassing field," i.e., an "assemblage" (*Inbegriff*) of the academic and practical knowledge required for the church's ministry.[13] Theology is subdivided by Schleiermacher into "philosophical theology," "historical theology," and "practical theology."[14] Historical theology, for example, shares with the academic study of history its commitment to the historical-critical method, so that the method of the historical theologian is no different from that of the historian in a non-theological line of inquiry.[15] In the same way, philosophical and practical theology share the methods of their cognate disciplines in the university. What unites these diverse methods and fields of inquiry into a single unit of study called "theology" is the goal of preparing professional leadership for the churches.

In Schleiermacher's scheme, historical theology includes biblical exegesis, church history, *and* dogmatics. As a historical discipline, dogmatics (*Glaubenslehre*) has as its datum an empirical phenomenon: a particular way of believing (*eine bestimmte Glaubensweise*), i.e., the Christian way.[16] The task of dogmatics in this view is descriptive: to illustrate for the present moment of history the internal coherence of the church's doctrine by showing its relation to the Christian experience of redemption. Schleiermacher thus attempted to secure a non-speculative foundation for dogmatics by assigning it to the final part of historical theology.

By contrast, philosophical theology is a "critical" task.[17] Its job is to formulate an adequate concept of the Christian church as a distinct form of religious community (i.e., the "essence" of Christianity). In order to do this, however, philosophical theology is necessarily engaged in discussion of questions that transcend the boundaries of Christian theology as such, namely, defining the nature of religious communities in general and delineating the various kinds of religious communities that have appeared in history.[18] Hence, the answer to philosophical theology's proper question builds upon the researches of the philosophy of culture ("ethics") as well as those of the comparative philosophy of religion.[19] In this way, the logic of philosophical theology's inquiry into the essence of Christian religion is essentially related to other disciplines in the university that study religion and religious communities from a non-theological point of view.

Since dogmatics, as the final part of historical theology, is a descriptive discipline, it must receive the definition of Christianity's essence from the labors of philosophical theology, which is a critical discipline. That the dogmatic task is assigned to historical theology whereas the definition of Christianity's essence is assigned to philosophical theology naturally leads to the question: What is the relation between dogmatics and philosophical theology, especially since the latter is necessarily bound up with non-theological approaches to the study of religion?[20]

In Schleiermacher's view, the inquiries of philosophical and historical theology are mutually corrective. Since Christianity is a historical phenomenon, the statement of its essence cannot be deduced *a priori*. By the same token, a purely empirical investigation of Christianity's history cannot yield a critical concept of its essence.[21] Hence, the descriptive work of dogmatics presupposes the critical conclusion of philosophical theology since the function of a definition of Christianity's essence is to distinguish the genuinely ecclesiastical material from heretical elements. Thereby dogmatics is able to work only with those materials that qualify as truly ecclesial. Conversely, the conclusion of philosophical theology is always to be tested by historical theology to insure that the definition of Christianity's essence is adequate to the empirical data as studied by biblical exegesis and church history. Indeed, the concept of Christianity's essence can only be tentative since it must constantly be revised in the light of a better understanding of Christianity's history.[22] In this way, historical theology provides philosophical theology with its material just as philosophical theology provides historical theology with its critical conceptual tools.[23]

According to this theological model, dogmatics is ecclesial in content and academic in form. In other words, the material content of dogmatics is determined solely by its relation to the Christian religious affections whereas the question of its academic character pertains only to the conceptual form, not the substance, of dogmatic statements.[24] With this non-speculative definition of dogmatics within the larger enterprise of theology understood as a "positive discipline," Schleiermacher believes he has found a way for theology simultaneously to respect the integrity of the church's faith and to respect the university's demand for academic intelligibility.

In this view, dogmatics is neither the product of independent philosophical speculation that works either deductively or inductively ("natural theology") nor is it the logical adjustment of doctrines supernaturally revealed in scripture and authoritatively expounded by the church's confessions ("orthodoxy"). The intention of Schleiermacher's alternative proposal is clear: to assume responsibility for the dogmatic task of the Christian church while taking seriously its character as a thoroughly historicized mode of thinking about a historically particular way of being religious.

A contemporary theologian can appreciate Schleiermacher's intention with respect to his understanding of theology in general and dogmatics in particular and yet question whether this is the best way to formulate a historicized model for dogmatics in relation to theology's other tasks. In other words, internal criticism of Schleiermacher's program is possible and, in my judgment, necessary. Specifically, it can be asked whether Schleiermacher's concern to historicize dogmatics is best served by his characterization of it as a "historical" discipline and his consequent placement of it within the field of historical theology. It seems to me that there is a difference between saying that dogmatic theology is a historicized mode of thought and that it is a historical discipline. Does not confusion result from Schleiermacher's placement of dogmatics within the discipline of historical theology, with the unfortunate consequence that it becomes difficult to grasp the relation of dogmatics as a descriptive enterprise to philosophical theology as a critical enterprise?[25] At least, this is my conclusion. But I emphasize that this is an internal criticism that respects and shares Schleiermacher's concern for a fully historicized understanding of the dogmatic task of Christian theology.

In place of this way of dividing the labor of theology, I believe that the commitment to historicize dogmatics is best preserved by those theologians in the liberal tradition who have modified this aspect of Schleiermacher's legacy by understanding dogmatics (or systematic theology) as a constructive and normative discipline.[26] In this revised formulation of the constructive or systematic task of theology, the critical attempt to give a definition of the essence of Christian faith (in Schleiermacher's terms, "philosophical theology") is integrated with the descriptive attempt at a comprehensive presentation of Christian doctrine for our time (in Schleiermacher's terms, "dogmatics"). Accordingly, the constructive task of theology should be understood as a hermeneutical enterprise that aims at a contemporary restatement of the meaning of Christian faith.[27] This revision of Schleiermacher's theological program thus moves in the direction of what Tillich called a "method of correlation."[28]

This historical study has analyzed the dogmatic theologies of both Calvin and Scheiermacher in the terms that have become familiar in discussions about a correlational method for theology in which the Christian faith is interpreted as the answer to the religious question of human existence as this is culturally formulated in different historical periods. In each instance there is a "fit" between some analysis of the religious question to be addressed and some construal of the meaning of Christian faith that is proposed as the answer to that question.[29] While these two poles of the correlation can be logically distinguished within the theological system, they cannot be separated from one another. The theological construal of Christian faith informs the analysis of the religious problem to be addressed, just as the analysis of the religious problem informs the particular construal of Christian faith which is proposed as the solution. The internal coherence of these theological systems, as well as their persuasive power in their respective historical contexts, can best be understood, I believe, as the successful outcome of this correlational endeavor.[30]

This is not to claim that either Calvin or Schleiermacher understood their own theological procedure in Tillich's terms.[31] But it is to suggest that the categories employed in arguments for a correlational method in theology may be fruitful, not only for the logical analysis of these two Reformed theologies, but also as a possible way to revise Schleiermacher's theological method that respects his intention to historicize Christian theology while avoiding the perplexities involved in his own statement of it.[32]

Such a restatement of theological method offers a way to answer the question whether and, if so, in what sense Protestant theology can be both an academic and an ecclesial enterprise in the contemporary North American situation, characterized as it is by the coming to maturity of the field of "religious studies" as an academic inquiry in its own right. In principle, theologians in the tradition of Schleiermacher affirm that Christian theology is properly understood as both an ecclesial and an academic discipline and, therefore, that the theological interpretation of Christian faith can and should be articulated in a way that is thoroughly engaged with the non-theological study of religion. This correlational commitment can be opposed by theologians for whom the confessional character of theology precludes any serious conversation with the secular study of religion.[33] For their part, scholars of religion can also object that the ecclesial character of theology precludes it from being in any sense a responsible participant in the academic study of religion. For these reasons, theologians who affirm the ideal of a "mediating" theology must take upon themselves the burden of clarifying to critics in both the church and the academy in what sense Christian theology is an ecclesial discipline and in what sense it is an academic discipline.

Theology, according to this model, is a critical function of the Christian church whereby it engages in reflection upon its life and preaching for the sake of the integrity of the gospel it exists to serve. Theology thus has a necessary "confessional" context in that it presupposes existential participation in a community of faith as well as commitment to a further constructive development of that religious tradition in relation to contemporary circumstances and challenges. As such, theology is not a sub-discipline of what is now being defined as religious studies in the university. According to the self-understanding of their discipline as a field of humanistic and social scientific study, scholars of religion may not pursue their inquiries with explicitly confessional commitments. By contrast, theology *is* an ecclesial discipline that acknowledges from the outset its rootedness in and its concern to develop a historically particular interpretation of human existence in its religious dimension.[34]

But if theology as a function of the church is an ecclesial discipline and, for that reason, not a sub-discipline within the field of religious studies, this does not mean that theology is not also, in an important sense, an academic discipline. Although theology as here defined is a confessional activity committed to the critical elucidation of a historically specific construal of the religious meaning of human life in the world, it nonetheless makes its appeal to human existence *qua* human. Because theology aims to interpret the Christian tradition so as to propose a normative answer to the human religious question, it is obligated to the same standards of academic excellence and intellectual integrity that are represented in the university. Such a theology must be open to an honest and forthright engagement with the academy's study of religion on its own terms with respect to the philosophical and historical issues necessarily involved in a comprehensive interpretation of the church's religious tradition for our own time.[35]

Schleiermacher's legacy has been an important factor in the emergence of the autonomous study of religion with which theology in his sense is to be critically engaged. Since his time, of course, the academic study of religion has undergone such tremendous development as a field of inquiry that the specific answers he proposed no longer suffice for those who continue to pose his questions. Schleiermacher's enduring significance, therefore, lies not in the actual correlations he himself made between the academic study of religion and theology, but in the development of a model for a self-critical theology that would be able to revise and correct itself in the light of new insights and questions arising from this attempt at mediation. With this in mind, it is appropriate to close this study with a few words about the disciplines of the "philosophy of religion" and the "history of religion" in today's academy and the relation of a contemporary Protestant theology to them.[36]

There are two important questions to be asked by the philosophy of religion that are relevant to the theologian. First, there is the question of definition: what do we mean by "the religious" as a dimension or aspect of human culture and experience?[37] Second, there is the qustion of truth: how are we to discuss and evaluate the claims of "the religions" to interpret this religious dimension?[38]

In the present-day intellectual pluralism of the academy, there is no consensus regarding these strictly philosophical questions to which theologians could appeal. It is not surprising, therefore, that theologians of differing persuasions avail themselves of contrasting philosophical views in their efforts to relate theology to the field of religious studies. In their polemics against liberal theology's effort to delineate a religious dimension of common human experience, Lindbeck and Thiemann are able to find philosophical arguments that lend extra-theological support to their theological positions.[39] There is nothing wrong with this procedure, provided that the strictly philosophical issues are clearly distinguished from the theological issues. Insofar as theologians are required by the logic of their inquiry to debate issues of a philosophical nature, it is important to recognize the philosophical pluralism that actually exists in today's academy as well as the inevitable circularity involved in relating contrasting theological positions to alternative philosophical viewpoints. This is not to say that philosophical argument among theologians is pointless; it is only to caution against underestimating the complexity of the issues involved for theologians of all stripes who seek to theologize in meaningful conversation with the non-theological study of religion, characterized as it is by a diversity of philosophical perspectives on the meaning and truth of religion.

The philosophy of religion must pose its questions regarding the meaning and truth of religion in a way that acknowledges the relativity of its own conceptual categories and perspectives. As a child of the Enlightenment, the modern philosophy of religion is just as historically conditioned as are the various positive religions that provide the data for its critical reflection. Hence, the problem of the historicity of religion cannot be solved by an ahistorical philosophy of religion oblivious to its own historical context in the modern West. This recognition of the thoroughly historical character of all thought, including modern philosophical thought, forces us to confront the inescapable fact there is no fixed place apart from the flux of history on which we might stand to decide questions of religious truth and value.[40] But the recognition of the thoroughly historical character of religious and philosophical truth-claims does not logically entail the conclusion that the questions and answers of the religions cannot be philosophically debated. It only requires more careful philosophical attention to the standpoint from which the philosopher asks about religious questions and answers. The import of the "linguistic turn" in recent Western philosophy is to point out that there are no "pure" descriptions of human experience since all such attempts, including efforts to define "the religious," are properly recognized as "interpretations" to be subjected to the critical scrutiny of hermeneutical considerations.[41]

Furthermore, the answers given by the philosopher of religion to these questions must always be subject to critical revision in the light of the empirical studies undertaken by the historian of religion.[42] The history of religion has not only contributed to our empirical understanding of the different religions; it has also called our attention to the difficulties involved in finding appropriate conceptual categories by which to compare the religions with one another.[43] The disciplined attempt at an unbiased description of the religions requires that the conceptual categories employed in the historical study of religion be controlled neither by the normative concerns of Christian theology nor by the standards of modern Western culture. The study of religions in relation to their own cultural and social contexts can serve as a critical tool in the struggle against religious and cultural imperialisms that denigrate the value and dignity of those who are different from us.[44] Only a consistent and self-critical application of historical method to the study of religion can allow for the genuine diversity among the religions as well as within the religions to come to expression. In this way the history of religion can assist us all in appreciating the complex plurality of the religious world with which it seems our age is destined to wrestle.[45]

A Protestant theology that seeks to articulate the meaning of Christian faith for our time in critical dialogue with the philosophical and historical questions of the academic study of religion will never complete its labors once and for all since new questions and challenges are always on the horizon. Nonetheless, such a theology will be well situated to grapple with what is sure to be a profound challenge to the Christian church in the twenty-first century: how to understand the universality of its religious claim in the light of the relativity of its historical witness in relation to the emerging global context of the new religious pluralism. It may even be the case that the challenge posed by religious pluralism to inherited modes of theological thinking will be as great as those once posed by the Reformation and the Enlightenment.[46]

Yet religious diversity is not only an external challenge facing the Christian church by virtue of its encounter with non-Christian religions. There are, and always have been, significant differences among Christians themselves that need to be addressed in the new spirit of genuine ecumenism.[47] An appreciative recognition of the theological diversity within Christianity itself can and should lead theologians in all the Christian traditions to articulate what each believes to be the essence of Christian faith. The answer that each gives to this question will also affect the response to the challenge of religious plurality beyond the boundaries of Christianity. Indeed, we may have to begin speaking of "Christianities" in the plural, both to acknowledge honestly the real differences that exist among the various construals of the essence of Christian faith and to allow for the further development of distinctive emphases within this complex Christian inheritance.[48]

Even within a given tradition, such as that of Calvin, there is plurality of interpretation regarding what is essential to that particular strand of Christian witness. For myself, the heart of the Reformed tradition lies in its "theocentric" interpretation of the meaning of Christian religion as faith in God.[49] Further development of this tradition in theology offers, I believe, the possibility of a *thoroughgoing* theocentric construal of Christian faith for our time. In this proposal, the traditional doctrines of christology and soteriology would have to be revised so as to make the point that human existence, if it is to be authentic, is to be oriented in devotion and service to the one God who is creator and redeemer of all that is.[50] Such a "reformation" of inherited doctrine would allow Christians to avoid idolatrous claims for the absoluteness of Christianity in relation to non-Christian religions without requiring that they surrender the universal claim upon human existence implied by the logic of monotheistic faith.[51] In this radically theocentric reformulation of the meaning of Christian faith as trust in and loyalty to God, it would surely be necessary to move beyond the explicit statements of Calvin and Schleiermacher, but a contemporary Reformed theologian committed to handing on their heritage to future generations can risk nothing less.

NOTES

1. Barth seems to acknowledge this aspect of Calvin's theology when he writes: "Calvin, too, will link the knowledge of God directly to self-knowledge only insofar as insight into our poverty, nakedness, and ruin through the fall compel us to ask after God. To this extent, but only to this extent, can human awareness of God be the object of theology for Calvin." *The Göttingen Dogmatics: Instruction in the Christian Religion*, vol. 1, ed. Hannelotte Reifen and trans. Geoffrey W. Bromiley (Grand Rapids: Eerdmans, 1991), p. 9.

2. I think that the most significant criticism of Barth's theology would have to be internal criticism that takes seriously his intention to find a theological method faithful to his christocentric construal of the gospel. In this respect, the two most important questions to ask of Barth's dogmatics concern his doctrine of scripture's authority and his exegesis of scripture's teachings. As John B. Cobb, Jr., writes: "The major presupposition [of Barth's theology] . . . is the assumption of the unity of Scripture. . . . It must be noted, however, that most Biblical scholars are impressed by the deep diversities of understanding that

characterize the Biblical writers even on such central questions as are decisive for Barth. . . . My point here is that in the formulation of the principle that guides Barth's exegesis of Scripture there is operating alongside Barth's openness to Scripture as such his hostility to some of the consequences of other interpretations of Scripture—consequences that lead to the inclusion, among the significant data of the theologian, of objects other than Scripture. Loyalty to Scripture is qualified by the predetermination that such loyalty must make itself exclusive. Hence, it is predetermined that aspects of Scriptural teaching that seem to point beyond Scripture do not really do so. The issue is, then, whether Scripture that is understood as testimony to revelation demands that exclusive status which Barth accords it, or whether this exclusive status is ascribed to it on considerations that are alien to Scripture itself. . . . Does Scripture teach the monism of grace and the exclusiveness of its own witness to revelation consistently? If not, Barth must employ selectivity and norms based on something else than the united witness of Scripture. These principles may still be found within Scripture, but their selection must point to some preunderstanding on the part of the man approaching Scripture. Then the question of the justification of this preunderstanding raises the whole range of issues that Barth's method is designed to circumvent. . . . If the method he proposes is humanly possible, we must acknowledge it at the very least as a stable, coherent, and intrinsically acceptable way to theologize. . . . If the criticism is valid, on the other hand, we must say that the ideal for theology held up before us by Barth is a false ideal." *Living Options in Protestant Theology: A Survey of Methods* (Philadelphia: Westminster Press, 1962; repr., Lanham, Maryland: University Press of America, 1986), pp. 193-97.

3. I see no reason to believe that Barth's material interpretation of Christian faith logically depends on his own statement of theological method. If Barth were willing to acknowledge that he does not have the Bible and the Reformation unambiguously on his side, he could still argue on immanent grounds that his christocentric theology is the most appropriate way to construe the gospel. As Cobb implies, this would require Barth to admit that he is engaged in theological *Sachkritik* of scripture and the tradition of Calvin, but this admission would undermine his quest for a theological method immune from the hermeneutical ambiguities of modern theology in general.

4. Tracy questions whether Lindbeck's rejection of the liberal paradigm can be explained solely with reference to the philosophical reasons Lindbeck adduces: "Lindbeck's problems with this 'liberal' tradition, I suspect, are finally less methodological or formal than his paradigm-analysis would suggest. His problems are substantive or material. . . . The hands may be the hands of Wittgenstein and Geertz but the voice is the voice of Karl Barth." "Lindbeck's New Program for Theology," p. 465. In a material vein, Tracy writes: "Insofar as this neo-orthodox tradition from Barth . . . makes the following two points, I agree with the critique: (1) no abstract religious a priori can account for the concrete *event*-character of Christian faith (and thereby its particularity as response to an event); (2) religions *can* be exercises in 'self-salvation' and as such fall under the Christian (and Jewish and Islamic) suspicion of 'idolatry.'" *Analogical Imagination*, p. 180, n. 8.

5. Note the first formulation by Barth of his two final questions to Schleiermacher in the "Concluding Unscientific Postscript": "Is Schleiermacher's enterprise concerned (a) necessarily, intrinsically, and authentically with a Christian *theology* oriented toward worship, preaching, instruction, and pastoral care? Does it only accidentally, extrinsically, and inauthentically wear the dress of a philosophy accommodated to the person of his time? . . . Or is his enterprise concerned (b) primarily, intrinsically, and authentically with a *philosophy* which turns away from Aristotle, Kant, and Fichte in order to locate itself in the vicinity of Plato, Spinoza, and Schelling... a philosophy indifferent as to Christianity and which would have wrapped itself only accidentally, extrinsically, and inauthentically in the garments of a particular theology, which here happens to be Christian?" *Theology of Schleiermacher*, p. 275.

6. As Hans-Joachim Birkner has pointed out in his very clarifying examination, the question of the relation of Schleiermacher's theology to philosophy can be adequately asked and answered only when his own categories and conceptual distinctions are observed and not confused with those arising from a different systematic perspective on these matters. Birkner, *Theologie und Philosophie*, p. 21. For Birkner, Barth's dichotomy between "theology" and "philosophy" is an instance of importing alien systematic categories into the interpretation of Schleiermacher (pp. 7-9). To his credit, Barth concludes his "Postscript" with this final question: "Are the two questions which I posed . . . (a) *correctly* formulated as such, i.e., so as to correspond to Schleiermacher's intentions? . . . Do these questions provide a basis for a meaningful and relevant discussion about the way he worked out the details of his position? Or are all the questions I have posed (b) *incorrectly* formulated, i.e., so as not to correspond to Schleiermacher's intentions? . . . Do they fail to provide a basis for a substantial and relevant discussion of the particular tenets and themes by which Schleiermacher worked out his position?" *Theology of Schleiermacher*, p. 277.

7. Schleiermacher, *Hermeneutics: The Handwritten Manuscripts*, ed. Heinz Kimmerle and trans. James Duke and Jack Forstman, American Academy of Religion Texts and Translations Series (American Academy of Religion, 1977; repr., Atlanta: Scholars Press, 1986).

8. Barth, *Church Dogmatics*, 1.2, pp. 284, 293. Of course, one can also ask whether Barth's theology is, in fact, free of material philosophical influences. See McCormack, *Karl Barth's Critically Realistic Dialectical Theology*, pp. 465-66. And in defense of the patristic dogmatic formulae, Barth writes: "By proving philosophical involvement we can reject the confessions and theology of any age and school, and we can do this the more effectively the less we see the beam in our own eye. For linguistically theologians have always depended on some philosophy and linguistically they always will. But instead of getting Pharisaically indignant about this and consigning whole periods to the limbo of a philosophy that is supposed to deny the Gospel—simply because our own philosophy is different—it is better to stick strictly to the one question what the theologians of the earlier period were really trying to say in the vocabulary of their philosophy." *Church Dogmatics*, 1.1, p. 378.

9. Gerrish comments: "Unfortunately, it is often assumed that to have a philosophical thought is un-Protestant, and that a good Reformation scholar should rise to the defense of the Protestant reformers if some possible influence from philosophy is suggested. I doubt if Zwingli and Calvin, at least, would have been anxious to have their honor maintained by this defense." He adds parenthetically: "I am not so sure about Luther." *Grace and Gratitude*, p. 37. Comparing the rather circumspect approach of Calvin with Zwingli's more enthusiastic embrace of the philosophers, Gerrish writes: "Although Calvin was inclined to be more cautious (he did not want the *mistakes* of the philosophers to be overlooked), he, too, insisted that all truth comes from God, whose Spirit is the one fountain of truth; it would therefore be mere superstition not to risk borrowing from non-Christian writers." Ibid., p. 33.

10. The acknowlegment by "postliberal" theologians of the necessity and legitimacy of *ad hoc* apologetics is a promising step toward moving beyond the stalemate of the usual methodological debates about "foundationalism." Notice what Placher says: "[P]hilosophers and theologians may sometimes wrestle with analogous problems, and when that happens, they can on occasion learn from one another without thereby presupposing any general theory about the relation of philosophy and theology. If something a philosopher has said happens to give me as a theologian a good idea, nothing necessarily follows about the priority of philosophy to theology." *Unapologetic Theology*, p. 13. Thiemann insists that this is Barth's way of appropriating philosophical concepts (*Revelation and Theology*, p. 173, n. 7). But is this not an apt description of Schleiermacher's relation to philosophical ideas? Lamm's analysis of the influence of Spinoza upon Schleiermacher's doctrine of God leads her to conclude: "While influenced by Spinoza and neo-Spinozism, Schleiermacher's doctrine of God cannot be simplistically interpreted as 'Spinozist' or 'pantheistic.'" *The Living God*, p. 227. The "postliberal" distinction between *ad hoc* apologetics and a "systematic" (i.e., foundational) use of apologetics is meant to open the door to conversation with philosophy while safegaurding theology's distinctiveness. The question to be asked, however, is whether this distinction between two types of apologetics really amounts to anything other than a declaration of good intentions. Can one specify on purely formal grounds how to distinguish an appropriate use of philosophy from an inappropriate use? Would theologians in the liberal tradition who are charged with "foundationalism" agree with the characterization of their theological methods as allowing philosophy to have the upper hand? And if, in a given instance, it could be demonstrated that a philosophy had imposed alien categories upon theology's subject-matter, would not the liberal theologian have to concede that the ideal of a correlational theology had been poorly executed in this case? See Tillich's statement in *Systematic Theology*, 1:6-8. The theological method I am seeking to articulate is neither a "revelational positivism" nor a "philosophical foundationalism."

11. This ideal of a theologian who embodies academic and ecclesial excellence in equal measure is called by Schleiermacher a "prince of the church." "If one should imagine both a religious interest (*religiöses Interesse*) and a scientific spirit (*wissenschaftlicher Geist*) conjoined in the highest degree

and with the finest balance for the purpose of theoretical and practical activity alike, that would be the idea of a 'prince of the church.'" *KD*, §9 (*BO*, p. 21).

12. *KD*, §1.

13. *KD*, §5 (*BO*, p. 20).

14. Ogden writes: "[F]rom the standpoint of its logic, [theology] is a field-encompassing field. Its unity is a unity-in-diversity involving three distinct moments, each centering in a logically different kind of question." "What is Theology?" in *On Theology*, p. 7.

15. For the classic statement of this requirement, see Van A. Harvey, *The Historian and the Believer: The Morality of Historical Knowledge and Christian Belief* (Philadelphia: Westminster Press, 1966).

16. *KD*, §1. In response to Lindbeck, Gerrish correctly points out that "Christian doctrines, according to Schleiermacher, are not about the prereflective experience underlying all religions but about the distinctively Christian way of believing, in which everything is related to the redemption accomplished by Jesus of Nazareth." "The Nature of Doctrine," in *The Journal of Religion* 68 (January 1988): 89.

17. A "critical inquiry" aims to discover the distinctive "essence" of an empirical phenomenon. *KD*, §32. See the recent study by Martin Rössler, *Schleiermachers Programm der philosophischen Theologie*, Schleiermacher-Archiv 14 (Berlin and New York: Walter de Gruyter, 1994), pp. 72-149.

18. "The point of departure of philosophical theology, therefore, can only be taken 'above' Christianity, in the logical sense of the term, i.e., in the general concept of a religious community or fellowship of faith." *KD*, §33 (*BO*, p. 29). In Schleiermacher's view, the same applies *mutatis mutandis* when seeking the essence of other religions: "[E]very particular mode of faith can be rightly understood only by means of its relations of coexistence and sequence with others." Ibid.

19. This is the question of the status of the so-called "borrowed propositions" (*Lehnsätze*) in the "Introduction" to the *Glaubenslehre*. Propositions §3-6 defining the concept of "church" as a religious community are borrowed from "ethics" whereas propositions §7-10 dealing with the diversities of religious communities are borrowed from the "philosophy of religion" (*Religionsphilosophie*).

20. Tillich writes: "[P]hilosophy of religion is an independent philosophical discipline . . . and in no sense a theological discipline. Schleiermacher was aware of this situation, and he spoke of propositions borrowed by theology from 'ethics'—ethics meaning to him philosophy of culture. But Schleiermacher did not answer the question of the relation of this 'borrowed' philosophical truth to theological truth. If philosophical truth lies outside the theological circle, how can it determine the theological method? And if it lies within the theological circle, it is not autonomous and theology need not borrow it." *Systematic Theology*, 1:30.

21. "The distinctive nature of Christianity no more allows of its being construed purely scientifically (*rein wissenschaftlich*) than of its being apprehended in a strictly empirical fashion (*bloß empirisch*). Consequently, it admits only of being defined critically (*kritisch*)." *KD*, §32 (*BO*, p. 29).

22. "Philosophical theology, it is true, presupposes the material of historical theology as already known; its own prior task, however, is to lay a foundation for the properly historical perspective on Christianity." *KD*, §65 (*BO*, p. 39).

23. It needs to be recalled that "philosophical theology" in Schleiermacher's sense does not involve a "proof" of Christianity since, in the nature of the case, there can never be a rational demonstration that a particular historical event has redemptive significance. *Gl.*, §11.5. Hans Frei correctly observes: "Schleiermacher . . . does not give priority to academic or philosophical theology, nor does he make philosophy the basis of theology. . . . Theology as academic enterprise and as Christian self-description in the Church must be correlated. Philosophy and theology must be correlated. External and self-description of Christianity must be correlated, and in each case, two factors are autonomously yet reciprocally related, but that reciprocity and mutual autonomy is not explained by any more basic structure of thought under which the two factors would be included." *Types of Christian Theology*, p. 38.

24. "The ecclesiastical value of a dogmatic proposition consists in its reference to the religious emotions themselves." *Gl.*, §17.1 (*CF*, p. 83). "The scientific value of a dogmatic proposition depends in the first place upon the definiteness of the concepts which appear in it, and of their connexion with each other." *Gl.*, §17.2 (*CF*, p. 84).

25. Tillich writes: "[Schleiermacher's] systematic theology is the description of the faith as it is present in the Christian churches. . . . This we call positivism; it is theology as a description of the empirically given reality of the Christian religion. But if this were all, then Schleiermacher would not have been a systematic theologian; he would have been a church historian dealing with the present conditions of the church. But this positivistic feature is counterbalanced—in a logically unclear way—by the fact that Schleiermacher begins with a general concept of religious community as it is manifested universally in the history of humanity. From this he derives a concept of the essence of religion. This is no longer positivism. It is a philosophical analysis of the essence of a thing. This presupposes constructive judgment about what is essential and what is not." *History of Christian Thought*, pp. 399, 402. In Cobb's analysis of theological methods, both Barth and Schleiermacher are considered as examples of "Theological Positivism" on account of their shared commitment to find a non-speculative basis for theology. He writes: "The effort of the nineteenth century was to distinguish the spheres of philosophy and theology in such a way that the former could not cast doubt upon the affirmations of the latter. . . . Twentieth-century theological positivism developed as both a continuation of and a reaction against this kind of nineteenth-century theology." *Living Options*, pp. 126-27. Cobb questions not only whether Schleiermacher and Barth were successful in their attempts to free theology from systematic dependence upon philosophy but also whether their methodological ideals in this respect could ever be implemented in actual practice.

26. The revised three-fold differentiation of theological inquiry into the logically distinct moments of historical, systematic, and practical theology embodies the intention of Schleiermacher's historicization of theology while

clarifying that systematic theology is a *normative* task. See Tillich, *Systematic Theology*, 1:28-34, 53, and Ogden, "What is Theology?," pp. 7-15. I am using "dogmatics" and "systematic theology" as synonyms as did Schleiermacher himself, even though he preferred the former designation on account of its ecclesial reference. *KD*, §97. In the English language, however, it is difficult to avoid the connotation of "authoritarian" associated with the term "dogmatic." But Gerrish insists on the importance of the older term. "I myself obstinately retain the term 'dogmatics' (or 'dogmatic theology') because, like Schleiermacher, I take the subject matter of the discipline to be the faith of the church, which in the Reformed tradition is embodied in the church's confessions. Admittedly, the confessions are less than dogmas, but 'dogmatics' conveys better than 'systematic theology' or *Glaubenslehre* the ecclesial anchorage of the discipline." "Errors and Insights," p. 70, n. 18.

27. See Tracy's proposal in *Analogical Imagination*, pp. 99-107.

28. Tillich writes: "Theology, as a function of the Christian church, must serve the needs of the church. A theological system is supposed to satisfy two basic needs: the statement of the truth of the Christian message and the interpretation of this truth for every new generation. Theology moves back and forth between two poles, the eternal truth of its foundation and the temporal situation in which the eternal truth must be received." *Systematic Theology*, 1:3. In his typology of theologies, Frei places Schleiermacher under the same type as Tillich, whom he calls "Schleiermacher redivivus." *Types of Christian Theology*, pp. 3, 68.

29. While I agree with Tracy that a correlational method for theology must be truly dialogical ("mutually critical"), Tillich's formulation (which Tracy criticizes) seems to be a better description of what a *systematic* theology intends to be, namely, a constructive proposal for how we might understand the Christian tradition as the bearer of an answer to the religious question of human existence (*Blessed Rage*, p. 46). When Tracy himself is describing "systematic" as distinct from what he calls "fundamental" theology, his own formulation is more traditionally Tillichian: "*Systematic* theologies . . . will have as their major concern the re-presentation, the reinterpretation of what is assumed to be the ever-present disclosive and transformative power of the particular religious tradition to which the theologian belongs" (*Analogical Imagination*, p. 57). Indeed, the term "correlation" could be somewhat misleading if by it is understood the bringing together of two static terms. It may be better simply to say that theology (i.e., the methodical explication of "faith" as an understanding of human existence in the world before God) is always constituted by *some* interpretation of the Christian tradition in *some* interpreted situation. The importance of the "correlational" motif is its ability to distinguish (not to separate) these two logically distinct types of interpretation for the sake of the critical analysis of any theological proposal. Unlike Tracy, I do not differentiate theology into the three sub-disciplines of fundamental, systematic, and practical theology; like Tillich and Ogden, I make no distinction between fundamental and systematic theology and I consider "historical theology" to have its own status as a sub-discipline next to systematic and practical theology. Cf. Tracy's comments on historical theology in *Blessed Rage*, p. 56, n. 1; p. 59, n. 30; p.

239. See also his clarification in *Analogical Imagination*, pp. 84-85, n. 28.

30. Tillich speaks of a "kerygmatic" and an "apologetic" element operative in every theology, including Barth's. *Systematic Theology*, 1:6-8. "Barth's greatness is that he corrects himself again and again in the light of the 'situation' and that he strenuously tries not to become his own follower. Yet he does not realize that in doing so he ceases to be a merely kerygmatic theologian." Ibid., p. 5. Tracy, too, draws attention to the implicitly correlational character of Barth's theology: "[S]ome understanding of the contemporary 'situation' and some, even if negative, appraisal of that situation will be employed explicitly or implicitly. The influence of the cultural shock of the post-World I crisis of European civilization was obviously influential upon (not, of course, determinative of) Karl Barth's rigorous stance against all appeals to common human experience or even to religious experience in the crisis theology of his *Romans*." *Analogical Imagination*, p. 60.

31. Gerrish correctly points out: "Like Troeltsch before him, Tillich held that the dominant religious question changes from one age to another as the religious sensibility changes, whereas Schleiermacher seems to have located the theological task in the quest for fresh expressions of a constant relationship with Christ—a relationship that he believed to be the same in him, in the less dialectically gifted members of his congregation, and in the apostle Paul." "The Chief Article—Then and Now," in *Continuing the Reformation*, pp. 35-36.

32. Tillich writes: "The solution which underlies the present system . . . accepts the philosophical and theological criticism of natural theology in its traditional sense. It also accepts the neo-orthodox criticism of a general philosophy of religion as the basis of systematic theology. At the same time, it tries to do justice to the theological motives behind natural theology and philosophy of religion. It takes the philosophical element into the structure of the system itself, using it as the material out of which questions are developed. The questions are answered by the theological concepts. The problem, 'Natural theology or philosophy of religion?' is answered by a third way—the 'method of correlation.'" *Systematic Theology*, 1:30. I agree with Frei's judgment that Tillich and Schleiermacher are exemplars of the same theological type. Hence, my appeal to Tillich is not a move away from Schleiermacher's ideal of a theology framed by piety but an attempt to reformulate that ideal so as to acknowledge that even a theology that strives to be "descriptive" of the Christian religious experience is never free of philosophical elements. Tillich's statement of theology's "two formal criteria" is clearly in the tradition of Schleiermacher: "This, then, is the first formal criterion of theology: *The object of theology is what concerns us ultimately. Only those propositions are theological which deal with their object in so far as it can become a matter of ultimate concern for us. . . . Our ultimate concern is that which determines our being or not-being. Only those statements are theological which deal with their object in so far as it can become a matter of being or not-being for us.* This is the second formal criterion of theology." *Systematic Theology*, 1:12, 14. In my judgment, the strength of Tillich's formulation of a correlational method lies in its sensitivity to critics on both the left and the right of the theological spectrum: those who suspect the tradition of Schleiermacher of surrendering philosophy to

theology (e.g., theologians in the tradition of Hegel) and those who suspect it of betraying theology into the hands of philosophy (e.g., those in the tradition of Barth). Tracy writes: "One may continue to find Tillich's articulation of the ideal for contemporary theology to be fundamentally sound. As Tillich expresses it in volume I of the *Systematics*, the ideal contemporary theological position would provide an *Aufhebung* of both liberalism and neo-orthodoxy." *Blessed Rage*, p. 45.

33. But, as has already been noted, this group does not include the "postliberal" disciples of Barth who are committed to responsible engagement with the discipline of "religious studies." Once again, this fact is indicative of an important convergence between the traditions of Barth and Schleiermacher in the contemporary situation which is too often obscured by the polemics among theologians themselves.

34. Theology's proper institutional location is, therefore, the theological seminary or the "divinity school" of a private university that understands its mission to include the preparation of leaders for the church. This does not mean, of course, that the study of Christianity is not also an object of inquiry for "religious studies."

35. Tracy writes: "The need for determining how we may have a 'confessional' position that is still open to 'public' discourse remains, I believe, the chief question for an adequate revisionist model for dogmatic theology." *Blessed Rage*, p. 87, n. 57. On the question whether theology belongs in a university, see the essay by Franklin I. Gamwell, "Should a University Include Theology?," in *Criterion* 36 (Autumn 1997): 18-27. Gamwell points out that this is no simple question since it presupposes an answer to two prior questions: "What is the nature of a university?" and "What is the nature of theology?" His conclusion is that while "it is false to say that Christian theology necessarily belongs in a university . . . [it] *may* be an activity of a university." Ibid., pp. 18, 25-26. When I speak of theology as "confessional," I am seeking to broaden the usual meaning of that term so as to make it a genuinely "public" (i.e., "non-internalist") discourse that could be pursued in the context of a university, should a university decide to include theology within its curriculum. This would not, however, obliterate the distinction between "religious studies" and "theology." See the recent study by Martin L. Cook, *The Open Circle: Confessional Method in Theology* (Minneapolis: Fortress Press, 1991).

36. "Religious Studies," like theology, is also a "field-encompassing field" of inquiry. I am using the terms "philosophy of religion" and "history of religion" to designate, respectively, the critical-conceptual investigation into the meaning and truth of "the religious" as an aspect or dimension of human culture and the empirical-comparative investigation into the differences evident among the various historic religions.

37. The notion of "religious experience" should be distinguished from that of a "religious dimension of experience." Smith writes: "The proper interpretation of religion in terms of human experience coincides with the correct description, *not* of religious experience, but of the *religious dimension of experience*. Among the many dimensions or 'worlds' of meaning in which experience is taken and through which it is understood, stands the religious

dimension, the dimension in which all is understood from the perspective of the worshipful being. This dimension marks man as the religious animal in the sense that he is the one being in whom the question of the purpose of existence as such becomes explicit both as a *question* and as a supreme *interest*. . . . Man is the one being in finite existence who asks about the quality of existence as such. The asking, moreover, is no purely theoretical matter such as is the case with questions that may or may not be answered in a man's lifetime. The question about the final purpose of the whole is at the same time a question to which every man *needs* some sort of answer as a basis for his *present* existence." *Experience and God*, p. 55.

38. This formulation suggests that it is necessary to ask both "What is *a* religion?" and "What is religion?" It is important to recognize that Lindbeck's discussion of theories of religion focuses on the question, "What is a religion?" When Lindbeck contrasts the "experiential-expressive" model with the "cultural-linguistic" model, this focus is evident. According to the former, "[d]ifferent religions are diverse expressions or objectifications of a common core experience." By contrast, according to the latter, "religions are seen as comprehensive interpretive schemes . . . which structure human experience" (*The Nature of Doctrine*, pp. 31-32). The implication is that the "experiential-expressive" theory reduces the various religions to a common experience which is then given diverse symbolic expressions in the historic religious traditions. The question to be asked, on strictly philosophical grounds, is whether two distinct issues have not been confused here: defining what "a religion" is and what identifies a religion as "religious." The correct insistence that an abstract definition of "the religious" not be mistaken for the concrete reality of "the religions" does not mean that the attempt at definition is misguided. As Smith argues: "From a nominalistic standpoint it is illegitimate to speak about religion in generic terms, on the ground that, while there may be a 'family resemblance' between the different religious traditions, we should properly bound our statements, confining them to an identifiable religion such as Christianity or Buddhism, and avoid the supposition of an 'essential nature' definitive of religion as such. . . . If these claims go unchallenged, a philosophical treatment of religion becomes impossible. But must we accept these claims? That religion in general or *überhaupt* does not confront us as an historical reality may be admitted at once; the point must even be insisted upon. That only individual or identifiable religious traditions can be said to have historical form, however, does not prove that there is no such thing as a *religious dimension* in human existence, nor does it prove that religions fail to have a generic structure that can be defined and illustrated. If a multitude of religions is admitted . . . then some basis must be found for denoting them by the same term. There is no contradiction involved in the claim that a set of phenomena can have a definite structure without that structure itself having a separate existence. . . . In fact it is only when a phenomenon is identified as being of a certain kind that we are in a position to show wherein its uniqueness is found." *Experience and God*, pp. 8-9. On the various attempts at definition, see Capps, *Religious Studies*, pp. 1-52.

39. Tracy's response to Lindbeck gives evidence of the extent to which

liberal theology's appeal to "experience" has been affected by recent developments in philosophy. Tracy argues that the liberal "experiential" paradigm for theology is not wedded to earlier Romantic views according to which language merely "expresses" experience: "The argument among explicitly hermeneutical theologians has been consistent: one can maintain the richer and broader understanding of 'experience' forged by the great liberals (both European and American) only by dialectically relating it to recent understandings of 'language' (and thereby, inevitably, also to history and society). 'Experience' cannot be understood on a Romantic 'expressivist' model (or any other purely instrumentalist model). But this crucial insight does not mean that we should, in effect, abandon half the dialectic by simply placing all experience under the new guardianship of and production by the grammatical rules of the codes of language. Insofar as these familiar hermeneutical claims hold, theologians can continue the liberal analyses of the broader notion of 'experience' without yielding to the earlier 'expressivist' temptations of that tradition. To do so, of course, theologians in the liberal tradition must become both explicitly hermeneutical and explicitly socio-political-cultural. But this, indeed, is exactly what most of them have become." "Lindbeck's New Program for Theology," p. 464.

40.   This requires a hermeneutical model of philosophy that fully recognizes its own historicity since, as Tracy points out, "the only ground upon which any one of us stand" is "the ground of real finitude and radical historicity in all hermeneutical understanding." *Analogical Imagination*, p. 103. See Placher's similar line of thought developed in his *Unapologetic Theology*, pp. 110-15. Barth wrote in a letter to Bultmann: "I am not an enemy of philosophy as such, but I have hopeless reservations about the claim to absoluteness of any philosophy, epistemology, or methodology." *Letters*, p. 105 (letter of 24 December, 1952). Thus the contemporary question of faith and reason can only be properly formulated as the attempt to correlate a thoroughly historicized conception of the theological task with an equally historicized view of philosophy's possibilities. Perhaps in our time we should supplement Schleiermacher's dictum "The Reformation continues" with another: "The Enlightenment continues."

41.   Smith writes: "The mistake embodied in the idea of religious experience . . . consists in the acceptance of an absolute distinction between immediacy and mediation, or between immediate experience and inference. . . . Absolute immediacy can never deliver what it promises because some form of mediation—concepts, language, symbols—always intervenes and makes it impossible to pass from the experience to the reality of God; inference does not suffice because it always takes the form of necessity, which means that God is not experienced, but that something else is experienced and that therefore God 'must' be real. The deficiencies of the two approaches point the way to a third approach, that of mediated or interpreted experience in which both experience and interpretation are interwoven." *Experience and God*, pp. 52-53. Note what Gilkey says about his own understanding of religious language: "The dependence of our view of our knowledge of God and so our language about him on Schleiermacher's view is obvious. There is a difference, however,

between that 'romantic' view and views characteristic of our own age, namely that whereas they assumed that thematization and so symbols could be drawn out of feelings . . . we do not. Rather, we see feelings, experience, or meaning as an interaction of symbols and life. . . . In this, we might claim, we approach Calvin, who, believing that God transcends all our talk about him, averred that he has 'lisped with us his children' and given us symbols with which to speak correctly of him." *Naming the Whirlwind*, p. 467, n. 25. See also Kaufman, *God the Problem* (Cambridge: Harvard University Press, 1972), p. 58, n. 14.

42. "Any understanding of what is religious that may inform the study [of religion] at the outset is tentative and heuristic, a way of identifying possibly fruitful questions, but any such understanding is a rough scaffolding subject to dismantling as the subject matter itself gives rise to more refined questions." *Liberal Learning and the Religion Major: A Report to the Profession*, Stephen D. Crites, scribe, The American Academy of Religion Task Force for the American Association of Colleges (Atlanta: Scholars Press, 1990), p. 11.

43. Troeltsch, whose deep engagement with the historical study of religion represents the further development of Schleiermacher's agenda for theology, says: "[T]hose constructions of the development of religion ventured by Hegel and Schleiermacher appear to us to be completely antiquated exercises of the imagination." Still, Troeltsch concludes that Schleiermacher's proposal for theology in relation to the historical study of religion only needs to be updated, not abandoned: "His program simply needs to be carried out consistently. Hardly any change is necessary. It need only be noted that since Schleiermacher's time, the methods and results of historical science have become more radical and have attained to more far-reaching conclusions." "The Dogmatics of the History-of-Religions School" (1913), in *Religion in History*, trans. James Luther Adams and Walter F. Bense with an introduction by James Luther Adams, Fortress Texts in Modern Theology (Minneapolis: Fortress Press, 1991), pp. 94 and 108, n. 5. Twentieth-century theologians have usually seen in the historical relativism of Troeltsch the culminating dead-end of liberal theology. Bonhoeffer expresses this view: in the conflict between the church and the modern world, the strength of liberal theology was "that it genuinely accepted the battle (Troeltsch), even though this ended with its defeat." *Letters and Papers*, p. 170 (letter of 8 June, 1944). By contrast, Cobb proposes that we recognize Troeltsch's "acknowledgment of relativity as a creative breakthrough of Christian faith itself" and points to H. Richard Niebuhr's work as a development of this positive legacy of Troeltsch. See Cobb, *Christ in a Pluralistic Age* (Philadelphia: The Westminster Press, 1975), p. 49, with reference to Niebuhr's *The Meaning of Revelation*, especially chapter one. Gerrish writes: "Why is revelation, as traditionally understood, a problem for historical thinking? The answer is that to view Christianity in historical perspective is to set it in a larger historical context, to see it as one religion among others, and that means reading the Bible with the same critical eye that we bring to our reading of any other book, sacred or secular. From a strictly historical point of view, there can be no reason to grant privileged status to Christian claims or Christian literature, even though we may have a special interest in them simply because they are part of *our* history. On the contrary, the

task will be to bring any religious claims whatever under the scrutiny of commonly accepted standards of inquiry. And this, as no one has seen more clearly than Ernst Troeltsch, is to remove Christian revelation entirely from the domain of the 'supernatural' (as usually understood). The temptation is always present, of course, to move from antisupernaturalism to naturalistic reductionism. But a realistic account of religious experience is not necessarily excluded by historical thinking: faith may be examined, at least hypothetically, as a response to a transcendent reality. What is excluded in principle is any untested assumption at the outset that Christianity is distinguished from all other religions as the sole recipient of an authoritative revelation, or as the object of a miraculous divine activity that is unparalleled in any other religious history." "[O]nly our provincialism has prevented us from facing a larger fact: that there are, as Troeltsch puts it, several nodal points in the history of humanity's encounter with transcendence, not one absolute center. Once Christian theologians fully acknowledge *this* fact, it is bound to make a difference to the way they go about their business, not least to the way in which they think of revelation." "Errors and Insights," pp. 69-70, 80. For an excellent critical discussion of the contemporary prospects for the concept of "revelation" in both senses of the word, i.e., as "original" and "decisive" (or "historical") revelation, see Wyman's essay, "Revelation and the Doctrine of Faith: Historical Revelation within the Limits of Historical Consciousness," in *The Journal of Religion* 78 (January 1998): 38-63.

44. Cobb criticizes the classical forms of nineteenth-century theology by saying that "the question of the distinctive essence of Christianity was subordinated to that of its superiority to other religions in such a way that the former question was inadequately treated. To determine the distinctive essence of Christianity, we should hold initially in abeyance the question of its relative value or excellence. Only when each religion is understood in its own uniqueness can questions of relative value be honestly treated." *The Structure of Christian Existence* (New York: The Seabury Press, 1979), p. 14.

45. In his last lecture, Tillich expressed his hope that systematic theology would become more explicitly engaged with articulating the Christian message in relation to the history of religions. "My hope for the future of theology," he said, is that there will be "a longer, more intensive period of interpenetration of systematic theological study and religious historical studies." After participating in seminars with Mircea Eliade, Tillich reflected upon his own systematic theology: "[I]n terms of a kind of apologia yet also a self-accusation, I must say that my own *Systematic Theology* was written before these seminars and had another intention, namely, the apologetic discussion against and with the secular." "The Significance of the History of Religions for the Systematic Theologian," in *The Future of Religions*, ed. Jerald C. Brauer (New York: Harper and Row, 1966; repr., Westport, Connecticut: Greenwood Press, 1976), p. 91. This lecture has also been included as an appendix to the new edition of Tillich's *Christianity and the Encounter of World Religions*, foreword by Krister Stendahl, Fortress Texts in Modern Theology (Minneapolis: Fortress Press, 1994), pp. 63-79. In this lecture Tillich stressed "the emphasis on the particular which the method of the history of religions gives to the systematic theologian."

The Future of Religions, p. 91. Tillich says that this insistence on the particular leads to "two negations: against a supernatural and against a natural theology." Ibid., p. 92.

46. Diana L. Eck proposes a helpful shift in imagery for how we think about religious change. She writes: "[O]ur religious traditions are more like rivers than monuments. They are not static and they are not over. They are still rolling—with forks and confluences, rapids and waterfalls. Where those rivers of faith flow depend upon who we are and who we become." *Encountering God: A Spiritual Journey from Bozeman to Banaras* (Boston: Beacon Press, 1993), p. ix.

47. As Tracy insists, "For Christian systematic theology, the first clue for an appropriate response to the radical pluralism of the contemporary situation is the need to reflect upon the pluralism *within* the Christian tradition in order to reflect upon the pluralism *among* the religious traditions or the pluralism *among* the analyses of the situation. . . . The emergence of the sense of a need for the other experienced in each classic Christian tradition as now necessary even to understand one's own particularity is the kairos in the recent emergence of ecumenical Christian theologies. The recognition that no classic tradition should abandon its particular genius in its entry into the conversation with the others is a central key for enhancing a genuinely ecumenical theology." *Analogical Imagination*, pp. 447-48. The historical delineation of the shift from Calvin to Schleiermacher on the question of Christian faith as religion has shown how closely related are the two problems of theological diversity within Christianity and religious plurality beyond the confines of the church.

48. Gustafson writes: "There are different ways of construing the world within the Christian theological tradition. There are persons within and outside the Christian community who would like to believe otherwise, but the literary and historical evidence belies them. . . . There are identifiable historical traditions in theology; each is distinguished by the persistent continuity of one or more central themes. . . . It suffices to say that in different theological ways of construing the world . . . critical judgments have been made in different historic strands of Christianity about which particular tenets are most central. ... The selection of particular tenets, if there is coherence to the strand, determines the ordering of other tenets, both theological and ethical." *Ethics*, 1:159-61.

49. For Gustafson's discussion of his "preference for the Reformed tradition" on account of its theocentric emphasis, see *Ethics* 1:157-94.

50. For a fuller account of what it would mean to revise contemporary Protestantism itself in light of this theocentric perspective, see Douglas F. Ottati, *Reforming Protestantism: Christian Commitment in Today's World* (Louisville: Westminster/John Knox Press, 1995). Ottati writes: "Reforming piety is theocentric because it affirms that, first and foremost, we belong to God, that God alone is God, and that God always already stands in relation to all. It is Christ-formed and even Christocentric in the sense that each of these affirmations in its fullness is both provoked by and made in Jesus Christ. . . . This particular strain of Christian piety accords with a certain understanding of Christian theology. . . . Reforming theology thus is reflection in the service of a theocentric and reforming piety." Ibid., pp. 43-44. See also Ottati's earlier study,

Meaning and Method in H. Richard Niebuhr's Theology (Washington, D.C.: University Press of America, 1982). In my own constructive development of such a theocentric theology, the dialectic of sin and grace (redemption) would constitute the axis around which human existence in faith is understood, while the point of redemption would be formulated as bringing the human being into appropriate relation to God as creator and the world as God's creation. "Jesus Christ" would be understood as the "decisive occasion" in which faith (the Christian understanding of human existence in the world before God) comes into clear focus.

51. On the idolatry of "henotheism" in Christianity, H. Richard Niebuhr writes: "No reformation remains reformed; no catholic church remains all-inclusive. The One beyond the many is confused again and again with one of the many. . . . Henotheism in Christianity tends to take one of two forms, the church-centered or Christ-centered form." *Radical Monotheism and Western Culture*, pp. 56, 58. According to Kaufman, "the functions of both humanization and relativization" are essential to a genuinely theocentric construal of reality (*In Face of Mystery*, p. 321). I am suggesting that a properly theological understanding of what the word "God" means can serve in our time of religious pluralism *to relativize* and *to humanize* the historic Christian tradition.

Bibliography

Primary Sources and Translations

Calvin, John. *Ioannis Calvini opera quae supersunt omnia.* Edited by Wilhelm Baum, Edward Cunitz, and Edward Reuss. 59 vols. *Corpus Reformatorum,* vols. 29-87. Braunschweig: C.A. Schwetschke and Son (M. Bruhn), 1863-1900.

_____. *Ioannis Calvini opera selecta.* Edited by Peter Barth, Wilhelm Niesel, and Dora Scheuner. 5 vols. Munich: Christian Kaiser Verlag, 1926-52.

_____. *Institution de la Religion chrestienne.* Calvin's French translation of 1560. Edited by Jean-Daniel Benoit. 5 vols. Paris: Librairie Philosophique J. Vrin, 1957-63.

_____. *Institutes of the Christian Religion.* English translation of the 1559 Latin edition. Edited by John T. McNeill and translated by Ford Lewis Battles. 2 vols. Library of Christian Classics, vols. 20-21. Philadelphia: Westminster Press, 1960.

_____. *Calvin's Commentary on Seneca's De Clementia.* With introduction, translation, and notes by Ford Lewis Battles and André Malan Hugo. Renaissance Text Series 3. Leiden: E. J. Brill, 1969.

_____. *Institutes of the Christian Religion: 1536 Edition.* Translated and edited by Ford Lewis Battles. Rev. ed. Bibliotheca Calviniana, vol. 1. Grand Rapids: Eerdmans in collaboration with the H. H. Meeter Center for Calvin Studies, 1986.

_____. *Institutes of the Christian Religion.* 1845 translation of the 1559 Latin edition by Henry Beveridge. Grand Rapids: Eerdmans, 1989. Reprint, 1994.

Calvin, John and Jacopo Sadoleto. *A Reformation Debate: Sadoleto's Letter to the Genevans and Calvin's Reply.* Edited with an introduction by John

C. Olin and a foreword by Lester De Koster. Harper and Row: 1966. Reprint, Grand Rapids: Baker Book House, 1976.

Schleiermacher, Friedrich. *Friedrich Schleiermachers sämmtliche Werke.* Edited by Ludwig Jonas, Alexander Schweizer, Friedrich Lücke et al. 31 vols. Berlin: Georg Reimer, 1835-1864.

_____. *Aus Schleiermachers Leben in Briefen.* Edited by Ludwig Jonas and Wilhelm Dilthey. 4 vols. Berlin: Georg Reimer, 1858-63.

_____. *The Life of Schleiermacher as Unfolded in His Autobiography and Letters.* Translated by Frederica Rown. 2 vols. London: Smith, Elder and Company, 1860.

_____. *Friedrich Schleiermachers Reden über die Religion.* Based on the first ed. of 1799 and noting changes in subsequent editions. Critical ed. by G. Ch. Bernhard Pünjer. Braunschweig: C.A. Schwetschke and Son (M. Bruhn), 1879.

_____. *Schleiermachers Sendschreiben über seine Glaubenslehre an Lücke.* Edited by Hermann Mulert. Studien zur Geschichte des neueren Protestantismus, Quellenheft 2. Giessen: Alfred Töpelmann (J. Ricker), 1908.

_____. *Die Weihnachtsfeier: Ein Gespräch.* Darmstadt: Wissenschaftliche Buchhandlung, 1953.

_____. *Der christliche Glaube nach den Grundsätzen der evangelischen Kirche im Zusammenhange dargestellt.* 7th critical ed., based on the 2d ed. of 1830-31. Edited by Martin Redeker. 2 vols. Berlin: Walter de Gruyter, 1960.

_____. *Kurze Darstellung des theologischen Studiums zum Behuf einleitender Vorlesungen.* 3d critical ed. based on the 2d ed. of 1830. Edited by Heinrich Scholz. Leipzig, 1910. Reprint, Darmstadt: Wissenschaftliche Buchgesellschaft, 1961.

_____. *Brief Outline on the Study of Theology.* Translation of the 2d ed. Translated by Terrence N. Tice. Richmond: John Knox Press, 1966.

_____. *Christmas Eve: Dialogue on the Incarnation.* Translated with introduction and notes by Terrence N. Tice. Richmond: John Knox Press, 1967.

_____. *Kleine Schriften und Predigten.* Edited by Hayo Gerdes and Emanuel Hirsch. 3 vols. Berlin: Walter de Gruyter, 1969-1970.

_____. *Schleiermacher's Introductions to the Dialogues of Plato.* Translated by William Dobson. London: J. & J. J. Deighton, 1836. Reprint, New York: Arno Press, 1973.

_____. *The Life of Jesus.* Translated by S. Maclean Gilmour. Edited with an introduction by Jack C. Verheyden. Lives of Jesus Series. Philadelphia: Fortress Press, 1975.

_____. *The Christian Faith.* English translation of the 2d ed. Edited by H. R. Mackintosh and J. S. Stewart. Edinburgh: T. & T. Clark, 1928. Reprint, Philadelphia: Fortress Press, 1976.

_____. *Kritische Gesamtausgabe.* Edited by Hans-Joachim Birkner, Gerhard Ebeling, Hermann Fischer, Heinz Kimmerle, and Kurt-Victor Selge. 13 vols. Berlin and New York: Walter de Gruyter, 1980-.

_____. *On the Glaubenslehre: Two Letters to Dr. Lücke.* Translated by James Duke and Francis Fiorenza. American Academy of Religion Texts and Translations Series 3. Chico: Scholars Press, 1981.

_____. *Der christliche Glaube nach den Grundsätzen der evangelischen Kirche im Zusammenhange dargestellt.* Study edition, based on the first ed. of 1821-22. Edited by Hermann Peiter. 2 vols. Berlin and New York: Walter de Gruyter, 1984.

_____. *Hermeneutics: The Handwritten Manuscripts.* Edited by Heinz Kimmerle and translated by James Duke and Jack Forstman. American Academy of Religion Texts and Translations Series. American Academy of Religion, 1977. Reprint, Altanta: Scholars Press, 1986.

_____. *Servant of the Word: Selected Sermons of Friedrich Schleiermacher.* Translated with an introduction by Dawn De Vries. Fortress Texts in Modern Theology. Philadelphia: Fortress Press, 1987.

_____. *Introduction to Christian Ethics.* Translated by John Shelley. Nashville: Abingdon Press, 1989.

_____. *On Religion: Speeches to its Cultured Despisers.* English translation of the 3d ed. of 1821. Translated by John Oman. 1893. New York: Harper and Row, 1958. Reprint, with a foreword by Jack Forstman, Louisville: Westminster/John Knox Press, 1994.

_____. *On Religion: Speeches to its Cultured Despisers.* English translation of the first ed. of 1799. Translated by Richard Crouter. 2d ed. Cambridge Texts in the History of Philosophy. Cambridge: Cambridge University Press, 1996.

_____. *Dialectic or, The Art of Doing Philosophy: A Study Edition of the 1811 Notes*. Translated, with introduction and notes by Terrence N. Tice. American Academy of Religion Texts and Translations Series. Atlanta: Scholars Press, 1996.

Ancient and Medieval Works

Anselm. "An Address (*Proslogion*)." In *A Scholastic Miscellany: Anselm to Ockham*. Edited and translated by Eugene R. Fairweather, 69-93. The Library of Christian Classics: Ichthus edition. Philadelphia: Westminster Press, 1956.

Aristotle. *Basic Works of Aristotle*. Translated by Richard McKeon. New York: Random House, 1941.

Cicero, Marcus Tullius. *De natura deorum*. With an English translation by H. Rackham. Loeb Classical Library. London: William Heinemann; New York: G.P. Putnam's Sons, 1933.

_____. *Tusculan Disputations*. With an English translation by J.E. King. Loeb Classical Library. London: William Heinemann; Cambridge, Massachusetts: Harvard University Press, 1971.

Denzinger, Henry. *The Sources of Catholic Dogma*. Translated by Roy J. Deferrari from the 13th ed. of *Enchiridion Symbolorum*. St. Louis: B. Herder Book Co., 1957.

Erasmus, Desiderius. *Ausgewählte Werke*. Edited by Hajo Holborn with Annemarie Holborn. Munich: C.H. Beck, 1933.

_____. *Opera Omnia*. Leiden, 1704. Reprint ed., London: The Gregg Press, 1962.

Lietzmann, Hans, Heinrich Bornkamm, Hans Volz, and Ernst Wolf, eds. *Die Bekenntnisschriften der evangelisch-lutherischen Kirche*. 4th ed. Göttingen: Vandenhoeck und Ruprecht, 1959.

Luther, Martin. *Luthers Werke*. Critical edition. Weimar: H. Böhlau, 1883—.

_____. *Luther's Works*. Edited by Jaroslav Pelikan (for volumes 1-30) and Helmut T. Lehmann (for volumes 31-55). 55 vols. Saint Louis: Concordia Publishing House; Philadelphia: Fortress Press, 1955-86.

_____. *Lectures on Romans*. Edited by Wilhelm Pauck. The Library of Christian Classics. Philadelphia: Westminster Press, 1961.

_____. *Martin Luther: Selections from His Writings.* Edited with an introduction by John Dillenberger. Garden City, New York: Anchor Books-Doubleday, 1961.

Melanchthon, Philipp. *Philippi Melanthonis opera quae supersunt omnia.* Edited by Carolus Gottlieb Bretschneider and Henricus Ernestus Bindseil. 28 vols. *Corpus Reformatorum*, vols. 1-28. Halle and Braunschweig: C. A. Schwetschke and Son (M. Bruhn), 1834-1860.

_____. *Melanchthons Werke in Auswahl.* Edited by Robert Stupperich in cooperation with Hans Engelland, Gerhard Ebeling, Richard Nürnberger, and Hans Volz. 7 vols. Gütersloh: C. Bertelsmann, 1951-75.

Migne, J. P., ed. *Patrologiae Cursus Completus.* Series Graeca. 161 vols. Paris, 1857-66.

_____. *Patrologiae Cursus Completus.* Series Latina. 221 vols. Paris, 1844-1900.

Plato. *Protagoras.* With an English translation by W. R. M. Lamb. Loeb Classical Library. London: William Heinemann; Cambridge, Massachusetts: Harvard University Press, 1977.

_____. *Phaedrus.* With an English translation by Harold North Fowler. Loeb Classical Library. London: William Heinemann; Cambridge, Massachusetts: Harvard University Press, 1982.

_____. *Timaeus.* With an English translation by R. G. Bury. Loeb Classical Library. London: William Heinemann; Cambridge, Massachusetts: Harvard University Press, 1989.

Roberts, Alexander, and James Donaldson, eds. *The Ante-Nicene Fathers.* 10 vols. Edinburgh: T. & T. Clark, 1867-72. Reprint, Grand Rapids: Eerdmans, 1980-83.

Seneca. *Epistulae Morales.* With an English translation by Richard M. Gummere. 3 vols. Loeb Classical Library. London: William Heinemann; Cambridge, Massachusetts: Harvard University Press, 1925.

_____. *De Beneficiis.* With an English translation by John W. Basore. Vol. 3, *Moral Essays.* Loeb Classical Library. London: William Heinemann; Cambridge, Massachusetts: Harvard University Press, 1935.

Schaff, Philip, ed. *The Creeds of Christendom, with a History and Critical Notes.* 6th ed., revised by David S. Schaff. 3 vols. Harper and Row, 1931. Reprint, Grand Rapids: Baker Book House, 1990.

_____. *Nicene and Post-Nicene Fathers*. 14 vols. New York: Christian Literature Co., 1886-1890. Reprint, Grand Rapids: Eerdmans, 1980-83.

Spinka, Matthew, ed. *Advocates of Reform: From Wyclif to Erasmus*. Translated by Ford Lewis Battles. Vol. 14, Library of Christian Classics. London and Philadelphia: S.C.M. and Westminster Press, 1953.

Statius. *Thebaid*. With an English translation by J.H. Mozley. 2 vols. Loeb Classical Library. London: William Heinemann; Cambridge, Massachusetts: Harvard University Press, 1928.

Tappert, Theodore G., ed. *The Book of Concord: The Confessions of the Evangelical Lutheran Church*. In collaboration with Jaroslav Pelikan, Robert H. Fischer, and Arthur C. Piepkorn. Philadelphia: Fortress Press, 1959.

Thomas Aquinas. *Aquinas on Nature and Grace*. Edited by A. M. Fairweather. Library of Christian Classics: Ichthus edition. Philadelphia: Westminster Press, 1954.

_____. *Summa Theologiae*. Latin and English. 61 vols. London: Blackfriars; New York: McGraw-Hill, 1964-80.

Virgil. *Aeneid*. With an English translation by H. Rushton Fairclough. 2 vols. Loeb Classical Library. London: William Heinemann; Cambridge, Massachusetts: Harvard University Press, 1986.

Zwingli, Huldreich. *Huldreich Zwinglis sämtliche Werke*. Edited by Emil Egil, Georg Finsler, et al. in cooperation with the Zwingli-Verein in Zurich. 14 vols. *Corpus Reformatorum*, vol. 88ff. Berlin: 1905-. The series was resumed in 1984 by the Theologischer Verlag, Zurich.

_____. *The Latin Works of Huldreich Zwingli*. Edited by Samuel Macauley Jackson et al. 3 vols. Vol. 1, New York: G. P. Putnam's Sons, 1912; Vols. 2-3, Philadelphia: Heidelberg Press, 1922-1929. Vols. 2 and 3 have been reprinted with the titles *On Providence and Other Essays* and *Commentary on True and False Religion*, Durham, North Carolina: Labyrinth Press, 1983, 1981.

Modern Works

Albrecht, Christian. *Schleiermachers Theorie der Frömmigkeit: Ihr wissenschaftlicher Ort und ihr systematischer Gehalt in den Reden, in der Glaubenslehre und in der Dialektik*. Schleiermacher-Archiv 15. Berlin and New York: Walter de Gruyter, 1994.

Armstrong, Brian G. *"Duplex cognitio Dei,* Or? The Problem and Relation of Structure, Form, and Purpose in Calvin's Theology." In *Probing the Reformed Tradition: Historical Studies in Honor of Edward A. Dowey, Jr.,* edited by Elsie Anne McKee and Brian G. Armstrong, 135-153. Louisville: Westminster/John Knox Press, 1989.

Bader, Günter. "Sünde und Bewußtsein der Sünde: Zu Schleiermachers Lehre von der Sünde." *Zeitschrift für Theologie und Kirche* 79 (February 1982): 60-79.

Baeck, Leo. "Judaism in the Church." In *Jewish Perspectives on Christianity,* edited by Fritz A. Rothschild, 92-108. New York: Crossroad, 1990.

Bainton, Roland H. *Here I Stand: A Life of Martin Luther.* New York and Nashville: Abingdon Press, 1950.

_____. "The Bible in the Reformation." In *The Cambridge History of the Bible,* edited by S. L. Greenslade, 3:1-37. Cambridge: Cambridge University Press, 1963.

James Barr. *Biblical Faith and Natural Theology: The Gifford Lectures for 1991 Delivered in the University of Edinburgh.* Oxford: Clarendon Press, 1993.

Barth, Karl. "Brunners Schleiermacherbuch." *Zwischen den Zeiten* 2 (1924): 49-64.

_____. *Die Theologie und die Kirche. Gesammelte Vorträge.* Vol. 2. Zurich: Evangelischer Verlag A. G. Zollikon, 1926.

_____. *Church Dogmatics.* Edited by G.W. Bromiley and T.F. Torrance. 5 vols. in 14. Edinburgh: T. & T. Clark; New York: Charles Scribner's Sons, 1936-77.

_____. *The Knowledge of God and the Service of God, according to the Teaching of the Reformation, recalling the Scottish Confession of 1560.* Translated by J. L. M. Haire and Ian Henderson. London: Hodder and Stoughton, 1938.

_____. *Protestant Thought: From Rousseau to Ritschl.* Translated by Brian Cozens from eleven chapters of *Die Protestantische Theologie im 19. Jahrhundert.* Harper and Row, 1959. Reprint, New York: Simon and Schuster, 1959.

_____. "The Word in Theology from Schleiermacher to Ritschl." In *Theology and Church: Shorter Writings 1920-1928,* 200-216. Translated by Louise Pettibone Smith with an introduction by T. F. Torrance.

London: SCM Press, 1962.

_____. *Learning Jesus Christ Through the Heidelberg Catechism.* Translated by Shirley C. Guthrie, Jr. Originally published in English as *The Heidelberg Catechism for Today.* Richmond: John Knox Press, 1964. Reprint, Eerdmans, n.d.

_____. *The Word of God and the Word of Man.* Translated with a new foreword by Douglas Horton. Harper Paperback, 1957. Reprint, Gloucester, Massachusetts: Peter Smith, 1978.

_____. *The Theology of Schleiermacher: Lectures at Göttingen, Winter Semester of 1923/24.* Edited by Dietrich Ritschl. Translated by Geoffrey W. Bromiley. Grand Rapids: Eerdmans, 1982.

_____. *The Göttingen Dogmatics: Instruction in the Christian Religion.* Edited by Hannelotte Reiffen. Translated by Geoffrey W. Bromiley. 2 vols. Grand Rapids: Eerdmans, 1991.

_____. *The Theology of John Calvin.* Translated by Geoffrey W. Bromiley. Grand Rapids and Cambridge, England: Eerdmans, 1995.

Barth, Karl and Emil Brunner. *Natural Theology, Comprising "Nature and Grace" by Professor Dr. Emil Brunner and the reply "No" by Dr. Karl Barth.* Translated by Peter Fraenkel, with an introduction by John Baillie. London: Geoffrey Blis: The Centenary Press, 1946.

Barth, Karl and Rudolf Bultmann. *Karl Barth-Rudolf Bultmann, Letters 1922-1966.* Edited by Bernd Jaspert. Translated by Geoffrey W. Bromiley. Grand Rapids: Eerdmans Publishing Company, 1981.

Barth, Peter. *Das Problem der natürlichen Theologie.* Theologische Existenz Heute 18. Munich: Christian Kaiser Verlag, 1935.

_____. "Die fünf Einleitungskapitel von Calvins Institutio." *Kirchenblatt für die reformierte Schweiz*, 40. Jahrg., nos. 11-13 (March 12, 19, and 26, 1925):41-42, 45-47, 49-50.

Battenhouse, Roy W. "The Doctrine of Man in Calvin and Renaissance Platonism." *Journal of the History of Ideas* 9 (1948): 447-71.

Battles, Ford Lewis. "God Was Accommodating Himself to Human Capacity." *Interpretation: A Journal of Bible and Theology* 31 (January 1977):19-38.

_____. "True Piety According to Calvin." In *Readings in Calvin's Theology*, edited by Donald McKim, 192-211. Grand Rapids: Baker Book House,

1984.

Baur, F. C. *Die christliche Gnosis, oder die christliche Religions-Philosophie in ihrer geschichtlichen Entwicklung.* Tübingen: C. F. Osiander, 1835. Reprint, Darmstadt: Wissenschaftliche Buchgesellschaft, 1965.

Bauke, Hermann. *Die Probleme der Theologie Calvins.* Leipzig: J. C. Hinrichs, 1922.

Bavinck, Herman. "Calvin and Common Grace." In *Calvin and the Reformation*, edited by William Park Armstrong, 99-130. Princeton Theological Review Association, 1909. Reprint, Grand Rapids: Baker Book House, 1980.

Bayer, Oswald. "Schleiermacher und Luther." In *Internationaler Schleiermacher-Kongreß Berlin 1984*, edited by Kurt-Victor Selge, 2:1005-1016. Berlin: Walter de Gruyter, 1985.

Beckmann, Martin. *Der Begriff der Häresie bei Schleiermacher.* Forschungen zur Geschichte und Lehre des Protestantismus 16. Munich: Christian Kaiser Verlag, 1959.

Behrens, Georg. "The Order of Nature in Pious Self-Consciousness: Schleiermacher's Apologetic Argument." *Religious Studies* 32 (March 1996): 93-108.

Benktson, Benkt-Erik. *Christus und die Religion: Der Religionsbegriff bei Barth, Bonhoeffer und Tillich.* Arbeiten zur Theologie 9. Zweite Reihe. Stuttgart: Calwer Verlag, 1967.

Berger, Heinrich. *Calvins Geschichtsauffassung.* Zurich: Zwingli Verlag, 1955.

Berger, Peter. *The Heretical Imperative: Contemporary Possibilities of Religious Affirmation.* Garden City: Anchor Press/Doubleday, 1979.

Beth, Karl. "Johann Calvin als reformatorischer Systematiker." *Zeitschrift für Theologie und Kirche* 19 (1909): 329-346.

Betz, Hans Dieter. "The Delphic Maxim ΓΝΩΘΙ ΣΑΥΤΟΝ in Hermetic Interpretation." In *Hellenismus und Urchristentum.* Vol. 1 of *Gesammelte Aufsätze*, 92-111. Tübingen: J. C. B. Mohr (Paul Siebeck), 1990.

Birkner, Hans-Joachim. *Theologie und Philosophie: Einführung in Probleme der Schleiermacher-Interpretation.* Theologische Existenz Heute 178 Munich: Christian Kaiser Verlag, 1974.

Blackwell, Albert L. "The Antagonistic Correspondence of 1801 between Chaplain Sack and his Protégé Schleiermacher." *Harvard Theological Review* 74 (January 1981): 101-21.

_____. *Schleiermacher's Early Philosophy of Life: Determinism, Freedom, and Phantasy.* Harvard Theological Studies 33. Chico: Scholars Press, 1982.

Bleek, Hermann. *Die Grundlagen der Christologie Schleiermachers: Die Entwicklung der Anschauungsweise Schleiermachers bis zur Glaubenslehre mit besonderer Rücksicht auf seine Christologie.* Freiburg: J. C. B. Mohr (Paul Siebeck), 1898.

Bohatec, Josef. *Budé und Calvin: Studien zur Gedankenwelt des französischen Frühhumanismus.* Graz: Verlag Hermann Böhlaus Nachfolger, 1950.

Bonhoeffer, Dietrich. *Letters and Papers from Prison.* Rev. ed. Edited by Eberhard Bethge. Translated by Reginald H. Fuller. Originally published under the title *Prisoner for God.* New York: Macmillan, 1967.

Bouwsma, William J. "The Spirituality of Renaissance Humanism." In *Christian Spirituality: High Middle Ages and Reformation*, edited by Jill Raitt in collaboration with Bernard McGinn and John Meyendorff, 236-251. Vol. 17 of *World Spirituality: An Encyclopedic History of the Religious Quest.* New York: Crossroad, 1987.

_____. *John Calvin: A Sixteenth-Century Portrait.* New York and Oxford: Oxford University Press, 1988.

Brandt, James M. "Ritschl's Critique of Schleiermacher's Theological Ethics." *Journal of Religious Ethics* 17 (Fall 1989): 51-72.

Brandt, Richard B. *The Philosophy of Schleiermacher: The Development of His Theory of Scientific and Religious Knowledge.* New York and London: Harper and Brothers, 1941.

Breen, Quirinus. "Humanism and the Reformation." In *The Impact of the Church Upon its Culture: Reappraisals of the History of Christianity*, edited by Jerald C. Brauer, 145-71. Vol. 2 of *Essays in Divinity.* Chicago: The University of Chicago Press, 1968.

_____. *John Calvin: A Study in French Humanism.* 2d ed. Chicago: Archon Books, 1968.

Brown, Marshall. *The Shape of German Romanticism.* Ithaca and London: Cornell University Press, 1979.

Brunner, Emil. *Die Mystik und das Wort: Der Gegensatz zwischen moderner Religionsauffassung und christlichem Glauben dargestellt an der Theologie Schleiermachers*. Tübingen: J.C.B. Mohr (Paul Siebeck), 1924.

_____. *Revelation and Reason: The Christian Doctrine of Faith and Knowledge*. Translated by Olive Wyon. Philadelphia: Westminster Press, 1946.

Brunner, Peter. *Vom Glauben bei Calvin dargestellt auf Grund der Institutio, des Catechismus Genevensis und unter Heranziehung exegetischer und homiletischer Schriften*. Tübingen: J. C. B. Mohr (Paul Siebeck), 1925.

_____. "Allgemeine und besondere Offenbarung in Calvins Institutio." *Evangelische Theologie* 1 (1934): 189-216.

Bultmann, Rudolf. "Karl Barth's Epistle to the Romans in its Second Edition." In *The Beginnings of Dialectic Theology*, edited by James M. Robinson, 100-120. Richmond: John Knox Press, 1968.

Capetz, Paul E. Review of *Barth and Schleiermacher: Beyond the Impasse?*, by James O. Duke and Robert F. Streetman, eds. *The Journal of Religion* 70 (July 1990): 467-69.

_____. Review of *Schleiermacher und die Bekenntnisschriften: Eine Untersuchung zu seiner Reformations- und Protestantismusdeutung*, by Martin Ohst. *The Journal of Religion* 72 (July 1992): 437-38.

Capps, Walter H. *Religious Studies: The Making of a Discipline*. Minneapolis: Fortress Press, 1995.

Christian, C. W. *Friedrich Schleiermacher*. Makers of the Modern Theological Mind. Peabody, Massachusetts: Hendrickson Publishers, 1979.

Clayton, John. "Theologie als Vermittlung—Das Beispiel Schleiermachers." In *Internationaler Schleiermacher Kongreß Berlin 1984*, edited by Kurt-Victor Selge, 2:899-915. Berlin and New York: Walter de Gruyter, 1985.

Clemen, Carl. *Schleiermachers Glaubenslehre in ihrer Bedeutung für Vergangenheit und Zukunft*. Giessen: J. Ricker'sche Verlags-buchhandlung (Alfred Töpelmann), 1905.

Clifford, Paul Rowntree. "The Place of Feeling in Religious Awareness." *Canadian Journal of Theology* 14 (October 1968): 217-221.

Cobb, John B., Jr. *Christ in a Pluralistic Age*. Philadelphia: Westminster Press, 1975.

_____. *The Structure of Christian Existence*. Philadelphia: Westminster Press, 1967. Reprint, New York: The Seabury Press, 1979.

_____. *Living Options in Protestant Theology: A Survey of Methods*. Philadelphia: Westminster Press, 1962. Reprint, Lanham, Maryland: University Press of America, 1986.

Collins, James. *The Emergence of the Philosophy of Religion*. New Haven and London: Yale University Press, 1967.

Cook, Martin L. *The Open Circle: Confessional Method in Theology*. Minneapolis: Fortress Press, 1991.

Cordes, Martin. "Der Brief Schleiermachers an Jacobi: Ein Beitrag zu seiner Entstehung und Überlieferung." *Zeitschrift für Theologie und Kirche* 68 (June 1971): 195-212.

Crites, Stephen D., scribe. *Liberal Learning and the Religion Major: A Report to the Profession*. The American Academy of Religion Task Force for the American Association of Colleges. Atlanta: Scholars Press, 1990.

Cross, George. *The Theology of Schleiermacher: A Condensed Presentation of His Chief Work, "The Christian Faith."* Chicago: The University of Chicago Press, 1911.

Crouter, Richard. "Hegel and Schleiermacher at Berlin: A Many-Sided Debate." In *Journal of the American Academy of Religion* 48 (March 1980): 19-43.

_____. "Rhetoric and Substance in Schleiermacher's Revision of *The Christian Faith* (1820-21)." *The Journal of Religion* 60 (July 1980): 285-306.

_____. "Schleiermacher and the Theology of Bourgeois Society: A Critique of the Critics." *The Journal of Religion* 66 (July 1986): 302-23.

_____. "A Historical Demurral." In *Barth and Schleiermacher: Beyond the Impasse?*, edited by James O. Duke and Robert F. Streetman, 165-68. Philadelphia: Fortress Press, 1988.

Curran, Thomas. "Schleiermacher wider die Spekulation." In *Internationaler Schleiermacher Kongreß Berlin 1984*, edited by Kurt-Victor Selge, 2:997-1001. Berlin: Walter de Gruyter, 1985.

de Greef, W. *The Writings of John Calvin: An Introductory Guide*. Translated by Lyle D. Bierma. Grand Rapids: Baker Book House and Apollos, 1993.

Despland, Michel. "The Theology of Schleiermacher." In *Karl Barth in Review: Posthumous Works Reviewed and Assessed,* edited by H. Martin Rumscheidt with an introduction by Eberhard Busch and an afterword by Hans Frei. Pittsburgh: The Pickwick Press, 1981.

DeVries, Dawn. *Jesus Christ in the Preaching of Calvin and Schleiermacher.* Columbia Series in Reformed Theology. Louisville: Westminster/John Knox Press, 1996.

Dierken, Jörg. *Glaube und Lehre im modernen Protestantismus: Studien zum Verhältnis von religiösem Vollzug und theologischer Bestimmtheit bei Barth und Bultmann sowie Hegel und Schleiermacher.* Beiträge zur Historischen Theologie 92. Tübingen: J. C. B. Mohr (Paul Siebeck), 1996.

Dilthey, Wilhelm. *Leben Schleiermachers.* Vol. 13 of *Gesammelte Schriften.* Originally published 1870. Göttingen: Vandenhoeck und Ruprecht; Berlin: Walter de Gruyter, 1970

Douglas, Jane Dempsey. "Calvin's Use of Metaphorical Language for God: God as Enemy and God as Mother." In *Archive for Reformation History* 77 (1986): 126-140.

Dowey, Edward A., Jr. *The Knowledge of God in Calvin's Theology.* New York: Columbia University Press, 1952.

_____. "The Structure of Calvin's Theological Thought as Influenced by the Two-Fold Knowledge of God." In *Calvinus Ecclesiae Genevensis Custos,* edited by Wilhelm H. Neuser. International Congress on Calvin Research 1982. Frankfurt: Verlag Peter Lang, 1984.

du Preez, J. "John Calvin's Contribution to a *Theologia Religionum.*" *Missionalia* 16 (August 1988): 69-78.

Duke, James O., and Robert F. Streetman, eds. *Barth and Schleiermacher: Beyond the Impasse?* Philadelphia: Fortress Press, 1988.

Dunkmann, Karl. *Die Nachwirkungen der theologischen Prinzipienlehre Schleiermachers.* Beiträge zur Förderung christlicher Theologie. Gütersloh: C. Bertelsmann, 1915.

_____. *Die theologische Prinzipienlehre Schleiermachers nach der Kurzen Darstellung und ihre Begründung durch die Ethik.* Beiträge zur Förderung christlicher Theologie. Gütersloh: C. Bertelsmann, 1916.

Dupré, Louis. "Toward a Revaluation of Schleiermacher's Philosophy of Religion." *The Journal of Religion* 44 (April 1964): 97-112.

Ebeling, Gerhard. *Wort und Glaube*, 4 vols. Tübingen: J.C.B. Mohr (Paul Siebeck), 1960-1995.

_____. *Word and Faith*. Translated by James W. Leitch. Philadephia: Fortress Press, 1963.

_____. *Luther: An Introduction to His Thought*. Translated by R. A. Wilson. Philadelphia: Fortress Press, 1970.

_____. "Schleiermacher's Doctrine of the Divine Attributes." In *Schleiermacher as Contemporary*, edited by Robert Funk, 125-175. Vol. 7 of *Journal for Theology and the Church*. New York: Herder and Herder, 1970.

_____. "Luther und Schleiermacher." In *Internationaler Schleiermacher-Kongreß Berlin 1984*, edited by Kurt-Victor Selge, 1:21-38. Berlin: Walter de Gruyter, 1985.

Eck, Diana L. *Encountering God: A Spiritual Journey from Bozeman to Banaras*. Boston: Beacon Press, 1993.

Edwards, Paul, ed. *The Encyclopedia of Philosophy*. 8 vols. New York: The Macmillan Company and the Free Press, 1967. S.v. "Spinozism" by Frederick M. Barnard, "Romanticism" by Crane Brinton, "Epicureanism and the Epicurean School" and "Epicurus" by P. H. DeLacy, "Stoicism" by Philip P. Hallie, "Pantheism" and "Spinoza" by Alasdair MacIntyre, "Deism" by Ernest Campbell Mossner, and "Schleiermacher" by Richard R. Niebuhr.

Elert, Werner. *Der Kampf um das Christentum: Geschichte der Beziehungen zwischen dem evangelischen Christentum in Deutschland und dem allgemeinen Denken seit Schleiermacher und Hegel*. Munich: C. H. Beck'sche Verlagsbuchhandlung Oskar Beck, 1921.

Eliade, Mircea. *A History of Religious Ideas*. 3 vols. Chicago: The University of Chicago Press, 1978-1985.

_____, ed. *The Encyclopedia of Religion*. 16 vols. New York: Macmillan, 1987. S.v. "Deism" by Allen Wood.

Engel, Mary Potter. *John Calvin's Perspectival Anthropology*. American Academy of Religion Academy Series 52. Atlanta: Scholars Press, 1988.

_____. "Calvin and the Jews: A Textual Puzzle." *Princeton Seminary Bulletin*, supplementary issue, no. 1 (1990): 106-123.

Engelland, Hans. *Gott und Mensch bei Calvin*. Munich: Christian Kaiser Verlag,

1934.

Febvre, Lucien. *The Problem of Unbelief in the Sixteenth Century: The Religion of Rabelais.* Translated by Beatrice Gottlieb. Cambridge, Massachusetts: Harvard University Press, 1982.

Fischer, Konrad. *Gegenwart Christi und Gottesbewußtsein: Drei Studien zur Theologie Schleiermachers.* Theologische Bibliothek Töpelmann 55. Berlin and New York: Walter de Gruyter, 1992.

Flückiger, Felix. *Philosophie und Theologie bei Schleiermacher.* Zollikon-Zurich: Evangelischer Verlag, 1947.

Foreman, Terry Hancock. *Religion as the Heart of Humanistic Culture: Schleiermacher as Exponent of Bildung in the Speeches on Religion of 1799.* Ph.D. dissertation, Yale University, 1975. Ann Arbor: University Microfilms, 1980.

Forstman, Jack. *Word and Spirit: Calvin's Doctrine of Biblical Authority.* Stanford: Stanford University Press, 1962.

_____. *A Romantic Triangle: Schleiermacher and Early German Romanticism.* American Academy of Religion Studies in Religion 13. Missoula, Montana: Scholars Press, 1977.

Frei, Hans W. *Types of Modern Theology.* Edited by George Hunsinger and William C. Placher. New Haven and London: Yale University Press, 1992.

Fuchs, Emil. *Schleiermachers Religionsbegriff und religiöse Stellung zur Zeit der ersten Ausgabe der Reden (1799-1806).* Giessen: J. Ricker'sche Verlagsbuchhandlung (Alfred Töpelmann), 1901.

Fuhrmann, Paul T. *God-Centered Religion: An Essay Inspired by Some French and Swiss Protestant Writers.* Grand Rapids: Zondervan, 1942.

Funk, Robert, ed. *Schleiermacher as Contemporary.* Vol. 7 of *Journal for Theology and the Church.* New York: Herder and Herder, 1970.

Gabel, Gernot U. *Schleiermacher: ein Verzeichnis westeuropäischer und nordamerikanischer Hochschulschriften 1880-1980.* Cologne: Edition Gemini, 1986.

Galling, Kurt, ed., et al. *Die Religion in Geschichte und Gegenwart: Handwörterbuch für Theologie und Religionswissenschaft.* 6 vols. Tübingen: J. C. B. Mohr (Paul Siebeck), 1961. S.v. "Reformation" by W. Maurer.

278   *Christian Faith as Religion*

Ganoczy, Alexandre. *The Young Calvin.* Translated by David Foxgrover and
Wade Provo. Philadelphia: Westminster Press, 1987.

Gay, Peter. *The Enlightenment: An Interpretation.* 2 vols. Originally published
1966 and 1969 by Alfred A. Knopf. New York and London: W. W.
Norton and Company, 1977.

Gerrish, B. A. *Grace and Reason: A Study in Luther's Theology.* Oxford:
Oxford University Press, 1962.

_____. *Tradition and the Modern World: Reformed Theology in the
Nineteenth Century.* Chicago and London: The University of Chicago
Press, 1978.

_____. *The Old Protestantism and the New: Essays on the Reformation
Heritage.* Edinburgh: T. & T. Clark, 1982.

_____. *A Prince of the Church: Schleiermacher and the Beginnings of
Modern Theology.* Philadelphia: Fortress Press, 1984.

_____. "The Nature of Doctrine." *The Journal of Religion* 68 (January
1988): 87-92.

_____. *Grace and Gratitude: The Eucharistic Theology of John Calvin.*
Minneapolis: Fortress Press, 1993.

_____. *Continuing the Reformation: Essays on Modern Religious Thought.*
Chicago and London: The University of Chicago Press, 1993.

Gilkey, Langdon. "Neo-Orthodoxy." In *A Handbook of Christian Theology:
Definition Essays on Concepts and Movements of Thought in
Contemporary Protestantism*, edited by Arthur A. Cohen and Marvin
Halverson, 256-261. Nashville: Abingdon Press, 1958.

_____. *Naming the Whirlwind: The Renewal of God-Language.*
Indianapolis and New York: Bobbs-Merrill, 1969.

_____. "An Appreciation of Karl Barth." In *How Karl Barth Changed My
Mind*, edited by Donald K. McKim, 150-155. Grand Rapids: Eerdmans,
1986.

_____. *Through the Tempest: Theological Voyages in a Pluralistic Culture.*
Selected and edited by Jeff B. Pool. Minneapolis: Fortress Press, 1991.

Gloede, Günter. *Theologia Naturalis bei Calvin.* Tübinger Studien zur
systematischen Theologie 5. Stuttgart: Verlag von W. Kohlhammer,
1935.

Gootjes, N. H. "The Sense of Divinity: A Critical Examination of the Views of Calvin and Demarest." *The Westminster Theological Journal* 48 (Fall 1986): 337-350.

Graby, James K. "The Question of Development in Schleiermacher's Theology." *Canadian Journal of Theology* 10 (January 1964): 75-87.

_____. "The Problem of Ritschl's Relationship to Schleiermacher." *Scottish Journal of Theology* 19 (September 1966): 257-68.

Graf, Friedrich Wilhelm. "Ursprüngliches Gefühl unmittelbarer Koinzidenz des Differenten: Zur Modifikation des Religionsbegriffs in den verschiedenen Auflagen von Schleiermachers *Reden über die Religion.*" *Zeitschrift für Theologie und Kirche* 75 (1978): 147-186.

Graß, Hans. "Schleiermacher und das Bekenntnis." In *Internationaler Schleiermacher-Kongreß Berlin 1984*, edited by Kurt-Victor Selge, 2:1053-1060.

Green, Garrett. "Challenging the Religious Studies Canon: Karl Barth's Theory of Religion." *The Journal of Religion* 75 (October 1995): 473-86.

Grislis, Egil. "Calvin's Use of Cicero in the Institutes I:1-5—A Case Study in Theological Method." *Archiv für Reformationsgeschichte* 62 (1971): 5-37.

Gruhn, Reinhart. "Religionskritik als Aufgabe der Theologie: Zur Kontroverse 'Religion statt Offenbarung?'" *Evangelische Theologie* 39 (1979): 234-255.

Gründler, Otto. "From Seed to Fruition: Calvin's Notion of the *semen fidei* and its Aftermath in Reformed Orthodoxy." In *Probing the Reformed Tradition: Historical Studies in Honor of Edward A. Dowey, Jr.*, edited by Elsie Anne McKee and Brian G. Armstrong, 108-15. Louisville: Westminster/John Knox Press, 1989.

Gunkel, Hermann, and Leopold Zscharnack, eds. *Religion in Geschichte und Gegenwart*. 2d ed. 5 vols. Tübingen: J. C. B. Mohr (Paul Siebeck), 1931. S.v. "Schleiermacher" by Georg Wobbermin.

Gustafson, James M. *Christ and the Moral Life*. Chicago and London: The University of Chicago Press, 1968.

_____. *Ethics from a Theocentric Perspective*. 2 vols. Chicago: The University of Chicago Press, 1981-84.

Hall, Basil. *John Calvin: Humanist and Theologian*. London: George Phillip and Son, 1956.

Hamilton, William. "The Death of God Theologies Today." In *Radical Theology and the Death of God*, edited by Thomas J. J. Altizer and William Hamilton, 23-50. Indianapolis: The Bobbs-Merrill Company, 1966.

Hammond, N. G. L., and H. H. Scullard, eds. *Oxford Classical Dictionary.* 2d ed. Oxford: Oxford University Press, 1970. S.v. "Delphic Oracle" by William Keith Chambers Guthrie and "Pietas" by William Chase Green.

Harnack, Adolf von. *Dogmengeschichte.* 8th ed. Reprint of 7th ed. (1931). Tübingen: J. C. B. Mohr (Paul Siebeck), 1991.

Harvey, Van A. "A Word in Defense of Schleiermacher's Theological Method." *The Journal of Religion* 42 (July 1962): 151-70.

_____. *The Historian and the Believer: The Morality of Historical Knowledge and Christian Belief.* Philadelphia: The Westminster Press, 1966.

_____. "On the New Edition of Schleiermacher's *Addresses on Religion.*" *Journal of the American Academy of Religion* (December 1971): 488-512.

Hegel, G. W. F. *On Christianity: Early Theological Writings.* Translated by T. M. Knox. Chicago: The University of Chicago Press, 1948. Reprint, New York: Harper and Row, 1961.

_____. "'Reason and Religious Truth': Hegel's Foreword to H. Fr. W. Hinrichs' *Die Religion im inneren Verhältnisse zur Wissenschaft.*" Translated by A.V. Miller. In *Beyond Epistemology: New Studies in the Philosophy of Hegel*, edited by Frederick G. Weiss, 221-44. The Hague: Martinus Nijhoff, 1974.

Heim, Karl. *Das Gewißheitsproblem in der systematischen Theologie bis zu Schleiermacher.* Leipzig: J. C. Hinrichs'sche Buchhandlung, 1911.

Heppe, Heinrich. *Reformed Dogmatics, Set Out and Illustrated from the Sources.* Revised and edited by Ernst Bizer. Translated by G. T. Thomson. George Allen and Unwin Ltd., 1950. Reprint, Grand Rapids: Baker Book House, 1978.

Hermann, Wilhelm. *Geschichte der protestantischen Dogmatik von Melanchthon bis Schleiermacher.* Leipzig: Verlag von Breitkopf und Härtel, 1842.

Heron, Aladair I. C. "Barth, Schleiermacher and the Task of Dogmatics." In

Theology Beyond Christendom: Essays on the Centenary of the Birth of Karl Barth May 10, 1886, edited by John Thompson, 267-284. Allison Park, Pennsylvania: Pickwick Publications, 1986.

_____. "Karl Barths Neugestaltung der reformierten Theologie." *Evangelische Theologie* 46 (1986): 393-402.

Hertel, Friedrich. *Das theologische Denken Schleiermachers untersucht an der ersten Auflage seiner Reden "Über die Religion."* Studien zur Dogmengeschichte und systematischen Theologie. Zurich: Zwingli Verlag, 1965.

Hillerbrand, Hans J., ed. *The Oxford Encyclopedia of the Reformation*. 4 vols. New York and Oxford: Oxford University Press, 1996. S.v. "Reform" by Konrad Repgen, "Reformation" by Mark U. Edwards, Jr., and "Reformation Studies" by John Tonkin.

Hinze, Bradford E. *Narrating History, Developing Doctrine: Friedrich Schleiermacher and Johann Sebastian Drey*. American Academy of Religion Academy Series. Atlanta: Scholars Press, 1993.

Hirsch, Emanuel. *Fichtes, Schleiermachers und Hegels Verhältnis zur Reformation*. Göttingen: Vandenhoeck und Ruprecht, 1930.

_____. *Geschichte der neuern evangelischen Theologie im Zusammenhang mit den allgemeinen Bewegungen des europäischen Denkens*. 5 vols. 3d ed. Originally published by C. Bertelsmann Verlag, 1949. Gütersloh: Gütersloher Verlagshaus Gerd Mohn, 1964.

Holl, Karl. *What Did Luther Understand by Religion?* Edited by James Luther Adams and Walter F. Bense. Translated by Fred W. Meuser and Walter R. Wietzke. Philadelphia: Fortress Press, 1977.

Huber, Eugen. *Die Entwicklung des Religionsbegriffs bei Schleiermacher*. Leipzig: Dietrichsche Verlags-Buchhandlung, 1901.

Huizinga, Johan. *Erasmus and the Age of Reformation*. Translated by F. Hopman. Princeton: Princeton University Press, 1984.

Hume, David. *Dialogues Concerning Natural Religion*. Edited with an introduction by Henry D. Aiken. The Hafner Library of Classics. New York: Hafner Press, 1948.

_____. *Hume on Religion*. Edited with an introduction by Richard Wollheim. Cleveland and New York: Meridian Books, 1963.

Jackson, Samuel Macauley, ed., et al. *The New Schaff-Herzog Encyclopedia of*

Religious Knowledge. 13 vols. New York and London: Funk and Wagnalls Co., 1908-1914. S.v. "The Reformation" by D. S. Schaff.

Johnson, William Alexander. *On Religion: A Study of Theological Method in Schleiermacher and Nygren.* Leiden: E. J. Brill, 1964.

Jones, Serene. *Calvin and the Rhetoric of Piety.* Columbia Series in Reformed Theology. Louisville: Westminster/John Knox Press, 1995.

Junker, Maureen. *Das Urbild des Gottesbewußtseins: Zur Entwicklung der Religionstheorie und Christologie Schleiermachers von der ersten zur zweiten Auflage der Glaubenslehre.* Schleiermacher-Archiv 8. Berlin and New York: Walter de Gruyter, 1990.

Kant, Immanuel. *Religion Within the Limits of Reason Alone.* Translated with an introduction and notes by Theodore M. Greene and Hoyt H. Hudson. New York: Harper and Row, 1960.

————. *Critique of Pure Reason.* Unabridged ed. Translated by Norman Kemp Smith. New York: St. Martin's Press, 1965.

Kantzenbach, Wilhelm. *Protestantisches Christentum im Zeitalter der Aufklärung.* Gütersloh: Gütersloher Verlagshaus Gerd Mohn, 1965.

Käsemann, Ernst. *Essays on New Testament Themes.* Translated by W. J. Montague. Philadelphia: Fortress Press, 1982.

Kattenbusch, Ferdinand. *Die deutsche evangelische Theologie seit Schleiermacher: ihre Leistungen und ihre Schäden.* 5th rev. ed. of *Von Schleiermacher zu Ritschl.* Giessen: Verlag von Alfred Töpelmann, 1926.

Kaufman, Gordon D. *God the Problem.* Cambridge, Massachusetts: Harvard University Press, 1972.

————. *In Face of Mystery: A Constructive Theology.* Cambridge, Massachusetts and London: Harvard University Press, 1993.

Kelsey, David H. *The Uses of Scripture in Recent Theology.* Philadelphia: Fortress Press, 1975.

Kempff, D. *A Bibliography of Calviniana 1959-1974.* Studies in Medieval and Reformation Thought 15. Leiden: E. J. Brill, 1975.

Kitagawa, Joseph M. "The History of Religions (Religionswissenschaft) Then and Now." In *The History of Religions: Retrospect and Prospect,* edited by Joseph M. Kitagawa, 121-143. New York: Macmillan, 1985.

Köstlin, Julius. "Calvins *Institutio* nach Form und Inhalt, in ihrer geschichtlichen Entwicklung." *Theologische Studien und Kritiken* (1868): 7-62, 410-486.

Kraemer, Hendrik. *Religion and the Christian Faith*. Philadelphia: Westminster Press, 1957.

Kraus, Hans-Joachim. *Geschichte der historisch-kritischen Erforschung des Alten Testaments von der Reformation bis zur Gegenwart*. Neukirchen Kreis Moers: Verlag der Buchhandlung des Erziehungsvereins, 1956.

_____. *Theologische Religionskritik*. Neukirchener Beiträge zur systematischen Theologie 2. Neukirchen-Vluyn: Neukirchener Verlag, 1982.

_____. *Rückkehr zu Israel: Beiträge zum christlich-jüdischen Dialog*. Neukirchen-Vluyn: Neukirchener Verlag, 1991.

Krusche, Werner. *Das Wirken des Heiligen Geistes nach Calvin*. Göttingen: Vandenhoeck und Ruprecht, 1957.

Kuhn, Thomas S. *The Structure of Scientific Revolutions*. 2d ed. Chicago: The University of Chicago Press, 1970.

Küng, Hans. "Paradigm Change in Theology: A Proposal for Discussion." In *Paradigm Change in Theology: A Symposium for the Future*, edited by Hans Küng and David Tracy, 3-33. New York: Crossroad, 1989.

Lamm, Julia A. *The Living God: Schleiermacher's Theological Appropriation of Spinoza*. University Park, Pennsylvania: The Pennsylvania State University Press, 1996.

Lange, Dietz. "Das fromme Selbstbewußtsein als Subjekt teleologischer Religion bei Schleiermacher." In *Schleiermacher und die wissenschaftliche Kultur des Christentums*, edited by Günter Meckenstock in connection with Joachim Ringleben, 187-205. Berlin and New York: Walter de Gruyter, 1991.

Lee, Sou-Young. "Calvin's Understanding of *Pietas*." In *Calvinus Sincerioris Religionis Vindex: Calvin as Protector of the Purer Reliqion*, edited by Wilhelm H. Neuser and Brian G. Armstrong, 225-239. Kirksville, Missouri: Sixteenth Century Journal Publishers, 1997.

Leith, John H. *An Introduction to the Reformed Tradition: A Way of Being the Christian Community*. Rev. ed. Atlanta: John Knox Press, 1981.

_____. *John Calvin's Doctrine of the Christian Life*. Louisville:

284   *Christian Faith as Religion*

Westminster/John Knox Press, 1989.

Leuze, Reinhard. "Sprache und frommes Selbstbewußtsein: Bemerkungen zu Schleiermachers Glaubenslehre." In *Internationaler Schleiermacher-Kongreß Berlin 1984*, edited by Kurt-Victor Selge, 2:917-922. Berlin: Walter de Gruyter, 1985.

Liebling, Hans. "Ferdinand Christian Baurs Kritik an Schleiermachers Glaubenslehre." *Zeitschrift für Theologie und Kirche* 54 (1957): 225-243.

Lindbeck, George A. *The Nature of Doctrine: Religion and Theology in a Postliberal Age*. Philadelphia: The Westminster Press, 1984.

Lobstein, P. "La Connaissance religieuse d'après Calvin." *Revue de théologie et de philosophie religieuses* 42 (1909): 53-110.

Löffler, Paul. "Selbstbewußtsein und Selbstverständnis als theologische Prinzipien bei Schleiermacher und Bultmann." *Kerygma und Dogma* 2 (1956): 304-315.

Macintosh, H. R. *Types of Modern Theology: Schleiermacher to Barth*. Originally published in 1937. Reprint, London: Nisbet and Co., 1962.

McGrath, Alister E. *Iustitia Dei: A History of the Christian Doctrine of Justification*. 2 vols. Cambridge: Cambridge University Press, 1986.

————. *Reformation Thought: An Introduction*. Oxford: Basil Blackwell, 1988.

————. *A Life of John Calvin: A Study in the Shaping of Western Culture*. Oxford and Cambridge, Massachusetts: Blackwell, 1990.

McCormack, Bruce L. *Karl Barth's Critically Realistic Dialectical Theology: Its Genesis and Development (1909-1936)*. Oxford and New York: The Clarendon Press of Oxford University, 1995.

————. "Revelation and History in Transfoundationalist Perspective: Karl Barth's Theological Epistemology in Conversation with a Schleiermacherian Tradition." *The Journal of Religion* 78 (January 1998): 18-37.

McLeod, Hugh. *Religion and the People of Western Europe, 1789-1970*. Oxford: Oxford University Press, 1981.

McNeill, John T. "Natural Law in the Teaching of the Reformers." *The Journal of Religion* 26 (1946): 168-82.

_____. *The History and Character of Calvinism*. Oxford: Oxford University Press, 1954, 1967.

Meckenstock, Günter. *Deterministische Ethik und kritische Theologie: Die Auseinandersetzung des frühen Schleiermacher mit Kant und Spinoza 1789-1794*. Schleiermacher-Archiv 5. Berlin and New York: Walter de Gruyter, 1988.

Meier-Dörken, Christoph. *Die Theologie der frühen Predigten Schleiermachers*. Theologische Bibliothek Töpelmann 45. Berlin and New York: Walter de Gruyter, 1988.

Moretto, Giovanni. "Angezogen und belehrt von Gott: Der Johannismus in Schleiermachers *Reden über die Religion*." *Theologische Zeitschrift* 37 (September/October 1981): 267-91.

Mühlhaupt, Erwin. *Die Predigt Calvins, ihre Geschichte, ihre Form und ihre religiösen Grundgedanken*. Berlin and Leipzig: Walter de Gruyter, 1931.

Mulert, Hermann. *Schleiermachers geschichtsphilosophische Ansichten in ihrer Bedeutung für seine Theologie*. Studien zur Geschichte des neueren Protestantismus. Giessen: Verlag von Alfred Töpelmann, 1907.

_____. "Die Aufnahme der Glaubenslehre Schleiermachers." *Zeitschrift für Theologie und Kirche* (1908): 107-139.

_____. "Nachlese zu dem Artikel: Die Aufnahme der Glaubenslehre Schleiermachers." *Zeitschrift für Theologie und Kirche* (1909): 243-246.

_____. "Neuere Deutsche Schleiermacher-Literatur." *Zeitschrift für Theologie und Kirche*, n.s. 15 (1934): 77-88.

_____. *Schleiermacher und die Gegenwart*. Frankfurt: Verlag Moritz Diesterweg, 1934.

Nelson, James David. *Herrnhut: Friedrich Schleiermacher's Spiritual Homeland*. Ph.D. dissertation, The University of Chicago, 1963.

_____. "Piety and Invention: A Study of the Dynamic Roots to Intellectual Creativity in Schleiermacher." In *The Impact of the Church Upon Its Culture: Reappraisals of the History of Christianity*, edited by Jerald C. Brauer, 293-331. Vol. 2 of *Essays in Divinity*. Chicago and London: The University of Chicago Press, 1968.

Neuser, Wilhelm. *Calvin*. Sammlung Göschen. Berlin: Walter de Gruyter, 1971.

Newman, Amy. "The Death of Judaism in German Protestant Thought from

Luther to Hegel." *Journal of the American Academy of Religion* 61 (Fall 1993): 455-84.

Nicol, Iain G. "Schleiermacher and Ritschl: Two Nineteenth-Century Revisionary Christologies." In *The Christological Foundation for Contemporary Theological Education*, edited by Joseph D. Ban, 137-157. Macon, Georgia: Mercer University Press, 1988.

Niebuhr, H. Richard. *The Meaning of Revelation*. New York: Macmillan, 1941.

_____. *Radical Monotheism and Western Culture, with Supplementary Essays*. New York: Harper and Row, 1960.

_____. *Faith on Earth: An Inquiry into the Structure of Human Faith*. Edited by Richard R. Niebuhr. New Haven and London: Yale University Press, 1989.

Niebuhr, Richard R. *Schleiermacher on Christ and Religion: A New Introduction*. New York: Charles Scribner's Sons, 1964.

Niesel, Wilhelm. "Schleiermachers Verhältnis zur reformierten Tradition." *Zwischen den Zeiten* 8 (1930): 511-25.

_____. *The Theology of Calvin*. Translated by Harold Knight. Philadelphia: The Westminster Press, 1956.

_____. *Calvin-Bibliographie 1901-1959*. Munich: Christian Kaiser Verlag, 1961.

Nösgen, Karl Friedrich. "Calvins Lehre von Gott und ihr Verhältnis zur Gotteslehre anderer Reformatoren." *Neue Kirchliche Zeitschrift* 23 (1912): 690-747.

Nowak, Kurt. *Schleiermacher und die Frühromantik: Eine literatur-geschichtliche Studie zum romantischen Religionsverständnis und Menschenbild am Ende des 18. Jahrhunderts in Deutschland*. Göttingen: Vandenhoeck und Ruprecht, and Weimar: Hermann Böhlaus Nachfolger, 1986.

Nuovo, Victor L. *Calvin's Theology: A Study of its Sources in Classical Antiquity*. Ph.D. dissertation, Columbia University, 1964.

Obendiek, Harmannus. "Die Institutio Calvins als 'Confessio' und 'Apologie.'" In *Theologische Aufsätze: Karl Barth zum 50. Geburtstag*, edited by Ernst Wolf, 417-31. Munich, 1936.

Oberman, Heiko Augustinus. *The Harvest of Medieval Theology: Gabriel Biel and Late Medieval Nominalism.* Cambridge: Harvard University Press, 1963.

————. "The Tridentine Decree on Justification in the Light of Late Medieval Theology." In *Distinctive Protestant and Catholic Themes Reconsidered*, edited by Robert W. Funk, 28-54. Vol. 3 of *Journal for Theology and the Church*. New York: Harper and Row, 1967.

————. *Forerunners of the Reformation: The Shape of Late Medieval Thought Illustrated by Key Documents.* Philadelphia: Fortress Press, 1966 and 1981.

Offermann, Doris. *Schleiermachers Einleitung in die Glaubenslehre: Eine Untersuchung der "Lehnsätze."* Berlin: Walter de Gruyter, 1969.

Ogden, Schubert M. *The Point of Christology.* San Francisco: Harper and Row, 1982.

————. *On Theology.* San Francisco: Harper and Row, 1986.

————. "Response to Josef Blanck: Biblical Theology in the New Paradigm." In *Paradigm Change in Theology: A Symposium for the Future*, edited by Hans Küng and David Tracy, 287-96. New York: Crossroad, 1989.

Ohst, Martin. *Schleiermacher und die Bekenntnisschriften: Eine Untersuchung zu seiner Reformations- und Protestantismusdeutung.* Beiträge zur historischen Theologie 77. Tübingen: J. C. B. Mohr (Paul Siebeck), 1989.

Olshausen, H. "Über den Begriff der Religion." *Theologische Studien und Kritiken* (1830): 632-650.

Ottati, Douglas F. *Meaning and Method in H. Richard Niebuhr's Theology.* Washington, D.C.: University Press of America, 1982.

————. *Reforming Protestantism: Christian Commitment in Today's World.* Louisville: Westminster/John Knox Press, 1995.

Otto, Rudolf. *Religious Essays: A Supplement to "The Idea of the Holy."* Translated by Brian Lunn. Oxford: Oxford University Press, 1931.

Ozment, Steven. *The Age of Reform 1250-1550: An Intellectual and Religious History of Late Medieval Europe.* New Haven and London: Yale University Press, 1980.

288   *Christian Faith as Religion*

Parker, T. H. L. *The Oracles of God: An Introduction to the Preaching of John Calvin.* London: Lutterworth Press, 1947.

————. *The Doctrine of the Knowledge of God: A Study in Calvin's Theology.* Edinburgh and London: Oliver and Boyd, 1952.

————. *Calvin's Old Testament Commentaries.* Louisville: Westminster/John Knox Press, 1986.

————. *John Calvin.* Tring, England: Lion Publishing, 1987.

————. *Calvin's Preaching.* Louisville: Westminster/John Knox Press, 1992.

Partee, Charles. *Calvin and Classical Philosophy.* Studies in the History of Christian Thought 14. Leiden: E. J. Brill, 1977.

————. "Calvin's Polemic: Foundational Convictions in the Service of God's Truth." In *Calvinus Sincerioris Religionis Vindex: Calvin as Protector of the Purer Religion,* edited by Wilhelm H. Neuser and Brian G. Armstrong, 97-122. Kirksville, Missouri: Sixteenth Century Journal Publishers, 1997.

Pauck, Wilhelm. *From Luther to Tillich: The Reformers and Their Heirs.* Edited by Marion Pauck with an introduction by Jaroslav Pelikan. San Francisco: Harper and Row, 1984.

Pelikan, Jaroslav. *The Vindication of Tradition.* New Haven: Yale University Press, 1984.

————. *Reformation of Church and Dogma (1300-1700).* Vol. 4 of *The Christian Tradition: A History of the Development of Doctrine.* Chicago: The University of Chicago Press, 1984.

Pfleiderer, Otto. *Geschichte der Religionsphilosophie von Spinoza bis auf die Gegenwart. Religionsphilosophie auf geschichtlicher Grundlage.* Vol. 1. 2d expanded ed. Berlin: Georg Reimer, 1883.

————. *The Development of Theology in Germany since Kant and its Progress in Great Britain since 1825.* Translated by J. Frederick Smith. 3d ed. London: Swan Sonnenschein and Co., 1909.

Pickle, Joseph W. "Schleiermacher on Judaism." *The Journal of Religion* 60 (April 1980): 115-137.

Piper, Otto. *Das religiöse Erlebnis: Eine kritische Analyse der Schleiermacherschen Reden über die Religion.* Göttingen: Vandenhoeck und Ruprecht, 1920.

Pitkin, Barbara. "Imitation of David: David as a Paradigm for Faith in Calvin's Exegesis of the Psalms." *The Sixteenth Century Journal* 24 (Winter 1993): 843-63.

Placher, William C. *Unapologetic Theology: A Christian Voice in a Pluralistic Conversation.* Louisville: Westminster/John Knox Press, 1989.

Postema, Gerald J. "Calvin's Alleged Rejection of Natural Theology." *Scottish Journal of Theology* 24 (November 1971): 423-34.

Preus, J. Samuel. "Zwingli, Calvin and the Origin of Religion." *Church History* 46 (June 1977): 186-202.

Proudfoot, Wayne. *Religious Experience.* Berkeley: University of California Press, 1985.

Pünjer, G. Ch. Bernhard. *Geschichte der christlichen Religionsphilosophie seit der Reformation.* 2 vols. Braunschweig: C. A. Schwetschke and Son (M. Bruhn), 1880-83.

_____. *History of the Christian Philosophy of Religion to Kant.* Translated by W. Hastie. Edinburgh: T. & T. Clark, 1887.

Quapp, Erwin H. U. *Christus im Leben Schleiermachers: Vom Herrnhuter zum Spinozisten.* Studien zur Theologie und Geistesgeschichte des neunzehnten Jahrhunderts 6. Göttingen: Vandenhoeck und Ruprecht, 1972.

Rahner, Karl. "Christianity and Non-Christian Religions." In *The Church: Readings in Theology,* edited by Hugo Rahner et al., 112-135. New York: J. P. Kenedy and Sons, 1963.

Redeker, Martin. *Friedrich Schleiermacher: Leben und Werk.* Sammlung Göschen. Berlin: Walter de Gruyter, 1968.

_____. *Schleiermacher: Life and Thought.* Translated by John Wallhausser. Philadelphia: Fortress Press, 1973.

Reill, Peter Hans. *The German Enlightenment and the Rise of Historicism.* Berkeley and Los Angeles: University of California Press, 1975.

Rendtorff, Trutz. *Kirche und Theologie: Die systematische Funktion des Kirchenbegriffs in der neueren Theologie.* Gütersloh: Gütersloher Verlagshaus Gerd Mohn, 1966.

_____. "The Modern Age as a Chapter in the History of Christianity; or, The Legacy of Historical Consciousness in Present Theology." *The Journal of Religion* 65 (October 1985): 478-499.

Reuter, Karl. *Das Grundverständnis der Theologie Calvins, unter Einbeziehung ihrer geschichtlichen Abhängigkeiten.* Beiträge zur Geschichte und Lehre der reformierten Kirche. Neukirchen-Vluyn: Neukirchener Verlag, 1963.

Richard, Lucien Joseph. *The Spirituality of John Calvin.* Atlanta: John Knox Press, 1974.

Ritschl, Albrecht. *A Critical History of the Christian Doctrine of Justification and Reconciliation.* Vol. 1. Translated by John S. Black. Edinburgh: Edmonston and Douglas, 1872.

_____. *Schleiermachers Reden über die Religion und ihre Nachwirkungen auf die evangelische Kirche Deutschlands.* Bonn: Adolph Markus, 1974.

Ritschl, Otto. *Schleiermachers Stellung zum Christentum in seinen Reden über die Religion: Ein Beitrag zur Ehrenrettung Schleiermachers.* Gotha: Friedrich Andreas Perthes, 1888.

_____. "Studien zur Geschichte der protestantischen Theologie im 19. Jahrhundert." *Zeitschrift für Theologie und Kirche* (1895): 486-529.

Roberts, Robert. "The Feeling of Absolute Dependence." In *The Journal of Religion* 57 (July 1977): 252-66.

Rohls, Jan. "Frömmigkeit als Gefühl schlechthinniger Abhängigkeit: Zu Schleiermachers Religionstheorie in der 'Glaubenslehre.'" In *Internationaler Schleiermacher-Kongreß Berlin 1984*, edited by Kurt-Victor Selge, 1:221-252. Berlin: Walter de Gruyter, 1985.

Rössler, Martin. *Schleiermachers Programm der philosophischen Theologie.* Schleiermacher-Archiv 14. Berlin and New York: Walter de Gruyter, 1994.

Roy, Louis. "Consciousness according to Schleiermacher." *The Journal of Religion* 77 (April 1997): 217-232.

Schellong, Dieter. *Das evangelische Gesetz in der Auslegung Calvins.* Theologische Existenz Heute 152. Munich: Christian Kaiser Verlag, 1968.

_____. *Bürgertum und christliche Religion: Anpassungsprobleme der Theologie seit Schleiermacher.* Theologische Existenz Heute 187. Munich: Christian Kaiser Verlag, 1975.

Schmidt, Kurt Dietrich. *Grundriß der Kirchengeschichte*. Göttingen: Vandenhoeck und Ruprecht, 1954.

Scholz, Heinrich. "Analekta zu Schleiermacher." *Zeitschrift für Theologie und Kirche* (1911): 293-314.

_____. *Christentum und Wissenschaft in Schleiermachers Glaubenslehre: Ein Beitrag zum Verständnis der Schleiermacherschen Theologie*. 2d ed. Leipzig: J. C. Hinrichs'sche Buchhandlung, 1911.

Schreiner, Susan E. *The Theatre of His Glory: Nature and the Natural Order in the Thought of John Calvin*. Studies in Historical Theology 3. Durham: Labyrinth Press, 1991.

Schultz, Werner. *Das Verhältnis von Ich und Wirklichkeit in der religiösen Anthropologie Schleiermachers*. Göttingen: Vandenhoeck und Ruprecht, 1935.

_____. "Schleiermacher's Theorie des Gefühls und ihre theologische Bedeutung." *Zeitschrift für Theologie und Kirche* 53 (1956): 75-103.

_____. *Schleiermacher und der Protestantismus*. Theologische Forschung—Wissenschaftliche Beiträge zur kirchlich-evangelischen Lehre 14. Hamburg-Bergstedt: Herbert Reich—Evangelischer Verlag, 1957.

_____. "Schleiermachers Deutung der Religionsgeschichte." *Zeitschrift für Theologie und Kirche* 56 (1959): 55-82.

_____. "Das Griechische Ethos in Schleiermachers Reden und Monologen." *Neue Zeitschrift für systematische Theologie und Religionsphilosophie* 10 (1968): 260-88.

Schützeichel, Heribert. *Die Glaubenstheologie Calvins*. Beiträge zur ökumenischen Theologie. Munich: Max Hueber Verlag, 1972.

Schwarz, Reinhard. "Lessings 'Spinozismus.'" *Zeitschrift für Theologie und Kirche* 65 (1968): 271-90.

Schweitzer, Albert. *The Quest of the Historical Jesus*. With a new introduction by James M. Robinson. New York: Macmillan, 1968.

Schweizer, Alexander. *Glaubenslehre der evangelisch-reformirten Kirche dargestellt und aus den Quellen belegt*. 2 vols. Zurich: Orell, Füssli, and Comp., 1844-47.

_____. *Die protestantischen Centraldogmen in ihrer Entwicklung innerhalb*

292 *Christian Faith as Religion*

der reformirten Kirche. 2 vols. Zurich: Orell, Füssli, and Comp., 1854-56.

Scott, Charles E. "Schleiermacher and the Problem of Divine Immediacy." *Religious Studies* 3 (April 1968): 499-512.

Seeberg, Reinhold. *Lehrbuch der Dogmengeschichte.* 4th rev. ed. 4 vols. Basel: Benno Schwabe and Company, 1953-54.

Seifert, Paul. *Die Theologie des jungen Schleiermacher.* Beiträge zur Förderung christlicher Theologie 49. Gütersloh: Gütersloher Verlagshaus Gerd Mohn, 1960.

_____. "Schleiermacher und Luther." *Luther: Zeitschrift der Luther-Gesellschaft* 40 (1969): 51-68.

Selbie, W. B. *Schleiermacher: A Critical and Historical Study.* London: Chapman and Hall, 1913.

Seltzer, Robert M. *Jewish People, Jewish Thought: The Jewish Experience in History.* New York: Macmillan, 1980.

Senft, Christoph. *Wahrhaftigkeit und Wahrheit: Die Theologie des 19. Jahrhunderts zwischen Orthodoxie und Aufklärung.* Beiträge zur historischen Theologie 22. Tübingen: J.C.B. Mohr (Paul Siebeck), 1956.

Shepherd, Victor A. *The Nature and Function of Faith in the Theology of John Calvin.* Macon, Georgia: Mercer University Press, 1983.

Slomp, Jan. "Calvin and the Turks." In *Christian-Muslim Encounters*, edited by Yvonne Yazbeck Haddad and Wadi Zaidan Haddad, 126-142. Gainesville: University Press of Florida, 1995.

Smith, John E. *Experience and God.* London and New York: Oxford University Press, 1968.

Smith, Samuel D. "John Calvin and Worldly Religion." *Lexington Theological Quarterly* 3 (July 1968): 65-74.

Smits, Luchesius. *Saint Augustin dans l'oeuvre de Jean Calvin.* 2 vols. Assen: Van Gorcum and Co., 1957-58.

Sockness, Brent W. "The Ideal and the Historical in the Christology of Wilhelm Hermann." *The Journal of Religion* 72 (July 1992): 366-88.

Spiegler, Gerhard. *The Eternal Covenant: Schleiermacher's Experiment in Cultural Theology.* New York: Harper and Row, 1967.

Spitz, Lewis W. *The Protestant Reformation 1517-1559*. New York: Harper and Row, 1985.

Stadtland, Tjarko. *Rechtfertigung und Heiligung bei Calvin*. Beiträge zur Geschichte und Lehre der reformierten Kirche. Neukirchen-Vluyn: Neukirchener Verlag, 1972.

Stalder, Robert. *Grundlinien der Theologie Schleiermachers*. Vol. 1: *Zur Fundamentaltheologie*. With an introduction by Jean-Louis Leuba. Wiesbaden: Franz Steiner Verlag, 1969.

Stange, Carl. *Christentum und moderne Weltanschauung*. Erster Teil: *Das Problem der Religion*. 2d ed. Leipzig: A. Deichert'sche Verlagsbuchhandlung, 1913.

Steinmetz, David C. "The Theology of Calvin and Calvinism." In *Reformation Europe: A Guide to Research*, edited by Steven Ozment, 211-232. St. Louis: Center for Reformation Research, 1982.

_____. *Calvin in Context*. New York and Oxford: Oxford University Press, 1995.

Stephan, Horst. *Geschichte der deutschen evangelischen Theologie seit dem deutschen Idealismus*. 2d rev. ed. by Martin Schmidt. Sammlung Töpelmann. Berlin: Alfred Töpelmann, 1960.

Stiewe, Martin. *Das Unionsverständnis Friedrich Schleiermachers: Der Protestantismus als Konfession in der Glaubenslehre*. Witten: Luther-Verlag, 1969.

Strauß, David Friedrich. *Die christliche Glaubenslehre in ihrer geschichtlichen Entwicklung und im Kampfe mit der modernen Wissenschaft dargestellt*. 2 vols. Tübingen and Stuttgart, 1840-41.

_____. *The Christ of Faith and the Jesus of History: A Critique of Schleiermacher's The Life of Jesus*. Translated with an introduction by Leander E. Keck. Lives of Jesus Series. Originally published in German in 1865. Philadelphia: Fortress Press, 1977.

Streetman, Robert F. "Romanticism and the Sensus Numinis in Schleiermacher." In *The Interpretation of Belief: Coleridge, Schleiermacher and Romanticism*, edited by David Jasper, 104-125. New York: St. Martin's Press, 1986.

_____. "Some Questions Schleiermacher Might Ask about Barth's Trinitarian Criticisms." In *Barth and Schleiermacher: Beyond the Impasse?*, edited by James O. Duke and Robert F. Streetman, 114-137.

294   *Christian Faith as Religion*

Philadelphia: Fortress Press, 1988.

Süskind, Hermann. *Christentum und Geschichte bei Schleiermacher. Die geschichtsphilosophischen Grundlagen der Schleiermacherschen Theologie. Erster Teil: Die Absolutheit des Christentums und die Religions-philosophie.* Tübingen: J. C. B. Mohr (Paul Siebeck), 1911.

Sykes, Stephen. *The Identity of Christianity: Theologians and the Essence of Christianity from Schleiermacher to Barth.* Philadelphia: Fortress Press, 1984.

_____. *Friedrich Schleiermacher.* Makers of Contemporary Theology. Richmond: John Knox Press, 1971.

Tamburello, Dennis E. *Union with Christ: John Calvin and the Mysticism of St. Bernard.* Columbia Series in Reformed Theology. Louisville: Westminster/John Knox Press, 1994.

Thiel, John E. *God and World in Schleiermacher's Dialektik and Glaubenslehre: Criticism and the Methodology of Dogmatics.* Basler und Berner Studien zur historischen und systematischen Theologie 43. Bern and Frankfurt: Peter Lang, 1981.

Thiemann, Ronald F. "Piety, Narrative, and Christian Identity." *Word and World* 3 (1983):148-59.

_____. *Revelation and Theology: The Gospel as Narrated Promise.* Notre Dame: University of Notre Dame Press, 1985.

_____. "On Speaking of God—the Divisive Issue for Schleiermacher and Barth: A Response to Frei and Sykes." In *Barth and Schleiermacher: Beyond the Impasse?*, edited by James O. Duke and Robert F. Streetman, 108-13. Philadelphia: Fortress Press, 1988.

Thomas, George F. *Religious Philosophies of the West.* New York: Charles Scribner's Sons, 1965.

Thomas, George Hasson. "Revelation, Faith, and Doctrine: A Study Based on the Theology of John Calvin, Friedrich Schleiermacher, and Karl Barth." Ph.D. dissertation, Vanderbilt University, 1961.

Thomas, John Newton. "The Place of Natural Theology in the Thought of John Calvin." *The Journal of Religious Thought* 15 (Spring-Summer 1958): 107-136.

Tice, Terrence N. *Schleiermacher Bibliography with Brief Introductions, Annotations, and Index.* Princeton Pamphlets, no. 12. Princeton:

Princeton Theological Seminary, 1966.

_____. "Schleiermacher's Conception of Religion: 1799-1831." *Archivio di Filosofia* 52 (1984): 333-56.

_____. *Schleiermacher Bibliography (1784-1984), Updating and Commentary*. Princeton Pamphlets, no. 101. Princeton: Princeton Theological Seminary, 1985.

_____. "Schleiermacher's Theology: Ecclesial and Scientific, Ecumenical and Reformed." In *Probing the Reformed Tradition: Historical Studies in Honor of Edward A. Dowey, Jr.*, ed. Elsie Anne McKee and Brian G. Armstrong, 386-407. Louisville: Westminster/John Knox Press, 1989.

Tillich, Paul. "What is Wrong with the 'Dialectic' Theology?" *The Journal of Religion* 15 (April 1935): 127-45.

_____. *Systematic Theology*. 3 vols. Chicago: The University of Chicago Press, 1951-63.

_____. *The Courage to Be*. New Haven and London: Yale University Press, 1952.

_____. *The Protestant Era*. Translated by James Luther Adams. Abridged ed. Chicago: The University of Chicago Press, 1957.

_____. *Theology of Culture*. London: Oxford University Press, 1959.

_____. "Answer to Karl Barth." In *The Beginnings of Dialectic Theology*, edited by James M. Robinson, 155-158. Richmond: John Knox Press, 1968.

_____. *A History of Christian Thought: From its Judaic and Hellenistic Origins to Existentialism*. Edited by Carl E. Braaten. New York: Simon and Schuster, 1968.

_____. *The Future of Religions*. Edited by Jerald C. Brauer. New York: Harper and Row, 1966. Reprint, Westport, Connecticut: Greenwood Press, 1976.

_____. *Christianity and the Encounter of World Religions*. Foreword by Krister Stendahl. Fortress Texts in Modern Theology. Minneapolis: Fortress Press, 1994.

Titius, Arthur. "Schleiermacher und Kant." In *Schleiermacher: der Philosoph des Glaubens*, 36-56. Six essays with a foreword by Friedrich Naumann. Berlin-Schönberg: Buchverlag der "Hilfe," 1910.

Torrance, T. F. *Calvin's Doctrine of Man*. London: Lutterworth Press, 1952.

Tracy, David. *Blessed Rage for Order: The New Pluralism in Theology*. New York: The Seabury Press, 1978.

_____. *The Analogical Imagination: Christian Theology and the Culture of Pluralism*. New York: Crossroad, 1981.

_____. "Lindbeck's New Program for Theology: A Reflection." *The Thomist* 49 (July 1985): 460-72.

_____. *Plurality and Ambiguity: Hermeneutics, Religion, Hope*. San Francisco: Harper and Row, 1987.

Tracy, James D. "*Ad Fontes*: The Humanist Understanding of Scripture as Nourishment for the Soul." In *Christian Spirituality: High Middle Ages and Reformation*, edited by Jill Raitt in collaboration with Bernard McGinn and John Meyendorff, 252-67. Vol. 17 of *World Spirituality: An Encyclopedic History of the Religious Quest*. New York: Crossroad, 1987.

Trillhaas, Wolfgang. "Schleiermachers Predigten über alttestamentliche Texte." In *Schleiermacher und die wissenschaftliche Kultur des Christentums*, edited by Günter Meckenstock in connection with Joachim Ringleben, 279-289. Berlin and New York: Walter de Gruyter, 1991.

Trinkaus, Charles. "Renaissance Problems in Calvin's Theology." In *Studies in the Renaissance*, edited by W. Perry, 1:59-80. Austin: University of Texas Press, 1954.

Troeltsch, Ernst. "Schleiermacher und die Kirche." In *Schleiermacher: der Philosoph des Glaubens*, 9-35. Six essays with a foreword by Friedrich Naumann. Berlin-Schönberg: Buchverlag der "Hilfe," 1910.

_____. "The Dogmatics of the 'Religionsgeschichtliche Schule.'" *The American Journal of Theology* 17 (January 1913): 1-21.

_____. "Renaissance and Reformation." In *The Reformation: Basic Interpretations*, edited with an introduction by Lewis W. Spitz, 25-43. 2d ed. Lexington, Massachusetts: D. C. Heath and Company, 1972.

_____. *Ernst Troeltsch: Writings on Theology and Religion*. Translated and edited by Robert Morgan and Michael Pye. Atlanta: John Knox Press, 1977.

_____. *Protestantism and Progress: The Significance of Protestantism for the Rise of the Modern World*. Fortress Texts in Modern Theology.

Philadelphia: Fortress Press, 1986.

_____. *Religion in History.* Translated by James Luther Adams and Walter F. Bense with an introduction by James Luther Adams. Fortress Texts in Modern Theology. Minneapolis: Fortress Press, 1991.

Verheyden, Jack. "The Knowledge of the Existence of God in Protestant Theology." *Dialogue and Alliance* 1 (Spring 1987): 27-40.

Vos, Arvin. *Aquinas, Calvin, and Contemporary Protestant Thought: A Critique of Protestant Views on the Thought of Thomas Aquinas.* Grand Rapids: Christian University Press-Eerdmans, 1985.

Vowinckel, Ernst. *Religion und Religionen bei Schleiermacher und Hegel: Eine Verhältnisbestimmung.* Erlangen: Verlag von Rudolf Merkel, 1896.

Wagner, Falk. "Theologie im Banne des religiös-frommen Bewußtseins." In *International Schleiermacher-Kongreß Berlin 1984,* edited by Kurt-Victor Selge, 2:923-944. Berlin: Walter de Gruyter, 1985.

_____. "Funktionalität der Theologie und Positivität der Frömmigkeit." In *Schleiermacher und die wissenschaftliche Kultur des Christentums,* edited by Günter Meckenstock in connection with Joachim Ringleben, 292-309. Berlin and New York: Walter de Gruyter, 1991.

Walker, Williston. *John Calvin: The Organiser of Reformed Protestantism (1509-1564).* New York: Schocken Books, 1969.

_____. *The Reformation.* New York: Charles Scribner's Sons, 1900.

Wallace, Ronald S. *Calvin's Doctrine of the Word and Sacrament.* Edinburgh: Oliver and Boyd, 1953.

_____. *Calvin's Doctrine of the Christian Life.* Grand Rapids: Eerdmans, 1959.

Warfield, B. B. *Calvin and Augustine.* Edited by Samuel G. Craig. Philadelphia: Presbyterian and Reformed Publishing House, 1956.

Webb, Stephen H. *Re-Figuring Theology: The Rhetoric of Karl Barth.* SUNY Series in Rhetoric and Theology. Albany: State University of New York Press, 1991.

Wehrung, Georg. *Der geschichtsphilosophische Standpunkt Schleiermachers zur Zeit seiner Freundschaft mit den Romantikern.* Strassburg i. E.: Buchdruckerei C. Müh & Cie., 1907.

_____. *Die philosophisch-theologische Methode Schleiermachers.* Göttingen: Druck der Univ.-Buchdruckerei von E. A. Huth, 1915.

_____. *Schleiermacher in der Zeit seines Werdens.* Gütersloh: C. Bertelsmann, 1927.

_____. "Religion als Bewußtsein schlechthiniger Abhängigkeit." In *Luther, Kant, Schleiermacher in ihrer Bedeutung für den Protestantismus. Forschungen und Abhandlungen Georg Wobbermin zum 70. Geburtstag (27. Oktober 1939) dargebracht von Kollegen, Schülern und Freunden,* edited by Friedrich Wilhelm Schmidt et al., 506-529. Berlin: Verlag Arthur Collignon, 1939.

Welch, Claude. *Protestant Thought in the Nineteenth Century.* 2 vols. New Haven: Yale University Press, 1972-85.

Welker, Klaus Eberhard. *Die grundsätzliche Beurteilung der Religionsgeschichte durch Schleiermacher.* Leiden and Cologne: E. J. Brill, 1965.

Wendel, François. *Calvin: Origins and Development of His Religious Thought.* Translated by Philip Mairet. New York: Harper and Row, 1963. Reprint, Durham, North Carolina: Labyrinth Press, 1987.

Wendland, Johannes. "Neuere Literatur über Schleiermacher." *Theologische Rundschau* 17 (1914): 133-143.

_____. *Die religiöse Entwicklung Schleiermachers.* Tübingen: J. C. B. Mohr (Paul Siebeck), 1915.

Wernle, Paul. *Johann Calvin. Der evangelische Glaube nach den Hauptschriften der Reformatoren.* Vol. 3. Tübingen: J. C. B. Mohr (Paul Siebeck), 1919.

Wilburn, Ralph G. "The Role of Tradition in Schleiermacher's Theology." In *Encounter* 23 (Summer 1962): 300-315.

Wilkin, Robert L. *The Christians as the Romans Saw Them.* New Haven and London: Yale University Press, 1984.

Wilkins, Eliza Gregory. *"Know Thyself" in Greek and Latin Literature.* Chicago: The University of Chicago Libraries, 1917.

_____. *The Delphic Maxims in Literature.* Chicago: The University of Chicago Press, 1929.

Williams, Daniel Day. "Liberalism." In *A Handbook of Christian Theology:*

Definition Essays on Concepts and Movements in Contemporary Protestantism, edited by Arthur A. Cohen and Marvin Halverson, 207-210. Nashville: Abingdon Press, 1958.

Williams, George Huntston. "Erasmus and the Reformers on Non-Christian Religions and *Salus Extra Ecclesiam.*" In *Action and Conviction in Early Modern Europe: Essays in Memory of E. H. Harbison,* edited by Theodore K. Rabb and Jerrold E. Seigel, 319-370. Princeton: Princeton University Press, 1969.

_____. *The Radical Reformation.* 3d ed. Sixteenth Century Essays and Studies 15. Kirksville, Missouri: Sixteenth Century Journal Publishers, 1992.

Williams, Robert R. *Schleiermacher the Theologian: The Construction of the Doctrine of God.* Philadelphia: Fortress Press, 1978.

_____. "Theodicy, Tragedy, and Soteriology: The Legacy of Schleiermacher." *Harvard Theological Review* 77 (July/October 1984): 395-412.

Willis, E. David. *Calvin's Catholic Christology: The Function of the So-called Extra Calvinisticum in Calvin's Theology.* Studies in Medieval and Reformation Thought 2. Leiden: E. J. Brill, 1966.

_____. "Rhetoric and Responsibility in Calvin's Theology." In *The Context of Contemporary Theology: Essays in Honor of Paul Lehmann,* edited by Alexander J. McKelway and E. David Willis, 43-63. Atlanta: John Knox Press, 1974.

Wobbermin, Georg. "Luther, Kant, Schleiermacher und die Aufgabe der heutigen Theologie." *Zeitschrift für Theologie und Kirche* 5, neue Folge (1924): 104-120.

_____. "Gibt es eine Linie Luther-Schleiermacher?" *Zeitschrift für Theologie und Kirche* 12 (1931): 250-60.

_____. *The Nature of Religion.* Translated by Theophil Menzel and Daniel Sommer Robinson with an introduction by Douglas Clyde Macintosh. New York: Thomas Y. Cromwell Co., 1933.

Wolf, Heinrich. *Die Einheit des Bundes: Das Verhältnis von Altem und Neuem Testament bei Calvin.* Beiträge zur Geschichte und Lehre der reformierten Kirche. Neukirchen Kreis Moers: Verlag der Buchhandlung des Erziehungsvereins, 1958.

Wyman, Walter E., Jr. *The Concept of Glaubenslehre: Ernst Troeltsch and the*

Theological Heritage of Schleiermacher. American Academy of Religion Academy Series 44. Chico: Scholars Press, 1983.

_____. "The Historical Consciousness and the Study of Theology." In *Shifting Boundaries: Contextual Approaches to the Structure of Theological Education*, edited by Barbara G. Wheeler and Edward Farley, 91-117. Louisville: Westminster/John Knox Press, 1991.

_____. "Rethinking the Christian Doctrine of Sin: Friedrich Schleiermacher and Hick's 'Irenaean Type.'" *The Journal of Religion* 74 (April 1994): 199-217.

_____. "Revelation and the Doctrine of Faith: Historical Revelation within the Limits of Historical Consciousness." *The Journal of Religion* 78 (January 1988): 38-63.

Yates, Frances A. *Giordano Bruno and the Hermetic Tradition.* Chicago: The University of Chicago Press, 1964.

Zachman, Randall C. "The Awareness of Divinity and the Knowledge of God in the Theology of Calvin and Schleiermacher." In *Revisioning the Past: Prospects in Historical Theology*, edited by Mary Potter Engel and Walter E. Wyman, Jr., 131-146. Minneapolis: Fortress Press, 1992.

_____. *The Assurance of Faith: Conscience in the Theology of Martin Luther and John Calvin.* Minneapolis: Fortress Press, 1993.

Zahrnt, Heinz. *The Question of God: Protestant Theology in the Twentieth Century.* Translated by R. A. Wilson. New York: Harcourt, Brace, and World, 1969.

Zeller, Eduard. *Stoics, Epicureans, and Sceptics.* Translated by Oswald J. Reichel. New and rev. ed. New York: Russell and Russell, Inc., 1962.

INDEX

Adam, 36, 40, 48, 51, 74, 83, 91, 169, 218-19

Albrecht, Christian, 149n116

Anselm, 65n99, 188n72

anthropocentrism, critique of, 5, 8, 118-19, 220, 233n41
See also theocentrism

apologetics, xi, xxiin20, 6, 60n47, 196n130, 223, 251n10

Aquinas, Thomas, 23n41, 57n31, 59n41, 61n55, 105n89

Aratus of Soli, 64n92

Arianism, 192n100

Aristotle, 61n54, 250n5

Athanasius, 192n100

atheism, 45-46, 63n72, 65n99, 65n100, 88, 129, 138n67, 230n22

Augustine of Hippo, 1, 20n4, 22n28, 29, 31, 54n17, 72-73, 91n3, 93n10, 94n12, 94n13, 98n44, 107n110, 186n65, 193-94n104, 201, 233n41

Baeck, Leo, 104n78

Baillie, John, 69n131

Bainton, Roland H., 92n4, 94n11

Barr, James, 57-58n33, 63n72, 227n2, 227n3, 235n48

Barth, Karl, 19, 233n41, 255n30
and Calvin, 14-15, 17, 57n31, 57n32, 60n43, 60n47, 67n123, 100n53, 101n61, 192n100, 198-200, 229n18, 230n27, 235n51, 238-39, 248n1
christocentrism of, 8, 14-15, 24-25n52, 238, 248n2, 249n3
Church Dogmatics, xii, 224
and liberal theology, xi-xii, xxn3, 4, 5-9
and natural theology, 8, 21n23, 21n24, 34, 55-56n24, 57-58n33, 58n34, 63n72, 68n127, 69n131, 200, 227n2, 227n3
and philosophy, 150n125, 233-34n45, 239, 250n5, 250n6, 250n8, 253n25, 255-56n32, 258n40

and postliberal theology, xv-xvi, xxin19, xxiin20, 249n4, 251n10, 256n33
and the Reformation heritage, xii, xvi, xxivn30, 10, 15-16, 25n53, 57n31, 60n43, 151n129, 195n129, 199, 221-25, 249n3
on religion, xi-xii, xxn6, xxn7, 4-9, 25-26n53, 101n61, 178n32, 198-200, 221, 223, 238
and religion, theories of, xxin18, xxi-xxiin19
and Schleiermacher, 4, 5-9, 21n14, 25-26n53, 198-200, 221-25, 234-35n47, 238-39

Barth, Peter, 29, 62n57, 67n122

Battenhouse, Roy W., 61n54

Battles, Ford Lewis, 52n3, 60n45, 61n49, 101n60

Bauke, Hermann, 53n11

Baur, Ferdinand Christian, 150n125

Bavinck, Herman, 65n96

Beckmann, Klaus-Martin, 187n70, 187n71

Behrens, Georg, 196n130

Benktson, Benkt-Erik, xxn7

Berger, Heinrich, 104n84

Berger, Peter L., 177n17

Bernard of Clairvaux, 95n21

Betz, Hans Dieter, xixn2, 64n88

Beveridge, Henry, 94n17

Bible
in Calvin's theology, 12-13, 32-33, 50-51, 74-76, 81, 84, 208
and continuity of Testaments, 84-85, 103n74
exegesis of, and dogmatics, 12-13, 32-33, 248-49n2
historical-critical study of, 3, 259-60n43
and knowledge of God, twofold, 75
in Reformation doctrine, 7, 31, 73-75
and religion, true, 71, 81
in Schleiermacher's theology, 12, 183n56, 189n81, 208, 228n13

302 *Christian Faith as Religion*

Biel, Gabriel, 91n3
Birkner, Hans-Joachim, 134n4,
188n76, 250n6
Blackwell, Albert L., 138n56,
139n70, 139n71, 181n50
Bleek, Hermann, 182n53
Bohatec, Josef, 54n16, 62n62, 63n76
Bonhoeffer, Dietrich, xii, xxn5, xxn6,
xxn7, xxin9, 20n1, 259n43
Börne, L.,136n19
Bouwsma, William, 53n11, 93n9,
104n84, 106n98
Bradwardine, Thomas, 91n3
Brandt, James M., 181-82n50,
231n30, 232n32
Brandt, Richard B., 140n77
Breen, Quirinus, 52n6
Brinton, Crane, 135n15
Brown, Marshall, 135n15
Brunner, Emil
on Calvin, 14, 15, 17, 57n31,
61n52, 62n56, 65n96, 105n93,
197-98, 200, 211, 221, 229n18
and liberal theology, xxn3, 4-5, 9,
10, 221, 225
Mysticism and the Word, 4, 20n6
and natural theology, 8, 34, 55-
56n24, 57n31, 58n34, 68n127,
69n131, 200
on Schleiermacher, 4-5, 9, 14-17,
150n125, 179n38, 197-98, 211,
222-23, 235-36n53
Brunner, Peter, 58-59n36, 101n59
Bucer, Martin, 67n124
Budé, William, 54n16
Bullinger, Heinrich, 67n124
Bultmann, Rudolf, 25-26n53,
196n129, 234n45, 258n40

Calvin
on conscience, 77, 96n25, 96n26,
96n27, 215, 230n23
on diversity, religious, 72, 82,
100n54, 101-2n66, 103n67,
106n98, 106n102, 155
on *duplex cognitio Dei*, 13, 14, 33-
34, 35, 36, 54-55n18, 58n35,
69n131, 75

on *duplex gratia*, 78, 203
on faith, 13-14, 17, 30, 51, 72, 76-
80, 81, 83-86, 89, 90-91, 95n20,
95-96n22, 96n32, 96-97n33,
97n34, 105n90, 202-3, 229n20
on false religion, 37, 72, 81-83, 87,
89, 90, 101n61, 202
on the gospel, 83-84, 202-3
on grace, 31, 78, 89, 203
and humanism, 7, 30-32, 51, 52n5,
52n6, 53n11, 54n16, 71, 90-91,
93n9, 94n16, 100n53, 104n84,
213
on hypocrisy, 81, 83, 88, 103n69
on idolatry, 81-83, 87-88, 106n98,
106n102
Institutes of the Christian Religion,
11-12, 29, 31-35, 37, 40, 48, 50-
51, 53n8, 53n9, 53n11, 54n13,
54-55n18, 59n41, 63n72, 63n78,
66n100, 66n117, 102n66,
105n89
on Islam, 82, 89, 101-2n66,
106n102
on Judaism, 82, 84, 85, 87, 88, 89,
102n96, 103n74, 103n75,
104n78
and natural theology, 14, 34-36,
49-50, 51, 55-56n24, 56n25,
57n31, 57-58n33, 59n39, 63n72,
68n126, 68n127, 69n131
on paganism, Graeco-Roman, 82,
102n66, 103n67, 106n98,
107n110
on piety, 12-13, 30, 32, 34, 47, 39-
40, 41, 50-51, 56-57n26, 59n43,
71, 77-78, 79, 80, 81, 82, 83, 87,
90-91, 97n34, 98n43, 98n44, 98-
99n45, 99n46, 103n71, 105n94,
202, 216, 217, 218-19, 229n20
philosophers, and relation to, 30,
41-48, 50, 62n60, 62n63, 63n76,
63n77, 63-64n78, 90, 98n44,
239, 251n9
Protestantism, and conversion to,
30-31, 51, 52n4, 52n5, 71, 90,
101n60, 106n97

Calvin (*continued*)
on the Reformation, 71-72, 88, 90, 91n1
on religion, 7, 41, 47, 57n32, 59-60n43, 71, 77-78, 79, 81, 82, 83, 85, 88, 89, 90-91, 91n1, 96n26, 97n34, 101n63, 103n71
on revelation, 17-18, 35-36, 49, 50, 59n40, 66-67n121, 69n131, 85, 91, 96n25
Schleiermacher's relation to, 19, 22n35, 23n40, 23n41, 24n47, 24n48, 24n49, 24-25n52, 53n11, 57n31, 109, 134n1, 136n20, 136n32, 149n119, 183n55, 190n87, 191n99, 191-92n100, 194n119, 196n130
scholasticism, and relation to, 31, 34, 52n7, 53n11, 90, 93n10, 105n89, 213
on *semen religionis*, 37, 38, 40, 40, 42, 43, 47, 67n123, 68-69n128, 81, 100n53, 134n1, 228n17
on *sensus divinitatis*, 14, 37, 41, 42, 43, 45, 59n40, 62n57, 63n73, 63-64n78, 105n94, 228n17, 232n34
on speculation, 12, 34, 45, 47, 75, 81, 91
on superstition, 47, 81-82, 87, 88, 101n63, 106n102, 107n110
and theological method, 11-15, 24n47, 24n48, 32-36, 37, 53n11, 54n13, 54n17, 54-55n18, 55n23, 56-57n26, 59n41, 60n47, 94n17, 229n19
on true religion, 29-3, 31, 71-72, 82, 86-88, 90, 206-208
Capps, Walter H., xxin9, xxiiin27, 257n38
Caroli, Pierre, 192n100
Christ. *See* Jesus Christ
Christianity, Schleiermacher on
as a "positive" religion, 157-65, 175
polemical nature of, 158-60, 163-65, 210

essence of, 160-63, 165-67, 175, 209-10, 241-42
Cicero, 14, 41-43, 47, 61n54, 63n76, 64n88, 66n116, 101n65, 107n110, 113, 136n20
On the Nature of the Gods, 41
Clarke, Samuel, 230n27
Clayton, John, 151n127
Clemen, Carl, 181n49
Cobb, John B., Jr., 248-49n2, 249n3, 253n25, 259n43, 260n44
consciousness,
of God, Schleiermacher on, 128, 154, 170-71, 209
self-, 127-29, 171, 209
Cook, Martin L., 256n35
Cop, Nicolas, 52n4
Cordes, Martin, 150n120, 150n122, 150n123, 150n124
Crites, Stephen D., 259n42
Crouter, Richard, 137n41, 140n80, 148n113, 234-35n47
Curran, Thomas, 150n125

de Greef, W., 54n13
deism, 112, 135n14, 179n40
DeLacy, P. H., 64n86
Democritus, 65n100
Denzinger, Henry, 92n7, 94n11, 97n39
Descartes, René, 55n23
DeVries, Dawn, 190n87
de Wette, W. M. L., 148n113
Dilthey, Wilhelm, 134n7, 139n69, 142n83
diversity, religious
and Christianity, 247-48
comparison of Calvin and Schleiermacher on, 206-11, 261n47
in Protestant theology, 211
See also Calvin, on religious diversity; pluralism, religious; Schleiermacher, on religion, diversity of
doctrine, Christian
liberal interpretation of, xv, xxiin22

doctrine, Christian (*continued*)
  postliberal interpretation of, xv,
    xxiin22
  Schleiermacher on, 133, 165-66,
    168-69, 236n53
dogmatics
  comparison of Calvin and
    Schleiermacher, 11-15, 197-201,
    206, 211, 220-21, 237-40, 241-
    43
  as constructive and normative,
    243, 253-54n26
  See also Calvin, *Institutes*;
    Schleiermacher, *Glaubenslehre*
Douglas, Jane Dempsey, 62n64
Dowey, Edward A., Jr., 33, 54n17,
  59n40, 61n49, 66n120, 66-
  67n121, 95n20, 96n25, 103n74,
  104n82, 105n90, 231n28
Drey, Johann Sebastian, 188n75
Dunkmann, Karl, 143n88
Dupré, Louis, 139n74, 147n104,
  149n117
du Preez, J., 100n54, 101n56

Ebeling, Gerhard, xixn2, 20n4,
  22n30, 23n39, 135n18, 137n43,
  146n103, 148n115, 191n100,
  235n52
Eck, Diana L., 261n46
ecumenism, xiii, xix, xxin11, xxin15,
  188n76, 261n47
Edwards, Jonathan, 22n28, 233n41
Edwards, Mark U., Jr., 93n8
Eliade, Mircea, 62n62, 144n92,
  260n45
Engel, Mary Potter, 54n17, 100n53,
  104n78, 105-6n94, 192n100
Engelland, Hans, 63n73
Enlightenment, the, xi, 2-3, 109, 201,
  203, 211, 240
Epicureanism, 41-43, 45, 46, 64n94,
  65n100, 66n102, 98n44
Epicurus, 42-43, 46
Erasmus, Desiderius, 31, 53n11,
  54n16, 55n19, 60n45, 90, 92n8,
  202

ethics. *See* morality
ethics, Christian
  Schleiermacher on, 174, 186n66,
    195n125, 232n32, 232n33
evil, Schleiermacher on, 171-72, 204
experience
  Calvin on, 62n56, 68-69n128, 238
  Christian, 133, 170, 190n87
  common human, 27n60
  comparison of Calvin and
    Schleiermacher on, 212-18
  liberal theology's concept of, xiv-
    xvi, xviii, xix, 257-58n39
  postliberal theology and, xiv-xvi,
    144n92, 186n65, 257n38
  religious, 141-42n82, 143-44n92,
    256-57n37, 258-59n41
  Schleiermacher on, 124-26, 129,
    133, 141n82, 143-44n92,
    147n104, 175, 238
  See also feeling; intuition

faith, Christian
  comparison of Calvin and
    Schleiermacher on, 18, 198-200,
    202-6
  comparison of Catholic and
    Protestant views of, 97n39
  implicit, 86
  as perfection of religion, 17
  and religion, concept of
    Calvin and Schleiermacher on,
      xvii, 220-21
    as material issue of theology,
      xix, xixn2
    in Protestant theology, xi-xiii,
      xvii, xixn2, 56n25, 100n54,
      201
  See also Calvin, on faith;
    Schleiermacher, on faith
Febvre, Lucien, 65n100, 230n22
feeling
  of absolute dependence, 110, 116,
    124, 126, 128-31, 160-61, 171-
    72, 204
  religious, Schleiermacher on, 116-
    17, 123-25, 126-27, 131-32

Feuerbach, Ludwig, xxi-xxiin19
Fichte, Johann Gottlieb, 138n67,
    140n77, 250n5
Flückiger, Felix, 150n125
Foreman, Terry Hancock, 135n18
Forstman, H. Jackson, 95n20, 95n21,
    135n16, 137n48, 176n6, 176n8,
    250n7
foundationalism, xvi, xxiin22,
    187n70, 251n10
Francis I, King of France, 31
Frei, Hans W., xxiin20, 150-51n125,
    180n46, 253n23, 254n28,
    255n32
Friedrich Wilhelm III, King of
    Prussia, 168
Fuchs, Emil, 139n75
Fuhrmann, Paul T., 92-93n8

Gadamer, Hans-Georg, 144n92
Gamwell, Franklin I., 256n35
Ganoczy, Alexandre, 52n4, 103n71,
    104n79, 106n100
Geertz, Clifford, 249n4
Gerrish, B. A., 23n42, 92n3, 138n66,
    259-60n43
    on Calvin, xxiiin29, 10-16, 22n32,
    22n35, 23n41, 53n11, 54n13,
    55n18, 61n52, 62n63, 62n64,
    97n34, 104n79, 191n100,
    227n1, 228n12, 231n30, 235-
    36n53, 236n54, 251n9
    on Reformation heritage, xxiiin29,
    10-16, 22n35, 23n39, 23n40,
    26n54, 251n9
    on Schleiermacher, 10-16, 22n35,
    23n39, 23n40, 23n41, 26n54,
    135n10, 179n38, 184n60,
    191n100, 228n12, 231n30,
    232n38, 252n16, 254n26,
    255n31
Gilkey, Langdon, xxn3, xx-xxin8,
    xxiiin28, 22n27, 223, 233n44,
    234n46, 258-59n41
Gloede, Günter, 59n39, 66n107
God, xii, xvi, 2, 4, 5, 8, 9, 12-14, 17,
    30, 33

comparison of Calvin and
    Schleiermacher on, 217-18,
    230n22
as creator and redeemer, 13-14
    (*see also* Calvin, *duplex cognitio
    Dei*)
Schleiermacher on, 121-25, 126,
    128-31, 172, 174-75
Goethe, Johann Wolfgang von, 110,
    155
Wilhelm Meisters Lehrjahre, 110
Graby, James K., 139n74, 181n50,
    184-85n60
Graf, Friedrich Wilhelm, 140n76,
    140n77
Graß, Hans, 189n81
Green, Garrett, xxin18
Green, William Chase, 98n44
Gregory of Rimini, 91n3
Grislis, Egil, 63n76, 66n116
Gruhn, Reinhart, xxiin19
Gründler, Otto, 105n90
Gustafson, James M., xxiiin28,
    182n50, 195n129, 232n33,
    233n41, 261n48, 261n49

Hall, Basil, 92n5
Hallie, Philip P., 64n86
Hamilton, William, xxin10
Harnack, Adolf von, 224
Harvey, Van A., 123, 139n72,
    139n74, 151n127, 252n15
Hegel, G. W. F., 25n53, 126, 131,
    143n88, 147n104, 148n113,
    150n125, 176n14, 182n53,
    256n32, 259n43
Hengstenberg, Ernst Wilhelm,
    142n87, 143n88
Heppe, Heinrich, 149n119
heresy, Schleiermacher on, 166,
    177n17
hermeticism, 62n62, 64n88
Heron, Alasdair I. C., 21n24
Hertel, Friedrich, 134n4
Herz, Henriette, 110, 182n53
Hick, John, 193n104
Hinrichs, H. Fr. W., 148n113

Hinze, Bradford E., 188n75
Hirsch, Emanuel, 138n67, 140n77
Holcot, Robert, 91n3
Holl, Karl, 51-52n2, 98n40
Huber, Eugen, 139n74
Huizinga, Johan, 92n8
Hume, David, 20n3, 230n22
Hus, John, 92n5

intuition, Schleiermacher on, 115-17,
    123-24
Irenaeus of Lyons, 193n104
Islam, 101-2n66, 179n43, 180n45,
    180-81n49, 249n4

Jacobi, F. H., 121, 131-32, 150n121
James, William, 145n93
Jesus Christ, xii, 4-5, 8, 9, 15, 17, 31,
    33
    Calvin on, 202
    Schleiermacher on, 159-61, 163-
        67, 169-70, 172-75, 204, 236n53
Jones, Serene, 56n26, 60n47, 65-
    66n100, 68-69n128, 228-29n18
Judaism, 102n66, 103n75, 104n78,
    162-65, 179n43, 182n53,
    194n119, 207, 209-10, 249n4
Junker, Maureen, 140n80
justification
    Calvin on, 80, 203
    Reformation doctrine of, 2, 51
    Schleiermacher on, 173

Kant, Immanuel, 12, 24n45, 110,
    131, 137n41, 138n67, 139n69,
    150n125, 176n14, 181n50, 213,
    215-16, 230n20, 230n22,
    230n27, 231n30, 233-34n45,
    250n5
Kantzenbach, Friedrich Wilhelm,
    135n13
Käsemann, Ernst, 189n81
Kaufman, Gordon D., 179n43,
    259n41, 262n51
Kelsey, David H., 95n20
Kierkegaard, Søren, 25n53
Kitagawa, Joseph M., 184n58

knowledge of God
    Calvin on, 12, 14, 34, 38-39, 76
        (*see also* Calvin, *duplex cognitio
        Dei*)
    and God's goodness, 39-40
    as necessary to faith, 77
    and piety, 48, 50
    and self-knowledge, 33-34, 37, 40,
        76-77
Köstlin, Julius, 55n18
Kraemer, Hendrik, 100n54
Kraus, Hans-Joachim, xxn6, 104n78,
    183n56
Krusche, Werner, 99n48
Kuhn, Thomas S., 20n5
Küng, Hans, 20n5

Lactantius, 64-65n96
Lamm, Julia A., 139n69, 251n10
Lange, Dietz, 181n50
law
    Calvin on, 79, 84-85, 98-99n45,
        99n46, 104n79
    Schleiermacher on, 183n55
Lee, Sou-Young, 56-57n26, 97n34,
    98-99n45
Lefèvre d'Étaples, Jacques, 31,
    62n62
Leith, John H., 26n54, 99n50
Lessing, Gotthold Ephraim, 121,
    138n66
Liebling, Hans, 150n125
Lindbeck, George A., xiv-xv, xxin11,
    xxin15, xxin19, xxiin22,
    144n92, 186n65, 246, 249n4,
    252n16, 257n38, 257-58n39
Lobstein, P., 61n51
Löffler, Paul, 234n45
Lombard, Peter, 93n10
Lonergan, Bernard, xxin11, 144n92
love
    in Calvin's theology, 79
    Schleiermacher on, 205
Luther, Martin, xvi, 1-2, 10-11, 13,
    19-20n1, 31-32, 51, 51-52n2,
    57n31, 71-73, 80, 90, 91-92n3,
    92n4, 92n8, 94n12, 97-98n40,

Luther, Martin (*continued*)
101n57, 103n66, 182n53,
188n77, 201, 205, 225-26,
251n9
Calvin's relation to, 10, 31, 32, 51,
71, 80, 90, 95n20, 104n79
"Ninety-Five Theses," 1
and Schleiermacher, 23n39, 23n40,
133, 151n129
Small Catechism, 32

Mackintosh, H. R., 190n87
Marheineke, Philipp, 148n113
Mariña, Jacqueline, 186n65
Maurer, W., 93n8
McCormack, Bruce L., 26n53, 233-
34n45, 235n50, 250n8
McGrath, Alister E., 52n3, 91n3
McLeod, Hugh, 20n2
McNeill, John T., 55n23
Meckenstock, Günter, 139n69,
181n50
Melanchthon, Philip, 62n62, 67n124,
99n51, 194n115
Mendelssohn, Moses, 121
metaphysics, Schleiermacher on,
26n53, 114, 117-18, 122-23,
125, 136n25, 148-49n116
method, theological, xxiiin28,
xxivn30
comparison of Calvin and
Schleiermacher on, 11-15
correlational, xxiin21, 54n17, 243-
44, 254n29, 255n30, 255-56n32
and liberal theology, xix
and material issues of theology,
xviii
Protestant debates about, xvi
and relation to theological system,
237-39
See also Calvin, and theological
method; Schleiermacher,
theological method of
modernity, xi, xiii, xv
monotheism, Schleiermacher on,
129-30, 160-63

morality
Calvin on, 215-16
comparison of Calvin and
Schleiermacher on, 215-16
Schleiermacher on, 114, 117-18,
125, 160, 215-16
Moravian Brethren, 111, 133, 135n12
Moretto, Giovanni, 176n4
Mossner, Ernest Campbell, 135n14
Mühlhaupt, Erwin, 95n21
Mulert, Hermann, 142-43n88,
149n119, 188n77
Muller, Richard, 52n7
mysticism, 4, 111

neo-orthodoxy
on Christian faith and religion, xi-
xiv, xvii, 17, 197
and criticism of Schleiermacher,
xi-xiv, 3-9, 200-1
historiography of, 9-10, 221-26,
235n48
See also theology, neo-orthodox
Nelson, James David, 134n7,
135n12, 135n17, 138n55
Newman, Amy, 182n53
Niebuhr, H. Richard, 151n129, 231-
32n30, 259n43, 262n50, 262n51
Niebuhr, Richard R., 22n28, 24-
25n52, 134n1, 146n103,
147n104, 190n87, 190n88, 224,
235n48, 235n49
Niesel, Wilhelm, 103n76, 222,
233n42
nominalism, 91n3, 257n38
Novalis, 135n16, 137n48
Nuovo, Victor L., 57n32, 63n77,
68n126, 101n63
Nowak, Kurt, 135n18, 137n48

Obendiek, Harmannus, 53n8
Oberman, Heiko, 26n57, 91n3, 92n5
Ockham, William of, 91n3
Offermann, Doris, 185n63
Ogden, Schubert M., xxiin21, 20n5,
26-27n59, 58n34, 68n128,
252n14, 254n26, 254n29

Ohst, Martin, 189n81
Operin, John, 103n66
Ottati, Douglas F., 261-62n50
Otto, Rudolf, 26n53, 137n36
Ozment, Steven, 52n7, 92n8

paganism. *See* Calvin, on paganism;
   philosophy, ancient;
   Schleiermacher, on paganism
pantheism
   Calvin on, 45
   and Schleiermacher, 121-25, 130,
      179n40, 218
   Spinoza's, 138n66
   Stoic, 64n94
papacy, the, 30, 73, 82, 88-9
Parker, T. H. L., 54-55n18, 59n41,
      67n121, 95n21, 103n77, 104n84
Partee, Charles, 54n16, 98n44,
      229n18
Pauck, Wilhelm, 92n6, 188n77
Paul, the apostle, 38, 44, 73, 76, 84-
      85, 87, 164
Pelagianism, 31, 72-3, 91n3, 202,
      215
Pelikan, Jaroslav, 22n29, 93n10,
      188n77
Pfleiderer, Otto, 138n66, 150n121,
      184n59
philosophy
   ancient, 57n32, 62n60, 63n77,
      98n44, 230n22, 251n9
   Calvin and, 41-48, 50, 90, 239-40
   pluralism of contemporary, 246
   and Schleiermacher, 131-32,
      239-40
   and theology, 134n4, 150-51n125,
      151n126, 187n70, 239, 250n5,
      250n6, 250n8, 251n9, 251n10
   See also religion, philosophy of
Pickle, Joseph W., 182n53
pietism, 135n12, 137-38n55, 228n12
   and influence on Schleiermacher,
      111-12, 119, 203, 214-15
piety
   comparison of Calvin and
      Schleiermacher on, 218-220
   See also Calvin, on piety; Calvin,

   on religion; knowledge of God,
      and piety; Schleiermacher, on
      religion
Piper, Otto, 137n54, 176n12
Pitkin, Barbara, 104n88
Placher, William C., xxin19, 187n69,
      251n10, 258n40
Plato, 60n45, 62n60, 62n63, 98n44,
      136n19, 250n5
pluralism, religious, xiii, xix, xxn8,
      247, 261n47, 262n51
Postema, Gerald J., 55n23
Protestantism
   and religion, concept of, 207, 208
   Schleiermacher on, 22-23n36, 168,
      208, 228n14
Preus, Samuel J., 59n40, 59-60n43,
      63-64n78, 101n66, 106n102
Proudfoot, Wayne, 141n82, 143-
      44n92, 145n101
Prussian Union Church, 11, 142n83,
      168, 208
Pünjer, Bernhard, 60n43

Quapp, Erwin H. U., 134n7, 139n69

Rabelais, François, 65n100
Rahner, Karl, 105n91, 144n92
Redeker, Martin, 22n36, 134n5, 137-
      38n55, 142n83, 176n8
redemption
   in Calvin's dogmatics, 14, 199
   in Schleiermacher's dogmatics, 14,
      162, 164-66, 169-70, 172-74,
      199, 204-5
Reformation, the Protestant, 1-2, 72-
      74, 92-93n8, 93n10, 201
   heritage of, xxiiin29, xxivn30,
      57n31, 58n33, 221, 222-23, 224,
      225, 235n52
   and Schleiermacher, 11, 167-68,
      200, 209, 225-26
   See also Calvin, on the
      Reformation; Schleiermacher,
      and Reformation heritage
regeneration, Schleiermacher on,
      172-73, 204
Reill, Peter Hans, 135n13

Reimer, Georg, 111
Reinhold, Karl Leonhard, 150n120
religion
    Calvin on, 7, 17-18, 37, 40, 47, 50
        (*see also* Calvin, on religion)
    Cicero on, 41-48
    comparison of Calvin and
        Schleiermacher on, 17, 200,
        212-221
    criteria for evaluating, 2, 3, 201,
        246-47, 260n44
    "cultural-linguistic" model of, xiv,
        257n38
    and ethics, Schleiermacher on
        relation of, 26n53, 136n25,
        231n30
    "experiential-expressive" model
        of, xiv, xxin11, xxiin22, 186n65,
        257n38
    history of, 183-84n58, 185n63,
        228n16, 245-47, 256n36,
        260n45
    liberal definition of, xi
    and metaphysics, Schleiermacher
        on relation of, 26n53, 136n25
    neo-orthodox repudiation of, xi-xii,
        5-6
    non-theological study of, xvii, 211
        (*see also* religious studies)
    philosophy of, 175n2, 245-47,
        252n20, 256n36
    Schleiermacher on, 17-18, 109,
        110, 113, 114, 115, 117, 118-19,
        121, 123, 124, 130, 131, 153-55,
        174-75
    systematic function of, 197, 199,
        220
religions
    non-Christian, 100n54, 101n66,
        106n98, 106n102, 147n107,
        179n43, 180n49, 183n58,
        195n119, 195n122, 228n16
    romantic critique of, 155
    Schleiermacher on, 153-57, 160-62
religious studies, xxin9, 244, 245,
    256n33, 256n34, 256n35,
    256n36

See also religion, history of;
    religion, philosophy of
Rendtorff, Trutz, 184n58
Repgen, Konrad, 93n8
Reuter, Karl, 100n54, 107n110
revelation, 231n30, 232n39, 259-
    60n43
    in Barth's theology, 5-8, 238
    in Calvin's theology, 199, 200, 207
    classical Protestant view of, xv
    and natural theology, 56n25
    and religion, xxin10, 26n53, 27n60
    Schleiermacher on, 128-29, 169,
        175, 200
    twofold meaning of, 17, 26n59
Richard, Lucien Joseph, 98n43,
    100n52
righteousness, Calvin on, 79, 80
Ritschl, Albrecht, 176n3, 181n50,
    227n3, 231n29, 231n30, 232n32
Ritschl, Otto, 134n4
Roberts, Robert, 145n101
Rohls, Jan, 145n101
romanticism
    and Schleiermacher, 110-13, 125,
        131, 175, 239
    and Schleiermacher on religion,
        117-19, 121, 154-55, 203
Rössler, Martin, 252n17
Roy, Louis, 145n93, 145n94

Sabellianism, 192n100
Sack, F. S. G., 120, 122-23, 138n56,
    181n50
Sadoleto, Jacopo, 10, 22n33, 99-
    100n52
salvation, 73-74
sanctification,
    Calvin on, 80, 203
    Schleiermacher on, 173, 204
Schaff, D. S., 93n8
Schaff, Philip, 195n129
Schelling, Friedrich, 140n77, 250n5
Schellong, Dieter, 99n46
Schlegel, Friedrich von, 110, 125,
    135n16, 136n19, 138n59

Schleiermacher, Friedrich
  on *Bildung*, 110, 113, 117-18, 124,
    135n18, 163, 176-77n16
  on conscience, 149n116, 171, 172,
    215
  on faith, 14, 17-18, 111-112, 133,
    151n130, 153-54, 161, 164, 165-
    74, 172, 175, 180n45, 183n58,
    187n70, 188n79, 190n87,
    194n115, 203
  on fetishism, 129, 160, 162,
    179n40
  Glaubenslehre (*The Christian
    Faith*), 11, 109-110, 120, 124,
    125, 139n74, 140n77, 142n86,
    143n92, 145n94, 145n101,
    147n104, 148n113, 148-49n116,
    150n125, 154, 160, 163, 164,
    165, 168, 182n53, 184n59,
    185n60, 185n63, 186n66,
    189n79, 191-92n100, 232n32,
    241
  on God, 110, 113, 121-25, 126,
    128-31, 140-41n81, 141n82,
    145n101, 146n102, 146-47n103,
    148n116, 149n117, 149n118,
    151n130, 154, 157, 162, 163,
    164, 169-74, 175, 181n49,
    182n53, 183n58, 190n87,
    191n97, 191n99, 191-92n100,
    193n102, 194n119, 195n129,
    196n130, 209
  on Islam, 162, 165, 179n43,
    180n45, 180-81n49
  on Judaism, 162-65, 167, 179n43,
    182n53, 183n56, 183n58,
    194n119
  on monotheism, 129-30, 160, 161-
    63, 179n40, 182n51, 193n101,
    194n119, 209
  on natural religion, 154-55,
    176n16, 180n45
  and natural theology, 192-93n101,
    227n3
  on paganism, Graeco-Roman, 121,
    147n107, 131-32, 163-64, 167,
    179n43, 181n49, 183n58

  and philosophy, 110, 120, 121-23,
    128, 130-31, 132-33, 134n4,
    136n19, 138n66, 139n69, 148-
    49n116, 149n117, 150-51n125,
    151n126, 165, 175-76n2,
    179n42, 183n58, 185n62,
    185n63, 187n67, 239, 253n23
  and pietism, and relation to, 111,
    119, 126, 134n7, 137-38n55,
    175, 195n125, 203
  on polytheism, 129, 147n107, 160,
    162, 163, 179n40, 181n49,
    194n119
  and Reformation heritage, xvii,
    xviii-xix, xxivn30, 3-19, 132-33,
    166-68, 188-89n79, 189n81,
    195n129
  on religion, 12-13, 109-110, 113-
    120, 120-21, 122-26, 128-29,
    130, 133-34, 139-40n76,
    140n77, 140n80, 140-41n81,
    141n82, 142n85, 143n89,
    143n90, 144-45n93, 145n101,
    146-47n103, 148n114, 149n117,
    150n125, 153-54, 160-65, 166,
    168, 170, 174-75, 179n40,
    180n45, 180n48, 181-82n50,
    184n59, 184-85n60, 186n65,
    186-87n67, 187n68, 187n70,
    190n87, 190n88, 190n92,
    192n100, 193n101, 193n102,
    195n125, 195n129, 196n130,
    217
    diversity of, 153-54, 155-57,
      158-65, 175, 176n10,
      178n31, 180n48, 183n58,
      194-95n119, 195n122, 208
    historical development of,
      160
    types of, 160-62
  on revelation, 17-18, 26n59, 121,
    128-29, 133, 141n81, 142n82,
    147n104, 149n116, 169, 174,
    175, 192n100, 194n119,
    195n124
  and romanticism, 110-13, 117-19,
    120-21, 125, 131, 142n85, 154-
    55, 175, 176n8, 177n16, 203

Schleiermacher, Friedrich (*continued*)
  on speculation, 12-13, 24n48, 126,
    149n17, 149n118, 165, 187n67,
    191-92n100
  Sittenlehre, 165, 186n66, 216,
    232n32
  Speeches, 29, 109-110, 113, 119-
    20, 122-23, 125-26, 130, 134n3,
    134n4, 138n56, 139n74,
    142n86, 143n92, 154, 155, 163,
    176n3, 176n4, 177n23, 183n58,
    184n59, 184-85n60
  theological method of, 11-15,
    24n48, 24-25n52, 133, 150-
    51n125, 151n127, 151n130,
    153-54, 160-61, 165-66, 186-
    87n67, 187n69, 187n70,
    189n81, 190n87, 191-92n100,
    216, 231n30, 240, 241-43
Schmidt, Kurt Dietrich, 135n8,
    135n14
scholasticism, 31, 52n7, 93n10,
    105n89
Scholz, Heinrich, 143n88, 151n130
Schreiner, Susan E., 64n94
Schultz, Werner, 136n19, 183-84n58
Schützeichel, Heribert, 105n89
Schwarz, Reinhard, 138n66
Schweitzer, Albert, 177n23
Schweizer, Alexander, 15, 26n55
Scott, Charles E., 145n101
scripture. *See* Bible
Seeberg, Reinhold, 91n2
Seifert, Paul, 23n39, 134n4, 183n58
Selbie, W. B., 141n81
Seltzer, Robert M., 182n53
Seneca, 30, 52n3, 62n61, 64n96,
    98n44
Senft, Christoph, 134n2
Shepherd, Victor A., 97n38
Simonides, 48, 113, 123
sin, Schleiermacher on, 171-72,
    193n104, 204
Slomp, Jan, 101-2n66
Smith, John E., 141n82, 256-57n37,
    257n38, 258n41
Smits, Luchesius, 93-94n10

Sockness, Brent W., 178n23
speculation. *See* Calvin, on
  speculation; Schleiermacher, on
  speculation
Spiegler, Gerhard, 151n127
Spinoza, Baruch, 121-22, 138n66,
    138n67, 139n69, 250n5, 251n10
  Ethics, 122
  and Schleiermacher, 122-23
Stadtland, Tjarko, 100n52
Statius, 66n105
Staupitz, Johann von, 91n3
Steinmetz, David C., 56n24, 67-
    68n124
Stiewe, Martin, 189n79
Stoicism, 41, 43-47, 64n93, 64n94,
    64-65n96, 230n22
Strauß, David Friedrich, 150n125
Streetman, Robert F., 146n102,
    192n100
superstition. *See* Calvin, on
  superstition
Süskind, Hermann, 179n38, 179n42
Sykes, Stephen, 180n46, 185n63

Tamburello, Dennis E., 95n21
theocentrism, 54n17, 98n43, 220,
    233n41, 248, 261n49, 261n50,
    262n51
theology
  Christian
    as academic, 244-45
    as confessional, 244, 256n35
    as ecclesial, 244-45
    Schleiermacher on, 240-41
  constructive, 237, 243
  historical
    and constructive theology, xviii,
      226
    Schleiermacher on, 240, 241-43
  liberal, xi, xv-xvi, xxn3, 233n44,
    235n50, 235n53, 249n4
    as heir to Reformation
      heritage, xix, 237
    (*see also* Barth, and liberal
      theology; Brunner, and liberal
      theology)

theology (*continued*)
  Lutheran, 19n1, 94n12, 104n79
  natural (*see* Barth, and natural
    theology; Brunner, and natural
    theology; Calvin, and natural
    theology; Schleiermacher, and
    natural theology)
  neo-orthodox, xxn3, xxin10,
    233n44, 234n46, 235n53
  philosophical, 187n69, 241-42,
    253n23
  postliberal, xiv-xv, xxin19,
    xxiin20, 251n10, 256n33
  practical, 187n69
  Protestant
    classical and liberal epochs of,
      xvii, 1-2, 3, 10, 13, 15, 201,
      224-225
    and ecumenism, xiii
    history of, xi, xvii, 201, 235n50
    and religious studies, 247
  Reformed, 104n79
    Barth and, 21n24, 25n53
    Schleiermacher and, 23nn38,
      26n54
  Roman Catholic, 97n39
  systematic
    historical comparison of, 19
    Calvin's *Institutes* as example
      of, 32
Thiel, John E., 149n116
Thiemann, Ronald F., xvi, xxiin20,
  xxiin22, 27n60, 180n46,
  187n69, 187n70, 246, 251n10
Thomas, George F., 138n66
Thomas, George Hasson, 235n51
Tice, Terrence N., 136n21, 149n116,
  184n60
Tillich, Paul, xi-xii, xxn7, 19, 20n1,
  25n53, 54n17, 61n51, 100n54,
  144n92, 144-45n93, 145n94,
  178n32, 186n65, 188n77,
  192n100, 227n2, 229n18, 232-
  33n40, 243-44, 251n10, 252n20,
  253n25, 254n26, 254n28,
  254n29, 255n30, 255n31, 255-
  56n32, 260-61n45

Tonkin, John, 93n8
Torrance, T. F., 106n94
Tracy, David, xxiin21, 27n61,
  144n92, 145n100, 249n4,
  254n27, 254-55n29, 255n30,
  256n32, 256n35, 257n39,
  258n40, 261n47
Tracy, James D., 93n9
tradition, Christian
  Gerrish's interpretation of, 10-11,
    16
  Schleiermacher on, 208, 235-
    36n53
Trent, Council of, 92n7, 94n11
Trillhaas, Wolfgang, 183n56
trinity, doctrine of the, 54-55n18,
  191-92n100, 195-96n129
Trinkaus, Charles, 61n54
Troeltsch, Ernst, 19n1, 23n42,
  185n63, 255n31, 259-60n43

Veit, Dorothea, 125
Verheyden, Jack, 230n27, 232n34
Virgil, 98n44, 151n126
Vos, Arvin, 105n89

Walker, Williston, 23n41, 107n113
Wallace, Ronald S., 96n22, 97n36
Warfield, B. B., 91n1, 93n10, 96n26
Wehrung, Georg, 134n7
Wendel, François, 52n5, 55n18,
  99n48, 103n74, 104n79, 104n82
Wendland, Johannes, 184n60
Wernle, Paul, 103n76
Wesley, John, 195n125
Wilken, Robert L., 98n44
Wilkens, Eliza Gregory, 60n45
Williams, Daniel Day, xxn3
Williams, George Huntston, 102n66,
  105n92, 106n102
Williams, Robert R., 145-46n101
Willis, E. David, 69n131, 94n26,
  100n53
Wittgenstein, Ludwig, 249n4
Wobbermin, Georg, 23n39, 146n102
Wolf, Hans Heinrich, 103n74
Wöllner, J. C. von, 120

Wood, Allen, 135n14
Wyclif, John, 60n45, 92n5
Wyman, Walter E., 23-24n42,
        192n100, 193-94n104, 260n43

Yates, Frances A., 62n62

Zachman, Randall C., 96n26,
        191n100
Zahrnt, Heinz, 21n22
Zeller, Eduard, 64n86
Zwingli, Huldreich, 59n43, 60n48,
        65n96, 73, 104n79, 251n9